Introduction to Philosophy and Applied Psychology

Conversational Topics in Philosophy and Psychology

A Book of Workshops

Lewis Schipper

University Press of America, Inc.
Lanham • New York • London

Copyright © 1995 by
University Press of America,® Inc.
4720 Boston Way
Lanham, Maryland 20706

3 Henrietta Street
London, WC2E 8LU England

Library of Congress Cataloging-in-Publication Data

Schipper, Lewis
Introduction to philosophy and applied psychology : conversational
topics in philosophy and psychology : a book of workshops / Lewis
Schipper.
p.   cm.
Includes bibliographical references and index.
1. Philosophy--Introductions. 2. Psychology, Applied.   I. Title.
BD21.S373   1995   100--dc20   95-3455 CIP

ISBN 0-8191-9891-9 (pbk: alk. paper)

Dec 28, 2002

Dear Jim & Bonnie,

Wishing you the best
in life.

To my wife Teodora

It was good meeting
you both:

Teodora Schopper
5466 Pounsett St.
Pitt. Pa. 15217
(412 - 422 - 1011)

Kae:
c/o Eric John Yaguen
294 Manalo Ext. Street
Puerto Princesa City 5300
Palawan Phil.
011 + 63 + 48 + 434 + 52 35

iii

Table of Contents

SECTION V. METAPHYSICAL FOUNDATIONS 187

SECTION VI. ETHICS 261

SECTION VII. THEORIES OF KNOWLEDGE 287

Acknowledgment

I want to express my thanks to Professors Edward Gelblum, Ronald Polansky, Tom Rockmore, and John Scanlon, who read various parts of the manuscript and made valuable comments. I am especially grateful to Professor Wilhelm S. Wurzer, whose highly valuable suggestions and critical comments greatly enhanced the quality and the scope of this project. I also want to express my appreciation and thanks to the participants (too numerous to be named individually) in my workshops on Applied Philosophy and Creative Learning, for their stimulating discussions and genuine quest for learning. I am very grateful to Professor Yu Xuan-meng for the inspiring conversations on many philosophical topics of mutual interest.

INTRODUCTION

The book is intended as an Introduction to Philosophy and Applied Psychology. It can also be used as a resource book in Counseling courses. The broad range of topics is viewed from an existential perspective. The purpose is to introduce the student to a variety of topics that would stimulate his or her intellectual interest and curiosity. The sessions are called workshops because they stress the interactive function of the teaching-learning process. Each workshop covers the essential ideas of the given topic. The aim is to experience learning in a new and creative way. The conversational topics introduce an innovative way of learning, teaching, and interacting, whereby individuals gain insight into themselves along with the acquisition of new knowledge. The exercises at the end of each workshop were designed with that purpose in mind. By connecting the inside of the person with the ideas explored in the subject matter, learning turns into a joyful experience. The book differs from other available textbooks in the broad range of its topics and in its innovative approach to learning. The reader will notice that Spinoza is given a prominent place in many workshops. No other philosopher has dealt with questions of human existence with greater depth and clarity. Spinoza was guided by a compassionate desire to help people understand themselves, and become more free. Freud called him the father of psychoanalysis.

We gain most from our learning, when we allow ourselves to be immersed in the learning activity, and enjoy it without any pre-conceived expectations of extraneous rewards. This intrinsic motivation is based on our intellectual curiosity, and on our desire to grow spiritually. We partake in the wisdom of the great thinkers in the received tradition, and our life is enriched by it. As we explore and understand that wisdom, we personalize it, and adapt it to our individual lives and experiences. This learning experience is a source of spiritual inspiration and beauty. We learn to master the thinking process itself. The book of workshops is designed for multiple uses and users. It should fill the need for the student who is trying to examine his or her own interests, before deciding on a major subject. For the student who has already decided on a major subject and knows what he or she wants to do, the book should help broaden his or her interest, and focus on some particular area within the broader field. If the reader's interest is aroused, he or she may turn to the original texts and pursue further study of the subject on his own. The teacher may use the book of workshops to introduce new material, to experiment with new ways of teaching and learning, and to break the routine of lecturing by using the method of peer group teaching.

(Briefly, the peer group method can be described as follows: A class of any size is broken up into small groups of approximately eight to ten members. Each group forms a closed circle, and elects a facilitator for the session. At the end of the session, the facilitators give oral reports of the group proceedings to the class as a whole. A general discussion follows afterwards. The teacher may also summarize his or her observations, and open the class for questions and discussion. The format is flexible and a number of variations and adaptations to special needs and circumstances are possible. It is important that the students are given the assigned readings ahead of time, and that they come prepared with written comments and questions. This greatly enhances the effectiveness of peer group learning. A session will usually consist of a combined two hour period).

The book also addresses itself to the adult person after college, the person who already has found a niche in his or her professional life. It is here, where the need for intellectual curiosity, and for meaningful conversation (based on ideas), is perhaps the greatest. It is my hope that the book will alleviate, and at least partially fill that need. The over-specialization and professionalization of our life has its drawbacks in terms of a narrowing down of our interests, the receding of our openness to the world at large, an arresting of our awareness of our spiritual needs, and a diminution of life in general. Wherever we turn, we find that there is a dearth of intellectual stimulation, and meaningful conversation. There is a quest for real conversation, conversation that is not merely based on a recounting of facts, but one that is based on a real sharing of oneself in genuine self-reflection, and exposition of ideas. A conversation that draws people in, rather than leaving them out, a conversation that does not leave people indifferent to themselves, to what they are saying, and to each other. People in various stages of life, regardless of profession or occupation, hunger for real discovery, for real learning, for closeness, for recognition, for being confirmed by another in a mutuality of human interests, and in a common desire for spiritual development and growth. We all seek intellectual stimulation in our ordinary life, as we live it day by day. We don't want the cultural stimulus to be confined and relegated to special events, where we buy a ticket, and where the structure is somewhat artificial.

The purpose of this book is to fill, at least partially, the need for intellectual stimulation. College students may use it as a guide to their interest. Others may use it as a background for learning and meaningful conversation. A few people come together for a couple of hours a week for the purpose of talking in a structured way on a certain topic from the history of ideas. The readings are called workshops because they provide the background material for conversation. They give structure to the conversation, and make sure that the conversation will not become loose, undisciplined, and trivial. One needs to guard against the ever present pull of habit of sloppy, and undisciplined thinking. People may choose a topic which they are going to discuss. The topics in the book stand each on their own, although the book is organized in sections according to various areas of interest. Any one workshop stands entirely on its own, and there is no prerequisite for the reading or discussion of any topic. The workshops are structured to provide an environment for real learning, where the individual learner can integrate and personalize what he or she learns. The participants will hopefully apply the ideas and the insights gained from these workshops, to their individual circumstances, and to their life experiences.

This takes us back to what really matters in life, and to what is really important to our well-being, once we have satisfied our necessary physical, and material needs. We are opening ourselves up to the expanse of the human spirit that bridges generations, centuries, places, and times. We are confronting the most fundamental aspects of our existence, and the most important questions of our life, namely, questions of meaning, purpose, truth, compassion, love. Everything else dwindles in importance relative to our spiritual needs and concerns. These needs have long gone unacknowledged, unmet, and forgotten to the point, that we don't feel their absence anymore, or even the need for them. That is the situation that most us, even the best of us, find ourselves in. This is quite characteristic of our general predicament of self-alienation. It exhibits the poverty of our commercialized life and culture. For the sake of our sanity, it is necessary to take initiative, and actively do something to counteract this trend. Otherwise we end up in a state of suppressed moral and spiritual distress.

The workshops provide a structured environment for the discussion and the internalization of ideas. Great ideas are eternal, and of lasting value. Optimally, the groups should provide an ideal environment for creative learning. An environment that is non-competitive, free from extraneous pressures and expectations, is appreciative and supportive of each other's contributions, is free of pretense or ego glorification, and where the participation is completely voluntary. The workshop participants are intrinsically motivated by a real desire for intellectual growth, and spiritual enlightenment. Sufficient flexibility is built in into the group process, and composition. There is the possibility of open-ended experimentation with methods of learning, with communicating effectively with each other, and the sharing of personal experiences and self-understanding.

Anyone can form a group among friends or strangers. What it takes, is to be motivated by a common desire for spiritual growth. The groups may be large or small depending on circumstance. From my own experience I found the ideal size to be between 5 and 10 participants. The participants agree each time on a topic, or they may select a list of topics for an extended period. The group may be open to newcomers for each session, or it may consist of regular and steady members. The group meets for about two hours a week, but the session may run for as long as there is a need, the time remaining flexible. People may meet at each other's homes, or in a public places (restaurants, lecture halls, salons, etc.). The facilitator may be the same or a different person each time. The participants may prepare the assigned workshop ahead of time, or they may just read it, and discuss it together. A person reads a paragraph aloud, opens it up for discussion and individual comments. Another person then continues with another paragraph, etc. Each group chooses and adjusts its procedure to what is most suitable for its needs. The workshop topics vary in length, they may take up one session, or may require a number of sessions. At the end of each topic there are suggested exercises. These exercises are designed to promote discussion, self-reflection, and self-expression. The topics are written in non-technical language, and the use of technical terms is minimized. The sessions differ from ordinary classroom experience in that, the attendance is completely voluntary, the participants are motivated by the intrinsic desire to grow intellectually and spiritually, and by the realization that true learning is a joyful and an inherently rewarding activity. All along with the new and creative learning experience, there is also the additional benefit associated with close groups, where people are free to be themselves, where they can remove the masks that they wear at work, or society at large, and where they can freely expose themselves without fear of being judged or rejected. The workshops help individuals relate to each other from the inner core of their true personalities, and thus bring about and promote the development of real friendship between them. Conversational groups based on a common desire for intellectual and spiritual growth should help, even if minimally, break down the alienation and self-alienation that is so pervasive in our society. We are alienated because we are totally driven by external and acquisitive values.

Most of our problems in education can be traced back to the alienation of student and teacher, alienation of student from the subject matter, and the predominance of extrinsic motivation propelled by external values resulting from the commercialized culture. People become divorced from life's essence, from their work, and from each other. Creative learning (and teaching) is the conscious self-involvement in the teaching-learning activity. The total focus is on the activity, (teaching, learning, listening, reading, thinking, and talking). We are immersed in the activity to the extent that we are not conscious of our separate existence. By doing this, we impose our personal imprint on the activity without being aware of it. Our activity becomes uniquely ours. We get connected with what we do, and with each other. We breathe life into what we do.

Our spiritual needs require that we open ourselves up to the possibilities imbued in us. True moral principles are inseparably linked to our professional and intellectual excellence. Our essence resides in our inner self. Intrinsic rewards, the unity of existence and essence, the active pursuit of truth and the love of truth, moral and intellectual integrity, the courage to be oneself and to go against the stream if necessary, the preservation of the integrity of our existence, the upholding of human dignity together with the belief in the divine right of every human being to the fullest unfolding of their natural capacities, all of this is part of our spiritual growth. It is also part of the love that is contained deep within everyone of us, but has been buried and shut up, without having had the opportunity to come out, and shine in our way through life. Intrinsic values lead to the affirmation of life in its most basic context. As a result, life is embodied with enthusiasm, vitality, and spontaneity. The recognition of our imperfections, limitations and transitoriness of our earthly existence frees us to live our life to the fullest. We are free to experience the joys of life inherent in life's essence.

The everyday environment is not conducive to spiritual growth and individual creativity. It emits subtle, and not so subtle messages that we are not needed, and that we can be easily replaced in our jobs or workplace. It is necessary that we structure our own environment where we can recognize each other's strength and creative contribution without being diminished by it. We must lend support, recognition, and appreciation for the individual's creative contribution expressed through the love of learning, and the affirmation of life.

SECTION I. LOVE AND FRIENDSHIP

Workshop 1. The Philosophy of Friendship: Aristotle, Cicero and Kant.

1. Aristotle on Friendship.

Exercise of virtue is, for Aristotle (384-322 B.C.),[1] the goal of life. The four cardinal virtues are: courage, justice, temperance, and love. (Corresponding Christian virtues are: love, faith, and hope. The fundamental Jewish virtue is charity). Friendship is a virtue. It is noble to be a friend to someone. Virtue is instrumental to the good life. The good is happiness itself. Happiness lies in living and being active, in conformance with virtue. We exist by virtue of activity, by loving and acting. In activity we actualize what is potentially in us. Aristotle distinguishes between two kinds of actions: Activity *(energeia)* where the end is in the activity itself, (walking for the enjoyment of walking), and motion, *(kinesis)* where the activity is for the sake of some end, (walking to work, walking to deliver a parcel, etc.) When we enjoy our work, we feel happy.

People need friends. With a friend, we are better able to think and act. The giving and sharing of ourselves (our plans, hopes, feelings, projects, beliefs, etc.) with someone we want to be with (a friend), frees creative energy within us, and stimulates us to noble pursuits. We need friends in order to enjoy the good life. We need to share ourselves with others. The happy man needs friends. Who of us has not experienced a sudden burst of creative energy when we were affirmed in our endeavor by another person whom we respect and like? When left to ourselves, even the strongest among us is often not strong enough to maintain a steady high level of energy and creativity that is required for the completion of a serious project. For this we need the comfort and the encouragement of a friend. We need to be strengthened in our confidence of ourselves, in the belief that what we are doing is right and worthwhile, and that we are able to carry out the task that we have assigned to ourselves or the endeavor that we are engaged in. That someone who is giving us encouragement and shows that he or she believes in us, is our friend. I can cite an example from my own experience: I was working on a project that required some novel approach to a problem. While I was thinking about my work almost all the time, I found it nevertheless difficult to crystallize my ideas and write them down. I tended to put off and procrastinate the work. One evening I had discussed my work with a friend and told him everything about my intended project. I was able to tell him all the yet unformed or partially formed ideas that were in my head. His response was highly encouraging. My friend was excited about my project. This gave me such a burst of renewed energy that I was able to write down my entire project that very evening. This shows the power of being affirmed by a friend. I am sure that others can cite similar examples from their own experience.

Aristotle discusses three kinds of friendships:

(1). Utility friendships: Such friendships are primarily intended for the sake of mutual benefit or convenience. Individuals weigh and calculate whether they get enough benefit from the friendship. The people who involve themselves with these forms of friendships to the exclusion of other forms, tend for the most part to be commercially minded, selfish, and calculating characters. They become friends chiefly for their own benefit, and not for the sake of the other. Since these friendships are based on the unenlightened and short term self interest of each of the parties, they will endure only when each of the two parties get the same or equivalent benefits from each other. Friendships of this kind are based on calculated self interest. We may call them selfish friendships. Such friendships are most common among politicians and businessmen. (We may add that relation between States are also regulated by each State's best interest.) Utility friendships are based on a balanced equality of benefits. However, when people use each other, they always want to get the better of the bargain. Therefore, there is a built- in source of conflict and friction in such relationships.

(2). Friendship based purely on pleasure: Friendships of this kind are engaged in primarily for the sake of the pleasure and the enjoyment that the participants derive from them. For example, the pleasure derived in friendships between young people, lover and beloved: the lover gets pleasure and the beloved gets attention. However when the bloom of youth passes, and the lover finds no more pleasure in the sight of the other, his or her interest in the other declines and the friendship between them passes. Pleasure friendships are often found among ready-witted people, between host and guest, or in general, when the two people enjoy some unique quality that comes to be expressed when they are together, as for example, story telling, or some other common interest.

(3). Character friendship: The highest kind of friendship is one that is based on the character and virtue of the two individuals. In character friendships, love is for the sake of the other, and not for the sake of oneself. The two people are alike in virtue. They share common tastes and views about the good, the beautiful, and the useful. They are harmonized in their feelings and affection for each other. They are more inclined to give than to receive. They find more satisfaction, and derive greater pleasure from giving than from receiving. The reciprocal affection for each other gives them the greatest delight. If love is a feeling, friendship is a state of character. Both are present in this highest form of friendship. Such friendships are most enduring, since they are based more on loving than on being loved. For loving is an activity, to be loved is a passivity. (Happiness lies in activity, not in passivity). However, individuals of highest character are unusual, and people who are capable of forming perfect friendships are rare. Therefore such friendships are rare. Most men seem to wish to be loved rather than to love. This is why so many men love flattery. The flatterer pretends to love more than he is loved.

2. Cicero's Treatise on Friendship.[2]

Cicero (106-43 B.C.) follows Aristotle in his views on friendship. Real friendship is based on character. Joys are enhanced and misfortunes are eased when shared with a friend. Friendship makes us stronger, and forbids despair. Friends admire each other's virtues and qualities of character. They are bound by intimacy of feeling. "Nothing inspires our love and affection like virtue and goodness." Although the advantages of friendship are numerous, reciprocal advantages do not form the basis for friendship. True friends do not use each other, and don't expect services from each other. They give to each other without expectation of return. The most important ingredients of friendship are honesty, and good will. A good friend will never display any pretense of feeling or make believe to the other, and he or she will never doubt their friend's rectitude of character. The character quality that is most essential to friendship is loyalty. Loyalty assures permanence and stability of the friendship. This is where many people fail. They do not possess such strength of character. They look down on others when they become prosperous and abandon their friends in time of distress, a time when their friends need them most. These are so called fair weather friendships. It is advisable that people choose their friends with care. They should not be too hasty in bestowing affection on another. It is necessary to get to know the other person, and be sure of his or her virtues and worthiness of character before one makes an emotional commitment to another.

3. Kant on Friendship.

Intimacy is restricted by the rule "that even the best friends should not become too familiar with each other,"[3] because it opens the possibility of loss of respect. And, once respect is violated it is irretrievably lost. According to Kant (1724-1804), love and respect are incompatible with each other, the one attracts, the other repels.

Moral friendship is characterized by complete confidence and openness, in so far, as it can subsist with mutual respect. People need friends. They are by nature social beings. People need to open up to one another, but they are also vulnerable. They are afraid of loss of respect, in case such openness is not reciprocated.

Exercises.

1. Perhaps the most important insight to be gained from the above discourse on friendship is the shifting of the focus from the nature of the other to the examination of myself, and of my ability to form and sustain a close relationship. Discuss.

2. We choose or happen to be friends according to our character predispositions and values. Do you agree or disagree? Why?

3. Do you actively take responsibility for the quality of the friendship that you form or fail to form?

4. Can you look into yourself with complete self-honesty, and without self-deception?

5. Only when we know ourselves can we know the other, and only when we are truly honest with ourselves can we be equally honest with another. Do you agree or disagree?

6. Additional exercises: We might want to ask ourselves some questions like the following: Why do I need a friend? Is it more important for me to have one special friend, many friends, or both? How do I become a friend with someone? Do I take the initiative in removing the barrier between me and the other, or do I wait for the other to do it? Have my friendship(s) stimulated me to be more active, to excel and to accomplish more? Which ones did, and which ones did not? Were they supportive of me? Was I insecure and vulnerable to loss of face or respect? Could I open up to my friend as I am open to myself? Could I fully trust my friend as I trust myself? Was (were) my friendship(s) fully reciprocated?   Does my friend know me, my character?   How well do I know myself?

Notes

1. Aristotle, *Nicomachean Ethics*. Books VIII &IX.
2. *Letters of Marcus Tulius Cicero With his Treatises on Friendship and Old Age*. Translated by E S Shuckburgh. The Harvard Cassics, edited by Charles W Ellliot, New York: P F Collier & Son, Volume 9, 1909.
3. Immanuel Kant, *The Metaphysics of Morals*. Introduction, translation and notes by Mary Gregor, Cambridge: Cambridge University Press, 1991. p. 261.

Workshop 2. The Philosophy of Love. The Art of Loving, by Erich Fromm.

The awareness of our separateness from other human beings and from the rest of nature is, according to Erich Fromm (1900-1980), a fundamental reality of our consciousness and of being human. Only people are conscious of this separation from the rest of nature. Animals are not. We are both part of nature, and apart from nature. The awareness of this separateness is the root cause of people's existential feelings of primordial anxiety and aloneness. The basic problem of human existence reduces itself to the question of how best to respond, deal, and overcome this fundamental existential reality or *Angst*. One of the ways of dealing with this problem is to conform to the peer group, and to follow routine ways of ordering one's life. This is indeed how most people act. They deal with their existential anxiety by suppression and denial of their individuality. This kind of response to separateness, namely, to blend and get lost in the group is most evident with adolescents.

A higher level response to existential anxiety is incurred by developing a productive and creative orientation to work and life. These responses however, are not normally made on the plane of consciousness. Erich Fromm states that, the most satisfying way of dealing with this universal problem inherent in human existence, is to seek union with another person or persons in love. "The desire for interpersonal fusion is the most powerful striving in man."[1] Love is a person's response to his or her separateness from nature. It is a way of uniting with nature, and a coming back to nature. In mature love, we unite with another human being, while at the same time, we preserve our integrity and individuality.

Mature love is an activity based primarily on giving, not receiving. Giving of oneself in love is the primary activity. Receiving or being loved is a passivity and secondary to love. To be loved is a natural consequence of love as an activity. Love is an activation of the powers of the soul which finds its natural expression in giving. To be loved is a passivity of the soul. True happiness lies in being active (in activating the powers of the soul), not in being passive. To love is to give.

What is giving?

To give is to give something of oneself, of one's powers, possessions, feelings, understanding, knowing, etc. To give is to give freely. Giving embraces the entire self. The entire self participates in the act of giving. Hence the joy of giving. True giving is most joyful to the person. It is the fountain and real source of true joy. It is the essence of joy. There is no greater joy than the joy of giving. This is most readily seen in the mother's giving and nourishing her baby. To give of oneself, whether materially or spiritually, is to perceive oneself as being rich. The more one gives of oneself spiritually, the more one shares oneself with another person in love, the greater one's true treasures, and the more one has to give. The more one loves, the more one can love. Love builds on love and giving builds on giving. This even applies to material goods. To voluntarily part with my possessions means to have the confidence and the conviction that these can be readily replaced, and even multiplied through my faith in myself, through my belief in my productive orientation and through my positive outlook on life. If this holds true for the parting with material goods, whereby the latter are not, at least not for the time being, available anymore to the giver, how much more does it hold for the giving of one's understanding, knowledge, feelings, and love, whereby the ability to give is itself conditioned on the act of giving? We can see why giving is the true spring of the greatest and most lasting joy. In this joy, one experiences one's true strength and potency. "Giving is the highest expression of potency."[2]

Love as an activity.

Love involves the entire person in its core. Love is active caring for the well being of the other person. It means being attuned to, and ready to respond to the need of the other. Love's activity expresses itself in active care. To love another means to respect the other as the person that he or she is, and not as the person that I want him or her to be, or what I imagine him or her to be. To love another is to know another. It is to see the other on the other person's terms, and not on my terms.   To love is to penetrate to the core of the other as much as I can penetrate into my own core. It is to penetrate into the secret of the other's being as much as I can penetrate into the secret of my own being. The act of love is an act of transcendence of the self. It is necessary that I know the other person and myself objectively in order to be able to love truly. To experience true love, I must overcome illusions, and an irrationally distorted picture I may have of myself or of the other. The more I overcome psychological distortions and illusions of myself as well as of the other, the more genuine and stronger will my love be.

Fromm maintains that love is essentially and perhaps primarily, a character orientation of the individual. Love signifies our relation to the world. It is not a question of whether I have found the right person with whom I can be in love. Neither is it a question of falling in love or finding the object of my love. This is indeed a common fallacy. Most people think that the actuality of love is a matter of finding the right person, Mister Wonderful or the Woman of my dreams.

Fromm never tires of stressing that love resides in the character of the person. The character orientation that we designate by love is an activity of the soul that expresses itself in all kinds of forms, such as, in mother's love, in brotherly love (for all human beings), in compassion for others, and of course, in erotic love. Erotic love rests on the exclusivity of the individuals in love. Erotic love is a craving for fusion with the essential being of the other person. It requires specific attributes and elements that exist between two people apart from everyone else.

It is a fundamental truism that the ability to love rests on the ability to love oneself. Self love and love for others are bound together. They are not opposites. Self love must however be distinguished from selfishness. Selfishness and self love are opposites. Selfish people are incapable of loving themselves or others. Selfishness is inimical to love. Love requires a totally honest relationship to myself and to the other. The latter means that I relate to the other from the center of my being. To the extent that I cannot or do not relate to myself or the other from the center of my being, I cannot and do not truly love. If I am not capable of a core relationship to myself or the other, I am not capable of love. Two people may remain strangers all their lives (in marriage) if they are unable to form a central relationship between them. Love is possible only if the two people can and do communicate with each other from the center of their individual selves. The latter means that they are perfectly honest with themselves and with each other.

The practice of love.

The practice of love requires discipline, concentration, patience, tolerance, sensitivity, understanding, and the supreme desire to master the art of loving.

1. The need for self-discipline.

Lack of self-discipline, and a tendency to self-indulgement is a common response to the routinization of work and life. Without self-discipline however, life becomes scattered and chaotic. Self-discipline is best defined as the ability to defer gratification. This ability is the mark of a mature person. The discipline must be voluntary, and it is necessary to experience it as something good, and inherently desirable.

2. The ability to concentrate.

The ability to concentrate is a necessary prerequisite for the learning and mastering of any art. We learn to be alone with ourselves, and derive joy from our being, regardless of what we do. We are not compelled to keep busy or have the need to do something. We learn to be fully concentrated in any activity that we are doing at the moment, (whether it is reading, speaking, listening, looking at a painting, etc.). Fromm maintains that, the ability to concentrate on any task at hand is a precondition for the ability to love.

3. The need to cultivate patience.

Patience is fundamental to the acquisition and mastery of any art. Most people seem to be habitually in a hurry. They are in a hurry to go nowhere. They don't know what to do with the time gained by being in a hurry. The development of intimacy between any two people requires patience, and the absolute avoidance of the use of any force whatsoever.

4. The desire for the mastery of love.

Although this would seem an obvious precondition for the evolution and the mastery of the art of loving, it is not as obvious and common as one would presume it to be. Without a strong desire to master one's trade, skill or art, one cannot gain excellence in anything. The supreme desire to be good, proficient, and to excel in one's profession, differentiates the master from the dilettante.

5. Relaxed alertness.

A state of relaxed alertness is best conducive to the evolution of love between any two people. The experience of having been exposed to a mature loving person will greatly facilitate the mastery of the art of loving. The art of loving presupposes the need to be objective in one's self-assessment. It is necessary to see people and things as they really are, rather than as one wants them to be. It requires us to be free from forming a subjective picture of reality, a picture that conforms more to our desires and wishes rather than to objective realty as it really is. It means that we have to avoid the practice of self-deception. Self-deception is ruinous to love. Love requires a state of inner alertness, vitality, and aliveness. It requires an active and productive orientation to life.

Exercises.

1. Do you have an awareness of "existential Angst"? How do you deal with it?
2. Do you know people who are compulsive busy bodies, cannot relax and enjoy plain being alive?
3. What does Fromm mean by a productive orientation? What does he mean "by relating to oneself or to another person from the core of one's being"?
4. Recall instances when you have experienced a core relationship either to yourself or to another, and describe, with as much detail as you can, how you felt about it.
5. Can you easily and freely speak about your feelings?

6. Are you aware of things that you cannot admit to yourself or to another?

7. Does the pain associated with those things or experiences inhibit your free access to yourself or to another?

8. Would you rather suppress certain painful experiences or ideas about yourself rather then overcome them and free yourself of them?

9. How do you react to constructive and well meant criticism of some aspect of your behavior?

10. Relate your personal experiences or observations to some of Fromm's key ideas of the practice of love.

11. Why does Fromm define love as a character disposition?

12. Why does he consider love as an activity?

13. Are there people who are not capable of love? Do you know any of them? Describe their characteristics.

Notes

1. Erich Fromm, *The Art of Loving.* New York, Evanston: Harper & Row Publishers, 1956. p. 18.
2. Ibid. p. 23.

Workshop 3. The Dynamics of Love and Friendship.

Alienation is the most pervasive aspect of our social environment. We cannot by our own efforts overcome self-alienation in an alienated culture. Even if we have a truly friendly disposition toward others, the friendliness will not last if is not reciprocated, or if it is met with indifference and coldness (on the part of our neighbor, co-worker, man on the street, etc.). However, while we cannot count on others' responses or friendly reciprocity, we must begin by changing our own way of relating to people. This will make it easier for us to initiate and form friendships. While it is true that our society is permeated with social indifference and human estrangement, we can nevertheless take the initiative and cultivate on our own an inner readiness to free ourselves from the all pervasive chains of social alienation. It will not change the social climate, but it will change our acting and feeling within that climate.

In order to be able to remove the barrier between me and the other, I must first learn to accept myself. The more I accept myself, the freer and less alienated will I be. The question of human alienation is thus connected to the question of self acceptance. I am estranged from myself to the extent that I do not accept myself, whether fully or in part. To accept myself is to know myself, and to love myself. As self-knowledge leads to self-acceptance, it diminishes the sense of self-alienation. When I accept myself, I am less touchy, less defensive, and less sensitive to outside criticism of me. I can more easily handle another's deprecating look, and respond less emotionally to a critical remark made to me or about me. I can afford to laugh it off, or to be more forgiving, more understanding, and more generous about its intended meaning. I will be less judgmental about the other person's character. But most of all, I will be able to evaluate personal criticism on its own merit, and hopefully benefit from it. I will learn to be more objective about myself, and will try to look at myself from the outside in rather than from the inside out.

To the extent that I accept myself, I am more free. I am free to be myself. I am not under any compulsion (conscious or unconscious) to compare myself to others who may be smarter (richer, etc.) than I am, or who have achieved more than I have. When I am free to be me, the person that I am, I will be more relaxed in my body and mind. My demeanor will be relaxed, my face will show inner contentment, and people will be drawn to me simply on the strength of my being there. Self-acceptance is also intimately connected with the development of interest. To the extent that I don't accept myself, I cannot really develop genuine interests, since these will reflect primarily my unconscious or conscious desire to seek approval from others, rather than my own true inclinations, dispositions or innate talent. It is in the use and development of my true inclinations and abilities that I can aspire to excellence and greatness. The use of my innate talent and abilities will show itself in the relative ease of mastering the particular subject matter or activity. This will bring me inner joy as well as recognition from the outside. Through the development and use of my true abilities, I will connect to myself and to the outside world around me in the best possible way.

The connection between intrinsic interests and self-acceptance is mutually reinforcing. I am likely to accept myself more if I enjoy my work (projects, etc.) more, and vice versa. In genuine interpersonal relationships, individuals affirm each other. The need to affirm the other and be affirmed by the other is the most fundamental need in all interpersonal encounters.

The alienated self can be traced in some measure to the Cartesian split between the mind and body. This sundering of mind and body in the western culture, has contributed to the accelerated development of the sharpness and precision of analytical thinking at the expense of wholistic thinking. It achieved great accomplishment in science and technology. It contributed to the special esteem to which analytical ability is held and the exaggerated material rewards that it commands. Intellectual sharpness and precision is rewarded in academic pursuits, even if it is applied to relatively unimportant minutiae. There is a tendency in academia to reward intellectual cleverness often at the expense of relevance. One builds a highly sophisticated structure that often ends up showing the merely trivial.

To the extent that we overcome alienation in our culture, we are able to shift our concerns away from the purely mechanical aspects of our life, and direct them towards the more real and more meaningful aspects of living. The quality of human relationships will become more important to people. It will be of greater concern to them. This quality will show itself in the feelings that people have for each other. People will be free to interact with warmth. They will be more free to show their feelings rather than to hide them. People will be less cold and less indifferent toward each other. Our capacity to love ourselves and others will be enhanced.

Alienation breeds misery, indifference, and even cruelty in human interactions. Cruel people are unable to love themselves or others. They can only act as if they love, without truly loving. If you only love your own (yourself, your family, your clan etc.) and you are indifferent to others, you cannot develop compassion which is the foutainhead of all love. Therefore your self-love will not be genuine. Your feelings are split in separate compartments, and you are less integrated as a person.

Reciprocity is at the center of human interactions. The initial attractiveness may have started through reciprocal liking. Factors in liking are: genuineness, openness, acceptance, trust, empathy, concern for others, unselfishness, altruistic actions, similarity of attitudes, interests, values, views, mutual affirmation, and esteem. "We like people that are similar to us, but it seems that we tend to love people that complement or complete ourselves."[1] The ability to communicate is of fundamental importance in the development of interpersonal relationships. When we are understood by another person, we feel less alone. Trust and mutual acceptance develop in the process of a continuing relationship between any two people, while shared values and interests are assumed to be initially given as the basis for a likely friendship to begin. But the latter are also not static. They grow and develop within a continuing friendship.

The dynamics of the relationship depends on the quality of the interplay and the nature of the interaction between the two people. Communication is at the base of the evolving quality of the relationship. Communication facilitates the build-up of trust and understanding between the two people. To understand and to be truly understood by another, is a most precious element in the building of a relationship. It requires patience, active and emphatic listening, and a total presence for each other. It culminates in the I-Thou relation.

If a person is consistently not being understood by the other (friend or mate), the relationship is bound to hit a rock, a barrier. It cannot evolve into a higher and truly gratifying level. The relationship is bound to deteriorate, and will eventually end. However, to really understand one another, we must allow time and never hurry a relationship. This is essential for the evolution of friendship. Over time, the relationship between any two people may grow or decline. People change and so does the relationship. A given relationship may be too one sided in terms of the individuals' capacity to give and receive emotional support. One person may be more self-centered than the other. He or she may may be less able or willing to listen or reach out to the other.

Any ongoing relationship with a degree of closeness is bound to encounter difficulties, and bumps on the road. How two people deal with their problems determines to great degree the direction of the relationship. If the two individuals have not found a way to constructively deal with their problems, their relationship is bound to suffer. It is important for people in a relationship to learn to anticipate problems, and deal with them even before they occur. In any ongoing relationship, conflict is inevitable. The real question is how the two people in a relationship deal with conflict. If they deal with it in a non-threatening way, conflict may lead to new perspectives, new discovery, and to new learning. Suppression of conflict however, will always be harmful to the relationship. When people are defensive, when they feel that they have to put the other person down in order to save their own (false) pride and ego image, conflicts will result. Some people may have a compulsive need to be always right, or critical of the other, etc. Such people do not truly desire to deal with their problems, and resolve their difficulties. The party that tends to be critical or self-righteous will not be able to affirm or really accept the other. If the relationship goes on despite all the odds, it will revert to a mere functioning or perhaps a comfortable routine.

When a relationship is close but insecure, it will abound in friction, conflict, lack of understanding and relative insensitivity. As a result, feelings will dry up. A silent power struggle may creep into the relationship. There may be some attempt at manipulation and competition within the relationship. The relationship will eventually end, if the parties are unable to get a handle on themselves, and deal with their problems in an honest and determined way.

A one-sided or self-centered relationship evidences itself in relative thoughtlessness and emotional neglect for each other. Thoughtlessness or non-caring is most destructive to the development of love between any two people. A lack of self-confidence on the part of one or both of the partners aggravates the situation. It leads to unnecessary misunderstandings and causes additional, superfluous problems which the parties are unable to handle, let alone, resolve. Briefly stated, insecurity leads to anxiety which leads to a loss of spontaneity and a loss of freedom.

Exercises.

1. What problem or problems do you most often encounter in your relationship(s)?
2. What is the nature of the problem? Is it based on a lack of communication and misunderstanding, or is it a question of a more basic difference in outlook?
3. What is the level of reciprocal trust in your ongoing (or past) relationships?
4. How close do you come to being open and free with the other person as you are with yourself?
5. Do you have any inhibitions in certain areas of communication?
6. Do you communicate your feelings not only bodily but also verbally?
7. Do you often feel that you are being judged? If so, can you express it?
8. In general, do you deal with problems in the relationship as they occur, or do you tend to procrastinate and suppress them?

Note

1. Zick Rubin, From Liking to Loving: Patterns of Attraction in Dating Relationships. in *Relationships and Development,* edited by Willard w. Hartup, Zick Rubin. Hillsdale, N..: L. Elbaum Associates, 1986. pp383-402. See also, Zick Rubin, *Liking and Loving; An Invitation to Social Psychology.* New York: Holt, Rinehart and Winston, 1973.

Workshop 4. Spirituality and Personal Growth. *The Road Less Traveled,* by M. Scott Peck.

Peck builds his argument from the basic premise that our understanding of ourselves and of the world we live in, may be truthful or distorted. Usually, it is a mixture of both. The greater the distortion, the less is there a correspondence between our beliefs, and the reality underlying those beliefs. Our actions nevertheless, are most likely to be based on what we believe to be true, rather than on what is objectively true. The gap between objective reality and our subjective understanding of it, will often show itself in our failure to reach desired goals. Subjective distortions and misconceptions of truth lead also to incongruities and inconsistencies in behavior, since the latter reflects a distorted view of reality, and a self-image that is out of line with the true self. Our distorted self-image cannot be confirmed and validated by others. This creates problems and inner conflicts, since we normally depend on the outside for the validation of our perceptions. In order to deal with, and resolve our problems, it is necessary to revise our understanding of ourselves, and of the world around us. We have to revise and change our reality map.

To face our problems with a willingness and determination to solve them, requires discipline, courage and time. It calls for a revision of our accustomed view of ourselves, and of the world. This is a very painful process since we may have to part and give up certain beliefs, images, or values that were dear to us, and in which we have put a great deal of emotional investment.

We must be willing to accept the necessary pain and suffering that accompany true growth. Emotional growth and the becoming of a more mature person is always painful. The first step in this process is a willingness to face up to the challenges of reality. It is a willingness to confirm that we have a problem, and that we are willing to face it, and deal with it. When we take the first step and recognize that we have a problem, we open ourselves up to inspection by ourselves. In counseling, we open ourselves up to the inspection by another. We allow ourselves to be challenged in our formerly held views of ourselves. To be open for the possibility of change and growth, requires that we put aside or bracket for the time being our previously held views, and allow them to be questioned and tested. This process can be, and usually is, very painful. Pain is always present when we go through the process of loosening our responses, and allowing them to become more flexible. For, as long as we hold on to outmoded and unreal beliefs about ourselves and the world around us, we avoid the pain of growth, but we also remain rigid, anxious, and insecure. We can overcome these only by garnering the courage to put aside (bracket) our outmoded, and unreal views of ourselves, and take a leap into the unknown. We confront our subjective and unrealistic perceptions of who we are. To be willing to face oneself, and allow oneself to grow is to love oneself. Peck defines love as "the will to extend one's self for the purpose of nurturing one's own or another's spiritual growth."[1] To extend ourselves in love is to get out of the confines of our ego, and to loosen up our ego boundaries. We want to expand and to give rather than to hold onto what we have.

When we fall in love, or when we experience an oceanic feeling in a mystical union with nature, the distinction between us and the other becomes blurred. We lose the awareness of differentiation between ourselves and the surrounding. At such temporary mergings with another in love or in a mystical union with nature, we lose the awareness of ourselves. We are not conscious anymore of our separate self. This brings with it a feeling of ecstasy and supreme bliss.

Before we can loosen up our ego boundaries, we must first know them. We must know ourselves before we can extend ourselves to another in love. A person who does not have well defined ego boundaries is not in a position to reach out to another in love. People with exaggerated dependency needs or with other neurotic disorders, are handicapped in their ability to express and give love. Their self-absorption and insatiable selfish needs for nurture and attention stand in the way of their readiness and ability to give themselves to another in love. Similarly with people who are not willing to accept the pain and suffering associated with growth. Such people cannot grow. For love, like any act of spiritual growth, is an activity, not a feeling. It is a readiness to accept the necessary pain and suffering that is part of our spiritual growth. To love ourselves is to open ourselves up to spiritual growth. It is to clear the path to growth. To love another is to help the other on his or her path to spiritual growth. This involves removing or putting aside all the obstacles on the way to growth. It means a willingness to look into ourselves objectively in order to recognize the inner impediments to our own well being.

True listening to ourselves or to another is an act of love. The ability to set aside our cherished notions of ourselves, and to truly listen to ourselves is an act of self love. The same holds for true listening to another. We don't let our preconceived notions and thoughts interfere with what the person is trying to communicate to us. We open ourselves up entirely to what the other is telling us. We truly hear the other person. This too, is an act of love. This kind of love takes place in counseling. In good counseling, there is true listening. One might say that counseling is listening. Good counselors have the capacity for true listening. When a person feels that he or she is truly listened to, it always makes them feel good. Genuine listening is very therapeutic. It involves a temporary bracketing of oneself, and a total acceptance of the other. And this is nothing less than an act of love. When there is no listening to one another, there is no love.

Unfortunately, a lack of true listening occurs in most marriages. Married couples for the most part, do not truly listen to each other. It is at this point that their love breaks down. To truly listen to another means, to make a disciplined effort to be fully present for the other. True listening, like love, is an activity. An activity that requires concentration, effort, and discipline. "Since love is work, the essence of nonlove is laziness".[2]

Self-centered or narcissistic people are unable to perceive the separatedness of the other. Therefore they cannot love. The unwillingness (laziness) to confront oneself realistically in order to open up avenues for personal growth, is evidenced through fear, the fear of self disclosure to oneself. It is the fear of knowing oneself. It is the equivalent of the non-love of oneself. As laziness is a form of non-love, so is fear.

Our personal world view evolves out of doubting and questioning. This doubting and questioning reveals our quest for truth. The practice of self- examination involves the desire to know the truth. To explore our most inner truths, we have to involve the unconscious. The unconscious will not lie to us. It knows who we really are. With the help of the unconscious we can bring the conscious into greater alignment with reality. Unrealistic or excessive needs hold us back in our ability to grow as spiritual human beings. We may have excessive dependency needs for affection, admiration, and approval. We may have unrealistic needs for self- sufficiency and independence, or we may have exaggerated needs for perfection and power. As spiritual people, we all have an inborn need to make a contribution to society, that is, to enrich other life with our life.

Exercises.

1. What does Peck mean by defining love as the "extending oneself for one's own and another's spiritual growth?"
2. How do you define spirituality? Do you consider yourself a spiritual being?
3. What are the manifestations of a spiritual person?
4. Do spiritual people evoke faith, hope, moral courage, sincerity, trust and peace?
5. Is spirituality bound up with religious practice, or is it independent of religion?
6. Would you agree that spirituality necessitates the total absence of cynicism?
7. What are your spiritual needs, and are you aware of them?

8. Does spiritual growth include bodily well-being , or is it restricted to the mind alone? Does it include the quest for objective truth, and the freedom to pursue it, regardless of established conventions or cultural prejudices?

9. What does Peck mean by defining love as "true listening".

10. Do you love yourself?

11. Do you make the necessary effort to listen to yourself, your friend, or your lover?

12. Do you listen to the warning signals that emanate from your body, and alert you of coming discomfort or disease? Do you heed them?

13. Are you willing to make the necessary effort needed to change your habitual life-style?

14. Do you agree with Peck that love is an activity, not a feeling?

15. Do you agree that non-love is laziness, and that fear in all of its forms (i.e. fear of self-disclosure, fear of truth, fear of others, fear of loss, fear of death), is also laziness? 16. Examine all these questions in light of your own experience, and most of all, be totally honest with yourself.

Notes

1. M. Scott Peck, M.D. *The Road Less Traveled: A New Psychology of Love, Traditional Values and Spiritual Growth.* New York: Simon and Schuster, 1978. p. 81.

2. Ibid. p. 131.

Workshop 5. *The I and Thou,* by Martin Buber.

"All actual life is an encounter."[1] The encounter is presence. Present or presence is not a question of time, i.e. what am I doing at the present moment, etc. For Buber (Buber, Martin 1878-1965), presence is a total absorption of the person in the actuality of life, that is, in the encounter. An encounter is always with a Thou. The world of I-It, is the world of functioning. The everyday "I" is surrounded by objects. The latter includes items of use, but it also includes other people. In the "I-It" world, others are viewed from the perspective of the I. Human relations are conducted on the principle of exchange, on the basis of *quid pro quo,* meaning what is there for me, or what do I get out of this connection between me and the other. The world of functioning, the "I-It" world, includes everything that is necessary or conducive to a so called, successful life, i.e. a good job, a promising career, an exemplary marriage, a display of material possessions, conspicuous consumption, etc. In the social sphere, it includes the world of institutions, technology, communication, and science. It covers all the progress that we have made in the technical and scientific areas of life.

The achievements in the fields of science and technology in the last century have been extraordinary, and their importance for potential human well-being cannot be doubted. There is nevertheless sufficient ground to question the direction that this development took. The extraordinary progress in the material sphere of life has not been matched by a reciprocal advance in the spiritual sphere of human existence. One might even be tempted to assert the contrary. Along with the advance in the technical potentialities of life, there has been a gradual deterioration in the actuality of living. Life in Western society has become poorer, not richer. And this, not only in the spiritual sphere. The pressures of living have increased, and the enjoyment of life has declined. Even leisure has been robbed of its inherent joy.

The philosophy of Martin Buber addresses itself to these very problems. Objects belong to the past, regardless of their present use. Objects consist in having been. If an individual's life turns around objects, he or she lives in the past. ..."in so far as a human being makes do with the things that he experiences and uses, he lives in the past, and his moment has no presence. He has nothing but objects; but objects consist in having been."[2] That is why a life centered around objects lacks joy. Joy can never be in the past. Joy can only come from life experienced as presence. But this presence is not available to modern man who is engulfed in the "I-It" world, the world of objects. It is in the world of objects that so called "progress" has been made. With each advance in the technical possibilities of man, the "I-It" world has encroached on the "I-Thou" world, and pushed it more and more into the background.   Clearly, objects ("the It") are necessary to life. ..."without It a human being cannot live. But whoever lives only with that is not human."[3]   Man needs to ask the basic question: What is life? What does it mean to live as a human being? What does it mean to be a person?

Buber's answer is both simple and profound. Life is joy. Joy is not pleasure. Pleasure can be had with objects. Joy can only be had in relation, in an I meeting a Thou. The "It" world is the world of objects. The "Thou" world is the world of relation, of encounter. For the human being, all real living is meeting. "All actual life is an encounter."   The encounter with a Thou is also a meeting with God. Only to a Thou can I be present with my whole being. The barrier of separation has been removed. The presence is all there is. To be with the divine signifies the full acceptance of the present. My whole being is present in the "I-Thou".

This is not the case with blind love. Blind love (or blind hatred) see only part of being. They can nevertheless, be a way to the openning of being. They point to relation. Indifference is worse than hate. ..."whoever hates directly is closer to a relation than those who are without love and hate."[4] A relationship always signifies a spiritual association. Love between the I and the Thou is a pure relation. In true love, one accepts the other as the other truly is. Love is not a feeling. It is the responsibility of an I for a Thou. "Feelings dwell in man, but man dwells in his love... love is *between* I and Thou."[5]

To say Thou to a another person is to affirm the other's being. To affirm another does not mean to agree with the other, or to be like the other. It means to partake in each other's being, that is, to open up to another, and to allow the other to open up to you. It means not to hide oneself behind appearances. It means to be true to one's authentic self. People hide behind appearances out of their deep need for affirmation. But to the extent that appearances hide rather than reveal people's true essences, any affirmation based on appearance will necessarily be shallow, and short lasting. It will, soon enough, be found out for what it is.

The world of "I-It", consists of individuals, not persons. To be an individual is to be different. Individuality means separation and difference from others. The individual is conscious of his uniqueness, of his being different, of his desire to stand out, and be distinct from others. To be a person however, means integration and sameness with others. It is a sameness that includes difference at its base. It is a sameness that is based on individual uniqueness and integration. It is not a suppression of individual talents and capacities. It is not a levelling or a merging with the crowd. Quite to the contrary, it means to feel the joy of participating in the common humanity that embraces, each one of us, as human beings. It means to develop our unique, God given faculties, in order to make a contribution to our common heritage. The source of this joy is open only to the person who has integrated his uniqueness with his humanity. It is not open to an individual who is stuck in his being different.

The world of the "I-Thou" consists of persons. It is only here, that an individual truly becomes a person. People cease to be concerned with appearances, with pure show, with how they compare to others, etc. They become persons in their own right. The split between subject and object has been overcome in the world of the "I-Thou." However, it is not a matter of simple choice between the two worlds. No one can exist purely in the world of "I-Thou". The choice between the two worlds is more a question of appreciating the need for the one (the "I-Thou"), and not get stuck in the other (the "I-It").

It is necesary to underline that the "I-Thou" refers to the interhuman, and not to the social sphere of existence. The world of groups and institutions, the social world, includes the world of the "I-It" as well as that of the "I-Thou". Social relationships may be characterized by genuine interhuman relationships, but they may also consist of relations that are exploitative in nature. In contemporary society, relations between people based on commodity exchange and the market, (the predominant characteristic of our social universe), express themselves more in work alienation and reification of consciousness, rather than in genuine interhuman relationships.

The sphere of the interhuman (as distinct from the social) is the sphere where people are really present to each other. In any interaction between two people there are three spheres: my sphere, your sphere, and the sphere of the "in between" you and me. Individual spheres are dominated by the individual perspectives. The sphere of the "in between" belongs to both. Buber's philosophy is the philosophy of the sphere of the "in between." It is the sphere where true and genuine dialogue between an I and a Thou takes place. In this sphere, the spoken (or unspoken) word is its living context. "Real dialogue is the way to existential truth."[6] In genuine encounter, I confirm you in your being as I am confirmed by you in my being. We need to be confirmed in our being.

Categories of genuine encounter:

Being present: I am present with my whole undivided being for you, in the here and now. I am exclusively present for you. I meet you with my whole being. I open myself up to you, and relate to you from the depth of my inner being. Each and every response to you comes from my real self. It reveals my inner self (my uniqueness) to me as well as to you. In meeting you (a Thou), I am becoming more alive. Meeting is the sphere where real living takes place. Aliveness is concrete and present in the encounter between me and you. This encounter points to the existential truth of you and me.

Engagement and exclusivity: My whole being is fully engaged in meeting you. I am here exclusively for you. I relate to you as the unique you that you are. I relate to you from the center of my own uniqueness. In this I affirm you as I affirm myself. (I affirm you even as I oppose you.) My whole being comes alive in meeting you. This is why Buber says that all real living is meeting. We become alive in meeting a Thou, whether it is a person, a thing, nature or God. Every true encounter holds a hidden significance for us. Every encounter is always in the concrete, between an I and a Thou. This concreteness derives not from the ideas that are exchanged between the two persons, but from the nature of the exchange itself, that is, from the nature of the dialogue. Whatever is said, expressed, acknowledged, disputed, whatever ideas or propositions are expressed and exchanged in the dialogue, is concrete by virtue of its aliveness. The dialogue is a living happening. In such dialogue, the two people are really present for each other. Each experiences the other from the uniqueness of their own being. This is the sphere of the "in between".

The encounter with God.

We encounter the eternal (God) only through a loving encounter with others, people, nature, or art objects. Art objects are creations of man's spirit. Man establishes a harmonious relationship to himself, and to the universe. This is the meaning of the I - Thou. By saying Thou, we learn more about the I.

"Every particular Thou is a glimpse into the eternal Thou". (Spinoza: God dwells in each mode.) Man finds God through his relationship with others. This is so, regardless, whether he is a believer or a convinced atheist. Similarly, no one finds God if he or she treats others like an It.[7] For no one can live without God. Whoever thinks that he or she does not need God, is simply missing a vital dimension of life. The question of God is not whether he exists or not, whether he is this or that, or not this and not that. God is the spiritual dimension that is absolutely necessary for life itself, and without which no life can have any meaning.

The biblical word Thou signifies the total immersion of the person in his or her dialogue with God. The dialogue is all absorbing. When you engage God in dialoque, there is nothing else. We have similar experiences when we contemplate natural phenomena with wonder and awe. We totally immerse ourselves in them. We experience Nature as Thou. For Buber, the encounter with another person is to experience the other as a Thou. It is to fully immerse oneself in the dialogue with the other. The sphere of the in-between,

betwen the "I" and the "Thou" is all that is. Nothing else exists for the
moment. This is where real life takes place. Life comes to its own
only in encounter between the "I" and the "Thou". This is where we
actualize our being. However, people ordinarily interact with others in
the form of "I"-"It" rather than "I"- "Thou". Thus, for the most part,
we are not fully experiencing life in all its potentiality, and promise.
To relate to another human being as an "it" is to reduce the other to the
status of a thing, an item of use (a knife, a spoon, a table, etc.). We
don't pay much attention to an item of use, we just use it. When the
thing, the "it" is no more useful to us, we just discard it, and replace
with another. But people, me and you, are not things. We are the
living humanity that is in us. Life is a meeting, a coming together of
people. When people relate to other people as they relate to items of
use, or merely by conveying information, or by being only "practical"
etc., they miss the fullness of life which only human beings can have.

When we relate to the other as "Thou", we absorb ourselves in the
meeting of the "Thou". The "Thou" becomes an all encompassing
totality. The meeting betwen the "I" and the "Thou" comes close to
being a totally absorbing reality. The "I" of my own person, and the
"Thou" of the other person become more like the all encompassing
totalities of Nature. Nothing else exists for the moment, but the "I"
and the "Thou". Each genuine encounter between an "I" and a "Thou"
is a total experience. Did you ever experience an immersion in Nature
to the point that you ceased to be aware of your separateness? In a total
experience, you are immersed in the event, the happening, without
being concerned with your separate existence, or your ego. Buber's "I"
and "Thou" encounter is a way of having a total experience. By
concentrating fully on the presence, by entering into a real dialogue
with the other, by affirming others in all their humanity, dignity, and
creativity, we come as close to life as the living reality that we are. If
we do not experience the living encounter between the "I"and the
"Thou", we miss out on life. Such fullness of life can be experienced in
a brief encounter between any two people, as much as, in an enduring
relationship betwen two people, as for example, in marriage. Suppose a
stranger asks for direction: when I respond to the stranger's quest for
help, with my total being, when at that moment my entire existence is
meant for him, I have had a real encounter, even if I should never see
that person again.

Exercise.

Observe your behavior. Describe the way you relate to other people. Be
specific. Is it more like an "I-it" rather than an "I-Thou"? Following

Buber, endeavor to change your relations with others, including incidental relationships, to "I-Thou" encounters.   Experience a real encounter with the other. It requires an affirming of the other, and a reaching out to the core of the other from the core of your own being. Give yourself sufficient time to practice core relationships with others. Describe your encounters.

Notes

1. Martin Buber, *I and Thou*. A new translation, with a prologue and notes by Walter Kaufmann. New York: Charles Scribner's Sons, 1958. p. 62.

2. Ibid. pp. 63-64.

3. Ibid. p. 85.

4. Ibid. p. 68.

5. Maurice S. Friedman, *Martin Buber, The Life of Dialogue*. Chicago: The University of Chicago Press, 1960. p. 59.

6. Maurice Friedman, *Encounter on the Narrow Ridge: A Life of Martin Buber*. New York: Paragon House, 1991. p. 157.

7. New York Times, Buber obituary, 6/14, 1965.

Workshop 6. Spiritual Formation. (Reflections on Van Kaam's Text on Fundamental Formation.[1])

Spiritual formation involves our desires and struggles for wholeness and integration. Life has to be understood and comprehended as a whole, not in parts. When life is viewed in parts, it is fragmented. Most of us have been conditioned to look at life (at our own person, family, friends, community, etc.) from the perspective of parts rather than the whole. The same holds with respect to learning. We fail integrate parts of what we learn into a knowledge of the whole. Our learning tends to be fragmented.

To form ourselves spiritually, to integrate learning and to acquire knowledge, we need to change our habitual ways of learning, and of living. A basic change of perspective and direction, is not however, a simple matter of decision or will. It requires the continuous application of mind, and body. It necessitates understanding, and faith. This holds true for any area of life. Faith manifests itself in the ever present longing for the whole, the holy. The inwardness of human existence is in faith. We aspire to wholeness. It includes the visible and the invisible in us.

We are formed by our beliefs, and our values. We are deformed by our fixations, and compulsions. We can heal ourselves by true faith, the faith in the wholeness of our nature. A walk in the woods, a spiritual opening to nature, is a healing experience. Life is an opportunity, a gift, a challenge. We have to make ourselves worthy of the gift of life. We must live our life in all its dimensions (vital, functional, spiritual, and cultural -historical) The transcendent dimension of life is to be of service to humanity. There should be a sense of wholeness in every act of life. Formative thought opens up the realm of the spirit. Deformative thought does the opposite. It closes and negates the realm of the spirit.

Attempt at self-inspection:

I am gripped by impulse. I am overcome by my pride form. My excessive pride deforms and debilitates me, in marriage, work, and family. I want everybody (my wife, my children, my friends) to admire and love me. I am dependent on the loving affirmation by others. These compulsive and dependent needs are the sources of my instability. Inner peace has eluded me. I am free in my heart, but not in my guts. Why is the road towards freedom such a tortuous one? I have to stop preaching to others. It is better to role model than to preach. I have to allow my potentialities (for love, for work, for joy, for friendship, for learning,) to unfold. I must open myself up to the transcendent. Without the transcendent, life simply doesn't make sense. I must open the source, the region of the great void, the region of the divine and the creative. Then I can feel the primordial power of nature within me. Can I, and will I, remove the blocks that close off the path to the future? There always lures the danger of the wish for the easy way out. Is my core form (the enduring structure of my personality) strong enough to assert itself in life's wholeness, and in the transcendent? Or am I ruled by my moods? (The mood captures the basic way in which a person is oriented to the world.) The quest for consonance, for faith, hope, and love is in me. The road is difficult. The (Jungian) deformative shadows accompany the formative faith.

However, mere awareness of the problems that stand in the way of integration and consonance, is not enough to accomplish integration and wholeness. We often think that the way to deal with problems of our behavior and inner conflict, is simply to become aware of them, and bring them out into the open, into our consciousness. Then they will somehow go away. But, no matter how difficult and painful such recognition may be, it will not bring about any real change. We often assume that change (the cure) lies in awareness. This is not the case, however. Even repeated recognition of the same problem is still stopping at the awareness level. It will not bring about a change in behavior or the resolution of inner conflict. Van Kaam teaches us, that in order to bring about formation, (i.e. change towards wholeness), it is necessary to repeatedly rupture the cycle of impulse and reaction, through appraisal, repetition and reiteration. This is the essence of Van Kaam's teaching. The road to inner freedom (formation) is not a one time (or even a many times) thing. It is a process. And the process never stops. Life itself is this very process.

Let me give an example: Suppose the person's problem is excessive pride and fragmented learning habits. The inhibiting effects of the pride form express themselves in certain tendencies towards oversensitivity, overreaction, impatience, quick and unfounded judgment, impulsive reaction and behavior, a certain unreadiness or excessive caution to take emotional risks in terms of opening oneself up to another person (or persons), and even within one's own family, a certain inability to control or shorten the impulse reaction time when one's pride has seemingly been affected (hurt).

With regard to the second problem, that of fragmented learning habits, one has to struggle with the practical implementation of the need to think problems through to the very end, and to replace formative for informative thinking. Past conditioning towards fragmented thinking and learning habits is very difficult to overcome. One must continuously and persistently practice it, in order to bring about change. Conditioned and acculturated habits of existence are the result of the total environment and the culture. They are deeply rooted in us. We cannot assume, that the cultural and environmental influences that shaped our behavior hitherto, will suddenly come to a stop when we make our decision to overcome them. To change our thinking from informational to formational thinking, and to correspondingly change our behavior from deformational to formational behavior, there is the actual need for a conscious exertion of effort, without let-up. Such effort is inherently difficult, and the danger of a relapse into the old ways, is forever present.

Contrary to informational thinking, which is shallow and fragmented, and which is practiced in our educational system, formational thinking is thinking from the perspective of the whole, and with a view towards the whole. The point made in the beginning, namely, that intellectual understanding of consonant living will not make living consonant, is worth repeating and ponder upon. It is a necessary first step. The rest (rupture, appraisal, repetition, and reiteration) is an immensely more difficult undertaking. The latter never really ends. I dont want to paint too dark a picture, or to be overly pessimistic about the ability of people to achieve consonace. Quite the opposite. By not understating the seriousness of the task, I am confirming the enormous excitement, inner joy, and happiness that accompanies us with every serious step towards wholeness. We are helped along in that journey by our increased ability to give and receive form, to give and receive love, to allow our core form to express itself and to live productively. The latter means to continuously activate, and reactivate our formation field. Life is an opportunity, a challenge and a gift. We need to be worthy of the gift of life.

Exercises.

1. What is consonant living?
2. Why is faith necessary for integration and wholeness?
3. What is the difference between formative and informative thought?
4. Why is form equated with the whole, and the whole with faith?
5. Awareness of the problem is a necesary but insufficient condition for the cure. Comment.
6. What does Van Kamm mean by: "rupture, appraisal. repetition, and reiteration?
7. Depict a problem that is holding you back from the enjoyment of life. Following Van Kamm, how would you deal with it in order to become more free?
8. Is spirituality to be equated with freedom?

Note

1. Adrian Van Kamm, *Fundamental Formation*. Formative Sprituality Series, Vol. 1. New York: Crossroad, 1983.

SECTION II. SELF-KNOWLEDGE AND SELF DEVELOPMENT: CONVERSATIONS WITH OURSELVES AND WITH OTHERS

Workshop 7. The Digression in Plato's *Theaetetus:* Self-Knowledge and the Portrait of a Philosopher.

The central question in the Theaetetus is what is knowledge? My concern here is with the problem of self-knowledge. More specifically, my question is, to what extent does the Theaetetus throw light on self-knowledge in terms of the meaning of the dictum "Know Thyself" and in its indirect allusions to the need to examine one's self-knowledge.

To know oneself, is in many ways, more difficult (more complex) than to know others (or the outside world). There is the multifaceted realm of the unconscious that operates on the level of the "self" which indirectly affects our judgment, and our ability to know. While all knowing is necessarily conscious, it is nevertheless conditioned and colored by the individual's unconscious. Any exploration of the question of knowledge involves also the question of self- knowledge. Thus, when Socrates asks Theaetetus the mathematician, what knowledge is, they are in a way exploring self-knowledge. What does the young mathematician know about the thing he is supposed to be good at, i.e, his own expertise? This is clearly an attempt at self-examination and self-scrutiny, namely, the need for the expert to examine, and explain his own expertise. The expert needs to raise his understanding (to square his opinion) in order to arrive at (to make it commensurable with) knowledge. The distinction between true opinion and knowledge is now raised. To know something requires giving an account of what one knows. That is, one needs to make knowledge intelligible to oneself and to others. This presupposes a deeper understanding of what one knows, an understanding that involves one's soul (one's self). If the account (or explanation) is merely a superficial one, (mere opinion which does not engage the soul), then such account is insuffficient for knowledge. One cannot stop at simple account giving. One must penetrate behind it, and be able to give an account of an account in order to arrive at knowledge. This presupposes reflective self-examination (self-knowledge) in a person's quest for knowledge.

Just as the entire dialogue of the Theaetetus is a way of answering the question of what is knowledge, the process of self-reflection, self-inquiry, and self-examination is a way (or more precisely, the way) of attaining self-knowledge. The latter deals with clearing the path to the truth about oneself (to overcome self-deceptions and delusions), rather than to get at the truth. However, in the processs of clearig the path, the truth itself will come out. Understanding along with the overcoming of one's prejudices and deceptions are not only a way to truth, but also a part of the truth.

More concretely, elements of self-knowledge include the following: knowledge of one's personal characteristics including physical features (how one appears to the outside), the knowledge of one's values (preferences, likes, dislikes, etc.), an awarenesss of one's capabilities (the powers of one's soul), the knowledge of one's interests, ideas, and ideals, as well as one's attitudes and inclinations.

Let us turn now to aspects of self- knowledge that can be gleaned from the text itself. There are a number of other person characterizations in the text, (Socrates asks about Theaetetus, Theodorus about Theaetetus, Socrates about Theodorus, etc.). Such characterization of other people usually reveals something about the person who is doing the characterizing. Thus, from Theodorus' description of Theaetetus to Socrates, we learn that Theodorus (being a teacher) knows how to judge people. We also learn that Theodorus, Socrates (and the Athenians in general) paid a great deal of attention to physical beauty in men, and that they are inclined to amorous relationships, (perhaps homosexuality). On this point , the translations differ somewhat: Thus, in the Mc Dowell text, we read: "If I had been handsome, I'd have been afraid to speak with emphasis in case anyone thought I was in love with him". In the Jowett translation, the same reads slightly differently: "If I had been a beauty I should have been afraid to praise him, lest you should suppose that I was in love with him."

From Theodorus' description of Theaetetus and his extraordinary qualities, (keen intellect, excellent memory, poise, devotion to knowledge, courage combined with gentleness), we not only learn that Theodorus knows Theaetetus, but also that Theodorus knows himself. Theodorus expresses, what he, as a teacher values in his students, and also the values that appeal to him as a person (moral and physical courage, gentleness, steadfastness, intellectual ability, and modesty.)

Throughout the entire dialoque, we find many instances of Socrates talking about himself: He practices midwifery, attends to men not women, watches over minds not bodies, and he can tell whether the young man's offspring is genuine or an imitation. He helps others discover "many admirable things in themselves" (150 d 5) provided that they stay long enough for delivery. Giving birth to knowledge and new ideas, requires a sustained effort (day and night), that is very painful not unlike the birthpangs of women in childbirth.

Socrates can also tell those who are pregnant with knowledge from those who are not. For the lattter, he tries to arrange proper matches. He sees Theaetetus as being pregnant, and reassures him that he is in good hands ("I am a midwife's son and an expert in midwifery myself"). He exhorts Theaetetus to be cooperative, and if something should turn out an imitation, he shouldn't get angry with him, because it is not an indication of ill will but of his (Socrates') inability to acqiesce in a falsehood, and obscure a truth. (151 d). Socrates is quite aware, that people tend to hold fast to their preconceived notions, and invest in them a certain degree of emotionality, which prevents them from seeing the truth. In the example with the dice (the question of relative and absolute change), Socrates exhorts Theaetetus to examine his thoughts and see whether they harmonize with one another. (The need to examine one's thinking not only with respect to external objects but with respect to oneself.) Examples from dreaming, (having wings and flying) and from a state of madness, (imagining oneself as God) are somewhat extreme examples of false perception and delusion. They are however, indicative of a wide range of possible self-deceptions, many of them less obvious and more subtle, likely to be hidden from consciousness itself.

Socrates describes himself as having no wisdom. He is only instrumental (like a good midwife) in having others generate ideas. "I have no wisdom in me" (150 c 7), and I am not at all wise myself (150 d). He portrays himself only as stimulating a discussion with the other person, and judging it on its merits. "I know no more than he does, apart from a tiny bit, enough to get an argument from someone else, who is wise and accept it in proportion to its merits"(161b5). Obviously, this bit of Socratic irony is used as a didactic device, to put the other person at ease, but one might rightly question its effectiveness because of its obvious exaggeration. However, the pinnacle of Socrates' ironic presentation of himself is reached in the Digression: the Digression is a multilevel presentation. It presents Socrates' (and Plato's) view of the (ideal-stereotype) philosopher, and a view of Socrates himself when the exaggerations are distilled from the presentation. Socrates uses the exaggeration (the extreme) to prove his point. (This is a common Platonic device.)

Let us briefly consider the picture of the philosopher as given in the Digression: Philosophers are never in a hurry. They pursue a subject to the end, until "they hit on that which is" (i.e. the essence). The philosopher is uninterested in practical things, his thoughts roam the entire cosmos ("in the depth of the earth" and "above the heavens"). His inexperience and lack of interest in practical affairs make him appear graceless, ridiculous, and awkward, (he doesn't see the pit in front of him"). He is so absorbed in his thoughts that he fails to notice his next door neighbor, or the beautiful maiden walking by. He does not care for position, high office, wealth or noble ancestry. Things that are important to most people appear silly to him. Because of this, he gets laughed at, (partly because he seems arrogant, and partly because he is absent minded.)

He is not interested in particulars (instances of justice or injustice), but in the investigation of justice and injustice themselves, or in human happiness in general, in order to understand their essence. The masses are only interested in the appearance of "the good" or "the just" but not in the good or the just, per se. But to be wise is to come as close to God as possible, and to become as just as possible. This is what differentiates the wise man from the rest of men. To know this is to know wisdom and virtue. People think that they are just and clever, and perhaps wise when they do things that appear just, good, and wise, in order to promote certain practical ends or desires. But the truth is that they deceive themselves, i.e. "they are just the sort of people they dont think they are" (176d6). The real penalty of injustice is not punishment. It is rather the falling into unhappy life patterns, "leading a life resembling themselves, evil men associating with evils" (177 a5-8).

Even people who seemingly live their lives in conformity with goodness, justice, and virtue, can be subject to unhappiness, if their behavior is motivated by self gain, (good fortune, good regulation, etc.). Apparently, the idea here is, that people should pursue good things (the good) for their own sake rather than for self- gain. Such people are still, at bottom, confused as to the meaning of true values (wisdom) and of life itelf.

The picture of the philosopher (the leader of the Chorus) and of Socrates, as given in the Digression, is clearly, an idealized self-portrait, not meant to be taken literally. The philosopher, like everybody else, must pay attention to his bodily needs, and to the business of everyday living. The purpose is rather to accentuate, and highlight the values that are most important to Socrates (and to the philosopher), and according to which he tries to arrange his life. He comes closest to a God by pursuing the good, and the just, not for the sake of earthly benefit, but for their own sake. For "in order to escape our mortal nature (and the evils of this region) one must become like a God, i.e. just and religious, with intelligence". Therein lies the secret of wisdom. If Socrates is not necessarily smart or clever or practical, he is certainly wise. He is the best model for his own dictum: "Know Thyself".

Assignment: You may want to read Plato's Theaetetus.

Workshop 8. Hegel's Master-Slave Dialectic: The Striving for Mutual Recognition.[1]

Hegel develops his master-slave model in the context of man evolving from the state of consciousness into the state of self-consciousness (individuality). The transition from consciousness to self-consciousness proceeds as follows: Self-consciousnes seeks absolute independence (freedom) and wants to be recognized as such by the other. One self-consciousness faces another. Several things happen: (a) In the transition from consciousness to self-consciousness, the self comes out of itself in becoming aware of something else, although it is not yet self-aware. (b) Self-consciousness loses itself by becoming another for the other. Then, (c) Self-consciousness regains itself by negating the other. It does not see the other as the essential being that it sees itself. Through this double supersession, self-consciousness becomes itself again. For Hegel, individualty requires recognition. But what we are depends on our relation to others. Individuality is gained not outside of, but within a social relation.

To place the above in more contemporary context, it would read:

At first, I am what I think myself to be. Then, I come to realize that I am what you think I am, (I am my appearance to you). However, in order to be certain of myself, I have to overcome (supersede) my appearance to you, (i.e. how I am perceived by others). But in so doing, I negate myself, since my appearance to you (the other's perception of me) is myself. Nevertheless, my appearance is an ambiguous otherness. I must free myself from it, and return to my true self again. I must therefore assert myself over you, and not accept my appearance to you as being me.

This dialectical movement, full of tension, opposition, negation, and supersession (i.e. negation of negation), goes on within each self-consciousness. Self-consciousness is now split. I am both the other (the self outside the self), while this other is really for me (for itself). I am thus aware that I am, and also that I am not, you. We recognize ourselves as we recognize each other. To put it differently, the awareness of the self is conditioned by the awareness of the other.

This recognition however, appears to be split into two extremes: me as being recognized, and you (the other) as doing the recognizing. In other words, one seeks recognition from the other on one's own terms, namely as being independent of the other, and as prevailing over the other. Self-consciousness excludes the other as inessential. It is in this being for self that it is to be an individual.

Thus, individual faces individual. Each one is submerged in the immediacy of life, and is thereby a negative reflection of the other, (the not self). They are not truly independent of each other. The truth of self-consciousness (individuality) however, lies in one's ability to abstract from oneself. This necessitates the overcoming of one's dependence or attachment to any given mode of existence, or indeed to life itself. The two self-consciousnesses have now to prove themselves, that is, they have to prove the truth of their own being as truly independent subjects. A life and death struggle ensues. Here Hegel extends the discussion into the meaning of freedom.

"...it is only through staking one's life that freedom is won."[2] To be free is to be willing to risk all. The individual who has not risked his life has not raised the certainty of his being for himself to truth. Only by a readiness and willingness to risk one's life does one prove that one's essential being is not for the sake of existing (appearing), that it is not a "submergence in the expanse of life", but rather, "that there is nothing present in it which could not be regarded as a vanishing moment" that is to be overcome, if necessary. One proves to oneself that one's life is not just pure being for self (i.e. existing), but rather, that one's life is being in itself, that is, the unfolding of the inherent powers of the self. "The individual who has not risked his life may well be recognized as a *person* but he has not attained to the truth of this recognition as an independent self- consciousness" (Phen. #187.)

However, the trial by death and life struggle does not resolve the question of recognition. Even if I survive the other's death, I cannot be affirmed by him. Recognition requires a living self-consciousness, not a dead one.

Hegel's dialectic now moves from death and survival to the confrontation between a pure self-consciousness, (one that is willing to risk his life), and one that depends too much on thinghood, that is, one that is attached too much to its mode of existence, and is therefore unwilling or incapable to give up its customary way of life for the sake of independence and freedom. The one becomes the master, the other turns into a slave.

The implication is that he who does not or cannot risk all including his life (i.e. material security, physical comfort, job, promotion, etc.) for the sake of independence and freedom, will end up being a slave. Hegel implies that, an individual who is too much attached to his mode of existence, cannot be truly free. He will become enslaved.

The dialectic goes on:

The master can now achieve his desire for complete independence and mastery of the other, by interposing the bondsman (slave) between himself and the external world. The lord's relation to the material world is now mediated through the bondsman and not through work. The bondsman works with the thing, (the material world, tools, nature), and the lord consumes the thing, (material goods produced by the bondsman).

However, the question of recognition still remains.

The master gets his recognition from a consciousness that negates itself, and thereby allows the other to negate it. Neither master nor slave can see himself in the other. (One is not satisfied from being recognized by one's inferiors. One seeks recognition from one's equals, professional equals, intellectual equals, etc.)

The dialectic continues:

As the lord gets to be dependent on the slave for his material needs, his independent consciousness eventually becomes the dependent (and servile) consciousness of the slave. The lord's consciousness turns into its opposite. The slave's consciousness also turns into its opposite. It manifests itself in the independent consciousness of the master. The master cannot do without the slave but the slave can do without the master. The slave is not bound to any external things. The initial complete subservience and dependence on the lord for his life and physical sustenance dissolves in the bondsman everything that was stable and secure in his life. It frees him from his fear of the "loss of thinghood" (attachment to the means of livelihood), since he has nothing to lose anymore. The shaking up of everything stable loosens the slave's attachment to his natural existence. This, however, is not yet enough to make the slave a free being. The slave will achieve this final awareness of himself as a free and independent consciousness, (as "a being for self"), through his work.

It is through work that the material world is formed and shaped. It is also through work that the slave learns to postpone desire, and hold it in check. Thus, the slave gains power over himself. He becomes aware of himself and of his power. He realizes that he can exist without the master, but that the master cannot exist without him. The slave becomes strong and independent. The master, on the other hand, by his self-indulgence, and by his inability to postpone gratification, becomes weak and dependent. Thus, the liberation of the slave and the enslavement of the master begin.

The liberation of the slave goes throgh several stages. These include service, fear, obedience, as well as work. Without the discipline of obedience and service, consciousness cannot really free itself. It would do so only superficially. Work would degenerate into mere skill, and consciousness would degenerate into a merely self-serving existence. Obedience and service signify a commitment to something higher than himself.

Freedom occurs when the slave overcomes his servile consciousness. The slave's liberation begins with the liberation of his mind. He rises to a universality that overcomes his own particularity. Thus the spirit (of man) comes into his own. The slave represents the truth of the master-slave relation. His own liberation will eventually give rise to a universal consciousness, and to the liberation of man's spirit, including that of the master.

The master will also rise above his self-seeking immediate advantage. By this, he will sublate *(aufheben)* his own self-seeking singularity and subject it to serve the good of the community. The dialectic ends with the finding, that the servant by freeing himself also initiates the completion of the master's freedom.

Exercises.

1. What lesson can you derive from Hegel's Master-Slave dialectic?
2. Self -consciousness meets self-consciousness, (individual meets individual). The opposition plays itself out initially within each self-consciousness. Steps in the dialectic are: (a) The individual first asserts that he is what he believes he is. (b) The individual denies himself and believes that he is what the other believes he is. (c) The individual incorporates the other into himself and asserts himself on a higher level. What does that teach you about who you are?
3. In this juxtaposition of individual against individual, in the striving of each to be recognized by the other, one ends up as master, the other as slave. He who is not inhibited by his attachments to his possessions (physical comforts, etc.), and even life itself, becomes the master. The one who cannot let go of his material dependencies and attachments, becomes a slave. Freedom, says Hegel, demands that we risk all for its sake, including life itself. He who is not willing or not capable to overcome his attachment to his possessions, including life itself, cannot be free. True freedom means first and foremost freedom from fear, the fear of losing what one has. Reflect.
4. Can you translate Hegel's insight into freedom and let it guide your life?
5. What does Hegel mean by the ability and the willingness to take risks?   Does he mean a willingness to face any risks, including irresponsible or reckless ones, or does he mean a readiness to take reasonable risks? Does the latter preclude risking one's life for the sake of freedom? Reflect and discuss.
6. Steps in the second dialectic: Master faces slave. (a) The slave works, the master consumes. The master depends on the slave for his physical needs. The slave depends on himself. The master cannot exist without the slave, the slave can exist by himself. (b) The master gets fat, lazy, and soft. The slave becomes disciplined, creative, and strong. The master's initial strength turns into weakness, the slave's initial weakness turns into strength. (c) The slave becomes free when he

overcomes his servile consciousness. The freedom that the slave has gained through his work, ennobles his spirit and makes him more generous. He can thus overcome his particularity, his pettiness and exclusivity. The slave helps liberate the master's consciousness along with his own, and together they reach a common universality in which the true human spirit of mankind asserts itself. Reflect.

Notes

1. G. W. F. Hegel, *Phenomenology of Spirit.* Translated by A. V. Miller. New York: Oxford University Press, 1977. # 178-228. pp. 111-138.
2. Ibid. p. 114.

Addendum: Some Applications of Hegel's Master-Slave Dialectic.

Hegel's master-slave dialectic can be applied to all situations of social inequalty, where there is dominance and submission. We will apply Hegel's model to the family, and illustrate it by a possible evolution of the relation between husband and wife.

Ideally, the family should provide a true home where love, security, and peace prevails. In the Jewish lore, the home is the indwelling of the divine. That is the ideal. But what is the real? Husband and wife are both aware of the potential imbued in marriage for the spiritual, emotional, and material development of each. The foremost need of any human being is to be recognized, acknowledged, and loved. "Self consciousness exists in and for itself when, and by the fact that, it so exists for another; that is, it exists only in being acknowledged."[1] Without acknowledgement, I cannot even exist "in and for myself". I lose the sense of myself and of my human essence. I am not capable to fully exercise my human potential and I will be reduced to a passive existence.

How truly sad it is, that so many people don't realize such a simple and basic truth as the need to acknowledge another human being's presence. When this happens in marriage, it is not only sad, it is tragic. The slippery road of sliding into a merely functioning marriage, where the two people go about performing their respective chores or functions, and where this functioning turns into a routine existence, starts when husband and wife begin to take each other for granted. This can happen imperceptibly, gradually, and without any of the parties noticing it. Yet, it may signal the beginning of the negation of the marriage, which if not caught in time, might lead to its destruction rather than to its sublation.

Traditional cultural stereotypes and roles, such as the husband being the provider and the protector, (with its ensuing macho image), and the wife being submissive and loving, are based on the misapprehension of the true meaning of love. Mature love "must be active and intelligent."[2] If conventional roles are allowed to become rigidified, husband and wife relationship may turn into one of dominance and submission. Neither husband nor wife are free to express their "being for self" into being "for one another". Marriage deteriorates into an empty shell, and it becomes its own negation. This leads to a master-slave situation.

When the woman is afraid to assert herself for fear of losing her husband (the provider), she turns into a slave. The husband slides into a situation whereby he increasingly takes advantage (perhaps unconsciously at first) of his wife's implicit fear of him, and he thus assumes the role of master. It is fear that played the crucial role in the original Hegelian master- slave model, and it is fear that operates the same way here. Fear turns the marriage into its opposite. The man turns into a tyrant, (even if only unconsciously, note the expression "tyrannical love"), and the woman withdraws into silent suffering, and perhaps self pity.

However, this is only a stage, (perhaps a necessary stage), in the final working out of the master-slave dialectic in marriage. The dialectic might either lead to the liberation of both husband and wife within the marriage, or it might lead to its dissolution.

The understanding of an ongoing master-slave dialectic in the marriage situation becomes a necessary condition for the restoration of the true marriage. It may bring the marriage back to itself. (The initial negation brings about its own negation.)

When the woman finally realizes her objective situation, when she finally sees and admits to herself that she is or has been a slave within the marriage, it signals the beginning of her liberation. Her consciousness turns into its opposite. She comes to realize her own strength and true independence, namely, that she can exist without her husband. She gets rid of the fear of being on her own.

This becomes a turning point for both husband and wife. The husband may now begin to realize his own bondage to the traditional stereotypes of what it means to be a husband. It might open his eyes to his lack of love and attention to his wife's real needs, and by extension to his own emotional needs. It might enable both husband and wife to open up to each other, and rekindle true intimacy and love. (However, if such a reawakening comes too late, it will lead to the formal dissolution of a marriage that was not a real marriage anymore, anyway.)

Through   constructive dialogue based on equality, acknowledgement, and mutual recognition, the initial liberation of the wife   also initiates the liberation of the husband.   The husband overcomes his traditional and cultural stereotyped notions, and is thereby able to express himself, and his feelings freely. Both husband and wife are can now grow together in love and harmony.

Exercises.

1. Are you aware of the full potential imbued in your marriage or relationship?
2. Can you express yourself freely in your marriage or relationship?
3. Can you detect any incipient power struggle in your relationship?
4. Do you try to satisfy each other's needs?
5. Are you thoughtful of each other's needs and desires, and can you anticipate them?
6. Are you trying to fully understand each other?
7. Do you help each other grow spiritually?
8. Is your marriage or relationship based on full equality and responsibility for the realization of the spiritual potential imbued in it? Discuss the above and similar questions with your partner.

Notes

1. Hegel, *Phenomenology of Spirit.* p. 111. #178.
2. Ibid. p. 255. # 425.

Workshop 9. A Conversation on *"The Art Of Thinking"* by Ernest Dimnet.

According to Ernest Dimnet (1866-1954),[1] living and thinking cannot be separated from each other. Mental processes, such as, feeling, thinking, remembering, willing, etc. cannot be separated from living. Our thoughts are either about ourselves or they are connected to ourselves. We can think creatively and constructively, or we may go around in circles. When we think compulsively, we go around in circles. Compulsive thinking dulls our mind and makes us unfree.

We lead a better and nobler life when we think clearly. We all wish to develop our thinking capacity to the extent possible. The stream of consciousness at any given moment is incoherent and chaotic. It consists of feelings, images, desires, resolves, representations, likes, dislikes, etc. We are conscious only of a a few of these. Of most of what goes on in our mind, we are not conscious. What we think at a given moment may be pleasant, unpleasant or neutral. For example, I may ask myself what do I think at this very moment? I say, I think of this or that or I think of nothing in particular. My mind is at standstill. I am at a mental lull. When we are at a mental lull, it is a good time to find out how our mind works. Am I inclined to think creatively or compulsively? Do I think clearly or confusedly?

Obsessions or compulsive thoughts are obstructions to thinking. They hinder the thinking process. When we are besieged with inner conflict, we cannot think clearly. We are not relaxed, our face shows tension, and we are not responding freely to stimuli in the environment. We are unable to fully appreciate the beauty of nature, or the beauty of a work of art. We are not fully appreciative of our surroundings. We fail to be wholly absorbed in what we to do at the moment. "Our mind is more inclined to be filled with incipient obsessions than with ideas."[2]

When we cannot let ourselves just be, when we do not fully accept ourselves, we hinder our capacity to think. If we pretend to be what we are not, we cannot think clearly. To be free, is first of all, to be free in our thoughts. Free thoughts are divine. They intoxicate us. To be free in our thoughts is to be closer to God as a free cause. We are the cause of our thoughts, as God is his own cause. Free thoughts when freely expressed give us an exhilarating feeling of joy. It is the joy of being, of creating, and of living.

When we are too sensitive, too preoccupied of how we are being perceived by others, our ability to think is inhibited. We tend to imitate the thoughts of others rather than to think our own thoughts. We thereby suppress our own being. We are not able to formulate or express our thoughts clearly. The longer we allow this tendency to suppress our own being to persist, the longer we deny our own person and refuse to accept ourselves, the more habitual the suppression of our own thinking becomes. Eventually, we lose the ability to think for ourselves, and we become more like mechanical beings.

To be free to think means, that we have to do away with any preoccupation of how our thoughts will turn out to be, whether they will be clever or stupid, profound or shallow. Thoughts by themselves (i.e. ideas) are never stupid. Stupidity is precisely the absence of thoughts. It is the inability to think that makes us stupid. When we preserve or restore our ability to think, we cultivate and train our mind. We make it stretch more than before. Our mind gets to be stretched, more elastic, and we become habitually more thoughtful. This is true, whether we are in solitude, (in conversations with ourselves), or in our interactions with others. We are more independent and less conforming. We do things not because we are expected to do them, but because we want to do them. We are less concerned with conformity or convention. To be able to think our own thoughts, to be our thoughts, is perhaps the highest achievement we can reach in life. Thoughtfulness is the highest form of life.

Children have this marvellous ability to be themselves. When we get older, we gain in experience, but this as Plato says "takes away more than it adds; young people are nearer ideas than old men."[3] When we repeat opinions of others rather than formulate our own thoughts, we obstruct our thinking capacity.

Similarly, with books. When we read a book that doesn't interest us, when we do not or cannot concentrate on what we read, we inhibit our thinking capacity. We should therefore read only what interests us. "Only read what gives you the greatest pleasure."[4] This way, we will always enjoy our reading, and we will develop our ability to fully concentrate on the task at hand. This will greatly enhance our thinking powers. "Good reading will save us from intellectual deterioration. To be able... to devote half an hour a day to religious or philosophical reading, or occasionally to a poet worth the name..."[5]

When we concentrate on any one particular thing, we eliminate all extraneous material, all noise, and all images that involuntarily intrude themselves into our consciousness. We are able to give our full and undivided attention to the task at hand. When we are nervous, we cannot concentrate. Our ability to think, and in particular to think clearly, is inhibited. When we are interested and fully concentrated, our thinking power is greatly enhanced. To think with clarity is to eliminate vagueness from our perceptual and conceptual field of vision. To think is to see with the inner eye. The mind is our inner eye, and the sharpness of our thoughts is like the sharpness of our vision.

Sublime thoughts come from the heart. People who are devoted, selfless, inclined more to give than take, are the ones that think great thoughts. Love opens up the intellect. Deep faith in life, and the nobleness of our pursuits stimulates our mental capacity. Petty irritations and selfishness are obstacles to thought.[6]

"Do not read good books...Only read the best."[7] Great books stimulate our best thoughts. Great books, great happenings, and great men lead to great thoughts. Through them, we commune with other thinkers, whether in person or in books.   In order to stimulate and enhance our capacity for critical thinking, it is necessary to develop the habit of complete comprehension. We have to grasp the main idea of the paragraph or the book that we have read, and reflect on it critically. It also means that we have to ask, and reflect on all the pertinent questions that we can think of. It is useful to see how the main idea is reflected and sustained throughout the text. "Never read, always study...we should study nothing that does not interest us."[8]

In order to enhance our thinking powers, we must develop the practice of asking questions. We have to engage our mind in the raising and solving of problems, until this becomes a habit. We must learn to pay critical attention to minor details, to be aware of small fragments of the landscape, of seemingly insignificant objects within our field of vision. We develop a sharp inner eye, like the painter who is paying attention to his painting. (Nothing escapes a painter's eye.)

It is necesary to mentally go over what we remember, and to complete what we have not sufficiently understood or comprehended. Such interiorization of knowledge will overcome or eliminate any intellectual inferiority that we might have felt. To be engrossed in the object of our reflection, means to think the object through, and go over the topic or question attentively, many times. When we reflect on something spontaneuously, we can use such spontaneous reflection to make our thinking more explicit, more deliberate, and more conscious.

We need to practice the enlargement of our conscious reflection *vis a vis* the unconscious. Whenever we move from the unconscious to the conscious, we reclaim a set of images for ourselves, images or ideas that have been there within us, but of which we had no previous awareness. There are many things of which we know very little, or of which we want to know more about. It is good to develop the habit of thinking about them, with frequent regularity. We need to make a continuous effort not to be hampered in our thoughts by oversensitivity, that is, by worrying about how others view or think about us.

It is good to develop the habit of keeping track of one's thoughts, and of what one learns. The greatest pleasures are those of the intellect, and facts are only worthwhile to the extent that they provide material for thought. When we see the connection between facts and ideas, we practice and make use of our creative imagination. We can connect to our past, and that of others. We can hold conversations with historical characters, and hold dialogues with great men. "To carry on a dialogue with one's self about those noble souls and keeping one's self alive by it..."[9]

By this, we get inspired to great thoughts, and to creative thinking. All creative thought is divine. "Our soul is an ocean."[10] There is infinite room in it for new, and creative ideas. Such ideas have one basic characteristic in common. They are all simple. "Simplicity is the characteristic of all creative notions."[11]

There are two fundamental requirements for intuitive and creative thinking. These are: to be oneself, and to find oneself. To be oneself is to be free of pretense, anxiety, and diffidence. To find oneself means to look for that part of the unconscious which is most fertile in the production of our thoughts, that is, where we can produce our thoughts with greatest ease and enjoyment. We find our real interest to lie with those things that we feel most at home with. When we feel at home with ourselves and with our environment, we are our natural selves. That makes us eloquent. It gives us the inspiration to do great things, and to have genuine thoughts. We are free from any subconscious need for fame, admiration, etc. These are all phantasms that intrude upon us. As we get closer to our unconscious, we discover treasures in it that have been hidden from us, for a long time. We become conscious of our power and of our freedom to be ourselves. We allow our intuition to come forth and to freely guide us to the truth in our life. When the mind reaches the truth, it reposes in it. We reach the contentment of the spirit.

Exercises.

1. Are you often inhibited to express your thoughts because you might be adversely judged by another?
2. Observe yourself: Determine when you have clear thoughts and when your thoughts are confused.
3. Dimnet defines stupidity not as having stupid thoughts but as the absence of thoughts. Do you agree? Do you agree that your own thoughts can never be stupid?
4. What does it mean to think clearly? Does clear thinking require that you follow through any given idea or thought to the very end?
5.   Do you agree with Dimnet that you will never feel inferior to anyone else as long as you follow through your own thoughts to the end?
6. Think of why you do whatever you do, why do you make plans or undertake certain projects that you wish to carry out? Are these projects of yours designed, consciously or subconsciously, to impress others, or are they exclusively designed for the joy and satisfaction that they will bring you?

7. Do you feel that you have to force yourself to work? Do you feel stress or pleasure in your work?

8. Are your unexpressed desires and aspirations internally or externally conditioned? In other words, are your desires and wishes truly yours? Or do you want to impress others with what you do or with what you can do?

9. Are you subjected to phantom needs for greatness, significance or fame?

10. Have you ever confronted such false needs?

11. What are the primary manifestations of your inner conflicts?

12. Do you think that inner conflict always manifests confusion, and a lack of clarity of thought? What is it that inhibits you from carrying out your thoughts to the very end, as far as you can go?

13. What is the nature of the threat to your ego and the pain involved in upsetting your self-image that you want to preserve under any conditions? Can you identify the threat and confront the pain?

14. Do you think that children are more clear in their thoughts than adults? If yes, why?

15. Do you agree with Dimnet that only in your thoughts can you be entirely free?

16. Have you ever felt intoxicated and exhilarated by your thoughts?

17. Do you agree with Dimnet's basic idea, that free and clear thinking depends on self-acceptance and on free being? And, that free being means to be without fear of how I am perceived by others?

Notes

1. Ernest Dimnet, The Art Of Thinking, New York: Simon and Schuster, 1931.
2. Ibid. p. 42.
3. Ibid. p. 75.
4. Ibid. p. 129.
5. Ibid. p. 86.
6. Ibid. p.122.
7. Ibid. 128.
8. Ibid. p.136.
9. Ibid. p.155.
10. Ibid. p.183.
11. Ibid. p. 182.

Workshop 10. Jean Piaget's Stages of Cognitive Development.

Piaget (Piaget, Jean 1896-1980) pioneered experimental studies in cognitive development of persons, from birth to maturity. He has greatly enhanced our knowledge in this area.

In the first two years the child develops sensory-motor skills. The child learns by trial and error. The infant coordinates his actions and perceptions into sensi-motor schemes. Sensory motor coordination and skills are not based on reflective abstraction. Based on sensory-motor intelligence, the child later develops logical thinking and cognitive structures. Structures with which the child learns to organize experience (biological structures) are given at birth. Perceptual discovery is based on inherited biological structures.

The period from two to seven years is the pre-operational period. This period is subdivided into the pre-conceptual period (two to four years), and the intuitive period (four to seven years). In the pre-conceptual period, the child develops the ability to use symbols through role playing, imitation, etc. The child is egocentric, believes in magic, and can be easily fooled. It can only deal with one variable at a time. The child cannot think logically. "Children are most like us in their feelings and least like us in their thinking."[1] In the intuitive stage, the child learns to classify objects. It begins to develop concepts of size, and order.

The period between seven and eleven years is the concrete operational period. Concrete operations are logical operations such as, classifications, symmetry, forming and the discovery of patterns, one to one correspondence, etc. These operations are limited however, to particular objects or materials. The child is unable to keep in mind more than one relation at a time. Intuitive actions are internalized and transformed into logical thought. The child intuitively repeats actions, but it can also reconstruct them anew. He or she does it through the process of reflective abstraction. In the concrete operational period, the child is egocentric. The child fails to differentiate between assumptions and facts. Objects are imbued with feeling. The child believes that natural phenomena are controlled by man. In adolescence, egocentricity takes on a different meaning. The adolescent thinks that others are primarily preoccupied with his appearance. He constructs an imaginary audience and reacts to it. The adolescent's primary emotional reaction is not guilt, but shame.

In the operational period, (following the concrete operational period), the child develops hypothetico-deductive thinking. Such thinking forms the intellectual core of human knowledge. Thinking is seen as processing information, a structured activity guided by feedback. (The science of self-regulating systems, living or not living, that is based on informational feedback is called cybernertics). Reflective abstraction at this stage gives rise to logico-deductive (mathematical) structures. The child applies cognitive structures to real world phenomena. These structures embrace discovery, exploration, inventiveness, critical evaluation, verification, etc. Human knowledge develops through the process of assimilation (opening) and accommodation (integration). The individual adapts himself cognitively to the environment. To assimilate means to transform what is new into what is familiar. To accomodate means to integrate the new with the familiar. For example, when length, width, and height have been transformed into the concept of size, the child has integrated knowledge. Formal operational thinking tends to be firmly established by the age of 15 or 16. At this age, the initial adolescent's egocentrism also tends to diminish. The young person is capable of developing intimacy with another. He or she can gradually integrate the other's feelings with his or her own. They can also begin to differentiate between their own thoughts and those of another. Both of these indicate a lessening of egocentricity.

Cognitive development in adolescence proceeds towards the ability to utilize symbols, to use combinatorial reasoning, to construct ideal situations, and to introspect. It is very important at this stage not to hamper the child's eagerness to learn. Education should not interfere with the child's own rhytm and pace of learning. Piaget differentiates between physical experience (P) and logico-mathematical experience (LM). LM learning provides the basic concepts for arranging and organizing experience. Reflection (interpretation, analysis, etc.) is its primary activity. In LM learning, we act on things. In P learning, things act on us. In education, we need to devote primary attention to LM learning. The discovery of logical truth is inherently satisfying. It is the source of intrinsic motivation. These mental activities are self rewarding and need not be externally reinforced. Curiosity and the desire for competence are additional motivational drives. We grow through conflict, change, facing obstacles, and problems. Conflict, and change are unavoidable in life as well as in thought. Any new learning or a new topic should be related to some concrete experience whenever possible. Through new learning, the child learns to act purposefully, think rationally, and deal effectively with the environment.

The years between six and twelve are crucial for later intellectual development. The child's perceptual growth proceeds through exploration, reorganization, schematization, and anticipation. Perceptual reorganization means the ability to mentally rearrange a given stimulus pattern or array of things. Perceptual schematization means to organize parts and wholes into schemata in such a way that they don't lose their individual significance. Perceptual exploration is the ability to scan or array a figure in such a way as to note all of its important features. Schematization is the ability to translate experience in to a well defined sequence of action, a schema. "A schema is a particular mental structure that is capable of generalization and transfer."[2] Assimilation is the process of incorporating new experiences into existing, and familiar cognitive schemata. Accommodation is the process of modifying an existing cognitive schema to allow for new experience. It consists of exploring, questioning, doing, reflecting, and experimenting. Perceptual anticipation is to anticipate similar figures or arrays in comparable circumstances. Formal operations consist in making use of assumptions, (even if only for the sake of argument), seeing many possibilities, forming theories, looking for general properties, seeing many points of view, stating general laws, inventing imaginary systems, and in general it means the ability to deal with a wide variety of complex relations. At the age of 14 or 15, the child reaches its peak of hypothetical thinking. Formal operational thinking is enhanced by cooperative tasks, (in discussion, and small group settings). Not all people attain the stage of formal operational thought, and the flexible problem solving associated with it.

Exercises.

1. To assimilate new knowledge is to incorporate new experiences into familiar cognitive schemata. Give examples from your own learning that illustrate assimilation of knowledge.
2.   To integrate and accommodate new knowledge is to modify existing cognitive schemata to allow for new experiences. Again, give examples from your own learning to illustrate how you integrate new knowledge.

Notes

1. David Elkind, *Children and Adolescents: Interpretive Essays on Jean Piaget.* New York: Oxford University Press, 1974. p. 51.
2. Ibid. p. 10.

Workshop 11. Some Aspects of Jungian Psychoanalysis.

Everything that pertains to our inner world that we are not aware of, is contained in our unconscious. It is possible to gradually widen the area of the conscious relative to the uncoscious. While nothing is foreclosed from the possibility of consciousness, there is a limit to the potential awareness of our psychic life. It is not posssible to become fully aware of our entire unconscious. We can enlarge the awareness of our inner world, we can push our conscious mind further, but we cannot entirely eliminate the unconscious. The unconscious is virtually limitless, and open ended. It contains everything that we once knew but have forgotten, and everything that we now know, but are not presently thinking about. All the repressed and forgotten thoughts and feelings, including the pain associated with them, are stored in our unconscious. Whatever we once felt, thought, wanted, experienced, etc. is never entirely lost. Instead, it has become part of our unconscious. This is what constitutes the personal unconscious. The person's unconscious is derived from his or her life experience.

In addition to this, basically Freudian, (Freud, Sigmund 1856-1939)) personal unconscious, Jung (Jung, Carl Gustav 1875-1961) developed the idea of the collective unconscious. The latter includes all those traits and qualities that we have collectively inherited from our culture and history. They are part of our collective experience. As inherited instincts and impulses, they are present in each one of us. We all share in them, but are not aware of them. The collective unconscious underlies our individual and personal unconscious. It is made up of archetypes or inborn tendencies that propel us to act in certain predetermined ways, without our being aware of the reasons and motivations for such actions. These archetypes form the deeper stratum of our individual psyche. They are collective, because they are not part of our personal experience. They are the common substrate (i.e. fixed qualities) of all human psyche. As we recede further and further into the collective unconscious and archetypes, they merge more and more with our physical world. According to Jung, the psyche is at bottom simply the whole unified world, whereby the physical and the mental are parallel and identical expressions of the same substance. There is a parallelism in the evolution of the physical and the psychical universe, both originating from the same source. This comes very close to Spinoza's idea of Substance (God or Nature), and the derivative psychophysical parallelism.

Humanity's beginnings and our entire past are a continuous substratum of our existence. This substratum molds our consciousness as much as the physical world around us. The psychic system like the physical body, has a prehistory of millions of years. Man's original mind forms the child's life instinct, and is imbued in its preconscious state. The child's mind at birth is not a *tabula rasa*. The collective unconscious (the original mind) is at the base of the individual psyche. Without it, the ego cannot develop. Consciousness awakens gradually in the child. Our myths are a channel to our primordial psyche. In these myths, the original fundamental instincts and archaic thought forms are still preserved. These myths speak to us in our dreams, in the form of symbols. Images of the original mind are highly numinous. They exert great power over us. They can both heal or destroy.

All aspects of human nature, (the good and the bad, the light and the dark, the creative and the destructive, etc.) are contained in the unconscious mind. Through the unconscious, we can get insight into ourselves. The unconscious both forms and transforms the person. We can change our psyche through the unconscious. ... "the unconscious is a *process*.... the psyche is transformed or developed by the relationship of the ego to the contents of the unconscious."[1] The self is the goal of all psychic development. The images of the unconscious are not subject to the laws governing spatio-temporal events. In our dreams, these images give us access to our individual unconscious. Through myths, they inform us about our collective unconscious. Our connection to the divine reveals itself in our myths.

We will now consider some of the central Jungian concepts:

The Self.

The Jungian self is a central archetype which denotes the totality of the personality. It embraces the conscious as well as the unconscious psyche. Just as the ego is the center of our conscious mind, the self is the center of the totality of our person. We can never fully reach the consciousness of the self. We may strive towards the realization of the self (in the form of creative self expression), but we can never fully reach it or express it. The totality will always remain beyond the possibility of its full realization. The process of individuation denotes the striving for an undivided whole, for self-fulfillment in wholeness, and self-completion. Individuation is not limited to the conscious embracing of one's ego. It is rather a process of embracing all humanity into the self.

In Jungian psychology, the self as the center, is symbolized by various images, such as those of a child, a circle, a mandala (the Indian picture of a magic circle), a square, or the number four (the four corners of the world). By meditating on these images we can get closer (connect) to our center. When the self is confused and disoriented, meditation on the magic circle or mandala, (divided into four parts, each of which is filled with specific content), represents universal order amidst psychic confusion. "The mandala is an archetypal image ...It signifies the *wholeness of the self.*" [2]

In the dream, the self often appears as a youth, the cosmic man (a human being that embraces the whole cosmos), or as the great man within. The image of the youth symbolizes the renewal of life or self renewal. The self may also appear as a crystal, which in its perfectly symmetrical arrangement indicates the union of spirit and matter. The presence of spirit in matter is part of Jung's concept of synchronicity. It signifies a coincidence of meaningful events which are not accountable by a causal relationships.

The soul.

The human soul contains all the accumulated images and experiences of mankind. God's image as an archetype is imprinted in the soul. The human soul can connect to God. It is inexhaustible in its non-spatial universe. It can span over all the cosmos and all time. The Jungian archetype is not determined with regard to content (something comparable to an unconscious idea), but it is present only with respect to form. In this sense it is more like an instinct.

The *Persona.*

The *persona* is "originally the mask of an actor".[3]   In our daily life, it is the image of ourselves that we project to the outside. When we become too closely identified with our *persona*, with our professional or the artificially contrived self, we lose the awarenes who we really are. When an unhealthy identification with the *persona* occurs, when we identify with something undesirable, we may anticipate the appearance of an opposite in a dream (to compensate for the above.)

The Shadow.

The shadow is often an unknown figure of the same sex appearing in a dream. It represents the dark side of our nature, the repressed part of our personality. Everybody has a shadow. The shadow contains all that we refuse to acknowledge about ourselves. It is part of our unconscious. Often we point to someone's bad behavior and become intensely emotional about it. We accuse the person of having some bad character traits that we find detestable. What we fail to do, is subject ourselves to the very same situation, and see whether we would indeed behave any differently. It is most likely the case that those negative character traits that we have assigned to the other person with such great outburst of emotion, reveal certain negative parts of our own personality that we dislike very much and have therefore suppressed. This is why we get so emotional about it. In other words, our emotional outburst and indignation often reveal our shadow. However, the shadow not only represents the negative and destructive side, but may also indicate the positive and the creative side of our nature. It contains certain ideals and values that we have failed to integrate within our personality and live up to them. The shadow exposes these high ideals and values to us. This usually happens in dreams. The shadow always appears in the same sex as the dreamer. It reveals to us what we potentially are or can be in terms of the good and the bad.

The *Anima* and *Animus*.

The anima is the feminine nature in man's unconscious. (*Anima*, the soul or breath of life.) The *animus* is the masculine nature in the woman's unconscious. The *anima* personifies certain female characteristics contained in man's psyche, such as, moods, receptiveness to the irrational, emotional warmth, softness, romance, and the occult. A man's mother has a decisive influence on the shaping of his *anima*. The *anima* is a source of an overflow of feeling that can be used either creatively, or self destructively.

Similarly in a woman, the *animus* in the unconscious, often takes the form of hidden convictions that are asserted with great force, some hardness in her character, some spontaneous and ready made opinions that shape the woman's outward behavior, etc. Similar to man's *anima*, the woman's *animus* is largely determined by her relation with the father. As is the case with the anima, the woman's *animus* can also be used in positive ways, namely, to bring out the creative possibilities contained in the self. The *animus* may reveal positive qualities, such as, courage, wisdom, spirituality, etc.

Synchronicity.

The Jungian concept of synchronicity denotes "the meaningful coincidence or equivalence of a psychic and a physical state or event which have no causal relationship to one another."[4] Examples of such coincidences are premonitions, telepathy, the materialization of a dream, etc. These phenomena are not subject to normal cause-effect relationships. Jung states: "Thus I found that there are psychic parallelisms which cannot be related to each other causally, but which must be connected through another principle, namely the contingency of events. ......It seems, indeed, as though time, far from being an abstraction, is a concrete continuum which contains qualities or basic conditions that manifest themselves simultaneously in different places through parallelisms that cannot be explained causally, as for example, in cases of the simultaneuous occurrence of identical thoughts, symbols or psychic states."[5]

Jung excludes the explanation of pure chance for the existence of such simultaneous occurrences. He compares these events to the discontinuities in physics, which are also mysterious in the sense that they are not subject to the laws of causality. The physicist, Wolfgang Pauli (1900-1958), has indicated that there might be an interrelation between the unconscious and certain biological processes. He pointed out, that if mutation of species was entirely random, and the evolution proceeded on the basis of the survival of the fittest, the biological evolution would have taken much longer than the known age of the planet. It is therefore possible that certain exceptional events have ocurred at certain times which have accelerated the random process of mutation.[6] This could be an example of synchronicity working in the universe. The simultaneous occurrence of the same discoveries in many fields of science is well known. The simultaneous discovery of calculus by Leibnitz and Newton may serve as a case in point. There are also analogies between Jung's unconscious and microphysics. In the latter, causal determinism breaks down, and is replaced by statistical laws of averages and probability calculus.[7]

Exercises.

1. Can you get access to your unconscious? Describe the ways of how you can do it.
2. Give examples of what Jung means by the collective unconscious.
3. In what sense is your unconscious different from another's unconscious? Can you relate to another's unconscious the same way as to your own?
4. What is Jung's *persona*? Describe your *persona*.
5. What is Jung's shadow? Discuss your shadow.
6. What is Jung's *animus* and *anima*? Describe them.
7. What is Jung's definition of the "self"?
8. What does Jung mean that through dreams one can get access to one's "self"?
9. Can you grasp your own "self" in terms of the totality of your being?

Notes

1. C. G. Jung, *Memories, Dreams, Reflections*. New York: Pantheon Books, 1963. p. 209.
2. Ibid. p. 335.
3. Ibid. p. 385.
4. Ibid. p. 388.
5. Ibid. p. 388.

6. Carl G. Jung, *Man and his Symbols*. New York: Doubleday & Company, Inc. 1964. p. 306.
7. For a fuller discussion of this, see, M. -L von Franz, *Science and the Unconscious*. in Carl G. Jung, *Man and his Symbols*. pp. 304-310.

Workshop 12. Wolpe's General Procedure for Self-Relaxation and Overcoming Anxiety.[1]

Wolpe's (Wolpe, Joseph) method consists in bringing the specific anxiety causing states back into our awareness at a time when we are fully relaxed. For example, when I am fully relaxed and without anxiety, I recreate my fear (of failing the exam, or of not getting the job, of being reprimanded by the boss, of being discovered for having done something wrong, of somebody bullying me in school or at work, etc. etc.). I bring back into my present consciousness the aroused anxiety that I felt previously in connection with some unpleasant event. While I feel relaxed and I am not facing the anxiety arousing event, I connect the state of relaxation with the events or thoughts that cause me to be anxious. I can practice this anytime I find myself getting anxious about anything. I purposefully bring back the anxiety causing event into my consciousness. Since the unpleasant event is only imaginary and not real, the corresponding emotional arousal will be lessened or non-existent. I can therefore associate my state of relaxation wth the anxiety causing events or thoughts. If I go on practicing this with anything that is the cause of my anxiety, and as I do this consistently, I gradually lose the state of anxiety that is connected with the anticipated (unpleasant) event. Systematic desensitization is a step by step procedure whereby the person is gradually exposed to increasing anxiety causing situations, at a time when he or she is fully relaxed. The overcoming of anxiety through full relaxation is gradually built up until it is almost reduced to zero.

My anxiety can also be reduced when I make a positive statement about myself. Thinking and feeling tend to overlap. They are in some sense the same thing. It is therefore possible for me to talk myself out of my anxiety or unhappiness. Conversely, it is also possible to talk myself into being unhappy. The latter is the basis for Ellis' (Ellis, Albert) rational-emotive psychotherapy. The goal is to teach people to see themselves in a more positive light. Self-awareness is often facilitated in group settings, such as, sensitivity or consciousness raising groups. Positive feedback from others greatly enhances our self-awareness, and it brings about a greater likelihood of a desirable change in our behavior.

We do not, as a rule, have the capacity to introspect accurately into the causes of our behavior. We tend to give incorrect explanations that seem to make intuitive sense. When we look at ourselves more objectively, we begin to notice the discrepancies between what we are, and what we would like to be. This causes some anxiety. On the other hand, when my focus on myself reveals something good and positive, it makes me feel good about myself. When we begin to focus on our self-awareness, feedback from another is of greatest importance. Our self-esteem is enhanced by positive feedback. When we have no feedback or when the feedback is negative, when we are being blamed or not understood by the other, our self-esteem suffers. When our self-esteem is high, we are more likely to assume responsibility for our actions and behavior. When our self-esteem is low, the opposite will be the case. This works in either direction. When we take responsibility for ourselves and for our behavior, our self-esteem is enhanced. Only when we come to accept certain truths about ourselves, can we begin to change. As a rule, we change our attitude and behavior more easily if we attribute the reason for the change to ourselves rather than to the outside. Outside prompting, or someone else telling us of our need to change our behavior, is usually not effective, and certainly not as effective as if we ourselves were the agent of our change. Changes in attitude and behavior necessitate an inner awareness and a readiness for change. We can, nevertheles, influence other people by making them aware of how they act in certain situations. It is necessary, under almost all circumstances, to use tact, good judgment and circumspection, in pointing out other people's inadequacies. It is important to make others feel, that the newly gained insight, has come from within themselves.

Anytime we turn our attention fully towards a given task at hand, there is an increase in energy level, and the performance of the work becomes that much easier and more enjoyable. This is also true when we practice a change in behavior. By concentrating fully on any one small aspect of behavior that we are determined to change, we gain in energy levels, and this enhances the prospect of successful change even more. The more we know ourselves and our emotional states, the more are we able to control them. "Everyone has the power, partially at least, if not absolutely, of understanding clearly and distinctly himself and his affects, and consequently of bringing to pass that he suffers from them" (Spinoza, Ethics). We cannot go beyond our limits. It is much easier to be aware of our external limits. It is more difficult to know our internal limitations. Our unconsciousness pushes us beyond our limit, and when we force our limitations, we act compulsively. When we seek to confirm our good or bad attributes, we will usually find enough information to support whatever we seek to confirm. In our conscious state, we can be more aware of our limits. When we work within those limits, we are operating within our reality. Our projects will be more reality oriented, and founded on a more solid foundation. We could therefore define reality to mean, the proximate grasp of the real possibilities imbued in our existence. This is what Spinoza had in mind when he equated reality with perfection. When we move outside of our real possibilities, we are acting compulsively. We are forcing our limitations.

The same pertains to relationships, to uncontrolled emotions, and expectations. When we build up unrealistic expectations about a relationship, we greatly inhibit its potential development, and more often than not, we will fail to develop intimacy. When we learn to live and operate within our limits, without giving in to excesses on either side, without contrived hubris and without despair, we also learn to love ourselves, and to accept ourselves. To value and esteem ourselves, to be tolerant to ourselves, to accept ourselves, and to love ourselves, is fundamental to our well-being. We cannot love life without loving ourselves. The wonders we seek outside are all within us. We experience our inner self in action and interaction, in our involvement in life. Without it, we are not fully alive. When we are not accepting ourselves fully, we tend to act, not according to our own desires but according to the wishes of others: Our self is a false self, and our existence is inauthentic.

Basic human realities consist of ourselves, other persons, and of our symbiotic interactions with them (talk). "The fundamental human reality is a conversation, effectively without beginning or end, to which from time to time, individuals make contributions. The structure of our thinking and feeling will reflect, in various ways, the form and content of that conversation."[2] Our material conditions (levels of living), and our spiritual values and beliefs, represent the two other (secondary) realities. The order of reality is, according to Harre, (Harre, Rom) structured as follows: (1) other people, (2) our interactions with them, (3) the conditions of material production, and (4) the system of our beliefs and values.

Exercises.

1. Describe events or thoughts that cause you anxiety.
2. List all the unspecified fears that you have. Be specific.
3. Select the fear that you encounter most often, and apply Wolpe's method of systematic desensitation. Combine it with deep breathing exercises.
4. Observe yourself and describe the results.
5. Do you usually deal with anxiety causing events by minimizing or avoiding your exposure to them? Can you also avoid anxiety causing thoughts?
6. List all the means by which you can overcome your fears.
7. Do you assume responsibility for your fears, or do you deny them and blame others for them?
8. Do you think that others can remove your fears, or do you think that only you can effectively deal with them?
9. How do you understand your reality? Is fear a reality within you? If so, does freeing yourself from this and other fears put you on a higher

level of reality? Does that give you an enhanced feeling of freedom? Is the movement from lower to higher levels of reality simultaneuously a movement from lower to higher levels of freedom? If the latter is true, does that mean that you can attain any level of reality and freedom? Do you have to stay within your reality in order to change it, (i. e. move to a higher level and be more free)?

10. Consider a specific area of your life that you want to change. Recognize all aspects of reality in the given area of your life. Take full responsibility for your situation and predicament. List all possible ways by which you realistically could change your situation to your liking. Test mentally or actually each one of these various possibilities. Do it diligently and consistently. Observe your behavior and carefully notice the results.

11. Do this exercise with respect to each of Harre's structure of reality, discussed at the end of the workshop.

Additional exercises:

1. How well do you listen to other people?
2. Do you tend to offer advice without being asked for?
3. What usually makes you angry or annoyed?
4. Can you easily admit guilt or failure?
5. Do you learn from your failures or mistakes, so as not to repeat them?
6. Can you easily compromise?
7. Do you act before you think or vice versa? Give examples.
8. Do you easily forgive and forget?
9. Do you get more pleasure from giving or from getting?
10. Are you spontaneous in your expressions and actions, or do you tend to inhibit them?

Notes

1. C. H. Patterson, *Theories of Counseling and Psychotherapy*. New York: Harper &Row Publishers, 1986, Chapter 5.
2. Rom Harre, *Personal Being; A Theory of Individual Psychology*. Cambridge, Mass.: Harvard University Press, 1984. p. 20.

Workshop 13. On Gestalt Therapy.[1]

Gestalt is the Whole, the Configuration, the Thought. Gestalt assumes completion. It could be the resolution of a problem, completing a script, or finding an answer to something that is bothering us. In any situation, there is always a figure and the ground. The figure is sharp, it is what we are focusing on. Everything else is the ground. Ground and figure interconnect. One helps define the other. When things are in context, part of my perception (I look at another person, etc.) is determined by the ground (the surroundings). My behavior is being defined by my situation.

Fritz Perls (1893-1970), the founder of Gestalt therapy, was a medical student at the University of Berlin, and studied psycho-analysis with Freud. In 1939, Perls went to South Africa. There he established the first Psycho-Analytic Center. Gestalt therapy is action oriented therapy. It is impossible to learn Gestalt therapy merely from reading about it, or by being passively exposed to it. One has to actively involve oneself in its practice and participate in workshops.

An important point in Gestalt therapy is that *we can only focus at one point at a time*. Neurotics are unable to focus on one thing at a time. We focus on the present with our five senses, in the *here and now*. We focus on what is happening now. We identify figures and pay attention to them. When we get in touch with our senses, we become excited by the things around us.   The present is always changing. We focus on the change, on what is happening now. When we focus on the present, we get very calm. "The past and the future only occur as they enter the present." [Kurt Lewin, (1890-1947)]. The future is what causes most people's problems, anticipation, and worry. Gestalt functions as a continuum of awareness, an awareness of the ever changing present.

We want to close (complete) things. If the gap between the action and the completion remains, if we have not completed our task for now, there is a degree of frustration associated with the gap. The frustration motivates us to want to close the gap. Gestalt therapy poses questions, and induces the person to resolve them. We try to identify and to close the gaps. Gaps are the things that are left incomplete within ourselves. The answers to all our questions lie within us. The therapist is actively involved in the questions but not in the answers. Everyone must take responsibility for his or her life.

The therapist functions as the director. The client is functioning by acting out the problem. In therapy, the client is figure, the therapist is ground. Feelings are just as legitimate as thoughts. Feelings are separate from thoughts, they have a life of their own. Feelings and thoughts are two levels of reality. Feelings are felt physically. When

someone hurts our feelings, we feel pain in our body. (Try to locate
your feelings in the body). We need to learn that feelings change.
Psychiatrists dull emotional responses with drugs. Drugs dull feelings,
they don't change anything. In Gestalt therapy, feelings speak. They
have to be worked with. They tell the person what is wrong. One
cannot medicate away psychological problems. Feelings manifest a
conflict. Locate the anxiety, describe it. "My feet feel warm and
heavy. Which foot feels the heaviest and warmest? Put your hand on
the foot. Visualize the warmth coming into your hand, how it infiltrates
your chest, etc. (Gestalt techniqes are practiced in therapy workshops).

Gestalt therapy centers on awareness. The immediate aim is the
restoration and expansion of awareness. Awareness is not the same as
consciousness. Consciousness is thought awareness, namely, to make
the unconscious, conscious. Gestalt awareness is the awareness of
one's feelings and sensory perceptions. It is to be aware of what one is
doing and feeling at the moment, (in the present). In Gestalt, we are
more interested in the perception of the person's present behavior rather
than in explaining it. There is a difference between intellectual insight,
(understanding of the causes of one's behavior), and emotional insight,
(expansion of awareness into present feelings and perceptions).

Repressing, negating or holding back of one's feelings lead to
muscular tension (Reich's character armor). It also leads to sensory
dullness, and a blurring of vision. The aim of gestalt therapy is to free
such pent-up feelings and bodily tensions. We want to restore
sensitivity, to bring back the sharpness to our senses, relax the tension
in the muscles, and to unblock the locked-up energy by relaxing our
body and increasing its awareness.

Gestalt therapy is most applicable to people who are unhappy with
the way they live and function, and who seek to change their behavior
in order to be more free and open for personal growth. Intellectual
insight and the talking about one's past, as practiced in conventional
therapy, can be a way of avoiding to deal with one's problems in the
present. It may thus lead to blaming, to self indulging, or to making
excuses for oneself.

Explanations and why questions, (why did you do this or why do
you feel that way), are usually avoided in Gestalt therapy. Gestalt
deals with the "what and how", not with why questions. It wants
desriptions, not explanations. The past is present in the here and now
in the form of body tension, compulsion, transference relation, etc.
Gestalt points to the possibilities that are inherent in the present and are
not entirely determined by the past. It points to the possibility of a
break in the continuity with the past. It is concerned with total
communication, with feeling, sensing and thinking. Gestalt pays
particular attention to body language. The person is forced to take
responsibility for what he or she wants or does not want to do. (Instead

of "I can't", one has to say "I won't," etc.) The full expression of any feeling releases energy and frees it for something new. A denial of feelings or a partial and limited expression of them, traps and clogs energy. Gestalt opens up the possibility for greater awareness, and the feeling of joy that comes with it. It reduces the heaviness of any previous moods, and it allows people to have fun and enjoy themselves.

The purpose of Gestalt is to reintegrate and reassimilate into our self the various pulls and conflicting tendencies stemming from the commands of the super ego. At the same time we are also aware of doing it. We thereby learn to better control our conflicts. By controlling and resolving our conflicts, we are able to make better use of the potential inherent in us.   Gestalt therapy helps people assimilate traits and values which they have adopted from their parents and significant others, in the process of growing up. These introjects (the super ego) have not been fully integrated into our conscious behavior. As a result, they continue to affect us and rule over us with an almost tyrannical force.

The self and the self-image: Normally, my self concept (what I think of myself) is the figure, and my real self is in the background, (the ground). To the extent that there is a gap between my real self and the image I have of myself, I am not capable of dealing realistically with problems. By reversing figure and ground, namely, by putting my weak self to be the figure and my self image (presumed strong self) to be the ground, I can begin to deal realistically with my problems. The figure is what I attend to. (I always attend to the figure). The ground is the background. When I attend to the concept and leave the real self in the background, I am divided.   When I attend to the real self and leave the self image in the background, I am integrated.   By integrating the various conflicting tendencies and pulls, I am more able to see the total situation, and thereby become whole again.   When we sharply differentiate between figure and ground, we can deal with problems effectively through the formation and destruction of Gestalts, i.e. through new figure-ground constellations.   Gestalt therapy allows successive figures to emerge and new figure ground relationships to unfold. People shape and discover themselves as they become more aware of themselves. Thus, they get to be in command of themselves.

Awareness is always accompanied by new Gestalt formations. Figure and ground form a clear Gestalt.   Frustrated or unmet needs interfere with this process. When we have unmet needs, our Gestalten are incomplete or poorly formed. The unmet needs remain unexpressed (incomplete Gestalten) and therefore demand attention. This saps our energy. It is through our senses, our feelings and our thoughts, that we experience ourselves and the world around us. Feeling , sensing, and thinking are the modes of our experiencing the environment. We can be alienated from any one of these. This is what is meant by self alienation.

In Gestalt therapy we increase our ability to express ourselves authentically, as we gain greater awareness of ourselves. We minimize self- deceptive or evasive behavior patterns. We allow ourselves to discover ourselves, to find ourselves, and to grow. Gestalt provides a safe environment for risk taking, and it aims at the avoidance of intellectualizing, psychologizing, lecturing, and advice giving. It mobilizes excitement, develops focus, and places responsibility on the person. By forming new Gestalten, people learn to be in touch with themselves, live with themselves, and accept themselves.

Exercises.

Take part and participate in a Gestalt workshop.

Note

1. For a good introduction to Gestalt therapy see, *Gestalt Therapy Primer*. edited by F. Douglas Stephenson, New York: Jason Aronson, Inc. 1978.

Workshop 14. Effective Interpersonal Communication.

Effective communication pertains to whether and to what extent the message given was received as intended. Communication between any two people is greatly facilitated by a sharing of values, beliefs, interests, comparability of intellect, and a general compatibility of background. The more two people have in common, the easier it is to reach out, and to communicate. The most important factor in effective communication between any two individuals is a willingness and readiness to listen to each other without prejudice, and without fixed prior notions or assumptions. This requires that the persons be free of defenses that inhibit the free flow of information between them. When people feel threatened, they put up defenses. When we communicate something to another person, we are trying to influence or change the other person's perspective, perception, understanding, beliefs or values. We may do this unintentionally or unconsciously. This is threatening to the other person's established inner equilibrium. The person's inner world, his or her basic system of values, may be called into question. Change is always destabilizing. Hence the fear and the defense.

Many situations may present this kind of threat to one or the other in the process of communication. For example, people may feel that they are being judged, evaluated, and appraised. They may think that the other acts from a position of superiority, that he or she is manipulative, calculating or dogmatic. They may feel less competent, less worthy than the other, or inferior to the other.   Sometimes the subject itself (i.e. what is being discussed) may be threatening to the person, and evoke defensive reactions.   Real communication is also blocked, when people feel that there is emotional distance between them, when there is a lack of respect for the other, or when there is a lack of interest and indifference toward the other. Tension between individuals will greatly inhibit their ability to communicate openly and honestly with each other.   When the atmosphere is emotionally charged, when each of the individuals rival for greater status or recognition, they cannot communicate freely and openly.   In non-threatening situations, people are open, flexible, and creative in their responses to each other. As the threat increases, they tend to close up, and distort information to fit their preconceived notions and prejudices. We don't want to let our stable system of beliefs and values be undermined.

People react defensively in different ways. We may avoid certain people or topics altogether, we may not want to expose ourselves if we fear embarassment or scrutiny, we may purposefully be ambiguous or non-commital, we may psychologically withdraw ourselves from the situation, be not involved, not reveal our true feelings and thoughts, we may not be serious in our conversation (not mean what we say), and we may assume body postures that indicate withdrawal (avoidance of eye contact, etc.). Similarly, we may talk compulsively and excessively in order to avoid confrontation, divert the conversation to less threatening topics, and avoid any real communication that affects our vital being and existence. We may obstruct any real and meaningful exploration of differences and exchange of ideas by a tendency to over-intellectualize the problem, or hide ourselves behind generalities, abstractions, and empty phrases.

Defences obstruct genuine growth, and inhibit true learning. To reduce defences we need to reduce the threat, and use discretion in our interactions with others. We need to cultivate interest, care, and involvement with the other. We need to be patient and understanding toward others. We have to avoid being aggressive, dogmatic, or arrogant. We must be open and curious about the views of the other. We must communicate as equals, be willing to listen and understand, as well as, to speak and be understood. We must be willing to respond, and invite feedback from the other. Non-evaluative feedback will help us discover more possibilities and new ideas, will make us more creative in our responses, and ultimately, will make us better understand each other. When we feel comfortable, secure, respected, and genuinely interested in each other, we freely respond and give objective, non-evaluative feedback to each other.

Reason is the true basis for any real communication between people. To be reasonable is to try understand each other objectively. When we fail to receive each other's messages as intended, when we misread, misconstrue, or misinterpret each other, reason remains the only way by which we can straighten out our misunderstandings. In case of misunderstanding or misconception, reason dictates that we ask further questions, in order to explain and clarify the content of the message. We cannot insist on our misconceptions and misconstructions and deny their falsity because they are ours, and because we have invested them with our ego. We cannot let our ego stand in front of and above objective truth. That is the meaning of letting reason resolve misunderstandings in the communication process.

When we are self-preoccupied or distracted, we do not hear the other's message. This is not different from physical noise that interferes with our ability to hear the other. Physical and psychological noise always interfere with effective communication. When we communicate with another person or persons, we interact with the other, and we also interact with ourselves. Communication is both interactive, (receivers send messages of their own to the sender, through verbal or nonverbal feedback), and intraactive (whereby both sender and receiver send and receive messages simultaneously).

Communication is either impersonal or developmental (interpersonal). In impersonal communication, the others are treated as objects. In interpersonal or developmental communication, the participants relate to each other as persons or subjects. Here the communication is more personal, and there is a gradual increase in the sharing of personal information. The individuals are more actively listening to each other, and they are more apt to use non-verbal signs. They are more perceptive of the subtleties of the expressed communication content, and are more sensitive to the reading and the interpreting of non-verbal clues. In this interchange, verbal and non verbal communication reinforce each other.

Factors in communication:[1]

Self concept. The self-concept is a set of characteristics that we ascribe to ourselves as particular individuals, and the qualities that we think we possess. A person's self-image is subjective, multidimensional, operates on many levels, and is difficult to change. One may have a positive or negative self image. People with a positive self image are usually supportive of others, while those with a negative self-image tend to be difficult or toxic in their relationships and interactions with others. We form our self concept in the process of growing up. The most important factor in forming a positive or negative self concept is the family environment from early childhood on. Our social interactions and early childhood experiences may have been primarily nurturing or alienating. This will largely determine whether we develop a positive or negative self-image. When we have a positive self-concept, we tend to be secure, self confident, self accepting, and have a high self-esteem of ourselves. The opposite is the case with a negative self-concept. Positive or negative self-concepts also relate to people's ability to accept objective reality or their need to deny it. The self-concept may thus be realistic or unrealistic, in various degrees. A realistic self-concept is flexible and capable of adjusting to change. An unrealistic self-concept is rather inflexible and resistant to change. Such people tend to refuse to accept and acknowledge a change in their objective circumstances or in the underlying reality of their situation. They are more concerned with preserving their self -image.

Our self-image is usually different from the way others view us. Other people see us more objectively than we see ourselves. People with an unrealistic self-concept tend to be too self-critical. They have a compulsive and irrational need to be perfect. This leads to self delusion and resistance to growth, as the following quotation will attest:

Immature and insecure parents cannot relate to each other in a balanced, give and take way. Children are frightened with insecure parents. Children that did not have a mature relationship with their parents and were not taught limits, grow up to be impatient, cannot set goals and work for them, cannot take pain, discomfort, hard work, disappointment, failure, unhappiness, stresses. They cannot accept weakness such as, dependence, or undecisiveness in themselves and in others. They become self-centered, selfish, without real interest in others.   They can only take, not give or share. They will not accept responsibility or keep promises. They will take advantage of others including their parents. Because they have been given things without exacting effort, they hold little appreciation for them.   Their entire value system, their goal and their purpose in life, has been distorted. (John Stewart, and Gary D'angelo, *Together Communicating Interpersonally,* Reading, Mass.: Addison Wellesley Publ. Co., 1975, p.6.)

Immature parents fail to set effective limits on the behavior of their children. In infancy and early childhood, a person grows to be secure if he or she has secure and mature parents. A gradual attainment of responsibility and independence makes the child happy. The child learns to trust itself, and be confident in its judgment. If we fail to trust ourselves, we will not be able to trust others. People who are mature have firm convictions, but remain flexible, open-minded, and amenable to change when change is called for. Immature people are often dogmatic, strongwilled, and overconfident. They usually lack sensitivity, understanding, and feeling for others.

The way we see things is affected by our senses, age, experience, the state of our health, stereotyped sex roles, occupational roles and transient factors, such as, fatigue and moods. Most importantly however, it is our self-concept that influences, colors, and affects our perceptions. The latter includes our unconscious projections. We tend to assume that others perceive things the way we do. We also tend to project onto others those qualities of ours that we do not approve of in ourselves.   And we are much more inclined to be critical of the other than to be tolerant or accepting of the other. We do not readily empathize with another's point of view. And we are more prone to remember being slighted by another than being affirmed.

We need to practice the art of listening. Listening is an art that we need to learn and to perfect. To listen actively is to listen with feedback. It requires that we confirm our understanding with the other. To listen attentively and actively means to hear the other, to attend to the other, to focus on what the other is saying, to remember, understand and empathize with the other. In order to be able to check our understanding with the other and to give feedback, we must also develop the ability to listen analytically and critically.   To listen to another means to consciously choose (decide) to listen, and to affirm the other by our listening. Most of us however, have poor listening habits. These include : pseudo listening (we only pretend to listen), self-centeredness (we are only interested in our own ideas), selective listening, (we respond only to part of the other's remarks, the part we are interested in), defensive listening, and insensitive listening, (we don't get the spoken message clearly, or we take it at its face value).

Relationships:

Relationships may be based on dominance-submission or on equality. Messages transmit information, but they also contain relational inferences. Relational messages convey approval or disapproval of the other, such as, "superiority, helplessness, friendliness, aloofness, sexual desire, or irritation."[2] A caring relationship consists in helping each other grow and self actualize. Self understanding is enhanced by sharing information with another. Expressing emotions to each other leads to greater intimacy and love. It also reduces stress caused by the perceived lack of freedom or ability to express one's feelings to each other.

Resolving conflicts depends largely on the attitudes of the partners. It depends on whether the two people choose to work together in order to understand each other and resolve their differences, or whether they prefer to deal with their problems separately, that is, apart from each other. The one will lead to integration, the other to polarization.[3] In discussing and solving problems, it is necessary to make sure that the agreement arrived at, is based on mutual understanding, and not on unexpressed coercion.[4] It is also necessary to guard against escalating the initial (perhaps minor) differences or misunderstandings.[5] Conflict resolution requires focusing on the problem, deescalating the problem, not letting the misunderstanding or difference drift without attending to it, (not burying the problem), and bearing foresight in the situation instead of being shortsighted.

A positive and affirming communication climate includes the need to acknowledge each other's presence, to be open-minded, to describe rather than criticize or evaluate the other, the use of "I language" instead of "you language", (for example, instead of saying, you smoke too much, one says, I am concerned about your health when you smoke so much), and most of all, to show interest in the other person's problems, and be honest.

Exercises.

1. Describe the most typical ways that you interact with others.

2. Which of the following defences are you inclined to use most often: being competitive, self-righteous, compulsive, excessively talkative, boastful, domineering, unbending, and dogmatic?

3. Do you consciously or subconsciously put other people down? Do you consciously or subconsciously always try to show how smart you are (or any other desirable attribute of character you think you possess, such as, intelligent, strong, kind-hearted, wise, knowledgeable, etc.)?

4. Describe situations that you experience as threatening to you. How do you handle the threat? Do you most often often feel the threat in your guts, i.e. you perceive it subconsciously rather consciously? Observe yourself and your reactions in such circumstances.

5. Do you avoid contact with certain people? Who are they? Describe their characteristics.

6. With people who are close to you, do you avoid discussing certain matters that are too sensitive or painful to you?

7. When you talk to your friend or lover, do you feel you are being understood, and vice-versa?

8. When you feel that you are not being understood, what do you do?

9. Do you reflect on the reasons why the other fails to understand you, and then try to discuss them?

10. Now, reverse the order, do you feel that you understand your friend or lover? And, if not, what do you do to remove the impediments to your understanding of the other?

11. Are you normally open, honest, trusting, and at ease with your friend or lover?

12. Do you feel that you are actively listening to the other?

13. Do you fully respect what the other is saying? Or, do you often anticipate what the other is going to say, based on your preconceived notions and opinions (prejudices) that you have formed of the other?

14. Can you reflect on yourself with objectivity?

Notes

1. This section is based on: Ronald B. Adler, Lawrence B. Rosenfeld, and Neil Towne, *Interplay, The Process of Interpersonal Communication,* New York: Holt, Rinehart and Winston, 1980.

2. *Interplay,* Ibid. p.158.

3. Ibid, p.265.

4. Ibid. p.266.

5. Ibid. p. 266.

Workshop 15. Teaching and Learning.

The need to enhance the effectiveness of the teaching-learning process, as is commonly practiced in our schools and universities, is widely recognized. Academic teaching and learning tend be formalistic and alienated. They do not engage the whole person in the process of teaching or learning. Learning tends to be mechanical. It consists primarily of feeding information and spilling it back. The emphasis is on extraneous motivation, i.e. grades, exams, etc. There is too much reliance on short term memory, and too litle concern with real comprehension and internalization of the material studied. Students forget quickly what they learn because they seldom get to the heart of the matter. The classroom environment does not, on the whole, stimulate intellectual exploration or give the student a sense of adventure. It does not excite the student to want to learn. It does not enhance the individual's intellectual curiosity. It does not bring about the sense of inner intensity that accompanies the joy of learning, the joy of thinking, and the appreciation of the power of the mind.

Every act of real learning is an act of self discovery. It is an act of the transformation of the self. The school environment, as is currently constituted, does not provide the needed atmosphere for such learning. Academic learning does not instill in the student a sense of admiration and passion for true discovery (self discovery), and genuine knowledge. It does not encourage thinking. It relies too much on memory. As the educational system is currently constituted, school learning does not cultivate respect for teacher or learner. It does not compel students to clarify their long term goals, values, priorities, or the broader aspects of life's purpose and meaning. It does not imbue them with the courage to self reflect, and to think for themselves. It does not diminish the need to imitate others. It does not show them the way to become true human beings, real people that are not ruled and determined by convention.

An education that is geared exclusively to jobs and practical applicability, tends to neglect the long term intellectual needs of the student. In order to address the latter, it is necessary to raise the intellectual achievement of the average student. It is necessary to place reflective thinking at the center of the educational process. This requires a renewed emphasis on the student, and on the way he or she learns. It highlights the need to subjectify and personalize knowledge. "Knowledge develops through a process of assimilation and accommodation" (Piaget). To assimilate new knowledge means to translate new information and new learning into terms familiar to us. We incorporate new information into existing frameworks. To accomodate new knowledge is, to explore it, question it, test it by trial and error, and modify our cognitive framework accordingly. Thus, we create new cognitive frameworks. To internalize, means to adapt the new cognitive frameworks, as a lasting part of ourselves.

We need a new learning environment, and a new concept of teaching. Teaching needs to be personalized. Theoretical knowledge needs to be applied and tested by self-understanding. Knowledge needs to be integrated with personal experience. The stress has to be placed on intrinsic rewards from learning, on the joy of learning, on the affirmation of life, and life asserting values. Teaching and learning must be made into a living and life oriented activity. There need be an openness to the new, the novel, and the unfamiliar. Experimentation and novelty need to be practiced and encouraged. In teaching and learning, we need to be open to new ideas, new methods, and new ways of thinking. Most of all, we must allow ourselves to be creative in our educational endeavors, and not be ruled by convention. We must create a learning environment that will lend support, recognition, appreciation, and encouragement to creative contributions on the part of teacher and student alike. An environment that will enable us to reach out to one another, to share, to give of ourselves freely, and not withdraw into mute privacy. An environment that will allow us to to be free to admit weakness as well as to appreciate strength.

Exercises in Creative Thinking:

To think through a given question means to carry all possible implications and ramifications of the problem to the very end. It is to allow ourselves the freedom to play with the idea or the problem. What are the implicit asssumptions underlying the problem? How would our consideration of the problem be affected if we were to make those assumptions explicit? How would our thinking be affected if we had made different assumptions? Do we subconsciously anticipate certain outcomes in our consideration of the problem? What options do we have in terms of possible alternative ways of dealing with the problem?

It is necessary to anticipate events that may bear on the solution of the problem, and incorporate those in our dealing with the problem. We need to examine our thoughts for the possibility of bias. Bias exists when we subconsciously or implicitly favor and expect certain solutions or outcomes. We must be aware of possible tendencies toward compulsion, fixation or deception, in order to prevent error in our thinking. Similarly, it is necessary to be aware of tendencies toward blocks in our thinking practices, which prevent us from being able to play freely with our thoughts, and to enjoy the process of pure thinking.

We need to practice concentration in order to focus our entire attention on the problem at hand. It is necesary not to get bogged down in irrelevancies that bear little on the problem under consideration. We are emotionally attached to our thoughts, and it is not entirely possible or desirable to disengage ourselves emotionally from our ideas. The point however is, that emotional bias creeps in to the person whose thoughts are not really his own, namely, an individual who is thinking primarily in the form of conventional stereotypes. When we think our own thoughts, when our thoughts are independent and creative, they are always accompanied with a feeling of joy. If we are mistaken in our thoughts, we can easily discard them, with the same feeling of joy. It is the joy of searching and reaching for the truth. When our thoughts are truly our own, we are not compulsive about them. Our thoughts are not biased. Our thinking is disciplined.

Questions that would enhance my ability to self examine, and to think critically:

How well am I aware of my subconscious drives and pulls?
How well do I know my priorities in life or in a given situation?
When and why do I act or behave compulsively?
What are my strenghts and weaknesses?
How well am I aware of my limitations or possibilities?
What part does money play in my subconscious, and conscious motivation?
How well can I discipline myself?
How much patience do I have with myself and with others? (Is my fuse short or long?)
How much am I given to flattery? to praise?
How much do I depend on recognition and emotional support by others in my work? How well do I respond to constructive criticism?
How persistent am I in my work? Do I tend to persevere and prevail, or do I tend to quickly lose faith and enthusiasm when confronted with difficulties or obstacles?
How genuinely am I interested in what I am doing?
Do I have a tendency to day dream or to act? Is there a gap betwen my thoughts and actions?
How well do I read?
How crisp is my expression, how clear and lucid is my thinking?
Am I genuinely interested in the other, or am I really primarily interested in myself? Am I self centered?
What do I really enjoy? (art, music, wit, elegance, good conversation, etc.)
How well do I converse?
What makes me tense or relaxed?
How dependent am I on the approval by those whom I love, honor, and respect? How does that interefere with my freedom to be me?

How well do I relate to others (family, friends, teachers, acquaintances, etc.) Is there a pattern to my relationships with others? Has this pattern endured or has it changed over time?

Do I differentiate knowledge from understanding? What have I learned from life experiences? What do I really know and understand?

What were the decisive influences in my life?

How sound were the choices I have made? over the years? in recent time?

How well do I articulate my needs, preferences, and desires to myself? to others?

How do I act and think in unfamiliar or novel situations?

What does it mean to be free? How free am I?

How well do I practice anticipatory thinking?

What are my biases, fixations, and deceptions?

How well do I think a problem through, and exhaust all possible implications and consequences within a given or alternative context?

How often do I examine my values in light of new experience and new knowledge?

How sensitive am I to my own feelings, and to those of others?

How honest, and open am I with myself and with others?

How well are my needs satisfied in the various spheres of my existence?

What are my minimum needs in the physical, emotional, social, intellectual, aesthetic, and ethical spheres of my being?

Am I expressing myself creatively in my life endeavors?

Am I still striving for creative self expression?

Workshop 16. The Power of Thinking and Acting.

The following are some of the ways of improving the power of thinking:

1. To go to the essence of things. It is necessary to conceptualize the problem and abstract from the problem.

2. The need to sharpen my awareness of things.

3. To be aware of what I am not aware. To be aware of my blindspots (inhibitions, compulsions, defenses, fears, anxieties, and deceptions). To detect vagueness and confusion in my reasoning. To be aware of my handicaps.

4. To perceive things objectively, without personal bias and wishful thinking. We must control our emotional responses to our situations. We need to be aware of likely double standards, and not put ourselves in a separate category from the other or others. We must be be sensitive to other people's feelings.

5. It is necessary to overcome defensive reactions as well as bad, sloppy, or rigid thinking habits. We should be aware of any tendencies to distort reality through internalized defenses. This is necessary in order to detect and correct error and not to deny it. It is good to invite feedback and resist saving face.

6. To be consistent in our reasoning.

7. To be alert to environmental cues.

8. To make right inferences from given premises.

9. To care and be involved with what we are dealing with.

10. To discriminate between good and bad, true and false, the important and the unimportant. To inhibit compulsive thinking. To take time to formulate ideas.

11. To think flexibly, adaptively, and creatively. Not to overstate or understate my ability to act in a given situation.

12. To overcome objective limitations, (money, time, age, etc), and subjective constraints (lack of hope, courage, etc.). To be free from the fear of failure. To have a sense of being in control over the situation.

13. To follow up our thoughts with deeds. To be self-confident, powerful, free, and joyous. To have a systematic plan (step by step) of how to carry out our designs. Not to give in to difficulty too soon, but stay with the intended design within the limits imposed by the reality of the situation. It is necessary also to have a back-up strategy and a fallback plan if the primary plan does not work out.

14. To avoid vagueness, mental confusion, lack of clarity, ambiguity, indecisiveness, and compulsive thought patterns. To know the consequences of my actions for myself and for others.

15.   To raise questions, to acknowledge mistakes, to express negative feelings, and to learn from our own mistakes as well as from those of others.

16. To be able to clearly articulate and express our strategy to ourselves and to others. It is good to formulate and consider alternative strategies. To listen, understand, and articulate objectively another's point of view. Not to force our opinion or point of view on others.

17. To think critically and creatively. The first applies to existing ideas and strategies, the second deals with new ideas and strategies.

18. To show forgiveness and grace to ourselves and to others.

19. To have a clear sense of values and a clear frame of reference with respect to things.

20. To have clear goals and a clear sense of direction.

21. To assume responsibility for ourselves, and not to blame others for our failures or shortcomings.

Workshop 17. On the Spinozist Unity of Mind and Body. Mental Habits and their Bodily Counterparts.

The human body is highly complex. It is composed of innumerable cells, with many different functions. What is visible from the outside is only a very small part of the body. We see the body muscles, the alignment of the muscles, the body posture, the protecting skin, etc. We don't see what goes on inside the body, its physiology, minute changes in functioning whether towards growth or decline, inclinations toward abnormalities or disease, etc. In many ways however, visible changes in body alignment and posture provide clues as to what goes on inside the body.

Spinoza's axiom of the unity of mind and body should therefore not be understood in a simple manner. The mind-body unity is a highly complex matter. The association of the mind and the body tells us that, body and mind, feelings and thoughts, are always and necessarily linked together, but the precise nature of the linkage (what idea or sequence of ideas are linked to which part or parts of the body), we cannot know. "The ideas of the modifications of the human body, in so far as they have reference only to the human mind, are not clear and distinct, but confused" (EII, 28). We can nevertheless, learn from what is visible to the outside in terms of mind-body association, and we can draw certain inferences as to what might go on inside our bodies developmentally, on a deeper level.

The most common aspects of the mind-body correlation are visible through body alignment, body posture, tension in the muscles, (facial muscles or muscles in the various parts of the body), etc. However, the mind- body unity is that between the mind (i.e. any idea) and the entire body. The body-mind link is for the most part invisible and unknown, but it is always there.

Individual people differ in terms of the inclination of various bodily parts to relative strength or weakness, respective high or low energy levels and intensities, etc. Therefore, the same mental events will not bring about the same bodily counterparts in different individuals. Different ways of dysfunctioning and disease will develop in different people because of the same or similar mental deformations and mental habits. For each individual, it is the weak link in the bodily chain of interdependent parts that will give first. If that weak part is not attended to, it will ultimately lead to a a general decline in body resistance and immunity, as well as, the onset of disease. The kind of disease however, whether it is an ulceration of the stomach, a respiratory ailment, or a particular kind of cancer, is body specific.

A healthy body is a free body just like a healthy mind is a free mind. The freedom of the person pertains to the ability of the individual to express himself in body and mind. The free expression of the individual's unique powers is his or her creativity. Individual uniqueness is the basis for the unfolding of our creative powers. I can express my creativity in my work, in play, in my relations with others, and in my life's projects. When I am expressing my creativity (i.e. myself) I feel free, fulfilled, and elated. When my creative powers are blocked, when I am unable to express myself (my unique self), I am unfree, weak, frustrated, and joyless. Most of the time however, we feel neither one, nor the other. We just go through the motions of everyday existence, where routine and the force of habit prevail.

Life demands that we get out of this comfortable slumber. We must be shaken out of our miserable little comforts that hinder us in our self-expression. Even to sink deeper into the abyss is better than to stagnate, and live mechanically. A sinking down eventually turns into a rising up. Routine living may go on forever.

To live in harmony with our essence is to be free. Why is it so difficult to be free? What are some of the mental habits that inhibit our freedom? These may include the following:

1. A failure to think through any idea or project to the very end, and the resulting failure to fully commit ourselves to it.

2. The intrusion of competing desires, projects and temptations. The inability to make up our mind. The person dwells in ambiguity.

3. Anxiety and fear resulting from an incomplete commitment. We are unable to give ourselves fully to our project or to what we do at a given time.

4. An unresolved idea or project creates frustration and conflict. It leads to a suspension of thinking, (non-thinking).

5. Our actions are thoughtless, repetitive, and indecisive.

6. We are not aware of the reasons for our actions and we do not reflect on them.

7. As a result, we lack self-confidence. This reinforces the general state of anxiety. We feel tension in our body.

8. Lacking self-confidence, we cannot fully accept ourselves and love ourselves. We neglect our appearance.

9. We lose touch with reality, and cannot objectivize our situation.

10. We depend more on the judgment of others, and less on our own judgment.

Visible bodily counterparts of these negative mental habits express themselves in the form of bad or shrinking posture, sloppy demeanor, facial and muscular tension, muscle weakness and fatique, shiftiness of mood, inattention or only superficial attention to our appearance, etc.

11. We tend to overlook and/or deny our own limitations and imperfections. The (tentative) bodily counterpart is expressed in unpredictable moods and feelings, alternating highs and slumps, etc.

12. We become increasingly self-centered. Possible bodily counterpart: excessive preoccupation with our appearance.

13. We lose the awareness of the spiritual and the transcendent sphere of life. The constant preoccupation with the here and now makes our body feel tight.

14. We are looking for meaning but we don't know where to find it. We don't know what gives meaning to life. We escape into drugs or cultural anaesthetics (TV, etc.).

15. We lack courage and we lack personal stature.

16. Inside of us there is mental chaos and confusion.

17. Our mind is not lucid and our body lacks poise.

18. We don't thave a clear sense of our integrity, and we don't have a sense of direction in life.

19. In freeing ourselves from an unreal self-image, we become stronger. (A false image is usually an exaggerated idea of myself in terms of some desirable character quality or qualities). We embrace our fears and gain in self-confidence. We don't want to deceive ourselves or any one else about our feelings. By accepting our fears, we open ourselves up to growth. Acknowledging and overcoming fear is a key to growth.

20. It is good to ask oneself at times: What am I doing now, and why am I doing it? Why do I have the need to write? Do I write because I have something worthwhile to say? Do I understand reality better than others? Do I write because I think a lot, and I don't want to lose the threads of my reflections? My reflections usually pertain to questions of human existence. By reflecting on these problems I have come to understand human existence better, and I want to share my understanding with others. Reflection requires tangible expression. I have to write down my thoughts. Writing is a form of doing, and thinking requires doing, because thinking without doing is not fulfilling. Writing makes thinking meaningful. Writing also expresses my unique self (my creativity).

21. It is necessary to share (talk, communicate) our work with others. This sharpens our senses, and stimulates our thinking. It will also bring us back to reality when we veer too far away from it.

22. Real work requires structure and discipline. This is important because retreat and inertia are always lurking from the side.

23. We need intrinsic satisfaction from our work. This is the primary source of our joy. To derive pleasure from our work is to be intrinsically happy with what we are doing.

24. We need to learn to accept ourselves realistically, and tone down any exaggerated expectations of ourselves.

25. If we persistently find it difficult to concentrate and commit ourselves to a given project, we must identify our basic conflict and resolve it.

26. Realistic and unrealistic needs: The need for greatness is an unrealistic (neurotic) need. It cannot be satisfied. The need for productive self-expresssion is a realistic need. It can be satisfied. Neurotic needs rob us of the enjoyment of life. They cripple our ability to do serious work.

27. Why do some people have a sense of mission? What is a sense of mission? Is it an unconscious drive for greatness? Is it a need for making a contribution to humanity? Is it a search for meaning? Or is it an inner rebelion against the oblivion of the mass?

28. Our compulsive drives may simply change direction when faced with life's realities. They need not be weakened or cease to be operative by this directional change. The new direction may be as unrealistic (compulsive) as the original one. We may simply not be able to face up to our phantasies (expectation of greatness) even when the objective conditions of our existence, and the subjective conditions of our powerlesness, have totally revealed themselves. We try at all costs to hold on to, and preserve our self-image.

29. To the extent that we need to justify our life, our existence, and our work, we are not free. As long as we have this uncontrolled need for significance or greatness, we will always act compulsively.

30. We have to overcome and get rid of such self-inflicted pressures. We should be able to live our life freely, without justifications, compulsions, or repayment of (imaginary) debts to ourselves and others.

31. We are caught in a double bind: We want to enjoy our work and not feel dejected when we don't work. Yet we feel compulsive about our work. The compulsion becomes a fixation. The fixation inhibits our work. We move in circles. We feel tension in our body. The tension further inhibits our work. The result is frustration and paralysis. This leads to sickness, physical deterioration, and decline.

32. We may lie to ourselves and deny the existence of these compulsions, and at the same time we are also aware that we ary lying to ourselves. We feel the grip of our compulsions and fxations in our bodies. We tense up our bodies.

33. How is one to make a final leap into freedom? This is our real challenge.

34. To affirm our innermost nature, and to express our real essence. That is the task ahead of us. To deny our essence is to negate ourselves. Self-negation is contrary to nature.

35. To be free is to accept ourselves. We accept ourselves by recognizing our need for productive (creative) self-expression. The realization of our innermost need is within us, not outside us. This realization depends on us, not on any one else. Compulsions alienate and hinder the realization of our innermost needs. Only those needs that can be realized from within are real. As long as we harbor traces

of our fixations and compulsions, our work will not be real, and our existence will not be a satisfactory one.

36. Freedom permits us to fully concentrate on the activity at hand, and allows the joy and intensity of our work to take a hold of us.

37. We need faith. Without faith life doesn't seem to make any sense. We need faith in the power of justice, despite its contrary manifestations in history. We need faith in the supreme force of a universal moral principle that ultimately guides human existence. We need faith in man's infinite possibility for courage, nobility, and moral justice. We cannot, however disregard history. The experiences of World War II and its aftermath have shaken the foundations of this faith. The certitude that man will ascend to morally higher spheres of existence has been subjected to great inner doubt. As a result, we experience inner crises and loss of direction. To get out of the latter, we must renew our faith in the moral principle as giving guidance to human existence. The need for faith brings out our essential humanity within us. It tells us that we, our actual individual existencies, cannot be the object of our lives. We need to have an elevated faith in something greater than our narrow, physical existence. This faith is our real essence. When our faith is affirmed, we experience a "high" state in life. When our faith is defeated, we experience the contrary. In the Jewish lore, there is the legend of the thirty six just and wise men, who are physically disguised but always present, and without whom the world could not exist. These just and wise men can be me and you.

38. Whenever we affirm our faith through our deeds, through our actions, we experience a state of elation and exhilaration. This may happen when we immerse ourselves in Nature, when we are witness to the greatness of others, when we express our inner truth in our actions, and when we interact with another person from the inner core of our being.

39. We need to know our values. Which values are life affirming, and which are not? Whatever contributes to the growth and the spiritual well-being of the person are life affirming values. Our self-development may be retarded or negated by our irrational drives, fears, and fixations, as much or more, than by an alienating social environment.

40. We need to know what our developmental values are. We need good physical health, good education, constructive habits, independence of mind and spirit, the ability to think clearly, the courage to be ourselves, not to be afraid to expose our presumed flaws and weaknesses, we need to respect ourselves, to have self-integrity, to respect others, to have a healthy respect for truth, to uphold self-dignity, to exercise self-control and control over the passions, to be assertive without being aggressive, to have a practical concern for our survival needs, to have a strong sense of identity and self-confidence,

to be caring and loving of others, to be tender and good hearted, to be
spontaneous and generous, to have compassion for the suffering of
others, to have a good sense of social justice and fair play, to have
wisdom, and be guided by moral principle.

41. In our daily life, in the way we live and act, we reflect our
values. Our values express themselves in our actions. They are the
actual, operative values. Suppose I catch myself cheating. I profess
strongly against cheating. But here I am doing it. Threre is a
contradiction between my professed value, and my operative value. I
must bring this contradiction into the open, and clarify my values to
myself. I have caught myself compromising my values for the sake of
personal advantage. What does this tell me about my professed values?
Among other things, it tells me that I deceive myself. What am I to do?
I have to change my behavior. Or, take another example: Suppose I
express a strong belief in social justice, but when confronted with
injustice or discrimination, I fail to do anything about it. What does that
tell me about my professed belief in social justice? It is not very
strong. How does that reflect on my integrity? Not very good. How
does that affect my respect for myself? I lose self-respect. This calls
for corrective action. I cannot live without respecting myself. To re-
establish my self-respect, I have to confront myself, and resolve any
value conflict.

42. The resolution of our value conflict depends on the awareness
of the conflict, and on the willingness to resolve it. The strength of the
desire to resolve personal conflict reveals our seriousness and
commitment to our beliefs. By making our values explicit to ourselves,
by spelling out the nature of our beliefs, we can clarify our values, and
assert them.

43. The question of principle: What is principled behavior? A
value that is not to be violated under any circumstances is a principled
value. When a principled value is at stake, (the honor of our parents,
the loyalty to a friend and family, or any other matter of principle), our
very freedom is at stake. At some (ultimate) point, when a high
principle is involved, we are ready to sacrifice everything including life
itself. It is true that prudence and the art of living dictate a certain
bending, a bending that is necessary if one is to go on with life.
However this bending must be consistent with our true essence, and not
violate our integrity. ("Absolutes do not permit one to live".)

43. There are two basic categories of values: material and
spiritual. Money is the universal expression of material values. All
other values are subsumed in the spiritual realm. When people are
guided by money as their chief value, the quality of their life will
suffer. Greed is insatiable. Spiritual values however grow stronger
with their satisfaction. The more we give, the richer we get. We
depend on human interactions for the fulfillment of our spiritual values.

We cannot consummate them alone. Our capacity for love, for aesthetic experience, for moral rectitude, and intellectual strength, grows with practice.

44. What we do from inner motivation, we do almost effortlessly (that is we don't experience the work as effort), and joyfully. The same happens when our work is appreciated by others, when others are supportive of what we are doing. In order to give our best, we need the stimulation and the support of people whom we respect. Sometimes all we need, is a word of encouragement from someone we trust and value. When we don't get the needed recognition of our work, our inner resources begin to decline, and our creative powers may dry up. The work becomes a drag on ourselves, and our discipline suffers.

45. To be interested in our work, means to have a sense of mastery and involvement with what we do. It is the relentless practice expressed as interest that makes us master our work. It is essential that we keep up our interest in our work.

46. Our thoughts need to be tested and steeled in practice. (As the Saying of the Fathers express it: "He whose deeds exceed his wisdom, his wisdom endures, but he whose wisdom exceeds his deeds, his wisdom does not endure."[1]

47. Our work, and our satisfaction from it, is the basis of our freedom. Our sense of direction is based on what we do, and freedom is not possible without direction.

48. The question of meaning, and of life's direction, is an evolving question. There are no final answers. Each of us is moved by different things. What is common to all of us is the need to give and receive love. A good conversation, a walk in the woods, a communion with nature, may galvanize our energies and revitalize our spirit.

49. From our body we emit clues to our inner feelings. The body does not lie. We give ourselves away in uncontrolled moments. Even the best actor cannot control his bodily and facial reactions all the time. We need to be attuned and alert to other people's bodily clues and uncontrolled facial expressions if we want to read other people correctly. A benign (and controlled) face may suddenly turn brutal, if only for a flash of a second. Behind the benign facade, there may hide an egocentric maniac. We are more apt to reveal our true intentions through our body language, no matter how strongly we may try to hide them. The body is the key to self- knowledge, and to the knowledge of others. If our inner and outer realities are congruent, our bodies will reinforce this perception. If there is dissonance, our bodies will also reveal it. The ability to read clues is an indispensable part of good thinking.

50. In communication, we need to rely on the spoken word. What cannot be expressed in words will be hinted by clues. We need to

overcome inhibitions that cripple our ability to communicate our thoughts and feelings honestly and truthfully to ourselves and to others.

51. Intimacy brings thinking, feeling, and acting between any two people closer together.

52. People's most basic self interest is to create optimal conditions for their growth and development. We have to exploit every opportunity that enables us to grow and develop emotionally, intellectually, profesionally, spiritually, and in every other conceivable way. It is necessary to overcome obstacles to our growth, whether imposed by the environment or by the unconscious self. We must ultimately depend on ourselves for our well-being. We must strive to be relatively independent of others. Self interest is not to be confused with selfishness. To the contrary, the two are not compatible with each other.

53. We need to cultivate the ability for rational decision making. We should avoid making decisions when we are under stress or in a state of anxiety. It is good practice to verbalize the nature of our anxiety or stress. This practice will reveal to us how well we tolerate uncertainty. We must learn to relax under pressure, and let our intuition come forth more effectively.

54. We must learn to think our own thoughts, and not be afraid of ourselves. We need to control our emotional responses, our self-preoccupation and egocentricity. We need to practice drawing proper inferences from given premises. We need to care and be involved with what we are trying to resolve. We need to overcome rigidity in our thinking habits, to be flexible, to restrain impulse, and to think objectively about any problem at hand. We need to test our assumptions, avoid unrealistic expectations, and overcome defensive reactions. To think creatively demands that we overcome objective and subjective constraints, and not be afraid of failure. We have to avoid vagueness and confusion. We have to discover weakness in our thinking, and learn to detect error. We need to practice not to give in to difficulty, not to quit, but carry out our will despite obstacles and hardships. We must learn to clearly verbalize our thoughts, our strategies, and designs. We need to accurately verbalize the other's objection to our point of view, and analyze their disagreement with us. We need to express accurately and objectively our ideas and feelings to others, as well as the feelings and ideas of others about us.

55. We must become aware of our blind spots, of our debilitating defenses, and of our tendencies to distort reality. We need to be alert and sensitive to environmental cues. We must learn to detect and correct error. We need to be aware when we are inconsistent in our reasoning, when we use wrong information, when we make wrong inferences, and when our assumptions are based on false values. If I can correct my errors without fear, I am not vulnerable to exposure. I have a

sense of being in control of myself. If my flaws are incorrectible, I am vulnerable.

56. It is always good to have an alternative plan or a back-up strategy in case intended outcomes do not materialize. This greatly reduces the fear of failure.

57. To think critically means: to compare alternatives, to calculate marginal costs and benefits, to ask hypothetical questions, to think of new ways to accomplish given objectives, to uncover discrepancies, to detect hidden assumptions, etc. Impulsive decisions should be avoided.

58. We must be careful to avoid overreactions and destructive defenses. We should not retaliate against perceived hurt, or use destructive criticism. We need to cultivate generosity and forgiveness.

59. People suffer from certain handicaps, when they are unable to think clearly and objectively about themselves. Inhibitions, fears, defenses, compulsions, fixations, deceptions, these are our blindspots. So is a lack of a clear sense of value. Our values provide us with a frame of reference for our thoughts. Without a clear sense of values it is not possible to think clearly. And so it is also with lack of purpose. Lack of purpose creates boredom, apathy, emptiness, and mental confusion. We feel lost. With purpose, we have vision. Vision enables us to have faith, and not to lose hope in the midst of adversity. A healthy organism exhibits purpose, direction, a sense of future, and vision. Existence integrates all these. Our soul needs strength of purpose. With strength of purpose, we feel self-assured. Purpose has to be based on reality, not on wishful thinking. If the purpose is based on unreality, it will lead to disillusion and despair. An unfulfilled realistic purpose will only strengthen our determination and commitment to it. It will lead to a re-thinking and a critical re-examination of the underlying assumptions of the reality of our situation. When we lose our sense of purpose and vision, we face a life crisis. We find ourselves without a clear orientation in life. To resolve the crisis, we must re-establish purpose and vision.

60. We need to be aware of the consequences of our actions. When we act compulsively, we are not aware of the consequences of our actions. We need to objectively reexamine our thinking, and avoid wishful thinking. We need to widen the areas of our thoughts, and not restrict our thoughts to familar patterns. We thus avoid going in circles.

61. In exercising moral judgment, we must avoid a double standard, and we have to be be careful not to put ourselves in a different category from the other. We must ask ourselves whether we can affect a realistic compromise in moral judgment, or whether we are inclined to act on absolutes, and to seek either /or solutions?

62. Extrinsic versus intrinsic motivation: If our motivation is primarily external, it will lead to alienation. Creative living is the opposite of alienation. Alienation means fragmentation. Creative

living leads to oneness and integration, the integration of body and mind, existence and essence, the particular and the universal. Creative living brings enthusiasm, vitality, and spontaneity to life.

63. Creativity is the most fragile of our faculties. It continuously needs nourishment and support. It requires simplicity, spontaneity, cheerfulness, and a relaxed state of mind. To be creative means: To have confidence in ourselves and in our work. To trust ourselves and others. Not to be afraid to admit personal inadequacy or shortcoming. To overcome compulsions and fixations. To experiment freely with new ways of learning. And to readily adapt ourselves to the demands of the environment.

64. What is wisdom? It is to assert and to choose life. To do the things that promote a tranquil mind and a healthy body. According to the Jewish tradition, charity and kindness is the highest wisdom. The wise man does not blame others or himself for his shortcomings. Only fools do that.

65. Our insecurity and faulty judgment about our future stem from a lack of self-knowledge and self-understanding. Bad habits and compulsive reaction patterns inhibit learning from experience.

66. Desirable character traits: internal control, ability to commit oneself, trusting, responsible, self-confident, decisive, the ability to delay gratification, capacity for sustained attention and concentrated effort, strong intellect and will, the ability to cope with reality, a willingnes to acept criticism, the ability to make up one's mind, to be firm in one's decisions, to be able to adapt to new situations, not to run from difficulty, and not to make the interest and motivation in one's work depend on external support and approval.

67. We experience tension if our actions are inconsistent with our self-image.

68. Do I usually know the reasons when I feel high or low? What gives me joy and what gives me sorrow? Do I know my irritations, annoyances, frustrations, pretensions, escapes, denials, defences, facades, and masks?

69. A noble mind and poised body, this is what I desire.

70. To be quick to discover deception.

71. Political activists often tend to be aggressive, self-centered, dogmatic, people I don't particularly like.

72. What I value most is innocence and love.

73. Any tinkering with one's self-concept or downgrading of one's self-image is anxiety provoking. Defense reactions will normally set in. Defenses derail objective self- assessment. (The image of a political activist versus an introverted thinker. An introverted thinker may have cultivated the self-image of a political activist. The two will eventually clash, since being an activist in thought is not the same as an activist in deed.)

74. Arguments, convictions, and expressed sentiments must be able to stand on their own merit. Excess emotion weakens the power of persuasion and appeal. Comprehension should be the source of the emotion, and not the other way around. To make rational choices means to be able to explain the choice to oneself and to others. People who do not have rational grounds for their convictions tend to be dogmatic. Criticism that expresses irritation or disappointment will bring about anger and resentment. It will not lead to behavior change or new learning. We must be especially careful not to use threats. They change the context of the interaction. Instead of learning through constructive criticism, we get a contest for power. Constructive criticism adresses itself to specific behaviors, never to the entire person. We need to make sure that we really and truly understand the other's criticism of a given aspect of our behavior or of our thinking, that we don't react defensively to it, that we don't avoid it by pointing out the other's same or similar failings, and that we respond to it attentively in order to find solutions, and learn from it.

75. A personal digression into self-reflection and analysis: My sense of mission, to bring justice to an unjust world, took on several transformations, when faced with its obvious unreality. The vision shifted gradually from political activism (to be a leader), to the thoretical field (provide answers for the world's problems), then to the existential field (to help the individual become stronger). While objective and subjective circumstances of my life completely defied the realism of my inner mission, I was not able to face up to its unreality openly, and consciously. I have compromised its essence for the sake of preserving my self-image. There were acute moments in these transitional stages when I would lose the will to live. The compromise (transformation of vision) somehow saved me from physical destruction. Or may be it was the other way around. I compromised my "mission" to save my life. I want to be free to live without justifications, apologies, debts to society, to myself or anyone. How am I to do it? How am I to be free? I want to enjoy my work and not feel dejected when I don't work. I am caught in a double bind. The compulsion to work has become a fixation. The fixation inhibits work. This creates bodily tension. The latter further inhibits its resolution (through work). The end result is frustration and paralysis. Eventually it brings sickness, physical deterioration, and disease. I have a strong need for communion with Nature, the oneness with the universe, and for sharing such transcendental experiences in intimacy with another. I need to share my inner self with another. I am interested in people, their joys and sorrows, and the circumstances of their daily life. This is behind my urge to travel.

76. To confront wishful thinking is to recall the event that precipitated the wishful thought. Wishful thinking is selective of those

aspects of reality that support the hoped for outcome. It leaves out all other aspects of reality. (For example, one doesn't want to accept the cold reality of a divorce prompted by incompatibility of personality and character. One thinks of the strong emotional bond that once existed between the two people, and one wishes to bring it back).

77. The meaning of freedom: to accept myself, and be free to be myself. The difference between self-consciousness and self-awareness: Self consciousness is inimical to freedom, self awareness is its precondition. Awareness implies objectivity and the ability to self control.

78. Growth is an excruciatingly slow and tedious process. It consists of repeated trials, efforts, and failures. Jenny (my daughter): "We stumble but move on."

79. Whenever I see a destitute, self neglected person, without hope and courage, a person totally defeated by life, I cannot help but think that the person was once a newborn baby, with the whole world open to it. When the child's life forces have been distorted and thwarted at a tender age, his character and future have already been badly affected.

80. A free man pleases himself, not others. Moreover, he pleases others by pleasing himself.

81. To direct our life forces into deep channels, not to dissipate them.

82. To be responsible is to act in good faith.

83. A cultured person is of noble mind. For a truly cultured person, nothing is spiritually meaningless. In a uncultured person, most everything is lacking in spiritual essence.

84. Cultural differences in child upbringing. Some (particularly Western) cultures stress independence, while Eastern cultures make children more dependent. A basic clash of values ensues.

85. We can know the causes of our anxiety if we are willing to look at them objectively. It feels good to unburden oneself in writing.

86. One is seldom aware of one's thoughtlessness. To be thoughtless is to be selfish. It prevents closeness. A person may think of himself or herself as caring, sensitive, and loving, but if he or she is thoughtless, their behavior will negate their self-image. Too much self-preocccupation leads to a disregard of the other's existence. Excessive sensitivity to oneself is often accompanied with a lack of sensitivity for the other.

87. A clue is a signal, and a subtle message that we emit through our bodies. A certain facial and bodily expression may forebode a change in attitude or a change in behavior. They may indicate approval or disappproval, acceptance or rejection. Clues signal feelings, and they demand attention. Clues help us widen the area of our self-awareness and the awareness of the other. Our body gives us clues about our state of health. By being attuned to them we may forestall

sickness. In a relationship, clues willl reveal our feelings to each other. They point to, and uncover any dissonance between feelings and behavior. The ability to detect, read, interpret, and act on clues, is the ultimate meaning of sensitivity. The fine art of reading and understanding subtle messages emanating from us, and from the other person, is what is meant by being sensitive to ourselves and to the other. We give ourselves away through clues because we can never sort out all our problems in life. Problems pertaining to our work, family, career, love relationships, friends, as well as our thoughts, indecision or doubts about them, all these come to the surface in the form of clues. If such clues about ourselves are ignored or go unnoticed, we pay a price later on in the form of mental confusion, depression, or sickness. If we ignore or do not notice the clues emanating from the person we are close to, closeness cannot be maintained, and the relationship will deteriorate. If however, we are attuned to the clues coming from each other in a relationship, and moreover, act on them, the relationship is bound to grow and become stronger. It leads to more openness, more affection, greater honesty, and a stronger commitment.

88. When we are ruled by false pride, minor misunderstandings cannot be clarified, and they instead become major problems.

89. Truth integrates experience. Falsehood and ignorance fragment it. To integrate experience means: to become more aware, more interested, more involved, to reduce anxiety and irrational fears, to be more sociable, more graceful, more poised and balanced, to be calm, relaxed, and at peace with oneself and the world. When experience is integrated, it is most intense, it is like being in a state of mental "high". The fear of facing an unpleasant truth (whether through cultural inhibition or bad upbringing) brings disssonance and fragmentation to all the people involved. This is especially important in marriage and family.

90. Depression inhibits action. The essence of depression is non-action.

91. It is necessary to have perspective with respect to oneself. One needs to step back and look at oneself from a distance. We can know the cause of our anxiety or mental anguish, if we are willing to look at ourselves objectively.

Note

1. *Tractate Avoth. Ethics of the Fathers.* Translated by Philip Blackman, F.C.S. New York: Judaica Press, 1964.

SECTION III.   THE PROBLEMATIC OF THE SELF

Workshop 18.   Concepts of Self.

1. Attitudes, Behavior, and Self-Awareness.

We become conscious of our attitudes, when we observe our behavior. We may be assertive, optimistic, and unafraid of difficulties. Or we may be timid, complaining, and withdrawn. We may be supportive and affirming of the other, or we may tend to be negative, and critical of the other. We may be all of these at different times. Our overall behavior may be relatively stable or unstable.

The way we view ourselves is called our self-concept. It consists of our conscious image of ourselves and the world. The self-concept is formed in infancy and childhood. Whether we experience ourselves as good or bad, and whether we develop a positive or negative self concept, depends on the consistency of the social and family environment. Our self may be integrated and cohesive, but more often than not, it may be fragmented and lacking in cohesion. It is also possible to have a number of self-relevant concepts that are not necessarily consistent with one another.

The self-image is relatively stable over time. We don't readily change our self-concept. Our actual behavior however is much less stable than the image we have of ourselves. On the whole, most people are not very consistent in their behavior. The reason for this inconsistency lies in the relative transiency of our feelings (passions) that so often determine and guide our actions. We may be sensitive at one time, and callous at another. Are our beliefs formed by our behavior, or is our behavior formed by our beliefs? Behavior and the underlying beliefs tend to reinforce one another. We learn about ourselves and get to know ourselves through our (direct and indirect) communication with others, and through our interaction with the environment. We incorporate others, our surroundings (the not-self) as part of ourselves. The self necessarily includes the not-self as part of itself.

We cannot normally identify ourselves with our conception of ourselves. We are not what and who we think we are. Our self concept does not tell us who we really are. There is a gap of diverse dimensions between what we think of ourselves and the way we really are. There is a gap between people's self-concept and their real self. To know ourselves involves knowing our intentions, our capacities, our inclinations, and our needs in relation to ourselves and others. Self-knowledge enables us to match our conduct with our intentions.

We make ourselves as we act. By our actions, we create our world. Our actions determine other people's responses to us. We can never exist separately from the world around us. How we perceive ourselves in the world makes a difference in how we live. We must learn to look at the world as it is in itself, not as we want it to be. Similarly, we must learn to look at ourselves the way we are rather than the way we think we are. We need to objectify our environment in order to correctly understand its meaning and significance for us. Such self-objectivization however, is very difficult. We are more prone to rationalize our actions rather than affirm them. We tend to blame others for our negative behaviors. We are not always, or for the most part, ready to assume responsibility for our actions. In finding faults and assigning blame, we tend to look for scapegoats. We are more readily apt to criticize the behavior of other's, and much less so our own. We readily criticize others and hasten to attribute their faults to some character flaws or adverse personality characteristics. We are much more hesitant to do the same to ourselves. (Recall Aesop's fable with the two sacks. We carry two sacks full of faults all the time. The sack with other people's faults we carry in front, the one with our own faults we carry in the back.)

When we begin to focus our attention on ourselves, we will more likely begin to notice our own shortcomings. We tend however, to rationalize and not attribute undesirable behaviors to factors operating within ourselves. We look for outside factors as causes for such behavior. We make excuses for our mistakes. We tend to avoid taking responsibility for our behavior. When we make excuses or deny our mistakes, we can neither learn from them, nor correct them. It is only when we stop being defensive, when we are more willing to admit our shortcomings, can we correct our failures, and learn from them. Thus we gain in self esteem and inner security. We become more mature. We do not depend on the immediate gratification of our desires. We gain in ego strenth and will power. We can more readily attend difficult tasks. We become more self-dependent, and less dependent on others. We move away from doing things to please others, and we are more concerned with doing things in order to please ourselves. We become motivated more by intrinsic rather than extrinsic rewards. Real self-acceptance is difficult. The road to self acceptance and self-relaxation needs to be found, learned, and repeatedly practiced. We will stumble many times, but the point is to get up, not to lose heart, and move on.

When we rationalize our faults, we tend to get emotionally aroused. We get excitable and irritable. We are unable to control these physiological states of arousal. We become excitable when we have vested (cathexed) feelings attached to certain outcomes or points of view. This is usually the case when there is a deficiency in our understanding of the particular event, phenomenon, or belief. We assume that we understand or know something without actually knowing it. For example, suppose I think that I fully understand a certain social problem or public issue, and that I also have worked out a solution to the problem. But, whenever there is a discussion of the given problem or issue, I get very excited and irritable. If there is disagreement, I cannot easily tolerate it. In all such cases, the emotional excitement is due to an insufficient understanding of the issue that I claim to know and be convinced of. (It is good to remember Nietzsche's dictum: "convictions are worse than lies".) We often take a definitive stand on a certain issues without having a complete and full grasp of all the factors bearing on the question. This lack of objective knowing is behind our irritation. The irritation discloses our inner insecurity. Individuals who have a full grasp of the problem (of any problem) can afford to remain calm, because they are very secure in their position. This can be generalized to all knowledge. The more thorough our knowledge, the more secure we are, and therefore the calmer we can afford to be.

2. Eastern (Buddhist) Concepts of the Self.

Buddhism negates the permanence of the self. It dismisses the conception of the self altogether. There is no stable, unifying core to our existence. The self has no identity other than thoughts and sensations. We consist of our sensations, feelings, perceptions, self-consciousness, and mental dispositions. There are states of consciousness, but there is no mind. Mind and body are aggregates of mental and physical states. The mental states consist of thoughts, feelings, perceptions and dispositions. The body consists of the four elements: earth, water, fire, and air. Of these, the physical is the more enduring than the mental. Our body may last a hundred years while our thoughts are transient and fleeting. There is no self sustaining substance behind the sense data. The sense data are the material things. There is no substratum or "thing in itself" behind them. The aggregate of mental states, or states of consciousness, is what we call the mind. Soul and body are not separate entities but coexist together as composite complexes. The self and the material world are always

changing. In the world, there is neither being, nor non-being, there is
only becoming. "There is incessant change, but at the same time there
is nothing that changes."[1] The nothing here refers to "nothing
permanent" that changes. There is no distinction between the process
of change and the thing that changes. The process is the thing, and the
thing is the process. All change proceeds according to cause and
effect. The effect is inherent in the cause, and each cause will
necessarily produce an effect. The self and the material world are
compared to the flame that consumes itself and to the river that flows
incessantly. Things are at a constant flux. There is no fixity. There is
only a succession of similar states. There is neither Being, nor non-
Being, there is only Becoming. A continuous coming to be and a
passing away.

The principles of impermanence and of no-self are basic to the
teachings of Buddha. Buddha's teaching is completely rational.
Nothing happens by chance. Chance is another name for a contingency
of causes unknown to us. There is no supernatural intervention in the
succession of states or things. There is only necessary succession.
Cause and effect are uniquely connected to each other. Necessary
succession is a universal law. Its actual operation however, depends
on certain conditions to be met. For example, if the conditions for the
burning of the wood are not satisfied, the wood will not burn. The
series of events connected with the burning of the wood will come to a
halt. This is the law of contingent causation. There are adequate
reasons why things are thus, and not otherwise. (The principle of
sufficient reason.) For any given occurrence, there are many
cooperating and contingent causes. The causes accounting for any
event are in principle knowable. The law of contingent causation is
universal and it holds everywhere. Everything in the universe is
impermanent and mutable. The aggregate of sense data is the thing,
and this aggregate continuously changes. If this is so, how can we
recognize objects? The Buddhist answer is that successive states are
not identical but similar.

And, if the self is impermanent and transitory, if it is only a
succession of aggregate states, how do we account for memory? The
Buddhist answer this by saying that each phase of human existence
potentially includes all the previous phases. The latter show itself when
the conditions are favorable. At each moment of existence, the
aggregate of all perceptions and sensations that make up our mental
state includes "all the potentialities of what preceded it.... though a man
is not the same in any two moments , yet he is not quite different.... The
self is not only a collective, but a recollective unity. It is on this basis
that Buddhism establishes moral responsibility."[2] Buddhism seeks to
alleviate universal suffering. The foremost need for man is to escape
suffering. Desire is the cause of man's suffering. It is rooted in the

self. When the self is removed, the selfish impulses will cease and there will be an end to suffering. The teaching of the no-self or the impermanence of the self will remove desire. Desire is rooted in ignorance. Ignorance leads to suffering. Suffering is rooted in desire which itself is rooted in ignorance. When ignorance is removed, desire will cease and the cause of suffering will be removed. Suffering will cease to exist.

Exercises.

1. Is there a the center to your being? What is it? Is there an the inner core to your personality? Can you reach that inner core of yours? Do you have ready access to it?

2. What is the first thing that comes to your mind when you think about yourself? By what qualities of character do you want to be known?

3. Do you often feel that others do not know you, that they do not know the real you?

4. What does it mean to know yourself as you really are, rather than as you think you are?

5. Is there a way to know yourself completely, fully, and truly? Or, is it more true to say that as your knowledge of yourself changes, you also change? How does this connect with the Buddhist notion of the impermanence of the self?

6. What does Buddhism mean by knowledge and ignorance?

7. Buddhism's main concern is cessation of suffering. What does it mean: "things change but nothing changes"? Is this a reference to suffering?

8. Buddhists say that right knowledge is a way to overcome suffering. Does right knowledge pertain to the theory of flux and the impermanence of the self?

9. Buddhism maintains that all is suffering, and even pleasure is but "attenuated pain."[3] Discuss why is this so, and what is meant by this.

10. In the Buddhist view of the impermanence of the self, is there no desire and no striving by the self, and therefore no suffering? How does the Buddhist impermanent self deal with personal memory and expectation, with past and future?

11. What is your view of suffering? Is it possible to avoid suffering in life?

12. The Chinese character for suffering is akin to crisis, seeing suffering as a challenge, and an opportunity to reach to the core of oneself. As a result, one gets spiritually stronger and purer. According to this view, one should not deny suffering, one must embrace it instead. Do you agree? Discuss the positive aspects of suffering.

Notes

1. M. Hiriyana, *Outlines of Indian Philosophy*.   London: George Allen &
Unwin, Ltd. p.142.
2. Ibid. p. 145.
3. Ibid. pp. 223-4.

Workshop 19. Marx and Lukacs on Alienation.[1]

In a capitalist (or for that matter any industrial) society, labor power and therefore the laborer who sells his labor power, is a commodity to be bought, and sold on the market. Labor becomes objectified, abstract, and measurable. The latter is very well demonstrated in time and motion studies. Labor as a commodity is stripped of all essential human qualities. The laborer does not own anything in the work place except his labor. He or she is not producing for himself or herself but for the businesss or company. Laborers are estranged from the product of their labor. They work only on a tiny segment of the total product, the most pertinent example being the assembly line. They are thereby estranged from the activity of their labor. What they do is of no interest to them. They are also estranged from the product of their labor, and from the activity of other laborers. By not being connected to their work and to the work of the others around them, the workers are estranged from their own vital essence, and the vital essence of their co-workers. This is the meaning of Marx's concept of alienation.   Alienation *(Entfremdung)* is the estrangement of the person from his or her human essence.

Every new machine and every new technology strips the laborer more and more of his yet remaining skills. It reduces the worker to a mechanical, unthinking, and robotlike functioning. He or she   truly becomes an appendix to the machine.   Entire clusters of skills that people once possessed, and which were part of their human essence and self esteem, have vanished without a trace. This is the double-edged sword of technology: Along with an increase in productivity and potential well-being, it also causes skill obsolescence, displacement of labor and unemployment, ecological imbalances, and other related problems.

The estrangement of the person from his or her work is perhaps the most basic problem of modern society. Since work does not provide people with an outlet for their absorbing and creative powers, since the workers are not engaged with their work, they lose the connection to their vital self. The person gets to be disconnected, divided, and estranged from himself or herself. Instead of affirming themselves in their work, they deny themselves in it. Productive life, life's most essential activity, and life itself, turn into a means of life. When the person is estranged from his or her life activity, he or she is also estranged from those around them. When people are estranged from themselves, from their essential nature, and from their humanity, they are also estranged from one another. Every relationship of a person to himself or herself is conditioned and expressed by their relationship to other people. This estrangement is the real meaning of alienation.

Human alienation leads to reification,*Verdiglichung*. Reification takes place when alienation has proceeded to the point where people are no more aware of their human essence. They treat themselves and others like things. In capitalist society, production is based on profit, and not on need. Needs do not determine production, only profits do. This does not mean that there is no connection between need and profit. It means that only those needs that translate themselves into effective demand get produced. A lot of public needs and poor people's needs don't get produced or satisfied. According to Marx, (Marx, Karl 1818-1885) in commodity production, i.e. production that is entirely based on exchange value, the place of the producer (the laborer) in it, is not clear to him (the laborer). Commodity production is veiled under a cloak of mystery. In it "social relations between men assume the fantastic form of relations between things."[2] Instead of men ruling over things, things rule over men. Through the magic of money, life becomes inverted. Man's existence turns around things (money). Existence becomes thing-like, reified.

Moreover, if consciousness is first and foremost the consciousness of one's existence, and if one's existence is dominated by things, then consciousness itself becomes reified. The commodity in its most generalized form, namely money, becomes the ruling principle between people, and the relations between them are governed by exchange value, the same principle that rules the exchange of commodities in the market place. Relations between people become objectified, like relations between objects. The commodity, the universal structuring principle under capitalism, enters man's consciousness and consciousness itself becomes thing-like. Its structure becomes reified.[3] If this is the prevailing condition in society, then people will not be aware of it. Persons functioning in an alienating environment, living in an alienated society, and being the product of an alienated culture (and education), never become aware of their alienation, and that of their environment. They tend to accept their condition as normal. They become unconscious of the destructive effects of alienation, and the ensuing effects of reification of human relations.

This is what Lukacs (Lukacs, Georg 1885-1971) meant by the "reified structure of consciousness." The person's consciousness becomes imprisoned in things. People's relation to others is based on exchange. Acquisition of things, and accumulation of money become the reason for being, the essence of existence. Things (money) become a fetish, an object of worship, and the source of self esteem. Life becomes inverted. What work cannot give, things will provide. When fulfillment cannot be found in work (activity), it will be sought in things. When self-esteem cannot be found in being and doing, it will be sought in having. Not the person, but objects (money) become the measure of all things. This is our social reality.

The root of the problem of alienation lies in the divorce of one's work from one's life. This can be seen even in education. Education has been reduced to commodity production. Its objective is to prepare people to function in the workplace, in a workplace that has been emptied of all human essence. Teachers and students have become reduced in the educational process to a mere routine functioning. There is little true learning, no real excitement, no joy of learning, and no striving for excellence in our educational system. In higher education, the system is overspecialized and highly fragmented. Each discipline or specialty develops within its own narrow and separate framework, without connection to the other specialties, and without regard to the needs of the person as a whole. The various disciplines are not integrated into an educational process that seeks to serve and benefit the student's life and his or her intellectual needs. The students are not taught or encouraged to integrate their academic learning with their life experiences. Our formal education does not provide the student with a wider perspective on life, that of one's own, and that of others. Neither does it give one a real grasp of one's natural, and social environment. Education as it is being practiced today does not address itself to the fundamental realities of life.

One might note that the term alienation is very general, and suffers from over inclusion. It includes too many shades of meaning, such as, loss of self, fragmented self, meaninglessness, anomie, despair, lack of community, etc. Man struggled with these problems throughout recorded history. In each historical epoch, certain aspects of human alienation take precedence over the others. In medieval times, sin was thought in terms of one's alienation from God. St. Augustine saw human nature as divided and fragmented. Man is in a fallen state, subject to, and surrounded by sin. Salvation was to be found in transcending the finite world of physical being, and in finding communion with God. The Greeks sought the answer to the dualism of man and nature in the state of social and individual harmony, in the pursuit of the good, and in the striving for human excellence. Man was forever seeking to be at home in his world.

Exercises.

1. Cite examples to support Marx's dictum that in a market economy, things rule over man instead of man ruling over things.
2. What does Lukacs mean by reification of consciousness?
3. When educators talk about academic excellence but make decisions on the basis of cost and returns, is this an example of the intrusion of reification into their minds and consciousness?

4.   When newspapermen routinely adjust their reporting to accommodate and placate advertising moguls, is this a form of alienation and reification of consciousness?

5.   When a professor's primary motivation for writing and doing research is the advancement of his or her career rather than the search for truth, is this also a form of self-alienation?

6.   What does Lukacs mean by reification of human relationships?

7.   When people and friends relate to each other on the basis of quid pro quo, is this evidence that interpersonal relationships have turned thing-like?   What happens to the human essence in this case?   Does reification deny human essence? Discuss.

Notes

1. Karl Marx, *Early Writings*. Translated and edited by T. B. Bottomore. New york: Mc Graw-Hill Book Company, 1964.

Karl Marx, *Capital*. Vol I. New York: International Publishers, 1967.

Georg Lukacs, *History and Class Consciousness*. Cambridge, Mass.: The MIT Press, 1971.

2. K. Marx, *Capital*. Vol. I. p. 72.

3. See Lukacs, Reification and the Consciousness and Proletariat. Ibid. pp. 83-222.

Workshop 20. J. Preston Cole, The Problematic Self in Kierkegaard and Freud.[1]

The relation of the self to itself is central to both Kierkegaard
(Kierkegaard, Soren 1813-1855) and Freud (Freud, Sigmund 1856-
1939). It is the cental question of human existence. What does it mean
to be "oneself"? What is selfhood? What is a person? What is
personality? All of these signify movement, strife, unrest, conflict,
tension, searching, and probing for answers. Existence is a struggle.
The self consists of many different selves, often in opposition to one
another. It is how we handle the struggle, how we face life's problems
that determines who we are as persons. For Kierkegaard the self is
subject to radical pulls from opposing forces operating within it. The
self is torn between two polar opposites, the ideal and the real, the
ordinary and the exalted, the free and the unfree, the independent and
the dependent, the strong and the weak, hope and despair. The
Kierkegaardian self is a dialectical relation between the immediate and
the transcendent, the ideal and the real, the finite and the infinite, man
and God. The infinite, the eternal, and the transcendent constitute the
higher Self. The finite, temporal, and the immediate constitute the
lower Self. The higher and lower self are concepts commonly used in
Eastern philosophy. For Kierkegaard, the self mediates and synthetizes
these polarities. "The self is a relation which relates itself to its own
self."[2]   The self is the active part of this relation, not the relation itself.
The self mediates the two polarities in freedom. Freedom or Spirit is
the essence of the self. The spiritual self is the self's essential mode of
being. It is the active part in the dialectical synthesis of the polarities
of the self's being. If that active component of the synthesis fails or is
non-existent, one ends up in fantasy or in a robotlike existence. The
Spirit presents the projected image of the self as possibility. The other
self (the finite and the immediate self) is the immediately given or the
required, namely necessity.   One cannot get too far away from
necessity (the reality of oneself and one's situation), lest one risks the
anticipated, and hoped for, great deed or project. For "one may lose
oneself in the fantastic if the resolve to do great things is not kept in
dialectical relation with a resolve to do that finite portion of the project
which is immediately at hand."[3]
The art of selfhood and of being oneself is the ability to incorporate
the transcendent into our ordinary life. While we live in the here and
now, with all the problems of concrete existence, to be oneself means
not to lose sight of the transcendent within us. Neither can we live our
life primarily on the spiritual plane without due attention to our
ordinary needs. The two poles (the finite and the infinite, the
immediate and the transcendent) need be synthetised in actual

existence.   Such synthesis is sustained in possibility not in probability.
It is sustained in freedom, not in compulsion. If one loses either pole
of the dialectic, one may lose oneself altogether. The transition from
essence to existence (becoming) is a possibility, not a necessity.
Change is a free choice. The process of becoming is the solving and
reconciling the relationship between possibility and necessity. The
synthesis of possibility and necessity designates a real person.
"Personality is a synthesis of possibility and necessity."[4] A real person
(a personality) is moved by the power of Spirit. In such a person, the
self always embraces both inspiration and a-spiration. "Spirit is the
fundamental power of Being."[5] The Spirit (the possibility of freedom)
is ontologically real, it is not an apparition or hallucination. The Spirit
is that synthesis between the finite, immediate self (the actual self), and
the projected image of the self, the possible self. One cannot however,
veer too far away from the real self, lest one gets lost in fantasy (reverie
or dream world). One has to stay connected to the real self, that is, to
the self that one is.   One cannot jump out of one's skin. One cannot
become someone one is not. Thus, for the self to become a self, one
must become the self that one essentially is. In other words, I can
aspire to be all that I can be, but I cannot aspire to be all that you can
be.

For Freud, the power of selfhood is the libido, Eros. The libido
consists of the sexual drive (the sex instinct, the preservation of the
species), and the ego drive, (the self-preservation instinct). The libido
can be restrained or inhibited through repression or through
sublimation.

The power of being (life) is in tension with the power of non-
being, (thanatos, despair or death.)   Eros, the power of life
continuously resists the power of non-being, the power of despair and
self-destruction. In Kierkegaard, the Spirit is the drive towards self-
determination, towards being all one is. In Freud, Eros is the power of
self-determination in life.   It is life overcoming death, being
overcoming non-being, faith against despair, the possible asserting
itself over the actual. In this sense, Kierkegaard's spirit and Freud's
libido are not different from one another. For Freud, the power of
selfhood is libido. For Kierkegaard, it is the Spirit. One can lose one's
selfhood in exceeding one's reality, one's real self. That may happen
when one gets lost in impractical endeavors, in irrelevant knowledge or
in unreal emotions, (cheap sentimentality).

Freud divides the self into the id, ego, and super-ego. The id
operates in the unconscious. It is the uninhibited part of the self. The
processes of the ego operate in the conscious. The ego consciously
inhibits the id. The superego are those inhibiting processes that
operate in the unconscious. The unconscious consists of both the id and
the superego. The conscious part of the self is what constitutes the ego.

Selfhood is an active, positive mode of being. It is a self that assumes responsibility for its own being. It is an active relation of oneself to oneself.

For Kierkegaard, the self becomes a self in the despair of defiance. In order to defy, one must affirm oneself. The despair of defiance is also a self-affirmation. It affirms being over non-being. Selfhood is contingent upon the power of the spirit, which is neither body alone nor soul alone. Spirit, for Kierkegaard, is a third power in man. The power of the spirit is decisive in Selfhood, in the self becomig its own self. The becoming of the "I", the person, is the actualization of possibility, the self assertion of being over non-being, the actualization of the self as spirit. "Spirit is the fundamental power of Being."[6] When necessity is left out of possibility, or when possibility is not included in necessity, the self turns into despair.

Kierkegaard's spirit is the power of the self to continuously determine itself. The power of being is always threatened by non-being. Life is threatened by non-life. Existence is threatened by extinction. Man's spirit is the power of life to assert itself over non-life. For Freud, the libido is the power of selfhood. Libido points to Eros. Eros, the life instinct, is always threatened by the inertia of non-being, thanatos. The life instinct manifests itself in the ego instinct. It assures the preservation of the individual. It is a defense against physical annihilation. The sex instinct safeguards the preservation of the species. The super ego functions as a defense against social extinction. The Kierkegaardian Spirit and the Freudian Eros represent both the same power of the self to assert it's own self against real and imaginary temptations and dangers of the not-self, (non-being). While, the aim and function of Spirit and of Eros are basically the same, they nevertheless represent different drives in their origin. It is the juxtaposition of nature versus history. "Libido is Spirit viewed from the perspective of Nature. Spirit is libido viewed from the perspective of history."[7] For Freud, selfhood is "a dynamic relationship between the id, the ego, and the super ego."[8] For Kierkegaard, selfhood is a dialectic or synthesis between the finite (the immediate, the actual), and the infinite, (the expansive, fantastic self). Without the immediate, the self is lost in reverie, in fantasy. Without the infinite, the self is lost in self-indulgence, in sentimental emotion, in irrelevant knowledge or useless information.

In Freud, the id represents man's primary psychic drives. The ego represents the secondary inhibiting impulses. They are the conscious checks on the omnipresent drives of the id. The super ego represents the unconscious inhibiting processes. It was formed through the child's identification with its parents, and it serves as an internalized norm for the person's behavior. In social (ethical) existence, it manifests itself as guilt or non-guilt. In Kierkegaard, selfhood is a dialectic between the immediate self and the transcendent self, necessity and possibility, the real and the ideal. Imagination is the medium by which the Spirit infinitizes existence. The content of the imaginary self is acquired in childhood, in the child's identification with hidden aspirations of the parents (the super ego).

Repression, for Freud, is a flight from an internal threat, a flight from pain. The defenses against an internal threat assume various forms: regression, reaction formation (one maintains the repression through the super ego), fixation (the arrested development of the ego at a certain stage), separation anxiety (the dread of loss of parental love or social rejection), denial, and sublimation. When the ego is dominated by the super ego, it exists in guilt. "It has fallen into the sickness of the self."[9] Psychotherapy is "reeducation in overcoming internal resistances."[10] It involves pain and suffering. The psychotherapist demonstrates his intellectual interest in the patient through interpretation. (Transference manifests itself in the affect of the patient for the psychotherapist.) Psychotherapy is a working through of the patient's resistances. To overcome resistance, it is essential not only that one knows himself, but more importantly, that one wants to know oneself. ..."the fundamental category (in knowledge and understanding) is becoming rather than being, history instead of nature, existence not essence."[11]

Exercises.

1. Do you experience within you tension between your (silent) strivings, hopes, (unexpressed) desires and the routine of everyday life, between your aspirations and the realities of your existence, between your potential and its realization, between essence and existence, between possibility and necessity? Reflect on this with self-honesty.
2. How do you handle this (dialectical) tension between the polarities of your inner self? Do you resolve it by day-dreaming, self-indulgence, and flight into fantasy? Or, do you try to formulate (realistic) projects which express your inner abilities and potential?
3. Give examples of one or more of such projects, and do you actually proceed to carry them out?
4. Do you feel happy when you self-indulge in fantasy and day dreaming?
5. Do you feel happy when you work on projects that express your inner essence and potential? Again, give examples.
6. What does it take to make you happy?
7. What does Kierkegaard mean by the "despair of defiance"? Defiance of what? Why "despair"? (Despair is when you don't see a way out of your situation any more.)

8. Do you agree with Kierkegaard that the Spirit is the fundamental power of Being? Can the Spirit assert itself through the "despair of defiance"?

9. It is your spirit that makes you a person, a personality. The spirit empowers you to synthesize existence with essence, the actual with the ideal, and it is your spirit that will make you free. The spirit always points to possibility, not necessity. The spirit signifies your power "to be" and to realize yourself. To be your possibility is to actualize your potential. Discuss.

Notes

1. J. Preston Cole, The Problematic Self in Kierkegaard and Freud. New Haven and London: Yale University Press, 1971.

2. Ibid. p. 11.

3. Ibid. p. 19.

4. Ibid. p. 25.

5. Ibid. p. 25.

6. Ibid. p. 17.

7. Ibid. pp.56-57.

8. Ibid. p. 60.

9. Ibid. p. 140.

10. Ibid. p. 185.

11. Ibid. p. 216.

Workshop 21. *Erich Fromm,* by Don Hausdorf.[1]

The sexual instinct is at the core of Freud's (Freud, Sigmund, 1856-1939) personality theory. This theory has been later questioned by Adler (Adler, Alfred, 1870-1937) and others. Another unresolved question dealt with the relative importance of heredity versus environment. Fromm (Fromm, Erich, 1900-1980) says that this is a false question, since the two always function together. For the same reason, he argued that the polarity of the "self" and "others" is a also a false polarity. True human needs, apart from the physiological ones, are according to Fromm, the need to grow, to develop, and to realize one's potentialities. Individual needs are however, in conflict with societal needs. Only in utopia do human needs and societal needs match perfectly.

Freedom for Fromm, consists in the absence (or removal) of all barriers between the "self" and "activity". In man, there is an inherent drive for life. To live is to be active. The essence of man is to produce, to create, to be productive. Man is formed by his activities. Actions, ideas, and character interact in man. Man is subject to two kinds of authorities: the authority of competence and knowledge, and the authority of power.

Contrary to Freud, Fromm maintains that neurosis results from man's failure to use his productive powers. In Freud, neurosis results from the blocking of sexual energy. Fromm poses the question of universal ethics. Does such an ethics exist? He answers the question positively. A universal ethics consists of "those moral norms whose aim is the growth and unfolding of man."[2] Church ethics serve the ruling classes. Religion is a compensation for frustrated needs. For Fromm, there is no absolute and eternal truth. Such truth is beyond man. Scientific knowledge is the optimal truth at a given historical period. ..."certain problems, arising out of particular historical dichotomies, may not admit any single correct answer."[3] Man needs faith. He needs something akin to a religious feeling. There are two kinds of faith: rational faith and irrational (religious) faith. Irrational faith is based on fear and ignorance. It is blind faith. Rational faith expresses a rational vision, and a strong belief in humanity. For Fromm, "the sacred and the secular are not necessarily contradictory."[4] Freud opposes religion in the name of ethics. Religion, for Freud, is "a replacement of infantile attachments and an obstacle blocking self-understanding. It obstructs and blocks self-understanding."[5] Fromm opposes cultural relativism. A sane society requires change in the social, economic, political, and cultural fields. He questions whether the profit motive, prestige, status or power is the principle incentive for work. He cites cases (The Boimondau experiment- a watch factory in

France) where work performance is not based on the profit motive. Capitalism alienates man. It perverts labor into a meaningless activity. But, work is a fundamental human need, and it needs to be a meaningful expression of human energy. This is one of capitalism's most basic contradictions.

Fromm opposes the centrality of sex in Eros. The truly erotic love transcends sex. The aim of psychology is the removal of distortions and illusions. To bring the unconscious into consciousness, means for Fromm, *"to transform the mere idea of universality of man into the living experience of this universality."* [6] Fromm has been influenced by Zen Buddhism. The goal of Zen Buddhism is like that of Socrates: Know Thyself. However, the method of Zen is more like that of the mystics: to know oneself from the inside. "Zen man is in direct communion with the great unconscious."[7]

Exercises.

1. Fromm's definition of freedom is the removal of barriers to activity. What does Fromm mean by being active? Think of all the barriers that inhibit you from being productive, and being able to express yourself creatively in your work.
2. Fromm defines neurosis as a blocking of the person's productive powers, namely, the inability to use one's life energy productively and usefully. Do you agree?
3. According to Jung, neurosis sets in whenever a natural function gets lost. (A natural function is one that is inherent in the person as a human being, for example, an ability to attend to a given task, the ability to concentrate, the ability to empatize, etc.) Do you see any difference between Fromm's and Jung's definitions of neurosis? Is a person's need to be productive a natural function? Think of yourself, and of your own need to be productive. Is work a fundamental human need?
4. Productive work is a goal oriented activity, it is oriented toward the future. Can a person live without a future?
5. When your work expresses your creativity and your inner self, you feel joy. When you are not connected to your work from the inside, you feel alienated. When you feel alienated from your work, life loses its meaning. Is this the reason why Fromm thinks that work alienation is the principle contradiction of capitalism?
6. Reflect on the nature of our society and its principle contradictions.

Notes

1. Don Hausdorf, *Erich Fromm.* New York: Twayne Publishers, 1972.
2. Ibid. p. 64.
3. Ibid. p. 63.
4. Ibid. p. 67.

5. Ibid. p. 68
6. Ibid. p. 108.
7. Ibid. p. 109.

Workshop 22. A Descriptive Phenomenological Approach to the Evolution of Interest.

"To know what one really wants is one of the most difficult problems that anyone has to solve."[1]

1. The Problem: How Do I Know What I Want to Do?

Most people think that they know what they want or would like to do. However, when confronted with the question directly, they are baffled to find out that they really don't know the "true" answer to this question. Why is this so? The answer to this is quite complex. It is a reflection of people's past life, and therefore, everything that they did, how they did things, and what they failed but intended to do, (i.e. their wishes, dreams, frustrations, etc.) as well as what they thought they were expected to do by those significant others in their lives. All of these conscious and unconscious manifestations of an individual's past, bear significantly on the answer to this simple question of why it is that most of us don't really know what we want, and correspondingly, we don't know what we want to do.

The fact that we are caught by surprise when confronted with the question directly and openly, indicates that we didn't want to deal with it, and perhaps, that we were afraid to face it, and thus to admit to ourselves our basic lack of direction, and the resulting lack of determination in the pursuit of internalized goals, that have not been made explicit to ourselves. In a way, it is a reflection of a lack of courage or faith in our ability to pursue and achieve what we really want. Thus, as long as we don't need to deal with it directly, as long as we don't need to confront it or face up to it, the dream and the wish, and the hope, and the illusion, they all remain with us, and our concrete reality, the work which we don't enjoy too much, the relationships that don't work out too well, the mechanics of daily life, all of these are easier to endure, if there is this romantic side to us, which somehow gives us slight comfort, and perhaps strength to carry on, despite all.

Thus, a simple confrontation in terms of what we want to do with ourselves, what we want for ourselves, and what kind of work would open up the creative aspects of our buried productive potential, will have a more lasting effect on us. There is the initial surprise of not knowing the answer to this simple question (of what do I want?), while all the time we were acting on the expressed or apparent premise that we knew what we want. ("If I only could do what I want or always wanted to do, etc."). The initial surprise that one has been going through life on a false premise of knowing oneself while the truth was that of not knowing oneself, that initial discovery may come as a slight

shock to some people, especially to those who have gotten into the
habit of concealing things from themselves, that means, those who
habitually deceive themselves, and who practice the art of self
deception.

After that initial startling discovery, there are two more basic
effects of this kind of self-confrontation. The first is a sobering up
effect. It takes away the illusions, false hopes, and all such private little
comforts that made everyday life more tolerable. This may put the
person in a down mood. The person will feel bad about himself or
herself. However, this is only an incidental aspect of the process. The
process itself could be the beginning of a real self-discovery through
self-confrontation. It could be a turning point that would make it
possible for us to act in accordance with our true nature, and that would
enable us to move forward on the way to greater freedom,
independence, and creative self-expression. We will become more
confident of ourselves, of our power, and of our possibilities. We will
depend less on others for our well- being. We will learn to reflect on
our experience in new ways. We will learn to integrate our
experiences, and apply them constructively, as we move from one
station in life to another. So, we come again to the question posed in
the beginning.

Once we realize that the answer to the simple question of what do I
want to do? is not simple, we can try to reflect on it for ourselves. We
can go about looking for the right answer in a systematic way. We can
start by examining the sources of our interests. What kind of things,
events, activities, etc. interest us? We can go through the entire routine
of our last days, weeks, months, etc. and try to find out what we were
interested in? For example, the boss came in with a new work project.
Did it catch my interest? Did it fire my imagination, did it pose a
challenge which I am anxious to meet? Say, I meet a new person. Do I
want to meet that person again? What was there special about the
person that aroused my interest? What kind of things am I drawn to?
What do I enjoy doing repeatedly, and never get tired of? What are the
things that I can do easily, and feel very comfortably with? What was
that book all about, the one I picked up and couldn't put aside, until I
finished reading it.

Suppose I find that nothing interests me, I have not been moved or
excited by anything. I am blase. Is that the end? The answer is
obviously not. Interests must be created, renewed, developed,
cultivated, and nurtured. To have interests means to be interested. It
means to actively engage oneself in life (in whatever form). To be
interested means to be engaged. This can be developed only by
practice. One cannot expect to have interest without the practice of self
involvement whose effect is the development of interest. Before we
have interests, we have inclinations. They are not differentiated. We

might be inclined to do one thing or the other. We choose to do this rather than that. As a result, we evolve an interest in what we do. Obviously, the inclination to do, both precedes our interest, and forms the basis for our interests.

The meaning of an inclination is that we choose to do the thing ourselves. It is not forced upon us from the outside. This is an important truth that we must learn to appreciate, namely, that interests cannot be forced on us. Thus the first step in examining our interest is to become engaged in the things we do. To be engaged is to give oneself totally to the single pursuit of the moment, whatever it is. However, we soon find out that we cannot do this no matter how determined we are. So we begin to discriminate. We discard those events, (things, phenomena, people, etc.) that we don't seem to be able or willing to engage ourselves with. But we must give them a real try. Only after repeated effforts can we come to the conclusion that they do not interest us. We will also find things that we tend to give more attention to. We will concentrate on these more and more. We will do this willingly, without any force or imposition from the outside or from the inside. These are truly our free choices.

Let me give some examples: To be engaged means to be fully concentrated on the activity at hand, that is, to give oneself fully to the experience of the moment. If I have a conversation with another person, I have to practice to be fully engaged with the other person in my listening, interacting, and focusing on that person to the exclusion of everything else. My present involvement becomes my entire one. I am completely absorbed in the activity of the moment. I am fully concentrated. To be engaged means not to be distracted. Just think of how many times you have been completely engaged in the moment. Think back as far as you can. You will find that children have that wonderful quality of total engagement in the moment. As we grow older we tend to lose it. Think of other people, your friends, acquaintances, your family, are they focused on what they do?

The ability to concentrate comes with practice. Full concentration brings about and develops interest in its wake. We cannot be interested in something that we have never tried, experienced, have not been exposed to, or encountered. Interests are acquired, not given. Our inclinations are given to us, they are with us all the time. They guide and direct our choices. We need to follow them up by our ability to absorb ourselves in what we do. All too often however, we are not fully listening or paying total attention to what we do. We are distracted, self-absorbed, and self- preoccupied. As a result, we sink into a morass of evasiveness and diffusion of energy imperceptibly, habitually, and surely. Then, when suddenly confronted with the question of what it is that we want to do, while we are thinking all the time about ourselves (being self- absorbed), we are not able to give a clear answer to this question. This is the paradox of self-preoccupation. Here lies the first answer to the initial question. We don't know what we want to do, because we have not developed the ability of being fully absorbed in the things that we do.

2. The Practice of the Art of Being Fully Engaged in What I Do.

2.1. The first requirement is: do only those things you want to do most. However, in order to prevent the lack of interest to be an expression of an unwillingness to become interested, it is necessary to articulate the reasons why this particular activity (book, etc.) does not interest you. I also have to make sure that my choice of interest is truly and freely my own, and is not a false choice that reflects the desire for approval or convention.

2.2. I have to allow for the possibility of making a wrong judgment. I must test my inclinations by allowing enough activity to make sure that I was not acting on impulse. This is especially important in matters of consequence to us.

2.3. The need to practice awareness. I have to catch myself as my mind starts to wander off. The sooner I catch my distractions the easier can I deal with them. To become aware of my distractions is to verbalize them.

2.4. To immerse oneself in the moment (or in the activity of the present) is to forget oneself completely. One shuts everything extraneous from one's mind (consciousness) in order to be fully absorbed in the activity at hand.

2.5. It is necessary to practice full concentration with small things, as with important things, until one becomes habituated to it. That is, until it becomes an automatic routine, and a way of life.

2.6. It is also good to observe and reflect on one's progress of this practice. It is desirable to set aside a time when one reflects on the daily events, and analyzes one's interest in them.

Through the practice of being absorbed in whatever we do, we soon find those activities that we enjoy, and the ones that we don't. We recognize our inclinations and see our interests aroused. We follow our interests and become involved in them. They become a source of excitement and pleasure. We want to talk about them, and share them with others. We want to become more knowledgable, and more competent in those areas that interest us. We begin to cultivate them, and leave out what does not interest us. When we read a newspaper or magazine, we quickly glance through it until we find something that interests us, then we stop and read it with care. We want to know everything about the things we are interested in. We do not feel the effort of getting to know or learn something that interests us. We can easily engage ourselves with what we do, and we derive pleasure from the activity.

3. A Phenomenological Account of Evolution of Interest Through the Method of Free Variation and the Use of the Transcendental Ego.

In phenomenology, we reflect on our perceptions and on our thoughts about them. We reflect on our mental states and describe them. How are our mental processes intentive? Are they temporal, motivational, or emotional? How are they different today from yesterday? Do they pertain to the past (retrotentive) or the future (protentive) ? What is their inner time? How does the inner time differ between different intentive processes? How can I use the method of ideation and free imaginative variation to get at the bottom of what interests me? Later on, I will attempt to use this method together with the method of phenomenological reduction, in order to identify my real interest or interests.

The exercise of a phenomenological reduction involves the suspension of all judgment about the existence of the outside world, of one's own prereflective "I", and of all the mental processes connected with it. When I brackct everything connected with the world, my own and that of others, I have performed a phenomenological reduction. "In this state my Ego becomes recognized as a transcendental Ego. This Ego lives through my normal, unreflective state anonymously, without self-recognition. I assume that each other person is his or her own transcendental Ego."[2] The outside and my inside world (consciousness) goes on as usual, except that I assume an attitude of neutrality (a suspension of judgment) toward them. Correlative with the outside world (the world of objects), and my experiences of them (my intentive mental states), I can subjectively construct an "as if" experience. From the perspective of the transcendental Ego, the world as it exists, appears to me strictly as the world *meant* and *experienced* by me, now. Each experience of the actual world becomes a phenomenon of experience for me. My universe becomes a universe of phenomena. The natural world as it exists for me derives its whole sense and meaning from me. Of this I can be apodictically certain. However, with respect to recollective intentive processes (events in the past), such apodictic certainty does not hold, because my motivational and emotional states are not the same each time. We can nevertheless use recollections from our past as a way to trace the evolution of our interests.

In each of our recollections from the past, there is a subject encountering an object. For each *noesis* there is the corresponding *noema*. For each intentive process that has been actualized, there are an infinite number of intentive processes that could have been realized, but were not. Similarly, for each object as it presented itself, there are an infinite number of ways in which the object could have presented itself, but did not. Such possibilities were actualizable but not actualized. Thus, I can tell each story of my recollected past in many different ways. Suppose, I do that, would there be an invariant, an "eidos", of a certain kind that is common to all stories? Let us find out by way of examples. We will tell stories, both fictional and factual, and subject them to free, imaginative variation. The stories are meant purely as examples of retrotentive processes in the search for the identification of interest. We will try to discern their *eidos,* the commom thread that bind them together.

Here are some of the stories:

When I was little, I lived on a street near the train tracks. I would always run after the train whenever a train was passing by. One time (I was about four), I kept on running, and got lost. In the evening my mother found me at the railway station. She castigated me, and embraced me with motherly love.

I am in grade school, (fourth or fifth grade). The teacher is reading a story: The story is about the adventures of Robinson Crusoe. I am totally immersed in the story. Suddenly, the bell rings, and the teacher stops reading. How I wished that the teacher had gone on reading, and that the bell never rang!

I am in the countryside on my summer vacation. I am about 12 years old. I walk with my uncle to a distant village. We walk through the rye fields just before harvest time. The seeds are ripe, and the stalks are golden. There is a breeze and the fields turn into a golden wave. I want to stay in the fields forever.

I sleep in the barn in the countryside. I hear beatiful chants at dawn coming to me from a distance. The chants come closer and closer. It is a group of peasant workers going to work on the fields of the lord of the manor.

I get up at dawn. I walk in the fields. I meet a shepherd boy with a flute. He plays the most beautiful songs. We stop and sit down on the grass. He cuts the bark from a tree and makes me a flute.

Since this is merely an illustration and an exercise, I will stop here. Let me try to discern the essential idea (the eidos) common to the above stories. What is the common thread (noetic-noematic unity) that binds these stories together? The unity in all of the above intentive processes pertains to the fascination for the exotic, for adventure, for nature, and a longing for the unknown. The common "eidos" in all of the above stories is the desire to travel and to see distant lands. Does that throw possible light on my primary interest in travel? Am I still interested in travel and in exploring foreign lands and peoples?

I could go on telling many more stories with many variations, with respect to time, content , fact, and fiction. Would they all show the same or a similar eidos, a common idea that binds them together? The answer is most likely yes. The reason for this is, that they would all be my stories, as told and experienced by me. In my own case, if I were to continue with this experiment in story telling, I would find that the essential ideas ("the eidoses") common to many different stories from my past, were: (1) The story itself, i.e. the love of story telling. (2) The love of travel. (3) The love of adventure. (4) The sense of wonder (philosophy). (5) An understanding and love of people. All these "eidoses" are my primary interests. My interest in psychology and philosophy was discovered almost accidentally through my exposure to these subjects in my last year of high school. The inclinations toward them were in me, and they came out strongly at the first opportunity of exposure. They were not however given a chance to ripen and develop because of outside conditions. Later on, I also developed a great respect for the sciences. However, these were secondary and tertiary interests that were extraneously determined.

Now, that I have identified my primary interests, let me subject them to further questioning. I don't want to take anything for granted. I have arrived at some kind of conclusion with respect to what my interests are, but I want to subject this very conclusion to a radical examination. I will do this, by way of suspending judgment about the validity of my conclusions.   I will use the method of a phenomenological reduction.

I am going to suspend judgment about the validity of my interest in travel. I am not sure whether I am really interested in travel. I don't even know what it means to be interested in travel. Am I interested in travel per se? Any kind of travel? Or, am I interested in certain kinds of travel, travel to certain countries as opposed to other countries? And, if so, why do I want to travel to those other places? Do I want to travel any time, or is the urge to travel stronger at one time than another? May be it is not really the travel or travelling that is behind my "interest"? May be that the need for travel is a cover for some other need that is in me, a need that (for whatever reason or reasons), I was not able to identify and express? Let me try to probe a little deeper. Is it possible that the urge for travel is not so much a desire to see and visit other places, as much as it is a way to "escape" from the place and the situation I find myself in, right now, in the present? Let assume that there is a certain validity to the notion of escape hiding itself behind the travel. But I am not sure. I will subject this "escape" to a further, phenomenological reduction. I am not certain that the urge behind my desire for travel is to escape my current situation, and I will suspend judgment about it.

I will go on with my search for the true urges that hide themselves behind my interest in travel. Suppose I say that an interest in foreign peoples is behind my interest in travel? What does interest in people mean? Am I interested in people's behaviors and customs, their rites and institutions, and the way they relate to each other? There are many opportunities to explore differences betwen ethnic groups right here, in the place where I live. Then why would I want to go to distant places for that purpose? I would have to discard the notion that anthropological considerations are behind my urge for travel.

I could go on looking for the true reasons behind my interest in travel, and continue to subject every one of them to doubt and to a suspension of judgment. Suppose I go as far as I can. What will I end up with? Without going through all the possible details of this exercise, I have come up with, the yearning for intimacy and love, as the final reason for my urge to travel. It is a romantic search for an ideal of love in an exotic place of the nether-nether land. It is search for an idealized form of intimacy. It is an intimacy that does not, and cannot exist. Can I doubt my desire for love? My desire for love is my essence. I cannot doubt it. I have come to the end of my investigation.

I will enter into the state of transcendental epoche. I will bracket everything. I will suspend judgment of the world around me, and of my own consciousness and desires. My Ego has now become a transcendental Ego, for whom the world exists not of actualities but of phenomena of beings. This phenomenal world exists now exactly as meant and experienced by me. My intentive processes, *noesis* and *noema,* have become unified. I can construct an "as if world", where all my experiences of objects, sensations, thoughts, and desires were entirely the way I meant and experienced them. I have reached a perfect unity of my intentive processes. On this noetic-noematic unity, I can proceed to build the world, and my place in it (my understanding of myself). This unity will in every single case, involve the subject (me) encountering an object (the reason for my presumed desire for travel). My search for truth has become unified.

4. Back to the Question of Why Study Interest?

It is my firm belief that interest is at the core of life. To have real interests means to live actively, productively, fully, and joyfully. To have interests means to be able to make independent choices that reflect one's own true self. Interest is the key to unlock the creative potential within us. It is also the secret of our intrinsic enjoyment and excitement of the work we do. Its ramifications are pervasive through the entire spectrum of our life. We relate better (more joyfully) to ourselves, to others, and to our natural environment. It seems that transcendental phenomenology might open the way for a systematic study of interest. Clearly, interest is personal, and therefore one has to investigate one's own past, (as well as the various influences that have shaped one's past), in order to trace one's interests. Phenomenological methods, such as, reflective theoretical observation, the method of ideation and free variation, as well, as the method of the phenomenological reduction, seem to be well suited for a systematic study of the evolution of interest.

I have been able to distinguish in this study between primary and secondary interests. Primary interests originate from within the person, for no obvious reason. In this sense they may be hereditary or inborn inclinations. These may be dormant within the person until given a chance to be aroused through exposure (whether by intent or accident.) We often refer to such primary interests as innate talent. It may very well be the case that innate talent is nothing but primary interest. Secondary (or tertiary) interests are prompted primarily by extraneous factors. The knowledge of one's primary interests should optimally guide the person in formulating his or her professional objectives. Our creative potential is likely to unfold most in the area of our primary interests. It is worth repeating that interest is fundamental to a person's creativity, to his or her self-confidence, to one's intrinsic enjoyment from work, and to one's productive contribution to oneself and society.

Exercises.

1. What are your primary interests? What are your secondary and other interests? Describe the difference between them.
2. Are you interested in your studies? in your work? Do you have any hobbies? What are they? What activities give you most pleasure?

Notes

1. Erich Fromm, *Escape from Freedom*. New York: Avon Books, p. 2.
2. I owe this formulation to Professor John Scanlon.

Workshop 23. The Way of the Tao.[1]

What is the Tao? The Tao is nameless and inexpressible. Once you express it or name it, it is not the Tao. Spinoza says: "All determination is negation." The Tao, like Spinoza's Nature, contains no negativity. It is boundless, eternal, invisible, and formless. It is absolutely infinite. The Tao is immanent in all things. It is the source and the mother of all things. The Tao is behind all manifestation and all differentiation. Only through non-discrimination and non-differentiation, when we overcome the split between subject and object, can we know the Tao. Only when we stop discriminating between phenomena, events, thoughts, and things, can we come to understand the Tao. We can feel the nothing behind all things, the nothing that is common to all things. That absolute void or nothingness that is behind everything, that ultimate reality behind all reality, is the Tao. The nothing, the great void that is behind things and objects, we can see with the third eye only. We can see it with the eye of the intuition, when our gaze is directed inward into the depth of our pure being, rather than being directed outwards, the physical universe and its manifestations. We see the Nothing that is behind everything. When we connect to the great Nothing, the Nothing behind all differentiation and all discrimination, we connect to the Tao. The Tao is everything and nothing. It is the nothing that is behind everything. It is nothing tangible or thinkable. It is not anything in particular. It is not any one form, object, or spirit. It is not directly accessible to our senses or to our imagination. It is the source of all things, of all creativity. The Tao is beyond anything that can be fathomed or formed. To see the formless behind all forms, the nothing behind all things, is to be in the Tao. That nothingness, ("I don't know how to name it, call it the Tao,") reveals the mystery and the origin of all things. It reveals the subtle reality that encompasses the manifestation of all things. This mystery is the mystery of the beginning of all things, the beginning prior to all things, the beginning of no beginning. It is the Tao.

The Tao reveals itself in action through non-action, or in non-action through action, *wu-wei*. The latter means not interfering with what is natural. It means letting nature freely come out, and express itself within us. It means going with nature, and not against nature. Any discrimination or learning that does not accord with nature (the Tao) needs to be unlearned. True learning is revealed in unlearning. We unlearn the artificial, the pretentious, and assent to the natural, the true. To learn, yet to unlearn, *wei wu wei*. In learning we accumulate facts or information, in study we reduce, we grasp the essence. The one informs, the other forms. Non-differentiation and no content, (the relaxation of body and mind) is a precondition for knowing (differentiation and content).

The willing of the non-willing: it signifies allowing nature to be. To be natural in view of the artificial conditioning that living brings about, requires a mental effort. It requires a mental discipline. To remain calm and tranquil in the face of a difficult and great task, is to allow nature to work with us. It is almost like letting nature do our work. That is the deeper meaning of action through non-action, or *wu wei*. In not searching for the Tao, one obtains the Tao.

The true self is a unity, the unity of nature, free from extremes. The inner self is intimate with its own nature. When you are intimate with your own nature, you are also intimate with nature, the Tao. You grasp the eternity of the present, the eternity of nothingness, of non-being. This nothingness is the non-being of being. It is the ultimate void, the unity of being and non-being. It is the going back to the origin, back to nothingness. That is the true reality. The truth of being is to be found in non-being. Nothingness makes being be, it makes being function. Being and non-being, emptiness and fullness, form and formlessness are all one. They are the same. Tao is the void, the nothingness prior to God. Tao functions through nothingness. "The glass encloses the nothingness in the cup. The cup functions through the nothingness". The wise man surrenders to the nothingness. This surrender is a passivity that is not a passivity, non-action through action, *wu wei*. The wise man connects to the highest spiritual reality, the reality of the Absolute, the void. It is the void that is not a void, a stillness that is not a stillness. It is a void that is most full and a stillness that full of movement. That is the profundity of stillness, the void, and the nothingness. An inner luminosity, an inner light, and absolute peace overcomes us. We open ourselves up to the mystery of mysteries, to the profundity of stillness, to the origin of all things. We reach the state of enlightenment, the Buddhist state of Samadha.

The Tao is eternal, nature is eternal. When I am one with the Tao, one with nature, I see things from the perspective of eternity, *sub species eaternitatis*. I see the one reality behind all differentiations. It is the reality that unites all the opposites. The opposites, (soft-hard, weak-strong,) are all parts of the whole, they belong to the whole. They act on each other and transform each other. The soft becomes hard, and the weak becomes strong. To maintain integrity it is necessary to bend (Chpt. 22). The bamboo bends and becomes straight. The iron rod bends and stays bent. Which of these is stronger? To bend is to become straight. To remain gentle is to be strong. This is called living according to reality. To abide with the origin is to never fall short in all of one's life (Chpt. 52). The principle of reversal *(fan)* is a guiding principle in the Tao. To understand the Tao is not to understand it. To not understand something leaves room for more understanding. Therefore, understand the Tao as if you don't understand it. To be aware of the positive, yet to abide in the negative, is to allow things to be, to let things happen. It means to accept whatever is, and not to worry. It is to be a man of high culture. The man of high culture balances the opposites in life. One-sidedness, tunnel vision and exclusion of everything that is not pertinent to the work in front of me, gives thrust and momentum, but it leads to barbarity. It tramples on everything that blocks my way. To remain in the state of original non-differentiation is to retain the innocence of a child. Yielding is the action of Tao. To think is to retain total openness, total yeilding, and total flexibility of the mind.

The wise man comprehends this differentiation, and applies it to his daily life. Thus, he asserts himself by not asserting, he has much by having less, he is strong by being weak, he is great by not endeavoring to be great, he is without pretense, and without complexities (pride or boasting). The wise man never works for what is great. He achieves what is great. The mind reposes in Tao. The wise man becomes his true self through selflessness. The man of Tao is free from self, he does not claim credit for any of his attainments, his self is the self of no-self. His achievement is that of non-achievement. He is not interested in fame, and he is free from ambition. He therefore lives fully and freely. He lives and does everything naturally, without compulsion, and without worry, i.e. through non-action. He allows his natural self to guide him. This is called every day-mindedness. It is living and acting with nature's rhytm. It is to be attuned to the rhytm of nature and hear the sound of stillness.

The man of compassion has no need to show compassion. He has no need for outward refinements, morality, and righteousness. Outward refinements (benevolence and justice, cleverness and profit), are replaced by the true compassionate inner self. To reach the great peace, the great compassion, the unity of the self with the universe, one must rid oneself of false moral teachings, and be one's true moral being, the original human nature. The original human nature is compassionate, not selfish. The true being identifies itself with the universe, the mother or the universal unconscious. ("I am nourished by the Mother," *Tao Te Ching*, Chpt. 20). The Mother is the origin. For Jung, the image of the mother is the symbol of the collective unconscious. Man and the world, subject and object are one in the collective unconscious. "The identity of opposites is characteristic of every psychic event that is unconscious."[2] The nourishing Mother is the same as the region of darkness, the great void, which one meets when one follows *wu wei*. This region of darkness is the source of all potentiality and of all creativity. The echo of Tao is inherent in the great attainment, the void. (*Tao Te Ching*, Chpt. 21.) Before differentiation there was *wu*, the thing. *Wu* is the non-differentiated chaos before separation of heaven and earth. "Look at it, nothing can be seen, listen to it, nothing can be heard, grasp it, nothing can be fathomed. Nothing can be determined, so we have no name for it."[3] The non-differentiated chaos, *wu,* is the origin of all things. It is the subtle reality of all things. It is the source of all spirituality, of all reality, of all tranquility, and of all creativity. To tranquilize one's mind, to nourish one's spirit, is to return to the source, to nature. (*Tao Te Ching,* p. 77.)

The Tao, the source of all things, of all manifestations, is in each thing. Each particularity contains the universality, the source. Each unconcealment contains the concealed. Each truth contains a truth that is still concealed, unknown. This truth (nature, Tao, Mother, origin, the great void, the nameless, etc.) cannot be exhausted. It is an inexhaustible and continually renewable source of vitality, and creativity. *Wu wei* is to act and yet to be free from action, it is to live in the world, and yet to be free from the entanglements of the world. It is a way of letting be, of letting come, of remaining tranquil. It is teaching without words. (The Tao led to the highest attainement in Chinese art and poetry.) It is dealing with life, engaging in life, without involving the ego self. The person is free from all attachments to things. He lets things be as they are. His actions are moral without claiming to be moral. The mind is cultivated to be free from all attachments (fixations and compulsions), to be free from the entanglements of the ego self.

Wu wei expresses the total person, and not any one aspect of the person. *Tao* and *Te* creates things, but do not possess them. "To see things according to things themselves is to follow one's nature *(hsing).* To see things accordindg to the ego self, is to follow one's passions *(ch'ing).* " Letting oneself identify with other beings leads to nature. Nature leads to spirituality. Spirituality leads to enlightenment."[4] Even in self defense (fighting), one's ego remains uninvolved and indifferent. This is when one's fighting strength is most manifest. When one experiences non-being, (the Buddhist Great Death, the mind of Satori, or the mind of the Tao), one is beyond being and non-being, beyond life and death. Life harbors death, and death harbors life.

The Tao dialectic stresses non-being, as the source of being, untruth as the source of truth, and non-thought as the source of thought. "Without intention I see the wonder of Tao, with intention I see its manifestations."[5] Intention refers to thought. Intention contains ambition, anxiety, willing, and desiring. The thought of no-thought is a state of contentment and freedom. Through the non-willing, I return to the original simplicity, my original nature, (emptiness, quiescence, tranquility, purity.) The sage (king, emperor) deals with things from the inner source, with love, not with force. (See Spinoza: "Minds are not conquered by force, but by love and highmindedness".) The man of the Tao never longs to be first in the world. He is humble towards people.   All hostility is dissolved. Harmony is achieved through humility. By being humble, one prevails over others.   The *Tao Te Ching* says: "Governing a large nation is as simple as preparing a dish of food.... When a greater nation is humble before a lesser nation it prevails over it."

The wise man does not hold on to things and therefore never loses anything. His thinking is free from calculation and will. He acts with foresight, before the event occurs, manages things before they are in disorder. He anticipates events instead of being caught by them. He is therefore free from failure. "That which is not yet manifest is easy to forestall.   Deal with a thing before it is there.   He is as careful at the last stage as at the beginning. "A journey of a thousand miles begins from where one stays." (*Tao Te Ching*. Chpt. 64.)

When one deals with others from compassion (love), one identifies with the other. One knows no fear. By identifying with one's opponent, one absorbs his strength. By not overextending oneself, (by not doing too much) one preserves one's strength. By not following blind ambition (wanting to be the first in the world), one can let one's talent develop and mature.   To be aware of defects as defects is to be free from defects. "He who recognizes sickmindedness as sickmindedness is not sickminded." (*Tao Te Ching*. Chpt. 71). This indicates the importance of knowing of not knowing. "The course of nature is to reduce what is overfull, and to supplement what is deficient" (Ibid. Chapt.77.) When one is free from selfishness, one shares with others.   One acts according to one's original, compassionate nature.   "The way of nature is free from intimacy", meaning nature is the source of things but not the things themselves. "Heaven and earth are not benevolent, they treat ten thousand things indifferently. Yet the good man constantly stays with the Tao". (Compare with Spinoza: One loves God without expecting to be loved by God in return.)

The Tao instructs the ruler not to rule by force. The ruler should rule by not imposing his seemingly certain knowledge on his subjects, for "Those who seek to rule a country by knowledge, Are the nation's curse. Those who seek not to rule a country by knowledge, Are the country's blessing. This is called the Mystic Virtue. When Mystic Virtue becomes clear, far reaching, And things revert back (to their source), Then and only then emerges the Grand Harmony".[6] To rule a country by knowledge is to make verybody accept the ruler's way of knowing what is good and right for the people, his way of governing. Not to rule a country by knowledge, means to allow people to think for themselves, and express their views about the right rule. This makes true knowledge proliferate. It allows the development of each person for the benefit of society as a whole. Freedom of thought and freedom of expression allow the unfolding of the creative potential of all the people.

Exercises.

1. Explain the meaning of *Wu-wei*.
2. Tao is the identity of opposites (form with formlessness, being with non-being, emptiness with fullness, the real void which is the most real.) Discuss.
3. What does it mean to live and act in accordance with nature's rhytm?
4. Tao is the source of all things but is not anyone of them. Comment.
5. The wise man asserts himself by not asserting, he is strong by being weak. To remain gentle is to be strong. To maintain integrity, it is necessary to bend. Explain.
6. There is one reality behind all differentiations. Explain.
7. The Tao, the source of all things is in each thing. Explain.
8. To understand the Tao is not to understand it. The principle of reversal is the guiding principle of the Tao. Explain.
9. It is necessary to see things according to the things themselves, without the ego-self. Explain.
10. To act with foresight is to be free from failure. Explain and give examples.
11. When a greater nation is humble before a lesser nation, it prevails over it. Explain.

Notes

1. *Tao: A New Way of Thinking,* A Translation of Tao Te Ching, by Chang Chung-Yuan, New York: Harper & Row, 1975.
2. C. G. Jung, *Integration of Personality*. Transl. by Stanley Dell, New York: Farrar, Straus and Giroux, 1939, p. 225.
3. Chang Chung Yuan, Ibid. pp. 72-73.
4. Chang Chung Yuan, Ibid. p.149.
5. Chang Chung Yuan, Ibid. p.129.
6. Lin Yutang , *The Wisdom of the Laotse*. New York: Random House, The Modern Library, 1948. p. 285.

Workshop 24. Spinoza and the Tao: A Rational-Intuitive Reading of the Tao Te Ching.

In this study we examine the affinities between the Philosophy of the Tao and that of Spinoza. We concentrate primarily on the respective metaphysics and ethics. Other topics, (i.e. theories of government) are left out. We argue that the Tao and *Natura naturans* (Spinoza's substance and attributes) are very similar to each other, and contain many common features. The basic difference between them lies in the apparent presence or absence of a systematic logical structure. Spinoza's thought is systematic and structured, while the Tao is less structured and less systematic. The Tao is composed as sublime poetry, while Spinoza's Ethics is written in the form of a rational deductive system. They both however, relate to the same essence. The distinction between Spinoza's God and the Tao is not a distinction of essence. Both philosophies are naturalistic. Neither the Tao, nor *Natura naturans* are outside nature. They are both in nature. The difference is more likely because of the disparity in historical epochs at the time of their conception. The Tao was conceived in China, in the sixth century B.C. Spinoza lived in Holland, in the seventeenth century A.D., an age of great strides in science. The similarity between the Tao Te Ching and Spinoza's Ethics also holds with respect to the Tao sage and Spinoza's wise man. The man in the Tao and Spinoza's free man share many common characteristics, but they are not identical.

1. The Tao and Spinoza's Substance.

The Tao Te Ching opens with the following lines: "The Tao that can be spoken of is not the Tao itself. The name that can be given is not the name itself."[1] We may best understand the unnameable essence of the Tao as Nature's cosmic principle, an infinitely creating and acting power in Nature. This power is pure being, pure undifferentiated content that is behind all being. It eternally originates within itself. It is the cause and the ground of all things. The Tao is not any of the things, but is behind all things. It is the cause of itself *(causa sui),* and of everything else. It is immanent in all being. It is everywhere. It is eternal and absolutely infinite. It is one, whole, and indivisible. This undifferentiated content is the ground of all differentiation, and of all being. It is the foundation of the physical universe, and the ground of all consciousness. Tao, the non-differentiated void, is the origin of all things, the void prior to differentiation and all change. The void is the chaos, the empty space, the original state of nature from which everything came to be. "Ever present and in motion. Perhaps it is the mother of all things. I do not know its name. Call it Tao."[2] (* Unless otherwise indicated all subsequent quotations are from this translation). The Tao cannot be named or determined in any way.

Spinoza's God, Nature, or Substance: (God, Nature or Substance are equivalent terms. We will use them intermittently and interchangably). Substance is self-caused. Nature is the cause of itself and of everything else. "By that which is self-caused, I mean that of which the essence involves existence, or that of which the nature is only conceivable as existent" (EI, Def. I). There is only one self-caused substance. If there were more than one substance, then one would depend on the other, and substance would not be self-caused. Substance expresses itself through its attributes. God's attributes are infinite, because God is absolutely infinite, an infinity of infinities. As human beings, we can only know two of God's attributes, the attribute of extension, and the attribute of thought. We know only these two, because we consist of them. Substance reveals its essence (existence) through its infinite attributes. ...."each attribute expresses eternal and infinite essentiality". "Attribute is that which the intellect judges to be the essence of substance." (Ibid, Def. IV). Each attribute has the power of substance. Attributes are indivisible, they are pure essence. Natura naturans (substance and attributes), is nature viewed as active. Natura naturata (modes of substance), is nature viewed as passive. (EI, 29. Schol.)

The unnameable is "the source and the origin of heaven and earth and the ten thousand things." The Tao is the source of the universe"[3] , and "the origin of the universe."[4] Is "ground" the same as "source" or "origin"? Ground means that without which there could be no consequence, without the ground nothing could come about. For example, when a flower is pollinated, a fruit develops. What makes a fruit develop after pollination? We would say, that nature makes it so. Nature is the ground. This example could be generalized into any of nature's events. Why do cells after conception, divide, differentiate, and develop into an organism? Science can only describe how natural processes occur. It cannot answer the question why nature acts in certain ways. All science can say is that nature acts that way. This eternally acting and creating power of Nature which is everywhere, behind all being and all manifestations, is the Tao. Without the Tao or Nature as ground, nothing could be, or be conceived. Is there a difference between ground, source, and origin? Source or origin could be continuous or not. The ground is necessarily continuous. Thus the ground is inclusive of the source and the origin.

In Spinoza, Nature is the ground. God's attribute of extension is the ground of all physical things. Extension is not matter. Matter exists in extension. Extension is indivisible, and does not consist of parts. It is the ground for the material world. It expresses God's power to produce motion and rest, i.e. physical energy. Motion and rest is an immediate, infinite, and eternal modification of substance. The laws of nature are inscribed in the face of the universe, *Facies Totius Universi*. The face of the universe is the mediate, eternal, and infinite modification of substance within the attribute of extension. Physical energy (motion and rest), and finite modes (things or bodies) interact according to the laws of nature.

Thought is the ground of the intellect. Thought makes the thinking of the intellect possible. It is the ground of all possible knowledge. The infinite intellect comprehends all reality, all possible knowledge, everything conceivable. Intellect is the immediate, eternal, and infinite modification of substance within the attribute of thought. *Idea dei*, (the idea of God), is the thought side of all things. It is the mediate, eternal, and infinite modification of substance within the attribute of thought. In God there is an idea of every conceivable thing. Every external thing has its mental counterpart, which is life. Thus everything in the universe is imbued with life. All of the universe is animated in various degrees. The degree of animation is compounded vertically, from the simplest to the most compound (complex) bodies. The human body is part of the infinite and eternal modification of substance in the attribute of extension. The human mind is part of the eternal and infinite modification of substance in the attribute of thought. Our mind is part of the *idea dei* , God's intelligence and his infinite intellect.

Although the Tao cannot be named, we are not necessarily wrong by identifying it with Nature's powers, that is with Nature as a whole. We are thereby not naming the Tao, but giving it another, more familiar designation. The Tao itself is also a designation of something that cannot be named. Names in the strict sense of the word, refer to differentiations or determinations. They do not pertain to the undifferentiated whole, the Tao or Nature. The Tao is both immanent in the differentiations (the ten thousand things), and is also prior to the differentiations. To be prior to all things means that the Tao is self-caused *(causa sui)*.

"Tao functions through its nothingness... And cannot be conceived as full of things...I do not know who created it, But it is likely that it existed before God."[5] Nothingness or emptiness, what is its significance? It is not an absolute void or literal nothingness, because out of nothingness comes nothing. It is obviously not the case with this nothingness, because out of it comes everything. Therefore nothingness or emptiness represent here a state of pure being, a state of absolute indeterminateness. It is a state of infinite freedom, infinite power, and infinite creativity. Such is the nothingness of the Tao, a nothingness that cannot be determined in any way. The Tao is the whole. This whole, indivisible, non-being or nothingness is the foundation of the universe. This prime force is the foundation of the physical universe, as well as, the foundation of all thought, the ground of all consciousness. The Tao as ground is not conscious of any particularity. It is neither conscious, nor self-conscious.[6] There is no awareness, and no concern with benevolence. "Heaven and earth are not benevolent, They treat ten thousand things indifferently".[7] Aubrey Menen (The Space Within the Heart) came close to this divine nothingness. He tells us that he came to know his true self only when his mind reached a state of perfect nothingness and perfect freedom:

"Our true self is not superior to other people; it is not inferior either. It is not touched by other people at all. It does not wish other people to be better or to be worse: it neither punishes nor praises. It can be totally indifferent to the world as if sleeping; or it can be awake and observe, but with the same indifference. "Not that, not that" say the Upanishads in the puzzling phrase which has echoed down the centuries. Now I saw its meaning. I was not that; nor anything that you could name in the world around me. I was not good, or bad.... I was not a success or failure...I sat on a stone bench, and felt a great peace descend on my spirit. I was a free man for the first time in my life. (Aubrey, Menen, *The Space Within the Heart.* New York: McGraw Hill Book Company, 1970. pp. 151-152.)

God is absolutely infinite. An infinitely and eternally creating power, infinitely and eternally active. God's essence is his existence, *causa sui.* God's existence is God's power. It is complete in itself. It involves no negation. God cannot be determined in any way. "All determination is negation, *"omni determinatio negatio est."* Nature reverberates with God's power and activity. Substance is immanent, absolute Being. It is infinite power, absolute perfection. God is immanent in nature. He is both creator and created. Existence is eternity. "By eternity I mean existence itself"...(EI, Def. VIII). Only substance exists.

Being and Nature are connected to eternity, not to time. God and the infinite modes are eternal. Eternity is outside time. Whatever is, is in Nature. There is nothing outside Nature. Modes exist because of substance. Substance is a necessary cause. God acts by the necessity of his nature. The universe could not be other than what it actually is. "From the necessity of the divine nature there must follow infinite beings in infinite ways" (EI, 16). God is not compelled to act by anything external to him. He is the only free cause. "God acts solely by the laws of his own nature, and is not constrained by anyone" (EI, 17). Nature alone is a free, and necessary cause. Freedom is the same as causal necessity. The laws of nature are eternal, the occurences are temporal. Reality is an all inclusive logical system and causal order. God is this very causal order. Everything in nature must be understood within nature's general order. The latter must be understood in terms of itself. Thus, ..."without God, nothing can be or be conceived" (EI, 15). Free will is incompatible with causal necessity. Will is a finite mode of thinking. It is always determined by other causes. People think that they act freely because they are not aware of the true causes behind their actions. The universe is orderly, rational, and intelligible. The same causal order prevails in bodies as in thought (ideas).

Infinite modes derive from substance. Finite modes derive from infinite modes. Things are modes of substance. "By mode, I mean the modifications of substance, or that which exists in, and is conceived through, something other than itself" (EI, V). Each of God's attributes express the eternal order of nature. They are all equivalent to each other. Thus, "the order and connection of ideas is the same as the order and connection of things" (EII, 7). Naturing nature *(natura naturans)* is immanent in all things. "God is the indwelling and not the transient cause of all things" (EI, 18). Each finite mode contains within itself some aspect of God's creative powers. Things exist in God, but they are not of God; *Panentheismus,* not *pantheismus.* In the universe of modes *(natura naturata),* nature discloses itself as negation. The world of manifestations, *(natura naturata)* is dialectical. It involves affirmation and negation. Each affirmation implies its own negation, (Tao Te ching 2: Reality is contradictory. Spinoza: All determination is negation"). Dialectics or the law of opposites is the essence of natured nature, *natura naturata* Opposites affirm each other. In each there is the seed of the other. With time, each is transformed into the other (the principle of reversal). The opposition of forces *(Yin* and *Yang)* are the causes for movement and change. Reality encompasses all contradictions, and all opposites.

Modes do not have a necessary existence. They depend on *natura naturans.* The existence of modes is entirely conditional. *Natura naturata* is in *natura naturans.* Together they are Nature. Non-existent modes are those that conform to the laws of nature, and therefore could conceivably exist. Fictional modes do not conform to the laws of nature, and therefore could not exist. Bodies continuously interact with respect to motion and rest. Changes in motion and rest follow sequentially. Here temporality or duration arises. Duration (time) arises with the advent of finite modes, the beginning of the universe. Spinoza deemphasizes time. Time (duration) is only related to modes whose existence is indefinite, and uncertain. Time is a submode of the human mind. It has no independent existence.

Our basic proposition is that the Tao and Spinoza's *natura naturans* (nature viewed as active), are essentially the same. The Tao is both immanent in the differentiated things (finite modes), and it is also prior to their differentiation. The priority is one of cause, not of sequence. To be prior to all things means that the Tao is self-caused, *causa sui.* The Tao is not any of the things, but it is behind each thing. It is self-created, ("I do not know who created it"), and eternal, (it existed prior to God, meaning prior to heaven, and prior to the universe). "God is prior to all things by reason of causality" (Ethics I, 17, Schol.), and "God is the indwelling and not the transient cause of all things" (EI,18). Thus, one may equate the Tao with Spinoza's *natura naturans,* the eternally active and creative principle in nature. In both the Tao and in Spinoza, God is referred to as infinite power. "God's power is identical with his essence" (EI, 34.).

The Tao is not divisible, and is not composed of parts. The Tao is the whole. The same holds for Spinoza's Substance. *Natura naturans* is the whole of any of its attributes, extension, thought, or any of the other of God's infinite attributes. Each attribute comprises the whole of substance. For the Tao, prior to God means prior to God's infinite and eternal modes, namely prior to Spinoza's motion and rest (physical power or energy), and prior to the laws of nature inscribed in the face of the universe.

The nameable, heaven and earth, and its forces *Yin* and *Yang,* are equivalent to Spinoza's (immediate and mediate) infinite and eternal modifications of Substance. These are motion and rest and the face of the universe. (Immediate and mediate pertain to the direction of causality, not to sequence.) *Yin* and *Yang,* (*Yin* -concentration and rest, *Yang* -expansion and motion), correspond to motion and rest (physical energy). Heaven and earth correspond to Spinoza's *facies totius universi,* the face of the entire universe. Together they give birth to the multitude of things, (finite modes). Heaven and earth and the ten thousand things make up Spinoza's *natura naturata.* Infinite modes derive from substance. Finite modes derive from infinite modes. "The Tao begot one. One begot two. Two begot three. And three begot the ten thousand things. The ten thousand things carry yin and embrace yang. They achieve harmony by combining these forces" (42).

The Tao Te Ching calls the wonder of the Tao and its manifestations a mystery. The valley spirit (6) is the (mysterious) mother spirit. The Tao is the mother (mother nature), the root of heaven and earth. It is concealed, barely seen. The human mind, while being able to comprehend the connection between the Tao and its manifestations, stands in awe before the wholeness of the Tao. We can see the Tao with the inner eye only. The inner eye is the eye of intuitive knowledge. With it we can see the concealed within the unconcealed. When our mind is calm and empty, it reflects the wholeness of nature. When it is engaged and inquisitive, it sees only the manifestations of the Tao.

Aristotle said that philosophy began with wonder. The Tao Te Ching and Spinoza's Ethics express the same sentiment. The philosopher (the sage) without intention sees the wonder of the Tao. With intention he sees its manifestations. The manifestations are the differentiations, the ten thousand things, Spinoza's finite modes. The philosopher-sage sees the Tao, the One, the undifferentiated unity behind the differentiation. The sage's mind is united with the whole of nature and he can see (intuit) nature as a whole. He comprehends "the union existing between the mind and the whole of nature."[8] Through the third kind of knowledge (intuition) the mind unites with nature, and reaches the highest state of blessedness, the intellectual love of god. The mind is totally at rest and without desire. "He has that peace which passes the understanding, but in which everything is understood."[9] Before that state is reached, there is still desire or intention. At the level of intention or desire, one sees only manifestations, appearances, or parts of the whole.

The above proves the similarity, if not identity, of the Tao with *natura naturans,* Spinoza's substance. Next, we take up the comparative ethics.

2. Spinoza on the Right Way of Life.

Our desires and endeavors follow either from the necessity of our nature, or from our being part of nature. Being part of nature means that we are subject to affects of others, (other modes). In the first case, we are the proximate cause of our desires. In the second case, other modes (individuals) are the proximate cause of our desires and endeavors. The former are actions, the latter are passions. Actions refer to mind and body. To the extent that we know the true causes of our actions, we are free. Otherwise, we are not free. In our actions, we affirm and determine ourselves. We are constrained when the cause for our action is outside us. When we don't have the power to act in accordance with our nature, we are constrained in our endeavors. Actions are always good, since they are based on the mind's power of reason, that is, on adequate ideas about ourselves and nature. Passions can be either good or bad. Passions are based on fragmentary knowledge, and inadequate ideas about ourselves and others.

Emotions are modifications of the body, together with the ideas of such modifications. Whatever the body feels, the mind is able to think, and vice versa. Neither one influences the other. They are both parallel expressions of the same substance. In body and mind we are connected to substance. There can be disharmony between body and mind. We need to understand our affects (emotions) by their primary causes. Pleasure is a passive emotion, but it enhances the power of the body. Pain is a passive emotion which reduces the power of the body. External causes may lead to destruction. Destruction, however, can never come from our inner nature.

The essential characteristic of any mode, human and non-human, is the endeavor to self-preserve, *conatus.* For man, self-preservation includes self-elevation. Our existential essence lies in our striving to actualize our unique, God given potentiality. (This striving expresses itself in the will to adequate ideas, called *Voluntas*.) Adequate ideas refer to substance, God. Inadequate ideas refer to imagination. The will, as an intellectual striving for adequate ideas, refers to the human mode. The consciousness of *conatus*, the striving for self-preservation and self-elevation, is desire. Desire is the fundamental affection from which all other affections are derived. **This desire is our essence.** Our essence lies in our striving. Our true desire lies in the striving for adequate ideas, to know ourselves and God.

This striving is good by itself. It is the affirmation of human existence, especially with respect to the body. (Descartes and the philosophic tradition tended to de-emphasize the human body.) Desire is rooted in power, not in morality. (Power is the will to an elevation of activity.) The will to self-elevation is the will to higher levels of reality, the will to greater perfection. Reality is perfection. Spinoza's theory of action is an affirmation of life, and of reason. Sorrow or suffering is a passive state, a state of lesser perfection. Suffering is a reduction of the power of activity. It does not inspire the unity of man and substance. The human mode experiences joy as the power of activity. The will to power is the will to love. Love inspires the transition to greater perfection. Hate inspires the transition to lesser perfection. Pain is a transition to a lower level of reality or perfection. The power of action is bound up with the world of affection. Action is not in the realm of pure reason. Action is a constellation of affection and reason. Desire is both emotion and consciousness. Desire is always antecedent to pleasure and pain. Pleasure and pain are passions. Feelings can be channeled into the direction of human freedom. Pleasure by itself does not produce active states. It does so only when accompanied by having adequate ideas. Spinoza's theory of action is a theory of self-preservation and self-elevation, an affirmation of the bodily and mental powers of activity.

Spinoza questions traditional views of good and evil. Traditional morality is based on imagination, not on truth. Good is what is useful to us. The good unites desire with reason. Spinoza's morality is a productive constellation of desire with reason. The unity of desire is inspired by reason. There is no clash between reason and instinct or impulse. There is no opposition between reason and instinct. Spinoza's notion of virtue is power. It is the power of understanding ourselves and God. The highest aim in life is to perfect the power of the understanding, the power of reason. Only therein can we find lasting happiness and the highest blessedness. Within the scope of our intelligence, within the limits of our intellectual ability and capacity, we can achieve adequate understanding of ourselves and of the rest of nature.

Whatever promotes the perfecting of reason and understanding, that is, whatever promotes our capacity to enjoy the rational life, **is good.** Whatever hinders it, **is evil.** Evil can only come from external causes. Man being part of nature is necessarily subject to its laws. We are subject to the afffections of others. Our power of action is enhanced when we are subject to influences that are in harmony with our own nature, when we associate with people that are in harmony with us. Similarly, disharmony will diminish our power of action.

Our self -interest lies in preserving our faculty for existing and enjoying the rational life. That is the meaning of self-preservation and self-elevation. Everyone has the right (by the souvereign right of nature) to advance his or her own interest. For man, there is nothing more useful than his fellow men who are led by reason. A rational social order is most conducive to man's well being. Envy or hatred are at variance with reason. Such people are to be feared in proportion to their power. However, **minds are not conquered by force, but by love and highmindedness.**

It is therefore useful to unite with others in bonds of friendship. Since men who live under the guidance of reason are few, (men are more prone to revenge than to sympathy), it is necessary to restrain oneself and not imitate the emotions of others. It takes **no small force of character to take everyone as he is....** and not imitate his emotions.

We need others, and our association with others will always bring us more advantages than drawbacks. We should always strive to promote harmony and friendship among people, to respect the rights and the customs of others, and to uphold justice, equity, and honor. Harmony should not be based on fear. Peace and harmony that is based on fear is insecure. Fear results from infirmity of spirit, and is not based on the exercise of reason.

Men are also gained by liberality, but it is the function of the state to provide for the poor, since no single individual has the power to do this. Lasting love is founded on man's character, on the freedom of his soul. All other love (especially carnal love based on lust) will easily turn into hate. Marriage should be based not on bodily beauty alone, but on the individual's character.

One can also achieve harmony through flattery, but such harmony is treacherous. Shame may also contribute to harmony when it is exposed, but the latter is painful, and therefore does not rest on reason. Indignation and self righteousness does not promote harmony between people. When men's intercourse is based on affirming each other's virtue or power, they will be stirred not by fear or aversion, but by the emotion of joy derived from the exercise of reason. For Spinoza reason does not have absolute power over the emotions. An emotion can only be controlled by a contrary emotion that is stronger than itself. Nature does not have a purpose, but man must have a purpose. Without a purpose, there is no freedom.

Spinoza sees a clear separation between man and beast. We may adapt nature for our use, for man's self preservation and self-elevation. The latter means that we must be concerned with the ecological impact of our behavior on the rest of nature. We must be aware of the short and long range ecological consequences of our behavior, both for ourselves and future generations.

For Spinoza there is no good or bad philosophy. There is only true philosophy. Causes in nature can be understood with clarity and distinctness. The order of ideas and of things is the same. Spinoza's intellectual intuition is founded on *ratio*, reason. His metaphysics is based on a mathematical and scientific mode of thinking. His ethics is derivative from his metaphysics. Above the second kind of knowledge, *ratio* and science, stands intuition, the third kind of knowledge. It is the highest mode of knowing, and the highest form of knowledge. Such knowledge increases the clarity of *ratio*. Intuitive knowledge culminates in *Amor Dei Intellectualis*, the intellectual love of God. It leads from pleasure to happiness, from *letitia* to perfect blessedness. The unity of the adequate idea with the love of God is perfect blessedness. Nature consists of true ideas, not of truth. The source of human freedom is to be found in the synthesis of knowledge and love. Nature's love of itself is also God's love of man because man is part of nature. To understand God is to connect to eternity. Nature is not in time. This understanding of God and of the self as being in God (nature) completes the transcendence of temporality. A state of perfect blessedness is reached.

3. The Tao Sage and Spinoza's Wise Man.

We approach the ethics of the Tao and that of Spinoza from the vantage point of contemporary life. Do the Tao and Spinoza's Ethics teach us the same or similar things about what constitutes the right way to live? Do they express similar notions about basic values, and about what is important and what is unimportant in life? Are these notions relevant to modern man living in an a post-industrial urban setting? In short, do they help us in deciding how to live our life today? The Tao Te Ching and Spinoza's Ethics were composed in totally different times, and cultures. The society of the Tao was pastoral, agricultural, and autharkic. In the seventeenth century, Holland was a very important commercial center, and was about to become the first capitalist country in Europe. The commercialization of the culture, and the corresponding capitalist values (commodity fetishism, excessive emphasis on material possessions) began to take a hold on society. They were replacing traditional, feudal, and patriarchical customs, and values. It was a time of transition that brought uncertainty into people's lives. Questions of life's meaning and purpose began to come into the fore. What does it mean to live well, and to live the right way? How is one to be alive, and derive joy from living? Are the sources of joy within us, or outside us? Are they spiritual or material? Spinoza's Ethics addresses itself to these problems.

The question of moral virtue, and of the right way to live is not specicific to any age or culture. The Tao and Spinoza's Ethics address the central question of meaning and purpose in life. For Spinoza, man's essence, *conatus*, consists in our desire to self-preserve and self-elevate. The free and uninhibited use of our physical and mental powers for the purpose of self-preservation and self-elevation is a source of joy and real happines to the person. Our real desire consist in understanding of ourselves and God (Nature), thus letting our potentialities freely develop and unfold. The desire to be free is our essence, our *conatus*. We realize our essence in self-understanding, by acting in conformity with nature, including our own nature. To act in accordance with nature means to live under the guidance of reason, and to be directed from within. For the Tao it means *wu wei*, acting by non-acting. It means to act according to our own calling, not some one else's. It also means to assume responsibility for our actions. This allows us to accept ourselves, to love ourselves, and exercise our powers naturally, without undue exertion. When we are relaxed and natural, when we are not constrained and artificial, we use our inner resources optimally and effortlessly. The sage does not forcefully interfere with natural processes. He does not use force (impose his will) on himself or others. He affects change within himself and others only by understanding, never by force. Acting by non-acting, *wu-wei*, is acting in accordance with nature. Action that accords with nature requires least physical or mental exertion, and it leads to the best results. (Nature never exerts itself). The sheer use of force (the use of will without understanding), even if carried out with the best of intentions, never resolves anything. It compounds the problem of evil. Force leads to more evil, and more ugliness. That goes for oneself, as well as, for others. In each of us there is an overflow of love and affection if we only knew how to open up to it.

To live well is to love life, to be useful and productive, to use our minds and bodies freely, and bring joy to ourselves and others. To give more is to have more. The more we give of ourselves, the more joy and love we have to give and share. People who are selfish and self-centered have little to give. "Minds are not conquered by force, but by love and highmindedness" (EIV, App.11). We can elevate ourselves through self-acceptance, through love of ourselves, and of others. The wise man of the Tao lets nature evolve, *wu wei*. He does not force nature. He understands and accepts the liberating force of nature. The wise man does nothing that is contrary to his nature or nature's own doing. To know this is to be strong. "Mastering the self requires strength" (35). To work with nature is to understand. The wise man does not distort reality by forcing his will on it. He allows nature to unfold its creativity to the fullest. This leads to highest results. To act in conformity with our nature is to experience joy in our action. This joy is derived from understanding, not from willing. "When the mind regards itself and its power of activity, it feels pleasure (EIII,53). Also, "Whatever we endeavor in obedience to reason is nothing further than to understand"...(EIV 26).

In life, it is necessary to discriminate between what is important and what is not important. What enhances our well-being is important. To think well of ourselves, to love ourselves, to be free and self-directed is important. What others think of us is less important. To be true to our selves is important. To impress others is not important. Learning is important. The ability to think ahead, to draw right inferences from given premises, to learn from others, to anticipate events rather than be caught by them, is important. To respect the teacher is important. To be clever is unimportant. "If the teacher is not respected , And the student is not cared for, Confusion will arise, however clever one is, This is the crux of the mystery" (27). To know this is to be wise. Cleverness is the opposite of wisdom. To be wise is to be far-sighted. Cleverness is always short sighted. The clever person is more concerned with the show, with how he or she appears to others. Clever people want to impress others. They look for quick results, and they seek immediate gratification. However, people who do not appreciate what is really important in life, people who look at life only from the perspective of the immediate and the short term, people who are not aware of the longer term consequences of their actions, such people necessarily end up being confused. The confusion arises from the confusion of ends and means. So-called clever people are really confused people.

The Tao teaches us that it is wrong to deny the (Jungian) shadow in us. We can surmount ugliness and evil not by denial or repression but to the contrary, by recognizing them wherever and whenever they appear. Only by living in reality can we realize our essence and our dreams. For Spinoza, reality is perfection. When we substitute the will for the understanding, when we force things on ourselves or on others, when through ignorance and lack of knowledge, we go against nature, we can never achieve our true desires. True desires are based on knowing, not on ignorance.

Disgrace and misfortune are unavoidable aspects of existence. The inability to accept misfortune and suffering is to deny reality. The sage accepts the reality of being human. He overcomes suffering and misfortune by caring and loving, and by helping others to overcome their adversities. By giving of himself in love, he conquers the human condition. Love is the strongest life giving force that we have. We give and accept love not by repression and denial, but by accepting ourselves and others willingly, and graciously. We do not pretend to be important, or to be somebody that we are not. (13)

For the Tao, to be free is to be free from the will to possess. For Spinoza, to be free is to know God and oneself. When one knows oneself and God, one does not need unnecessary things. One is free from self-involvement, vanity, pride, and other entanglements of the ego. Nature creates without possessing. The sage, being free from the will to possess, allows his nature to be fully creative. He teaches by living (without words), and he does not claim credit for his achievements, (for what he does). "Work is done, then forgotten, Therefore it lasts forever" (2). Work that is free from the insnarement of the ego expresses the necessity of one's nature. Such work is the expression of our inner creative powers. It always brings joy in its wake. It expresses the creative force of the Tao or *Natura naturans* within us. Therefore, the achievements of the sage's work last forever. The sage's work has enriched our understanding of ourselves, and of nature. The sage sees things from the perspective of eternity *(sub species aeternitatis)*, not from the transitoriness of everyday life. The sage's existence is synonymous with his achievements, and since his achievements are synonymous with nature, they last forever. They are eternal. Spinoza's wise man does not dwell on his being wise, he does not claim credit for his natural endowments (natural gifts or talents), he does not rest on his achievements, his work is done but soon forgotten so that he can go on to other work, and since his work is entirely free, that is, it conforms to his nature, it is also part of nature, partaking in the truth of nature, and therefore it lasts forever.

The Tao admonishes the sage to "merge with the dust" (4). A "merging with the dust" may have several meanings: 1. The Tao urges us to experience our own nothingness. A Dionysian, intoxicating, self dissolving, death experience prepares us for the fullness of life. The experience of death enhances the experience of life. By removing the fear of death, we assert life. 2. The Tao tells us to merge with the multitude, and overcome our ego. We should not think that we are superior or inferior to anyone else. 3. It is a call to be flexible, adaptable, respectful, and understanding of the multitude. This is similar to Spinoza's advice to the free man to show respect for the multitude, and the common man. (EIV,70, Schol.) 4. To merge with the dust is a quest for a complete union with nature. It is to reach a state of blessedness, a state of pure acquiescence, of total peace, and infinite tranquility. It is a merging with the Tao that culminates in the intellectual love of God. It is to reach the quiescent center within us that gives us poise and steadies us through the turbulence of life (26). It allows us to fully partake in nature's creative energy. For Spinoza, virtue is the power of understanding of self, and God. The highest aim in life is to perfect the power of understanding, the power of reason. "From the third kind of knowledge arises the highest possible mental acquiescence (EV, 27). The pure self is a state of total tranquility. It is a state before limitation, before action, and before words. The sage is spontaneously benevolent in the sense that he does not feel superior or inferior to others. He is pure self, just as the pure self of any other. (See Aubrey Menen, p.3). He transcends qualification or determination. He is not intentionally benevolent (does not try impose his views on anyone) but is spontaneously benevolent (accepts men as they are). This applies equally to Spinoza's free man.

When people live in conformity with nature (the Tao), they don't need conventional morality or formal precepts about how to accept others, and be good to others. Their morality is based not on duty, but on self-knowledge, and freedom. The man in the Tao and Spinoza's free man is moral from the inside, his virtuous behavior flows from his character, not from any external rules. When men lose their innocence, conventional morality becomes necessary. Rules of conduct are a protection against man's wickedness, and his immorality. The same with the family. The need for filial piety came about because of the decline or the absence of natural love, and natural piety within the family. "When the great Tao is forgotten, Kindness and morality arise" (18). Conventional morality arises only after differentiation, when people see themselves as unequal. The sage transcends this differentiation. His benevolence comes from his identification with nature, and with other selves. "The good which every man, who follows after virtue, desires for himself, he will also desire for other men, and so much the more, in proportion as he has a greater knowledge of God." (EIV, 37). The free man's morality is a morality of being, not a morality of rules. The latter is needed by those who are not free.

Body and soul derive from the same source, the Tao or Nature (10). Through the practice of yoga (proper breathing exercises), one can purify one's mind and body, retain the suppleness of a newborn, and achieve full concentration. Suppleness of body and mind, easy adaptability to change, and an openness to growth, signify youthfulness. Rigidity of mind and body, an inability to adapt to change are signs of old age. True aging is not necessarily synchronized with a person's chronological age. People young in years may already be old to the extent that they are rigid in their thinking and living patterns, if they cannot readily adapt to environmental changes, and are stultified in their ability to learn and grow. On the other hand, people old in years may retain their youthfulness, both physically and spiritually, to the extent that they remain flexible in spirit and body, and are not slaves to adverse habits and past conditioning. Therein lies the supreme importance of relaxation, concentration, and purification of mind and body through daily exercise and self-discipline (yoga).

There is a hierarchy of greatness in men. The highest (the best) are those that work for the good of the people (the community) without being known or seen. These are the highest rulers and sages. They work in obscurity, they are totally devoid of any desire or need for credit or recognition. In the Jewish lore there is a legend that at any given time, there are thirty six wise and righteous men upon whom the world rests. In Hebrew they are called LAMED VAV meaning thirty six. They are among us but no one knows who they are. They are not even aware themselves who they are. According to the legend, they are the pillars of the world. Without them the world would have long perished. That is what the Tao means by, "the very highest are barely known to us." (17)

The best way to influence others is not by telling others what to do, or by giving explicit advice to others, often without being asked. In doing this, we are indirectly telling others that we know better what is right or or good for them. Thus we show our "superiority", and expose our vanity. We are exposing our own weakness by our presumed generosity, advise, and kindness that no one asked for . This is why such help is almost never effective. The most effective way to help others is to listen attentively, and to express love, understanding, and active concern for the other's well being.

We help others by listening and understanding even if we feel that the others are wrong. We can indirectly and discreetly suggest possibilities for change, and thus point out any self-destructive behavior patterns. By our acceptance of others, we help them get a better understanding of themselves. To be trusted one must trust others. We come back to what was already said before. "Minds are not conquered by force, but by love and highmindedness" (EIV, App.11.). Whoever does not trust, cannot be trusted. Even if I have had bad experiences by trusting others, even if I have been cheated or lied to, it is still more important that I not lose my trust. It is better to trust and suffer rather than not to trust. Without trust there cannot be love. And without love there cannot be happiness.

The sage is ahead by not trying to be ahead. He endures by not trying to endure. He is detached from possessions. He identifies with all of nature (everything and everybody). Thus he is one with all. "When you are one with the Tao, The Tao welcomes you" (23). Thinking and being are one. The Spinozist unity of mind and body is expressed here. To listen and hear the sound of silence. Talk is not always good or necessary. One may exhaust oneself in superficial or empty talk. "To talk little is natural" (23). Nature never puts on a show. Nature is. Virtue is Nature. Spinoza: "Virtue is power". "When you are one with virtue, The virtue is always there" (23). Because the sage, and Spinoza's wise man, are not out to fulfill themselves, they attain fulfillment. Life's contradictions are resolved by the man in the Tao. "I am different, I am nourished by the great mother." (20). The Tao *(Natura naturans)* is the great mother. It is the source of all creativity.

Taoist virtues, (8, 22, 25,) such as, gentle loving kindness, truth, justice, competence, prudence, getting to the heart of things, ("In meditation go deep into the heart") (22), a firm anchor in reality, a quiescent center, ("The still is the master of unrest") (25), self-discipline and self-mastery, all these apply equally to Spinoza's free man. Similarly, "Yield and overcome; Bend and be straight; Empty and be full; Wear out and be new; Have little and gain; Have much and be confused." (22). Such are the deep and hidden truths. To yield and overcome means that it is wiser to yield to one's opponent, whether in an argument or fight, especially, when the opponent acts from passion or by naked force. Such irrationality will eventually be exposed. Thus, one overcomes by yielding.

"Bend and be straight." Blind force almost never brings about the desired result. Once force is used, it is impossible to restore the previous condition. You cannot rectify it. If you bend an iron rod, you cannot make it straight again. If you bend a bamboo stick, it will straighten out. The Tao advises to be flexible. If you make a wrong move, it will not be fatal. You can repair it. To be rigid is to be short-sighted. To counter force by not-force is to be far-sighted. To penetrate into the truth of things one must look underneath the surface. What seems to be strong often turns out to be weak, and what appears to be weak may turn out to be strong (36). Iron resists, the bamboo gives, iron is rigid, the bamboo is flexible. Which is weak, and which is strong? Which perishes, and which endures? The rigid perishes, and the flexible endures. Thus, strong is weak, and weak is strong. To bend and be straight, to overcome by yielding has implications for every sphere of human endeavor, such as, politics, family, work, interpersonal relations, etc.

The soft overcomes the hard is a recurring theme in the Tao. "The softest thing in the universe overcomes the hardest thing in the universe" (43). The mind is stronger than any physical power. It is spaceless, it can enter where there is no room. We win and conquer through understanding (yielding), and not by the use of force. The use of force may bring seeming returns, but these eventually end up in self-defeat. Only understanding (knowledge of self, God, Nature, love, and highmindedness) bring lasting benefits to the person.

The Tao compares the good to water (8). Water is the softest of all things, it penetrates where nothing could enter. Water purifies everything, and flows everywhere. It benefits the ten thousand things, giving life to all things. The Tao advises the sage to be gentle, adaptable (like water), and show kindness to everybody. The sage should treat others with dignity and respect, he should go to places others reject, and show kindness and friendship to those who are abandoned by others. The sage must go to the heart of things, ("go deep into the heart"), he must carry understanding to the limit, and is not to shy away from difficulty. The free man, as well as, the man in the Tao, is competent in his work, and is not prejudiced against anyone. The sage knows the proper timing for action, when to act and when to postpone action.

The Tao emphasizes intuitive knowledge. "Without going outside, you may know the whole world, the sage knows without travelling...He sees without looking..."(47). Through intuitve reflection, one penetrates into the essence of things. For Spinoza, this desire, the intellectual striving for adequate ideas, is our essence. The source of striving, lies in body and mind. It culminates in highest affection, *amor dei intellectualis*. It is the will to an elevation of activity, to self-elevation, to higher levels of reality, and to greater perfection. (Reality is perfection). The sage and the free man achieve the highest level of intuitive knowledge, by knowing God and themselves.

It is better to anticipate events rather than be caught by events. "Trouble is easily overcome before it starts. The brittle is easily shattered;... A journey of a thousand miles starts under one's feet". (64) It is necessary to exercise caution and act with prudence. The Tao advises against excess of any kind. "The five colors blind the eye."(12) Any excess is self-defeating, and self-destructive. This applies to sensual as well as mental excess (aberrations of body or mind). It is necessary to overcome, and not be misled by the temptation of the senses. "Better stop short than fill to the brim."(9) It is not desirable to accumulate things in excess of need. Greed inhibits satisfaction and true accomplishment. One is never satisfied with what one has but one always wants more of everything. This brings misery and unhappiness. Excess leads to its opposite. It leads to loss. It is better to stop in time rather than try to capture all. Greed is an affliction of the mind, and a passion. It is not in accordance with nature. A greedy person is a slave to his passion. The person is therefore not free to follow his true essence. The sole pursuit of external goals (fame, riches, and sensual pleasures) is self-defeating. The pursuit of fame compels us to order our lives according to the opinions of others. The pursuit of riches makes us insatiable, or sad when frustrated. The pursuit of sensual pleasure is always followed by extreme melancholy. "All the objects pursued by the multitude (fame, riches, or sensual pleasures) not only bring no remedy that tends to preserve our being, but even act as hindrances, causing the death not seldom of those that possess them, and always of those that are possessed by them."[10] ...the acquisition of wealth, sensual pleasure, or fame is only a hindrance, as long as they are sought as ends, not as means;[11]

The Tao emphasizes the importance of the void, the nothing, the non-action, and the non-being. " Thirty spokes share the wheels hub; It is the center hole that makes it useful."(11) The usefulness and effectiveness of function and action of anything derives not from its fullness, not from overextending oneself and exaggerating the immediate and tangible results, but from its emptiness, that is, by retaining the void, the measure, by relaxation of effort, and by the understanding of the intangible, invisible, longer term consequences of one's actions. Every peak is followed by decline. It is necessary to know when to retire and leave space for others. It is better to retire at the peak of one's career, and not carry on the work beyond one's natural capacities. When one tries to extend one's work beyond one's optimal time span, one's fortune will decline.

The Tao criticizes pretense. (22)   It is better not to put on a display, not to show of, not to boast, and not to pretend. People's intelligence shines through not by will or force, but by their being relaxed, and acting naturally. Otherwise one dissipates one's energies on trivial things, on things that are not important to one's spiritual growth and well-being. What is important in life is to live in conformity with our nature, to know ourselves, and the Tao (God), to experience the joy of living, to feel nature's powers within us, and to utilize our creative potential for the enrichment of all life.

"A truly good man is not aware of his goodness"...(38). When you are aware that you are virtuous, wise, good, or smart,   you are none of these.   When you are conscious of your good qualities, you put a separation between your natural self, and the image of yourself. You do not allow your excellence and goodness to express themselves naturally. Therefore you are not what you think you are. When you try to be all those good things, you will not be them, even if you appear to be them.

One should avoid unnecessary complexities in life. One ought to choose the simple over the complicated. The simple is the essence, the complicated is the show, the appearance. Pretense is superfluous and unneccessary baggage. Life is better and easier without them. The essence is for me, the appearance is for the other. Do I live for myself or for the other? (24). "Fame or self: Which matters more?" (44)   "Be an example to the world", unite with Nature and the Tao. Know differentiation (honor, manifestations, distinctions of wealth, power, knowledge, etc.) but keep to the simple, stay humble, be understanding, and receptive to all human experiences ("Be the valley of the universe!"). Whenever you feel accomplished and sophisticated, always remember that compared to true knowledge (knowledge of the Tao) you know very little, therefore leave yourself open and return to the uncarved block, to the state before knowing.

The Tao describes the human qualities of the enlightened sage (15): he is watchful, alert, courteous, accommodating, yielding, simple, pure, hollow, (acknowledging that he lacks knowledge or that others may know more than he does, and therefore he is always ready to listen, and learn from others). Neither is he afraid to mix with the common people lest he be influenced or subverted, and thus become like them. His purity, tranquility, self-confidence, and inner calmness rest entirely of his knowledge of himself and the Tao (God). This knowledge is indestructible. "Observers of the Tao do not seek fulfillment." By not seeking fulfillment, by not acting for the sake of an anticipated end-result, by acting only from the necessity of his nature, he totally enjoys his work, and remains fulfilled by it. The sage remains still while acting, he is not moved or perturbed by the expected outcome of his action, he remains calm and unexcited. Thus, the sage, by not seeking fulfillment remains fulfilled. The Tao like Spinoza advocates the need to gain insight into oneself, and to have self-understanding. "Knowing others is wisdom, knowing the self is enlightenment"...(33). To achieve enlightenment, one has to accept disgrace and misfortune willingly. "Accept being unimportant. .... Accept misfortune as the human condition. Misfortune comes from having a body. ... Love the world as your own self; then you can truly care for all things." (13). A firm and constant mind (a mind that knows reality) is an open mind and "with an open mind, you will be openhearted" (16).

The man who struggles to be himself, and who cannot accept artificial ways of living, will often experience pain and suffering. (20) The Tao advises him not to try to imitate others, or be like others. "Give up learning, and you will put an end to your troubles". You must accept yourself and be yourself. Listen to others, but follow your own instincts. You be the judge of what is good for you. Don't depend on others for your self-worth, and inner well-being. The resolution of life's contradictions involves pain and suffering. We cannot avoid it. We cannot overcome suffering by force, by sheer will, or by denial. We can overcome suffering only by understanding. "Self approval is in reality the highest object for which we can hope" (EIII, 53). Pain and suffering are necessary aspects of spiritual growth, the way to inner strength, and inner freedom. When we unite with the Tao, we realize that we are different, we are nourished by the great mother. We have reached the divine, creative powers within us. The great mother, (Spinoza's Natura naturans), is the source of all creativity.

We need to cultivate a balanced approach to life. (28) We ought not neglect any of life's dimensions. A strong mind and healthy body require the satisfaction of our emotional needs. Man needs the support and warmth that come from a woman's care. We need to go back to being a child. At times, we long for mother's warmth and security. But we must never neglect our heart. The mind should never be developed at the expense of the heart. If we do that, our mind becomes arid, it dries up. We lose the source of creativity and divinity within us. These come from the mother. "Great thoughts come from the heart."[12] Nietzsche: "If you lose your heart you soon lose your head too."[13] True knowledge does not consist in accumulating or adding information (facts). The carved block does not require much cutting. One who merely collects information and facts without going into the root of anything, does not know much. Often we have to unlearn what we have learned. This is clearly the case in therapeutic counseling. But, one who goes into the root of things (the Tao), knows much by knowing few things. Knowing the Tao, he knows everything. This illustrates the (Taoist) proposition that "more is less, and less is more". There is too much accumulation of knowledge, and not enough (self)-understanding. Spinoza: "The more we know an individual thing, the more we know know God". We gain true knowledge by going into depth of few things, not by accumulating facts, and staying on the surface of many things.

Laughter is part of the Tao. The fool is closer to the Tao than the average. The foolish student hears of the Tao and laughs aloud. If there were no laughter, the Tao would not be what it is"(41). Appearance and reality are not the same (41). Going forward seems like retreat; The easy way seems hard; The truth of things is beneath the surface (concealed). "The Tao is hidden and without name." What is hidden will eventually become apparent, (the principle of reversal). The creative principle is the principle of reversal. The Tao (the Way) operates through the principle of reversal. The weak are (potentially) strong and the strong are (potentially) weak, "Great talents ripen late" (41). The man who knows how to live is not concerned with death. Spinoza: "The wise man thinks about life and not on death". "He who knows how to live can walk abroad Without fear of rhinoceros or tiger....Why is this so? Because he has no place for death to enter"(50). ...."remaining in touch with the mother, Brings freedom from the fear of death". (52) Spinoza: That part of the mind which is in touch with God (having adequate ideas about nature) never dies. It is immortal.

The Tao has a specific ecological message (29). Nature cannot be changed. Nature regenerates itself. It provides its own means for self maintenance. It can never be exhausted. If left alone, (if not interfered with by man), nature eternally nurtures itself. "The universe is sacred. You cannot improve it. If you try to change it, you will ruin it. If you try to hold it, you will lose it."(23). The ecological implications of the Tao are very much the same as those found in Spinoza. Nature is perfect. It is extreme folly, and arrogance to want to improve the universe. The wise man does not force nature to follow his way. He accepts the vagaries of nature. In nature there is a season for everything. Things are sometimes up, and sometimes down. The wise man does not despair when things are down, and he does not exaggerate his importance (exhilarate) when things are up. In good times and bad times, he maintains his balance and measure. When one tries to improve upon nature, one ends up ruining it. If you recklessly plunder nature's resources, you will lose everything.

In the knowledge of self and God (the Tao), the mind rests at peace (16). In the union of the self with the whole of nature, we leave the realm of the finite and merge with the infinite. The mind returns to the source, to the stillness of nature. The finite universe of time and duration is transcended. We come to view things from the perspective of nature itself, a perspective of eternity,*(sub species aeternitatis).* The (sage's) mind partakes in nature's immortality. His mind and heart are one. Both derive from the same source. A mind that is united with the whole of Nature (that is one with the Tao) is eternal. By uniting with the whole of nature, the sage survives the death of the body. (This part of the mind remains after the body dies.) "The human mind cannot be absolutely destroyed with the body, but there remains of it something which is eternal" (EV, 23). Also, "Whatsoever the mind understands under the form of eternity, it does not understand by virtue of conceiving the present actual existence of the body, but by virtue of conceiving the essence of the body under the form of eternity" (EV, 29).

In this essay, I have shown the affinity and similarity between the Tao and Spinoza in their respective metaphysics, in their views on morality, and in their derivation of the latter from the former. We know that Spinoza had no access to the great Chinese classic, the Tao Te Ching. (The Tao Te Ching had not been translated to any Western language in Spinoza's time.) The Tao preceded Spinoza by over 2000 years. How can we understand the appearance of two so great and original philosophies entirely independent of each other, and yet retaining the same essence? I can only think of one answer to this question. Nature, *natura naturans* and the Tao are eternal. Truth and human wisdom derived from Nature and the Tao, are the same, regardless of time, culture and place.

Notes

1. *TAO; A New Way of Thinking,* A Translation of Tao Te Ching, with an Introduction and Commentaries, by Chang Chung Yuan. New York: Harper & Row, 1975.
2. *LAO TSU TAO TE CHING.* A New Translation by Gia Fu Feng and Jane English, (25). New York: Vintage Books, A Division of Random House, 1972.
3. Ibid. Chang Chung Yuan transl.

4. Paul Lin, *A Translation of   Lao Tzu's Tao te ching   and Wang Pi's commentary*. Ann Arbor. Center for Chinese Studies, University of Michigan, 1977.
5. Chang Chung Yuan transl. Chpt. 4.
6. See: Lewis Schipper, *Spinoza's Ethics: The View From Within*. New York: Peter Lang Publishing Inc. 1993. p. 28.
7. Chang Chung Yuan Transl. Chpt. 5.
8. Benedict De Spinoza, *On the Improvement of the Understanding,The Ethics, Correspondence*. Translated by R. H. M. Elwes. New York: Dover Publications, Inc. 1955. p. 6. (Note: All quotations from Spinoza's Ethics are from this translation.)
9. Menen, Ibid. p. 169.
10. Spinoza, Ibid. p. 5.
11. Ibid. p. 6.
12. Ernest Dimnet, *The Art of Thinking*, New York: Simon and Schuster, 1931.
13. Walter Kaufman, *The Portable Nietzsche*. New York: Penguin Books, 1976, p. 201.

SECTION IV. POLITICAL PHILOSOPHY

Workshop 25. An Outline of the Political Philosophy of Spinoza.

Spinoza's political philosophy deals with the scope, function, and meaning of a rational government. The State is seen as the guardian of justice, security, and freedom of the people.   Unlike Plato, Spinoza does not think that philosophers are best qualified to be rulers. Philosophers are not fit to rule because they tend to idealize human nature, they "conceive of the passions... as vices into which men fall by their own fault"...they conceive of men, not as they are, but as they themselves would like them to be."[1] Spinoza intends to deduce politics "from the very condition of human nature, ...not to mock, lament or execrate, but to understand human actions; ....to look upon passions, such as love, hatred, anger, envy, ambition, pity, and the other perturbations of the mind, not in the light of vices of human nature, but as properties"[2] that we must understand rather than judge.   Spinoza's approach to political science is objective and dispassionate, free from wishful thoughts and ideological prejudices.   Society is part of the system of Nature and underlies its laws. The task of political science is to understand changes in social systems, and their corresponding laws of motion. Power is the decisive factor in politics. Politics deals with the distribution, maintenance, and shifts in political power.

It is commonly assumed that Spinoza's political philosophy lacks historical perspective. Spinoza's political philosophy is derived from his metaphysics. Nature, including human nature, is to be understood as part of a logical system of necessary laws. A timeless ideal constitution that conforms to the true order of nature would serve as a model for the best State, (a State based on reason).   Spinoza's political philosophy fails to account for the evolution of new forms of social organization, and historical change in general.[3] I would argue that this is not an entirely true account of Spinoza's political philosophy. While the ideal objectives of the State always remain ther same, namely, to enable people to live under the guidance of reason, and to pursue rational aims in life, the very same conditions however, are necessarily bound up in time. They are historicaly determined. Societies as much as individuals are part of the universe of finite modes *(natura naturata)*. Their existence is historical. Finite modes exist in time. The conditions of their existence evolve in time. Only *natura naturans* is eternal and unchanging. The latter represents the realm of absolute freedom. The art of government, like the art of living, is to optimize conditions for human self-realization in freedom. The State has to be designed with a view of serving the needs, the interests, and the desires of the people, and not the other way around. The State should be organized in such a way as to provide the necessary conditions for the achievement of human freedom. This objective is true for all time. However the conditions that will make this realization possible, differ among societies, times, and places. The conditions of realization of human freedom are themselves products of human history. History is implicitly included in Spinoza's political philosophy through the world of *natura naturata*. Spinoza believes that democracy is the best form of government:

> I think I have now shown sufficiently clearly the basis of a democracy: I have especially desired to do so, for I believe it to be of all forms of government the most natural, and the most consonant with individual liberty. (Benedict de Spinoza, A Theologico-Political Treatise, Chap. XVI. Transl. by R.H.M. Elwes. New York: Dover Publications, Inc. p.207.)

1. Natural Right and Power.

Spinoza distinguishes between natural rights and civil rights. Natural rights are those that inhere in the mode's right to exist and continue in existence by its being part of nature. Such rights are divine. They are given by nature, not by man. Natural rights however, extend only to the mode's power to exist and to operate. In the state of nature, right and power are the same, ..."every natural thing has by nature as much right, as it has power to exist and operate;... any man has as much right over nature as he has power."[4] Man's desires, whether based on reason or passion are part of his nature, and actions derived from them constitute his natural right. "Nature forbids nothing but what no one wishes or is able to do."[5] People are only independent to the extent that they can guard themselves against oppression by others. While man in the state of nature is not bound by any laws and therefore seems to be free, he nevertheless lives in perpetual fear of others. Individuals in the natural state are always threatened by others. Therefore, their power and freedom are fictitious, not real. Since, ..."nothing is forbidden by the law of nature, except what is beyond everyone's power," people can do no wrong. Right and wrong, justice and injustice do not apply here.

2. The Formation of the State.

States are organized in order to protect people's lives and property. Individuals give up certain liberties in order to gain greater freedom, namely, peace, security, and freedom from fear. Everyone pursues his or her own interest, and the ability to live in peace, and be free from fear is each highest interest.   People gain power when they form associations. They have more power collectively than individually. "If two come together and unite their strength, they have jointly more power, and consequently more right over nature, than both of them separately, and the more there are in alliance, the more right they all collectively will possess."[6] Fear is the greatest impediment to freedom. Fear inhibits an individual's power and his right. Likewise, people depend on others for the sustenance of life. For, "without mutual help, men can hardly support life and cultivate the mind." Men combine "to protect themselves, to repel all violence, and to live according to the general judgment of all..."This right, which is determined by the power of the multitude, is generally called Dominion."[7] Natural rights cannot be conceived without general rights applicable to all.   The state determines what actions constitute right and wrong, lawful or unlawful. Wrong-doing cannot be lawfully committed, since it is forbidden by law. Similarly, with justice or injustice. These notions apply only to the organized State, not to the state of nature. A just man does not appropriate to himself that what belongs to another.

The civil state is designed to remove general fear, and prevent general sufferings. Reason dictates that everyone should obey the general laws, since as long as men are liable to passions, they cannot remain independent, and cannot maintain peace. Even if an ordinance appears to some one as unreasonable, he or she must still obey it, since "the harm is far compensated by the good which he derives from the civil state."   Human power is determined more by the power of the mind than by the power of the body, and "those men are most independent whose reason is strongest, and who are most guided thereby." The same holds for the State. "That commonwealth will be most powerful and most independent, which is founded and guided by reason."[8]

3. The Functions of Government.

The government's primary functions are: to maintain public order, to secure peace, to care for the welfare of the people, to protect the rights of individuals, to cultivate justice and charity, and to maximize opportunity for the full development of the bodily and mental powers of all the people. Freedom of thought, and the safeguarding of individual liberties are considered necessary requirements for the flourishing of the arts and sciences. The government must see to it that the people live in freedom, not in fear. The object of rule is to control people's passions, to minimize conflict between individuals or groups of people, and in general, to assure harmony in the community. The laws of the State are to be based on reason. The State aims for the good of all citizens. The object of the State is to protect people against violence, and to provide optimum conditions for the smooth functioning of the economy. Poverty and the perception of injustice are the main causes of discontent in society. Laws are good only to the extent that they promote the essential interests of the people, that is, to be free to pursue rational aims. There are no moral rights or duties per se. Rights and duties are to be understood only in the context of their applicability to peoples lives. When the law threatens the basic interest of any group of people, they may disobey the law, in so far, as they have the power to do so.

4. Limits on Government.

What are the powers of government? The government should not act contrary to natural right. Natural rights are divine rights. They are in accordance with reason, and the way of nature. The powers of government are coextensive with its rights. Spinoza: "Force is to be guided by reason if it is to become power." The government has no right to intrude into areas of people's conduct which it has no power to enforce, i.e. the minds and thoughts of individuals. When the government is guided by reason, it is most powerful. When the government imposes unreasonable laws, it is to that extent weakened. What the government cannot enforce, it has no right to enforce. Rights and powers are coextensive with each other. Equating right with power effectively determines the limits of government. A system of checks and balances is necessary to provide stability, and to guard against the usurpation of power by anyone group of people or branch of government.

The state cannot enforce things that are abhorrent to human nature. It cannot force a man to bear witness against himself, to force certain beliefs on him, to love one whom one hates or to hate one whom he loves, etc. If the government tries to enforce unreasonable laws, its power and its right are correspondingly diminished. It will cause people to conspire against it. Just as people in the state of nature are unfree in proportion to their fears, so is the State less free the more it has reason to fear its own citizens. The State cannot force its citizens to act in self-destructive ways. A free multitude is guided by hope, not by fear. Macciavelli has shown how cautious a free multitude should be of entrusting its welfare absolutely to one man. Spinoza concurs with this argument against totalitarian rule.[9]

The State should not impose opinions or certain (preferred) ideologies on the people. The State has the right (i.e. power) to suppress subversion that threatens the social order, but it has no right (power) to impose its own orthodox beliefs on society. (Spinoza did not forsee the enormous propaganda apparatus, and the power of the political State to shape public opinion.)   Laws that do not serve the general welfare should be broken. That determination however, must be made by the people in conjunction with the powers of the State. It should not be left for any private person to do so. The ends of the State are encoded in the civil laws. Civil laws are to guarantee peace, harmony, justice, and good will among the citizens. They are to bring peace and guard the security of life.   "A human life is defined above all by reason, the true excellence and life of the mind."[10]

5. Relations Between States.

Relations between States are ruled by self interest. In this it is comparable to the state of nature.   A State is independent only to the extent that it can protect its citizens against aggression by another State. If a State is endangered by another State, if it fears the other State's power, or if it depends on another State for its own peace and security, to this extent is the State not free. States enter into contractual relationships for mutual protection and gain. While States can make war on one another unilaterally, they need the concurrence of other States for the maintenance of peace. This is the reason why States enter into treaties with one another. However, if the interests of a State are no longer served by the treaty it has entered to, the State may break it. It cannot be said, in such a case, that the State has acted perfidiously or treacherously. Moral terms do not apply to relations between States. The more States are bound together by mutual treaty, the less is each one endangered by fear of the remainder, and the less will each one have the authority to declare war.

6. The State and Religion.

Spinoza believes in the separation of State and religion. The State cannot have dominion over any one's mind, nor can it prevent anyone from the love of God, from charity to his neighbors, from performing harmless rites, etc. The State should not prevent anyone from practicing his religion.[11] Religion plays a positive role in society to the extent that it makes the ignorant, (i.e. people who cannot reason), act virtuously. Religion, however, cannot contradict or oppose the aims of the government. Religion should complement the objectives of the State. The essence of true religion is to love God, and to live in accordance with reason. The love of God cannot express itself in destructive passion. A truly religious man will desire for others what he desires for himself. *Conatus* or self-preservation is the striving for the fulfillment of one's nature. Man's true good lies in the development of his natural powers. Man's natural powers are anchored in reason. Reason is man's real power. Man's essence, his striving for self-preservation, lies in the striving for intellectual perfection, and in the love of God. Man must use reason in order to overcome compulsion and passion.

To love God is to strive for intellectual and moral perfection. To perfect one's mind is to know oneself in relation to God and Nature. Morality consists in reason overcoming passion. To the extent that men are rational they are also moral. *Conatus,* self-preservation and the seeking of one's true advantage, lie in man's ability to follow reason. The essence of each mode is to self-preserve, and to seek what is to its advantage. This is the law of nature. The law of nature compels a mode to pursue its own advantage. For man, to pursue his or her advantage is to live under the guidance of reason. The latter may be called the divine natural law. The divine law of nature affirms the necessity of reason to underlie men's actions. Since men's actions are determined by what they perceive to be to their advantage, rather than by what is to their advantage, people who are ignorant of their true advantage, are predominantly ruled by passion instead of reason. This is why religion has an important role to play. Moral conduct exemplifies true and universal religion. The essence of religion is the practice of charity and justice. True religion, by making man adhere to moral precepts subordinates passion to reason, and thus bridges the gap between the two. In this way, religion complements the laws and aims of the State.

Exercises.

1. Unlike Rousseau, Spinoza says that people in the state of nature are unfree. Discuss.
2. What are, according to Spinoza, the proper functions of the State?
3. What are the powers of the State?
4. What does Spinoza mean by saying that the rights of the State are coextensive with its powers?
5. Can the State control an individual's thoughts? Does the State have the power to deny freedom of thought?
6. How does it relate to freedom of expression? Can the State deny freedom of expression? If the State does that, does the State undermine its own effective rule, and thereby weakens its power?

7. What is, according to Spinoza , the essence of religion? Is this esence the same for all religions? Can we therefore speak of a universal religion?

8. Can the above be reconciled with religious intolerance, opposition, and religious wars?

9. What is the true function of religion?

10. How would Spinoza view religious fundamentalists, religious cults, and the religious far right?

11. What is the State's role with regard to religion? What is the fundamental relation between the State and religion? Should there be a State sponsored religion? In case of conflict between the State and religion, should the State have the final power to decide between the two? Does that mean that in the separation of State and religion, the State always assumes the leading role, and religion is subordinate to the State?

12. Do you agree with Spinoza that love of God has to express itself in actions toward others, in charity and justice, rather than in mere words?

13. Can racism, bigotry, and hatred be part of religion?

Notes

1. Benedict de Spinoza, *A Political Treatise*. Transl. by R.H.M. Elwes. New York: Dover Publications, Inc. 1951. p. 287.

2. Ibid. pp. 288-289.

3. See, Stuart Hampshire, *SPINOZA. An Introduction to his Philosophical Thought*. New York: Viking Penguin Inc. 1987. pp.145-147.

4. Ibid. p. 292.

5. Ibid. p. 294.

6. Ibid. p. 296.

7. Ibid. p. 297.

8. Ibid. p.303.

9. Ibid. p.314.

10. Ibid. p.314.

11. Ibid. p.305.

Workshop 26. The Political Philosophy of Jean Jacques Rousseau.

Rousseau (1712-1778) raises problems of the modern unsettled self: the rational and the passionate side to man. Our intellect is not big enough, and the passions are too strong. People are different and unequal. He attacked the ordinary intellectuals, and their overemphasis on talent. Man is a historical being. The nature of man evolves in history. For Rousseau, the contrast is between nature and history. In the old philosophy, the contrast is between nature and convention, between physis and *nomos* (the laws).

Is man rational or a-rational? Rational means to think rationally about ends. A-rational means to think rationally about means. If man is a-rational, a-political, and unequal, the strong will take advantage of the weak. For Hobbes (Hobbes, Thomas 1588-1679), man is a-rational, a-social, but equal in the sense that they can kill each other, especially with the use of firearms. We need to get out of the state of nature, a state of war of all against all, and form a commonwealth based on social contract. Hobbes advocates a liberal monarchy, ruled by the consent of the governed. To enable the citizens to pursue their own interest and accumulate wealth, a strong government is necessary. It doesn't matter whether the government was formed by force, or by common consent. Justice will eventually come about, when the citizens are free to seek their own good, and become wealthy. The government is legitimate when the people live up to the social contract.

Rousseau is reacting against Hobbes' political views. The making of laws belongs to the people. The people are the souvereign. They are the ultimate authority in society. The authority of the people expresses itself through the general will of the people. The government is there to execute the will of the people. The magistrates form the executive branch of government. They are to carry out the general will of the people. The general will is based on the unanimous expression of the will of the people. This requires a relatively small community where people are in a position to know one another, whether directly or indirectly. All people have to consent to the common rule. (In the utilitarian view, people may sacrifice the rights of some for the good of the many.) The magistrates (the government) have to execute the people's laws. The people, as citizens, make the laws. As subjects, they are bound to adhere to them, and obey them. For Rousseau, freedom is the most important virtue of all. Commerce, wealth, or possessions are not, for Rousseau, the highest virtues. ("Man is everywhere born free, but ends up in chains.") Freedom is incompatible with excess property. Freedom means not to be dependent, not to live at the discretion of another. The general will keeps the people from becoming dependent.

People give up private rights in order to gain social rights. One gains freedom by giving up freedom. The general will represents the common good. It seeks to establish principles of justice in the commmunity. It makes people free and protected. It is based on the collectivity. When people form factions, there is no general will. The general will must be general, it cannot deal with particulars. The laws must be general. The law giver (like Moses) is great, because he expresses the general will. Before the general will, there was only a multiplicity of private wills. Everyone must agree to enter the new society. The general will is its highest expression. The general will cannot err, but the people can be deceived, and it is sometimes necessary to force one to be free. Rousseau would limit the acquisition of property in order to check unlimited accumulation. Private property has to be regulated by the community.[1]

In 1749, on the way to visit Diderot in jail, Rousseau took part in an essay contest on "Whether the revival of the arts and sciences improved morality." His answer was that the arts and sciences did not improve morals but corrupted them. He won the contest. Natural man (in primitive society) is not greedy or corrupt. He is compassionate, he has natural pity, and a good heart. Man is good by nature, it is society that corrupts man. Natural man does not abuse nature. When reason comes in, we get corrupted by selfishness. Study corrupts people. Arts and sciences provide a veneer of respectability. They become a tool of the ruling class. There are learned people however, who combine learning with virtue. As the arts and sciences flourish, desires get stronger. Rousseau did not advocate a return to the state of nature. Once a society has been corrupted, the arts and sciences help lessen corruption. They distract people from doing bad things. The academy has a positive role to play. The arts and sciences also soften people's character. Rousseau was the first to raise questions of authenticity, sincerity, hypocrisy, alienation, and historicity. He was the first one to discuss childhood problems, "children are not little adults". He dealt extensively with romantic love. He put the person at the center of things. Modern man takes a personal approach to things. Rousseau was a modernist. Courage is an important virtue for Rousseau. The ultimate test of virtue is courage. Ignorant people, at least, don't try to rationalize their vices. Big society is bad for virtue, because people don't know each other. In small societies, people are more virtuous.

Rousseau questions the fruits of enlightenment. He questions man's faith in science and technology. He worries about the results of technology. (Compare this with ancient Greece. In ancient Greece, the Sophists were the enlightenment people. They were satisfied with conventional answers. Plato, Socrates, and Aristotle look more like anti-enlightenment thinkers. The arts and sciences don't tell us about the good and the beautiful. They foster desires.)

In the second Discourse, Rousseau holds out the possibility of the science of man.[2] He lists three periods in the development of man: (1) The jungle man. Man has no mind. (2) The savage (or natural) man. Man has love, reason, morality, compassion, but no jealousy. Man in the state of nature is concerned with survival. He has compassion for other men. The natural man is robust, calm, not afraid, and not driven to achieve. He depends on himself. His needs are limited, and he can easily satisfy them. He does not plan for the future. He does not compete with others. Man's natural pity is at the base of all other social virtues, such as, generosity, mercy, humanity, benevolence, and friendship. For Hobbes, man is by nature fearful, and therefore needs religion. For Rousseau, man is by nature not fearful. He does not need religion.

Rousseau's natural man is conceivable when nature is generous. When man cuts down the forests he ruins nature. Land becomes less fertile and eventually turns into desert. Natural resources become scarce relative to the needs of a growing population. Man has to devise ways to use existing resources more efficiently. Civilization begins with the coming of the arts and sciences. According to Rousseau, iron and wheat (the development of metallurgy and agriculture), civilized man, but ruined the human race. It made man greedy. As men forge iron, other men are needed to feed them. Agriculture had to produce enough to feed the industrial worker.

With the coming of the arts and sciences, (the development of industry, agriculture, and the institution of private property), man begins to rank himself not only on the basis of possessions, but also on the basis of intellect, beauty, strength, skill, talent, merit, etc. There appear ostentation, avarice, deceptive cunning, ambition, dependence, pretentiousness, and unhappiness. By comparing himself with others, man becomes unhappy. Comparisons are at the root of man's unhappiness. (Primitive man is neither happy, nor unhappy, he is free and wants to remain free.) Man becomes two faced and crooked. "One never knows with whom one is dealing." Only in critical situations does man show his true face. All the social ills stem from private property and incipient inequality. The worst that can happen to man is to see himself at the discretion of someone else.

Reason brings corruption and decadence, but it also holds out the prospect of a true morality and perfection. The Geneva city-State can serve as a model for the good community. It represents a return to nature on a more rational basis, with a new morality that is based on reason. Rousseau contrasts nature versus history. In old philosophy, nature was contrasted with convention, customs and laws. Rousseau initiates a new view of history, it is a kind of relativism based on history. Human beings are changing historically. Man makes himself.

Passions originate in needs. The Social Contract is formed when people alienate themselves and their possesions in order to achieve a kind of moral equality. One acquires a legitimate title to one's possessions, and it protects them and one's life. The general will is the standard of legitimacy. If the government is to weak, it cannot assert the general will. If it is too powerful, it will impose itself on the general will. For the government to function effectively, some right amount of force is necessary.

The traditional political question was, what is the end of human life, and what form of government would contribute most to that end. Rousseau maintains that the role of government is to provide security. For Hobbes and Locke (Locke, John 1632-1704), the role of government is to protect property. For Rousseau, there are three maxims of good government: The government has to listen to the general will (the people), it has to enforce the general will (the authority of the people), and it has to watch over the finances (it has to practice fiscal responsibility). This will make virtue rein. Virtue is defined as the conformity of private will to the general will.

Exercises.

1. Rousseau was the first to view man historically. Man is both a product of history and a maker of history. Man makes himself. What does that mean to you?
2. Rousseau had a great aversion to human faults and weaknesses, such as, greediness, dishonesty, duplicity, and lack of moral courage. Do you feel the same as Rousseau?
3. Rousseau did not have the faith in science and technology that the enlightenment had. What are the human questions and needs that science cannot answer?
4. Rousseau saw in civilization a corrupting influence on man. Was he right or wrong? Explain.
5. What are Rousseau's social and political views? How relevant are they to our society today?
6. What does Rousseau mean by the general will?
7. Freedom is for Rousseau the highest virtue. Explain Rousseau's understanding of human freedom. How does the general will of the people express that freedom?
8. What is the difference between Rousseau and Hobbes in their view of man in the state of nature, and in their assumptions about the nature of man?
9. Why is Rousseau considered a romantic? What does "to be a romantic" mean to you?

Notes

1. Jean Jacques Rousseau, *On the Social Contract.* in The Basic Plitical Writings. Translated and edited by Donald A. Cress. Indianapolis/Cambridge: Hacket Publishing Company, 1987. p.148.
2. Discourse on the Origin of Inequality. Ibid. pp. 25-81.

Workshop 27. An Introduction to Marx and Marxism.

There is a single central vision in all of Marx's (Marx, Karl, 1818-1883) writings. This vision is the fulfillment of the human being and its self-realization. Marx's theory provides an analysis of the real condition of human self-realization. There are two basic forms of human practice: (1) alienating activity, and (2) activity that results in the fulfillment of a fully human individual. Human realization must be practical and concrete. Religion is a realization of the human essence in fantasy. It is the illusory sun. Philosophy should be practical. Philosophy must be in the service of man. Philosophy cannot be neutral. It must engage itself on the side of the human being. There can be no wholly neutral philosophy. To claim to be neutral is to perpetuate the fraud of the status quo.

There are two views of Marxism: the orthodox or received view of Marxism, and a view of Marxism as humanism. The latter is based primarily on Marx's Early Writings and the Paris Manuscripts *("The Economic and Philosophical Manuscripts of 1844").* [1] The received view holds that Engels' and Marx's views are the same, that Engels is the authoritative interpreter of Marx, and that there is a continuity between Marx and Engels (Engels, Friedrich, 1820-1895). Subsequent "official" Marxism was largely based on this view. Alienation, "the complete domination of living men by dead matter" is the problem of capitalism in the short run. "Self objectification of labor (production of wealth) has the character of self dehumanization of man." In the long run, the capitalist system is not viable, due to the increasing incompatibility (contradiction) between the relations of production and the mode of production.

Hegel (Hegel, George Wilhelm Friedrich, 1770-1831) also views labor as the essence, the self conditioning essence of man. But for Hegel, labor is the labor of Spirit, abstracted from the concrete reality of man. For Marx, labor (object creating activity) is fundamentally social. The reality of others is revealed to man through the object of labor. "The subject-object interchange with nature is human collectivity." This interchange is historical. "History is a process of man's self- creation through his labor." The essence of man is an ensemble of social relationships. This is a socio-historical view of man.

Human alienation pertains to the relation between the worker, the product, and society. For Marx, all society can be understood as the worker's product, as the product of labor. Whoever does not understand this does not understand the society he or she lives in.

Kant: (Kant, Immanuel, 1724-1804) we can only know what we produce.

We can distinguish four types of alienation: (1) from product, (2) from activity, (3) from species being (alienation of the self), and (4) from other people.

Opposition between product and work: The product is an objectification of work, appropriation is alienation. (Proudhon: [Proudhon, Pierre Joseph, 1809-1865] property is theft.) There is an inversion between product and worker. In the normal case, the product depends on the worker, but in capitalism the worker depends on the product. Alienation is disunity, one part rules the other. Division of labor is equivalent to the alienated form of man as a species being. Political economy conceals alienation because it does not examine alienation in the process of production. Productive activity as a basic human need is not fulfilled in the capitalist productive process. Nobody performs this activity freely. You don't identify with it, and you are constrained by the system, (passive). In capitalism, the human being is displaced by money as an actor.

Marx's critique of Hegel's dialectic and general philosophy: For Hegel, mind alone is the true essence of man. Labor, for Hegel, means abstract, mental labor. Human life (man) is equivalent to self-consciousness. Spirit is abstract thought. Opposition is viewed as between consciousness and self-consciousness, between object and subject, between abstract thought and sensible reality. Negation of negation is an abstract and speculative expression of the historical process.

Marx: The idealists overlook social reality. Real historical process is not the same as the speculative view of the historical process. Hegel makes a double error: He conceives things in their thought form only, and he vindicates problems on the mental level. There is the social world, and the views of the social world. Hegel considers and solves the social problem on the level of thought only. He thinks that he can resolve problems of practice through speculative thought. He substitutes illusion for social reality. Hegel takes ideas for the things, but objects are not the same as the thought of the objects. Hegel's achievement is that he grasps human creation as the process of labor. Labor is the essence of things, but Hegel has somehow failed to grasp the negative aspects of labor, the alienation in the labor process. Idealism can be characterized as thought preceding being. In materialism, being precedes thought. Materialism defines itself as a science and a negation of idealism, whereby idealism is ideology (false consciousness). Marx is neither idealist, nor materialist, but encompasses both of these perspectives.

Marxist theories of social change: The most often cited view is that Capitalism will perish by its own contradictions, that revolutionary overthrow of the capitalist system is inevitable. Capitalism will fall on its own weight when the contradictions within system reach a level that will inhibit its own functioning, and the people will not tolerate it any longer. The prevailing (capitalist) institutions will have to be modified, or the system will undergo a revolutionary transformation. This is a causal analysis of social change. The principal contradiction in Capitalism is that between social relations of production and private appropriation. All the other contradictions stem from this contradiction. Other contradictions of Capitalism are: recurring crisis, depression and cyclical unemployment, production for profit versus production for need, the tendency toward concentration of production, monopolization of markets and the resulting decline in competition, inflation and monetary crisis, relentless exploitation of vanishing natural resources, and the ecological destruction of the environment, urban decay, capital flight and long term structural unemployment, the use of the machinery of the State for the private aims of the big capitalists, namely, to distribute income in favor of the rich and wealthy, and many other problems connected with capitalist production. The second view of social change presents a voluntarist or intentionalist analysis. People act to realize their own good. This view stresses the role of the revolutionary party in bringing about social change. The proletariat as a class will abolish all classes. ("Philosophy is the head, the proletariat is the heart".) This view is connected with Lenin. Luxenburg, Rosa, (1871-1919) denied Lenin's (Lenin, Vladimir Ilyich, 1870-1924) role of the party. She relied on spontaneous revolutionary activity of the proletariat. In Marx one can find both views. In Marx's Capital,[2] the inevitability of revolution is upheld.

Materialist versus speculative method of analysis:

The materialist method starts from the concrete (the here and now), and advances toward the abstract. Marxian analysis proceeds from reality (earth, concrete, real) to the concept. Speculative philosophy starts from the abstract, and advances toward the the concrete. It begins with the concept and goes to reality, (it descends from heaven to earth). Hegel sees the revolutionary potential in self- consciousness. He begins with the concept (the abstract), and goes towards the concrete (reality). Marx rejects this view. For Marx, truth must prove itself in practice, in real activity. Practical, critical, revolutionary activity is the criterion of truth. Dialectical materialism is the road to truth. Subject and object interact dialectically in the historical process. In all metaphysics, thought remains contemplative, and the object is untouched by it. In dialectics, the problem is to change reality. The economic structure plays a primary role. The analysis must begin here. Truth must grasp the whole of reality. Partial views are inadequate.

Historical materialism seeks to unravel the laws of motion of social development toward higher forms of social organization. Historically changing economic institutions and the corresponding changes in patterns of resource allocation are the cornerstone of Marxist economics. Social change and development take place through class conflict, tension, stress, and struggle brought about by the built-in contradictions within society. The study of contradiction is the essence of Hegelian and Marxist dialectics. The emphasis of Marxist economics on objective laws of motion operating historically and independently of human consciousness or will, has contributed to a dogmatic and rigid view of social change. In a sense, there is a similarity between conventional economics that treats social categories, such as, efficiency, costs returns, prices, etc. as natural categories, and the Marxist view that considers the laws of social evolution as natural laws.

Marxist philosophy is anchored in the concrete reality of the process of production. One begins from non-arbitrary real premises that are verifiable. Human beings produce the means of subsistence. These represent the material conditions of production. There is no fixed human essence. With the division of labor, conditions of production change. The largely agricultural society gives way to landed property. The latter is converted to a form of capital. Traditional mores and values tend to be displaced by a society where capital furnishes the social glue that keeps people in their place.

History is characterized by a series of (historical) social stages that reflect the mode of production. These stages can be summed up as follows:

Tribal ownership - elementary division of labor.

Ancient communal and State ownership. As soon as there is private property (ownership of land, etc.) divisive forms of society appear.

Feudalism - division of town and country. The conditions of life determine what in fact occurs. There are no higher laws. Production of ideas is directly interwoven with material activity. What we think is a function of what we do.

In Capitalism, the chief contradiction is between relations of production and the mode (forces) of production. Commodity fetishism: relations between persons appear as relations between things. Historical materialism: Relations of production are the key to the understanding of the historical processs, for every society. The real basis for the development of law (and the superstructure) is a change in the power relations between classes, (the base).

Exercises.

1. What do you understand by a Marxist analysis of society?

2. Commodity production is the essential feature of capitalist production. Profits and markets determine production. How is this related to peoples' needs?

3. Explain the meaning of "contradictions in Capitalism" i.e. in the capitalist mode of production.

4. Why would, according to Marx, socialism replace capitalism?

5. Is it true, that according to Marx, capitalism will have to develop to its highest stage, and exhaust all its potential possibilities for the satisfaction of human needs, before it would be replaced by a higher form of social organization in the form of socialism? Was this indeed the case in Russia and the other socialist countries?

6. Was the system that replaced capitalism in these countries a socialist system in the Marxian sense? Or, was it a form of State Capitalism based on brutal force?

7. Can Marx be blamed for the consequences of Marxism?

8. How pervasive is alienation, in all its forms, in our society? Does it intrude into all our social and cultural institutions, education, religion, and modes of social interactions?

9. What is Marx's vision of a communist society?

Notes

1. Karl Marx, *The Economic and Philosophical Manuscripts of 1844*. Moscow: Foreign Languages Publishing House, 1979.
2. Karl Marx, Capital. Vol. I, II, III. Moscow: Foreign Languages Publishing House, 1962.

Workshop 28. Marx's Concept of Human Needs.

The most basic human needs are those that are necessary for human life and existence. These are man's vital needs. History begins with the production of means to satisfy man's material needs. The reproduction of the material condition of life constantly creates new needs. The family is the first social unit (social relation) in the production and the satisfaction of needs. With the increase in population and the development of new needs, new social relations develop, and the family becomes a subordinate unit in the production process.

As population increases, available resources are insufficient to satisfy all the needs of the people. It becomes essential to increase production and the productivity of labor. To enhance productivity, investment in capital goods becomes necessary. This requires additional saving. The small family unit does not provide enough saving that are necessary for the investment in capital goods. It therefore hampers the development of the means of production. There is insufficient saving for investment in capital goods. Eventually, a small class of the population comes to control the productive resources in the community. The owners of capital satisfy their consumption needs at the expense of those who who are without capital, and who only own their labor. By appropriating part of the laborer's product, they are able to accumulate more capital and bring about greater capital development. A small class obtains a monopoly on the development of the means of production. The majority is excluded from ownership of productive resources (capital), and from economic development. They are reduced to mere toilers, working for those that own the capital resources.

Commodity production creates new needs along with the means of their satisfaction. The growth in human needs and the means of their satisfaction are both historically conditioned. Production not only produces the new need but it also creates the consumer for the new need. Marx: (Marx, Karl 1818-1883) "Production not only produces the object for the subject but also the subject for the object." It produces not only the consumer but also the mode of consumption. Expansion of production (based on private property andthe profit motive) depends on the expansion of the market for its products. The latter becomes increasingly geared to the creation of new, (artificial) wants rather than to the satisfaction of genuine human needs. "Capitalism is the pimp that by constantly producing new objects creates an unending stream of new needs which make people prostate themselves. It serves as an alien force for the expansion of capitalist production."[1] Men and women are increasingly subjected to new wants. They come to be dominated by things. People become dependent on things, and things establish an alien power over them. While a minority dwells in luxury, the majority can barely satisfy its most elementary needs. The working poor are reduced to an inhuman existence. Capitalism has failed to meet the human needs of human beings.

In capitalism, human needs have been reduced to economic needs in the form of effective market demand. The market determination of need in the form of effective demand expresses the alienation of human needs. The end of production in capitalism is the creation of exchange value, i.e. to produce use value for the capitalist (profit). The division of labor expresses labor's alienation in the production process. The laborer works only on a tiny part of the total product. The laborer has no relation to the value he produces. Optimally, the development of the productive forces should reduce labor time, and create more wealth for all. In capitalism however, the development of productive forces become themselves a means to the enhancement of profits for the capitalist class. The worker's work is not lightened or reduced. Along with the increase in wealth, there is also the reproduction of poverty. Alienated labor is at the base of man's alienation in society. The needs of capital displace the needs of people. The laborer exists for the reproduction and the expansion of capital.

The profit motive also intrudes into the educational system. In a capitalist society, the educational needs of people are determined by the requirements of the market. The capitalist system rations research according to the profit motive, and the market exchange system also dominates scholarship. The system inhibits universal acccess to knowledge. To satisfy the needs of capital (i.e. profits), wants are artificially enhanced and created. Such manipulated needs and false wants do not necessarily satisfy true human needs, and indeed, they may hinder the optimum development of the person. At the same time, the satisfaction of man's vital needs (nourishment, clothing, a culturally attainable level of housing, health care, etc.) are retarded, and not sufficiently met. Large segments of the population are excluded from potential social wealth, and are forced to live in near poverty conditions. Yet, the satisfaction of people's basic needs is a prerequisite for the realization of all of their (sublimated and unsublimated) needs. True human needs (non-alienated needs) are by necessity free needs. They are not survival needs. They are not related to material goods. They are free needs whose satisfaction is conditioned by the satisfaction of man's necessary needs. The expansion of unneeded consumer goods hinders the expansion of free time, and the satisfaction of true human needs. The individual becomes enslaved to these one-sided needs. People's needs are reduced to the need to have more and possess more. Marx sums it up as follows: "The less you are...the more you have. The quantity of money becomes its sole effective quality."[2] True human needs (spiritual, aesthetic, and moral needs) are directed toward other people seen as ends, and not as means. In an alienated society, man is a means for the satisfaction of another man's private ends (greed). The humanization of man's needs means that the highest object of man's need is man himself. The nobility of man is the true end of man.   Human needs are directed towards humanity at large. For Marx, material wealth is a precondition for the development of human wealth. Human wealth embraces the free and many sided activity of human beings. It consists in the development of the creative capacities, and the vital senses of every individual. For Marx:

> the realm of freedom begins only where labor which is determined by necessity....ceases; ...Freedom in this field can consist in socialized man, the associated producers, rationally regulating their interchange with Nature;....and achieving this with least expenditure of energy...Beyond it begins that development of human energy which is an end in itself, the true realm of freedom, which, however, can blossom forth only with this realm of necessity as its basis. (Capital III, pp.799-800.)

In a communist society of associative producers, labor time will cease to be the measure of exchange value, and exchange value will cease to be the measure of use value. Unlimited progress in the sphere of material production will transform physical labor into supervisory, scientific, and intellectual labor. Technological progress underlying the production of desired levels of material goods become a condition for the availability of true human wealth, rather then a source for the accumulation of material goods. True human wealth consists in the free time necessary for the pursuit of higher level human needs. Man will be able to excel in many things. The division between manual and intellectual labor will be overcome. The social division of labor will cease, and the class division of society will disappear. Individuals will be able to freely choose their position at work, and remuneration will be according to need. "From each according to his capacity and to each according to his need." Remuneration according to need reflects the basic uniqueness of individuals. A communist society does not proclaim a levelling and an absolute equality of people. Work will become man's vital need, and the needs of socialized human beings will alone determine production of material goods. The realm of freedom replaces the realm of necessity. .."beyond production, begins that development of human energy which is *an end in itself, the true realm of freedom.*"[3]

There are major shortcomings in this communist vision. It exhibits an excessive faith in moral incentives, an excessive faith in technology, and a insufficient recognition of the role that   specialization and division of labor play in productivity and the efficient use of scarce resources. The communist vision portrays an unrealistic confidence in the ability of society to supply any level of material needs deemed necessary for the unfolding of human freedom.   More importantly however, Marx's vision leaves out human passions as determinants of human behavior.   Human passions will not simply disappear in a communist society. Marx does not deal with the question of human passions. He overstates the importance of the material sphere and its ability to transform human consciousness.   The dictum   "being determines consciousness and not vice versa" is too dogmatic and one-sided. Nevertheless, Marx's utopian vision expresses the most noble aspiration of humanity. This vision will forever remain a measure of the possibilities imbued in man as a social being.

Exercises.

1.   What does Marx mean by free and necessary needs? free and necessary labor? necessary and free time?
2. Why does Marx call free needs human needs?
3. What is the difference between realm of freedom and the realm of necessity?
4. Now, think of your own situation. How do you relate the realm of freedom and the realm of necessity to yourself?
5. Do you feel that all or most of your time is taken up by necessity or by freedom?
6. Do you feel that all or most of your needs are necessary needs? What are your free or human needs? Are you fully aware of them?
7. Make a list of all of your free needs. How well do you satisfy each of them?

Notes

1. Karl Marx, *Economic and Philosophic Manuscripts of 1844.*   Moscow: Foreign Languages Publishing House, 1979. p. 147.
2. Karl Marx, Ibid. p. 147.
3. Karl Marx, *Capital.* vol. III. Moscow: Foreign Languages Publishing House, 1962. p. 800.

Workshop 29.   Critical Theory.

The fundamental question in critical theory is how does philosophical reason relate to society and the good life? In critical theory, society itself is the object of theory.   The function of philosophical theory is to promote social change for the betterment of the people. In the Greek view, thought and action are inseparable. To know is to act. Philosophy is indispensable to the good life. Hegel focuses on the relation of thought to the social context in which thought originates. Reason grasps what is essential in experience. It is the product of the actual when grasped conceptually. "The owl of Minerva begins its flight at dusk." The future can only be known through a dialectical understanding of the present. We comprehend after the fact, a-posteriori. The comprehension of what has been is necessary in order to be able to anticipate what can be. What can be, follows from what has been. Theory (and philosophy) comes in after the fact.   Hegel: Ideas realize themselves in the practical. "What is actual is rational, what is rational is actual". Reason realizes itself. What occurs has an intrinsic rationality. (It served as an an apology for the Prussian State.) He criticizes Kant's a-priori conditions for knowing, "you can't swim without going into the water." Hegel's interest lies in the social use of reason. Reason realizes itself in actuality. What occurs has an intrinsic rationality. Thought and being, subject and object interact and condition each other.

Only history can resolve the antinomies of philosophy, the subjective and objective dimensions of being. Subjective dimensions are human freedom, values and ideals.   Objective dimensions are causality or necessity in nature and in history. The resolution of the antinomies means the reconciliation of the opposition between the individual and society, between self-interest and moral choice. On the level of thought, it means the unity of subject and object, thought and being, man and nature.

Marx: "Communism as a fully developed naturalism is humanism, and as a fully developed humanism is naturalism. It is the definitive resolution of the antagonism between man and nature, and between man and man. It is the true solution of the conflict between existence and essence, between objectification and self-affirmation, between freedom and necessity, between individual and species. It is the solution of the riddle of history and knows itself to be this solution."[1]
The function of philosophy is to provide conceptual knowledge of what is the case. All philosophy can be reduced to the relation of thought (subject) to object. Consciousness is defined in terms of subject seeking to comprehend the object. Idealism claims that the subject conditions the object. The materialist position (Engels) holds that to know,

means to know what is independent of us. This is known as the reflection theory of knowledge, the object as reflected in the subject. Marx criticizes Hegel's philosophy as dealing with knowledge in the abstract. Hegel's philosophy fails to grasp its object (social action). Thought (subject) is its object. Hegel's theory deals with formal relations, with variables of logic.

Hegel fails to grasp how human activity occurs. His thought is too abstract. A human being must be understood in terms of his own activity. The person is active. Work, labor, is real human activity. Hegel upheld the centrality of work, but he had an alienated view of human activity. For Hegel, true ideas will substantiate themselves. Marx's answer to Hegel is: don't just theorize, instead, change the world. Hegel's philosophy is alienated from social reality.

For Marx, thought is determined by the social context. People are the product of their environment. Capitalism blocks free expression of human capacity. A distorted social context produces a distorted view of social reality. Philosophy will reinforce the status quo.

Lukacs (Lukacs Georg 1885-1971): we must search for the most general framework. We must look for a deeper perspective in the prevailing general view. A false general view may hide a deeper perspective that is true. Knowledge must be grasped in a wider context. The economic structure plays this wider role. Analysis must begin with the analysis of the commodity structure of society. Lukacs sees in Marxism a method which leads to true results, a method to transform society.

In contrast to Descartes' (Descartes, Rene, 1596-1650) epistemology (theory of knowledge) which centers on the individual, Marxist epistemology centers on class. Forces of history operate independently of man's psychological awareness. Subjective views are only partially aware of the essence of the whole society. Partial views are fragmentary. They lead to false consciousness. They don't induce people to act. (We are reminded that for the Greeks to know is to act.) Social distortions prevent people from understanding social reality. Partial views are not adequate. Knowledge of social reality is manipulated and distorted by the ruling class via capitalist ideology. Transformation of society is prevented by blocking knowledge. To know, is to grasp the whole, a perspective of the whole is needed. Marxism provides this perspective. Marxism deals with historical processes rather than with isolated events. Bourgeois thought does not grasp the whole of social reality. It is partial, narrow, and falls short of totality. Bourgeois perspective cannot explain human action. For Lukacs, reality has to be seen from the perspective of the proletariat. The proletariat is the real subject of history.

For Kant, knowledge is only of appearance. Kant does not bridge the subject- object relation. We don't know the "thing in itself". Hegel also failed to bridge the subject-object dichotomy. He used a transcendent concept, the absolute Spirit in history. Lukacs maintains that the concept of the proletariat can bridge the gap between subject and object, man and the world. Only the slave can be aware of the master-slave relationship. When the proletariat becomes conscious of reality, reality will change. False consciousness is an awareness which does not reveal the truth about oneself. True consciousness is the consciousness of the deeper structure of social reality. The difference is one between appearance and reality. Marxism is seen as a conceptual instrument that allows us to analyze society in its totality. It does not deal with individual objects but with historical processes. (Who acts in history? Not Hegel's Absolute Spirit, but the social class.) The social class, not the individual human being is the real motor of history.

Exercises.

1. What does the term "critical theory" mean to you? How do you understand it?
2. Marx said that philosophers have only interpreted the world, the point however, is to change it? What do you think is the proper function of philosophy?
3. What is Marx's chief criticism of Hegel?
4. Define the meaning of terms "idealism" and "materialism".
5. How do you interpret Hegel's dictum: "the actual is rational and the rational is actual"? Are people's and Government's actions always rational?
6. According to Hegel, the Absolute Spirit operates in human history. What is Hegel's Absolute Spirit?
7. Does critical theory allow for a separation between theory and praxis? Or, is it necessary that theory be tested, refined, and confirmed in praxis? What does praxis mean in this context?
8. If theory abstracts from concrete reality and deals only with pure thought, is such theory really neutral with respect to the status quo? According to Marx, theory that is divorced from praxis serves the interests of the ruling class. Is this the essence of Marx's criticism of academic philosophy? What do you think about it?

Note

1. Karl Marx, *Economic and Philosophical Manuscripts.* Moscow: Foreign Languages Publishing House, p. 155.

Workshop 30. Max Horkheimer, *The Eclipse of Reason.*

"Philosophies that look exclusively to an inner process for the eventual liberation end as empty ideologies."[1] Horkheimer (1895-1973) examines the concept of rationality in advanced industrial society, a society that inhibits the better life more and more. The kind of reason that we have is shaped and conditioned by the society we live in. In other words, cultural values shape reason itself. Horkheimer differentiates between subjective and objective reason. The main difference between subjective and objective reason lies in the proposition, that subjective reason does not question purpose. "The idea that an aim can be worthwhile (noble) in itself without a necessary gain or advantage, is alien to subjective reason." Objective reason aims at evolving a hierarchy of all beings, including man and his aims. A man's life is reasonable if it is in harmony with the totality, the world around him. In objective reason, the emphasis is on ends rather than on means.

Socrates held that reason should determine beliefs, that it should regulate relations between man and man, and between man and nature. The objective content of reason is to attain moral truth. Enlightenment substituted reason for religion, but ended up emptying reason of its objective content. Hume, (Hume, David 1711-1776) the father of modern positivism, eliminated all general concepts (values) from reason. Liberal ideology of the industrial age identifies reason with self interest. Great ideals and universalist concepts, such as, freedom, humanity, justice, equality, etc. have lost their objective truth. Calculative logic (pragmatism) has replaced objective truth. Science can be used to serve the devil as well as the good. Positivism identifies truth with science. The positivists confuse the scientific method with truth itself. Science has turned into dogma. It eventually stops (inhibits) all (free) thinking. However, so called facts are often merely surface phenomena. Weber (Weber, Alfred, 1868-1958) sharply differentiated between scientific knowledge and values. Interests of social classes cannot be reconciled by science.

"If by enlightenment we mean the freeing of man from superstition, (emancipation from fear), then the denunciation of what is currently called reason is the greatest service reason can render."[2]

Exercises.

1. Do you agree with Horkheimer, that the difference between subjective and objective reason is that between means and ends? Explain your understanding of the difference.

2. Is it possible to use rational means toward irrational ends? And, can one use irrational means toward rational ends? Give examples from history, and reflect on the significance of this problem.

3. In your own life, do you reflect as much on ends as on means?

4. Do you think that subjective reason has taken a hold of our society in the form of narrow sef-interest, efficiency and "technique"?

5. Can there be rationality in the part, and irrationality in the whole? Consider the interests of a single corporation and the interests of the State. Are the two necessarily compatible?

6. What about military spending in excess of genuine defense needs? Is excess military spending (such as had occurred during the Reagan-Bush years) a waste of scarce economic resources for the country as a whole, while at the same time they are a source of great profits to individual firms and corporations? Who ends up paying for it? Did the excessive military spending of the Reagan-Bush years make our country morally and economically stronger or weaker?

7. What did ancient Greece understand by "reason"? How did enlightenment change this understanding of reason?

8. Do universal notions, such as, freedom, justice , equality, human dignity, etc. belong to the realm of reason, or do they merely reflect personal values and preferences?

9. What is, in your view, the connection between reason and logic? Is there a necessary connection between them?

Note

1. Max Horkheimer, *The Eclipse of Reason.* New York: Oxford University Press, 1947. 2. Ibid. p. 182.

Workshop 31. Government and Public Needs.

The ancient Greeks thought that the main object of government was to secure the good life for its citizens. The Romans supposed that the chief object of government was to secure and maintain efficient administration. For the Stoa, universal government was to be based on universal law, and justice. In Machiavelli (Macciavelli, Niccolo 1469-1527), power itself becomes the end of the State. The principle of "reason of State" (raison d'Etat), the guiding principle of a totalitarian State, was first enunciated by Machiavelli. For the totalitarian State, the end justifies the means (any means). The birth of the secular national State signifies the beginning of modernity. In the Middle Ages, laws were made not by legislators, but by judges. The French Protestants of the 17th cent. (the Huguenots), viewed government as a compact between the people. The people are the sovereign, political rule is a trusteeship, and the people have a sacred right to resist unjust rule.

Locke's (Locke John 1632-1704) *Two Treatises of Government* provided the theoretical foundation for the modern liberal state.[1] The right to rebel against unjust rule, has in its own way, contributed to the stability of the State. By giving the people the right to oppose tyranny, it assured the viability of the liberal State. Locke's political philosophy served as a basis for the American political system. The ruling principles of the American Constitution are: inviolability of property, limited government, and inalienable rights of individuals. The public sphere includes education, health, defense, public safety, social welfare, and the infrastructure.

Government responsibilities in the modern welfare state extend to the following:

Public safety and order.

A viable economy, and providing economic opportunity for all.

Education, health, public welfare, and the care of the indigenous.

Public investment in people, and infrastructure.

Resource conservation, and ecological balance.

Distributive justice, and a fair distribution of the cost of government.

Rights and responsibilities of individuals.

The government is a servant of the people. The public must trust the government. For the government to rule effectively, public trust is of prime importance.

Efficiency and fairness are proper evaluative criteria of the nature of the government and its proper functioning. The latter includes the human quality of administration, rights and responsibilities of individuals, the vigilance of the electorate, and the right to repeal bad rule.

Exercises.

1. What are, in your view, the proper functions of Government?
2. Can you arrange these functions in a sequential order according to their respective importance?
3. Consider the local, state, and federal government. To what extent do they fail to fulfill their proper functions, or fulfill them only minimally or inadequately?
4. How would you improve the functioning of your government? Make a list of suggestions.
5. In your mind, does the bureaucracy enhance or hinder the proper functioning of government? Is government bureaucracy necessarily inefficient or wasteful? Or, is it more a question of leadership and morale?
6. Is inefficiency specific to government operations, or is it a general by-product of any large scale organization?
7. Does inefficiency relate to a general lack of accountability and personal responsibility? How accountable are public officials to the electorate? How accountable are corporate executives to the shareholders?

Note

1. Locke's *Two Treatises of Government* . London: Cambridge University Press, 1967.

SECTION V.
METAPHYSICAL
FOUNDATIONS

Workshop 32. Early Metaphysical Speculations: A Brief Review of the Presocratic Philosophers.

The poetic concept of fate *(moira)*, is the precursor of the philosophical concept of necessity. In Greek mythology, even the Gods are subject to fate.

Western philosophy was born in Miletus, southern Ionia, on the shore of the Mediterranean sea. The first philosophers, Thales, Anaximander and Anaximenes were Ionians from Miletus. They asked questions about nature and the source of all things in nature. If philosophy arose out of wonder (Aristotle), these philosophers truly wondered about nature and the nature of things. They were *phusikoi*, philosophers of nature. (*Phusis* - designates nature as a whole, as well as the nature of things: what things are and how they come into being).The Milesians were materialist monists. They looked for one substratum from which everything came to be. Thales of Miletus (600 B.C.) conjectured that water is the source of all things. Water is the fundamental substance, one underlying reality, a substratum or cause of everything. It is the material principle *(arche)* from which everything is derived. He also said that magnets have souls and that the world is full of Gods. Thales was a naturalist. Nature *(physis)* was opposed to convention *(nomos)*. It is nature versus convention.

Anaximander (610-546B.C.) named the originative substance *Apeiron,* the indefinite, the infinite or the unbounded. The *Apeiron* is infinite in extent and has no definite chracteristics. This view of ultimate reality is similar to that of the Eastern Tao and to Spinoza's substance or Nature. The *apeiron* is the *arche,* the material principle from which everything gets started. The original stuff that formed the world was indefinite, without any internal distinctions. Anaximander, through the use of *apeiron* , is saying that not everything can be accounted for naturalistically.   God forms the world initially. (In theology God is there and controls everything.)

For **Anaximenes** (6th cent. B.C.), air is the underlying nature of everything. Air holds up the earth. Hot and cold, (rare and dense) are the moving principles of everything. Reality is made up of contraries, hot and cold. Motion is reduced to rarity. Locomotion is a wave of density. In wave motion, energy moves but no body moves, (each little part of water stays, but energy passes). Air is everywhere. All matter is animate, the air is the animator, (hylozoism).

Xenophanes (570-475 B.C.) main fragment is about wisdom. He is dubious about a naturalistic account of the world. He is sceptical of Milesian cosmogony and cosmology. He criticized common religious practices and maintained that there is one God, a single, non-anthropomorphic deity. He is more of a poet than a philosopher, a real predecessor of Plato.

Heraclitus (5th cent.B.C.)

One of the most important presocratic philosophers is Heraclitus. He was born in Ephesus, after the middle of the sixth century. He was unconventional, and full of riddles. In antiquity, he was referred to as the "dark" or the "obscure" one. Heraclitus continued in the tradition of the Ionian natural philosophers. The one, underlying substance in the universe, is fire.   Fire is the *arche* of the universe. Fire burns all, brings all into being. Like Xenophanes, Heraclitus was critical of the prevalent religious practices. God was identified as the cosmic fire. The first principle of knowledge and existence is *logos*.   Is the world the same as our cognizance of it?   The truth is close to us but we fail to comprehend it. Nature likes to hide."*Men should try to comprehend the underlying coherence of things: it is expressed in the Logos, the formula or element of arrangement common to all things*".[1] Fire is another name for   *logos*. *Logos* is the plan of the universe, the unity of the world process. Humans may apprehend or misapprehend it. "The fundamental truth about nature is this: the world is an eternal and ever changing modification of fire..."[2] Wisdom consists in grasping the *logos* of things. The *logos* maintains measure, proportion, and equilibrium in the universe. It makes things coherent.   Behind all the diversity, opposition, and contradiction, there is the undelying unity of the *logos*. *Logos* reconciles the opposites. "The path up and down is one and the same." (Fr. 200.)   Unity and diversity are related.

Opposites are necessary and depend on each other. Health and rest are good only if we recognize disease and weariness. Hot and cold form a single entity (temperature). They cannot exist without each other. The same things produce different effects. Pigs like mud (fr. 13), and donkeys prefer rubbish to gold (fr. 59). The unity of things lies beneath the surface. Things change but they remain the same. Heraclitus emphasized universal flux (everything is changing), and the notion of contradiction. *"Gods are mortal , humans immortal, living their death, dying their life."* [3] The common sense distinction between mortals and immortals, men and the gods, life and death does not hold. Life turns to death and from death arises life. There is ceaseless flux within the apparent rest. The river flows and the flow is the river. The river could not be identified without the flow. The flux makes the continuity of things possible. It is the world process. Everything is changing but the *logos* is always the same. The opposites are united in the *logos*. Nature and convention, being and thinking, oppositions are both real and unreal, they are and they are not.

Pythagoras and the Pythagoreans. (Late 5th cent. BC.)

   Pythagoras was born on the island of Samos, before the middle of the sixth century. He was an Ionian Greek who moved to Italy. The Ionians are materialist (natural, scientific) thinkers. The Italians are more idealists (religious-ethical) thinkers. Pythagoras was a wanderer. He believed in reincarnation and the transmigration of souls. There formed around him a circle, a mathematical group, (the Pythagoreans). The Pythagoreans sought to explain things in terms of structure or form, not in terms of perception as the materialists did. For the Pythagoreans, everything is number. The world is numbered. Pythagoras wrote nothing. He initiated the "philosophic way of life". Number is seen as the essence of things. For example, No. 4 stands for justice (a square, each side treats the other equitably). No. 5 is marriage, (the lowest junction of odd and even). The odd is limited which is good, even is unlimited which is bad. "Odd is correlated with Rest...Even is correlated with Motion;"[4] Limit means to be the same as itself. Unlimited means to be other than the other. The right no. is 7. (There is mystic significance in ancient lore, including Judaism, to number seven, as seven days of the week, seven spheres of heaven, etc.) The perfect no. is 10. (ten fingers, base 10, sum of 1+2+3+4). Numbers translate into geometry: 1=point, 2=line, 3=plane, 4=solid. They also translate into knowing: 1=intuition, 2=demonstration (from premise to conclusion), 3=opinion (superficial), 4=perception. The Pythagoreans applied the number theory to music, (*harmonia* and ratio). *Harmonia* as a principle of order in things. The ultimate principle is one, the principle of limitedness. Out of the one, numbers are generated, the one and the infinite dyad. (For the early Greeks, two is the first number, one is not a number. One is the principle of number.) The Pythagoreans account for things by mixing of the elements. There is no one substratum such as air or water.

Parmenides of Elea.

Parmenides was born about 510 B.C. in Elea, a Greek city on the coast of Italy. Parmenides is the most crucial presocratic philosopher. The philosophers before him were all monists, after him they are pluralists. Parmenides' poem, deals with the way of truth, and the way of seeming, *(doxa)*. He is a youth led by a chariot to the Goddess that reveals everything to him. There is the way of being, and the way of seeming. Being is immutable, the kind of entity that can be known. The primary purpose of the poem is to show that the belief in the reality of the sensible world is mistaken. One cannot think intelligibly of changeable things. Parmenides talks about objects of knowledge that are forever unchanging. The way to truth is about ultimate being. Intellect or thought is moving towards being or truth. Being is unchanging, definite, has limits, and is a finite sphere. How does the unchanging Being connect with the world of change and diversity? It connects through the transition to the way of seeming. The distinction is between opinion and knowledge, or appearance and reality. The way of seeming is perhaps the best we can do. In Metaphysics, one can be a realist (viewing things as they are). In Physics, one gives an instrumental (fictional) account of things. The Eleatics were the founders of dialectics, *(elenchos* = refutation, it is what Socrates does). The dialectical tradition is often linked with Zeno and Parmenides.

Zeno (born ar. 490 B.C.).

According to Aristotle, Zeno is the founder of dialectics. He is the father of sophism, of argumentation. Zeno's argument is a defense of Parmenides' view of being as definite and unchanging. His argument is based on *reductio ad absurdum*. Motion is potentially infinitely divisible, but not actually infinitely divisible. Achilles and the tortoise: You let Achilles go first to where the tortoise is but the tortoise will have moved away, etc. Thus he will never catch up. Zeno is showing that motion is a paradox. (The thing that is moving is not in the place it is, and it is not in the place it is not.)

Melissus (about 400 B.C.).

Melissus follows Parmenides very closely, but with some changes. In Parmenides, Being is a finite sphere. In Melissus, Being is infinite, because if it were finite, then what is outside it? Also, if Being is infinite, it is partless, and therefore it is more truly one. Space is a plenum, it is full of eternal stuff. Space is coextensive with Being. There is nothing outside space, the boundless one.

Empedocles (early 5th cent. B.C.).

Empedocles is a contemporary of Melissus and Anaxagoras (500-428 B.C.). According to Aristotle, Empedocles started rhetoric. Water, air, fire, and earth are the four roots. They correspond to winter, spring, summer, and fall. He linked those with the four humors. Water - phlegm, air - blood, fire - yellow bile, earth - black bile (melancholy). Empedocles is important to the medical tradition. When the four humors are well balanced, they form a healthy person. This is also expressed in terms of character: sanguine, melancholic, phlegmatic, and choleric. Blood is homogeneous. It is composed of a ratio of all four elements. (Therefore, one should not spill blood, etc.) He also introduced love and hate. Love unites the four roots. The four roots are mixed together in the sphere of love. Strife separates them. There is a cosmic cycle of love and strife. The mixing of the four roots produces variety. The ultimate deity is in the sphere of love. It is a non-anthropomorphic idea of God. The mind is a perfect mixture. Therefore it is receptive to all. Love imbues the world with value. Love is harmony, (a formal principle). It is the formula for mixing. Strife seems to be the principle of stress, nothing wants to stay where it is. It leads things to separate. The living organism is coherent (love). When it dies, it decomposes, (strife). Strife is not merely negative. It enables the renewed composition. Empedocles uses harmony for love. Plato changed it to eros. The sphere of love is the ultimate intellect. Aphrodite (love) gives birth to the eyeball - seeing -theoria - philosophy. Unlike Parmenides, Empedocles maintains that the senses are a way to knowledge, when properly used. Cognition or perception is from like to like. Affluences are delicate mixtures of air, fire, water, and earth. There are affluences from everything. Things flowing out through the pores and flowing in through the sense receptacles. (This later becomes Aristotle's theory of cognition. The mind becomes informed, likened to what it cognizes. We cognize like by like.) Blood travels through the pores. The main center of human cognition is where the blood concentrates around the heart.

Anaxagoras (500-428 B.C.).

He came from Asia minor, and lived many years in Athens. Anaxagoras theory of matter is that everything is in everything, except mind. Substance is eternal. Nothing can come from nothing, there is no *creatio ex nihilo*. There is something of everything in everything, (but something is more predominant.) There is no pure gold. What we call gold is predominantly gold. Nothing comes into being nor perishes. Things compose or decompose. Whatever the offspring has, must be in the seed. No two things are alike except the portions of mind. The mind is pure and unmixed. It is infinite, self-ruled, and controls everything. Mind is cosmic energy.

Democritus (460-370B.C.) and **Loecippus** (5th cent.B.C.).

Leucippus and Democritus are the two atomists. Democritus was a contemporary of Socrates. Parmenides conclusion that void or empty space cannot be ("since Being is, void can only be where being is not, and therefore cannot be)" was refuted by the atomists. "Not being exist as much as being."[5] Existence is not to be confused with material existence only. Space exists as well. Democritus developed the atomic theory of matter. There is an infinite number of atoms, but not an infinite number of shapes. The atom is uncuttable, indivisible, and unchanging. Atoms are scattered in the void, and are ceaselessly moving. They have unchangeable features: size, shape, weight, (so called primary qualities). They do not possess changeable (secondary) qualities, like color, heat, odor. The cosmos is finely ordered, like a jewel (cosmos means jewel). Atoms differ in shape and arrangement. Objects are aggregates of atoms. Qualitative differences between objects are accounted for by the quantitative differences of the conglomerates of atoms. No two atoms can ever touch. There is proximity, but they do not touch one another. In the atomic world, there is no direction, no real up or down.

Epicurus. (342-272 BC.)

Epicurus took over the atomic scheme from Democritus. Atoms move at the same speed but in different direction. If more atoms move backwards than forwards, their vector sum would give a slow motion. Also, when atoms collide, they swerve. The swerve introduces a degree of indeterminacy into the outcomes of physical events. [In this he came close to modern subatomic physics where Schrodinger's (Schrodinger, Erwin 1887-1961) principle of uncertainty holds]. For Epicurus death is nothing. When one understands the atomic theory of matter, one is not afraid of death. Epicureans are atheists. There is no after life, and there is no fear of death. Once you give up the uncertainty of the outcome, fear leaves you. Epicurean ethics is to seek pleasure and avoid pain. Pleasure is not to be interpreted as carnal pleasure. Epicurus advises to seek enjoyment in life, and not aspire to what is beyond one's natural powers and abilities.

For exercises, see workshop 33.

Notes

1. G.S. Kirk, J.E.Raven, and M.Schofield, *The Presocratic Philosophers.* Cambridge: Cambridge University Press, 1987. p. 186.
2. Jonathan Barnes, Early Greek Philosophy. New York: Viking Penguin Inc.1987. p. 39.
3. Ibid. 117.
4. Reginald E. Allen, *Greek Philosophy: Thales to Aristotle.* New York: The free Press, 1966. p. 9.
5. Ibid. p.16.

Workshop 33. The One-Many Problem in Ancient Greek Philosophy.

What is the nature of ultimate reality? Is it one or many? The earliest philosophers grappled with this question.

Thales of Miletus thought that water is the material principle or substratum from which things come into being, and into which they perish. The substance (water) persists but it changes its qualities. Water is the underlying reality which is the cause of everything. This position is called materialist monist.

Anaximander held that *apeiron* (the infinite or indefinite) was the originative principle of all existing things. The *apeiron* was not precisely defined but the implication was that not everything can be accounted for by one material substratum. The world is accounted for by heat. The eternal hot and cold are the causes of generation of things. They are the moving principles of change. If we take heat to represent energy (or eternal motion and rest), than the latter is the cause of all change in the universe. According to Anaximander, the originative substance of the material world is air. Through condensation and rarefaction, air takes on different forms (fire, wind, cloud, water, earth, stones). Change comes through motion in the air. Motion is eternal. Hot and cold are the moving principles of change.

In **Xenophanes**, the One is God, who himself is motionless, but who is the source of all motion and change in the universe, ("he shakes all things by the thoughts of his mind"). Parmenides was supposed to be his pupil.

Heraclitus was concerned with the unifying reality that underlies all change and multiplicity. There is unity in the diversity of things. The flux metaphor ("everything is in flux") may be interpreted on several levels of meaning: (1) Change that balances out. (2) Change is constant, there is unity in action, and not all motion is apparent. (3) There is ceaseless flux within apparent rest (Plato's interpretation). (4) Motion as being, (Heidegger's view).

The underlying coherence of things, i.e. unity in diversity, is expressed in the *Logos*. *Logos* is the plan of the universe which reconciles all opposites. There is never any real, absolute division between opposites. Opposites are different phases of a single process, (hot and cold continuum, night and day, parent- child-procreation, etc.). God (the *Logos*) ensures that change is proportional and measured. The total plurality of things form a single determinate unity. ("The unity of

things lies beneath the surface"...)   Fire is the originative stuff ("The
world is an ever living fire"). This may express a materialist monist
view (Aristotle's belief) or, it (fire) may be another name for *Logos*.
The latter could mean fire as illumination, and this would express a
non- materialist view.

For **Pythagoras** and the **Pythagoreans**, things are represented
by numbers. Numbers are seen as the formal causes of things.   The
ultimate principle is One. It is the principle of limitidness. Out of
one, numbers are generated. (One itself is not a number, it is the
principle of number).   Numbers are generated from one and the
indefinite dyad. To be limited means to be the same as itself. To be
other than the other is the unlimited. (Aristotle interprets limit as the
formal cause, and the unlimited as the material cause of things.) The
Pythagoreans account for the plurality of things by mixing. They are
idealist pluralists in distinction from the Ionians who are materialist
monists. The Pythagoreans are the first mixers.   Ratio (limit) is the
principle of mixing.

For **Parmenides**, being is truth. Truth consists in the knowledge
that being *is* and non- being cannot be. It is impossible to know what
is not (what does not exist).   Neither can there be becoming (coming
to be), or perishing. This is so, because what is coming to be must
have previously not been, (thus analogous to what is not), which is
rejected as impossible. Similarly with perishing, (going from being
to non-being.) "It never was nor will be, since it is now, altogether
one, continuuous". And, why, if it came to be, did it happen at one
time rather than another? Therefore, "it must be either completely or
not at all".   All reality is one, changeless, without beginning and
without ending, being fixed in the same sphere forever. Parmenides is
trying to apprehend being as being (as truth) that is unchanging and the
same everywhere, ("continuuous in all directions"). This truth (about
ultimate being) can be fathomed by thought. For, "the same thing is
there to be thought and is why there is thought". Reality (truth) is
whole and changeless... "there neither is nor will be anything else
besides what is".
The world of change and diversity, the coming to be and the
perishing, being and not being, changing place and altering... are only
names given by mortals who mistake opinion (convention) for truth.
They named two forms (light and night) of which neither one is being.
Mortal opinions are based on the belief in the two sensible forms, light
and night, out of which all sensible appearances are produced.
However, the senses which see plurality and change do not point to
the truth. Truth is only given by thought of being, as necessary, and
non-being as imposssible. All the multiplicity of things, and the

changing world which mortals suppose to be real, is in reality only One which alone truly is. There is being and nothing else. "What is is, and what is not is not". Being is one, unchanging and eternal. Change is impossible because it would be contradictory, (being changing into non-being and vice versa.) How then are we to explain the phenomenon of change and plurality? Being, that is immutable and one, appears as mutable from a finite human perspective. We cannot deny change in the realm of appearances (i.e. seeming). The problem of one and the many is resolved on the level of truth versus appearance. It depends on whether we consider things from a final and immutable perspective or from a finite one.

Anaxagoras saw the world as an original mixture of all things together. The original mixture contained the four elements (air, water, earth, fire), and innumerable seeds. Air and aither (fire) held the original mixture together. Each thing, except mind, contained a portion of everything, but it was determined by its predominant feature. Except mind, no two things are alike. Mind is infinite, and self ruled. It is all by itself, and it is mixed with nothing. Mind is an abstract principle that controls the cosmos. It arranged all things (the air, the aither, the hot and the cold, the dry and the moist, etc.) and their separation. The separations (except mind) were not complete since each thing is what it contains most. All opposites come out from one another (hot and cold, dry and moist, etc.). They must have therefore been present in one another all the time. The mind is incorporeal, but it also is the finest and purest of all things. Anaxagoras is a dualist. Mind is the cause of motion, and of coming into being. The original single substance was a mixture of all things. The plurality of things developed from these two: separation of elements in matter, and the mind controlling it.

For **Empedocles**, the four roots, fire, earth, air, and water are the irreducible material elements from which all other things are formed. The four elements are equal to each other, but each prevails at different times (seasons). They intermingle, run through one another, become different at different times and yet are the same. The four elements are at the root of all living, and non living things. The difference in the various things lie in the different ratios of their elements. Love and strife alternate in the cosmic cycle. The four roots get mixed together in the sphere of Love. It leads to unity. Strife gets eveything to separate and fall apart. It leads to diversity. Blood is composed of the elements mixed in equal proportions and it accounts for our ability to think, and have an unbiased view of the world.

The Atomists: Leucippus and Democritus.

The Atomists held that only atoms and the void are real. All differences between physical objects can be explained in terms of differences in shape, arrangement, and position of atoms. The atoms are ungenerated, unalterable, and indivisible. The void is that which separates the atoms, and without which no movement would be possible. The atoms are infinite in number, with different shapes and sizes. They are in continuous motion. This gives rise to collisions leading to change, (i.e. combining into compound bodies, and separating into atoms). The compound bodies acquire or possess various qualities.   Qualitative changes are mere   (quantitative) displacements of immutable units (atoms).

The atoms are the basic elements (corpuscular chunks), and the many diverse things arise from their combinations and separations. The full (atom) and the void, are the material causes of existing things. The difference in their elements (shape, arrangement, position) are the cause of the diversity of things. Objects are conglomerates of atoms, and all qualitative differences depend on quantitative differences alone. This may be seen as a response to Parmenides, as a way to reconcile the one with the many.

Plato's dialectic centers on the theory of Forms. (How much Plato subscribed to his own theory of Forms (Ideas) is an open question. He criticizes it in his Parmenides. (Things partake in forms, but forms also partake in each other.). The Platonic Forms are essences or archetypes in which particular things participate. The Forms are absolutely perfect, immutable, unique, and independent. The Form exists by itself. Ideas are timeless and spaceless.   They remain perpetually like themselves, cannot come into being or pass away, they are eternally the same. Individual objects are homonymous with the Ideas and similar to them. Objects participate in the Forms. They come into being, pass away, and are always in motion.

In the Timaeus, Plato argues that the physical world has the form of becoming, and not that of true being. We can know nothing certain about it. We can only know what is probable about the sensible universe. We know nature not by truth but by belief. The world of the senses is subject to mere opinion. The Forms are the only entities that are accessible to knowledge. They are the standard for the sensibles. Things can both be like and unlike each other, but ideas cannot be qualified by their opposites, (i.e. likeness is the same as itself, it cannot participate in unlikeness). There is plurality of concepts (forms). The many sensibles (individual objects) share, relate or participate in each form. Individual objects are subsumed under their corresponding ideas.

The world of sensibles is the world of seeming (opinion, doxa), and the world of ideas is the world of truth (episteme).

Aristotle criticized Plato's theory of Ideas, especially, the notion that Ideas have a separate and independent existence. Plato posits two elements to be present in the ideas and in all existing things: the one and the indefinite dyad. (Aristotle, Metaphysics I, 1087b12.) From the one and the indefinite dyad, numbers arise in an natural manner. Plato identified the One as the idea of the good. Within the realm of ideas, the One (the Good) is the highest idea. The plurality of ideas is correspondingly arranged in a hierarchical order.

In Aristotle, Being *(to on)* is used in many senses: (1) as *"ousia"* or the "what" of things, (2) as qualities, quantities or affections of things, i.e. predicates of *ousia*. Only *ousia* is substance. All other categories depend on substance *(ousia)* for their existence. Each thing (table, etc.) is the true *ousia*. It is a composite of matter and form. We know the thing through its essence (i.e. its intelligible structure). "To have knowledge of the individual is to have knowledge of its essence" (Metaph. 61031b7-8:19-23.).

Ousia is the result of a process. The table came into being and it will perish. Change *(metabole)* and process *(kinesis)* is what we experience in the world. Aristotle identified four causes of change: formal, material, efficient and final.

Nature is not a mere mixing and unmixing of elements. Natural processes exhibit certain ends *(tele)*. The egg will grow into a chicken. End is not purpose. Nature has no purpose. Only man has a purpose. Each thing has an impulse to become what it can be. (The acorn strives to become an oak tree, etc.) Men desire to know. They have the power of *nous*.

Ousia is an activity. Aristotle distinguishes between two kinds of activities: (a) *energeia* (these have ends in themselves), and motion *(kinesis)*, which is for the sake of some end. Being is *energeia*, an activity which has its end in itself. Even the unchanging and eternal being is an activity *(energeia)*. Processes take place by motion *(kinesis)* and change *(metabole)*. Each particular motion is caused by another particular motion. But motion in general has no efficient cause. Motion like time has no beginning. The unmoved mover is the *arche*, (the principle) of motion in general. It is like a natural law, not a physical cause. The unmoved mover is both the formal, and the final cause of motion. Since the *arche* has no temporal beginning, an infinite regress is not possible. The circular motion of the heavenly bodies have no temporal beginning.

The unmoved mover moves the world not by force but by attraction. This comes close to the Platonic Idea of the Good. In every natural process there is the urge to perfect one's being. The drive for perfectability is built in in Nature. *Nous,* the power to know, is the highest power in the world. Aristotle thinks that the stars are a greater embodiment of *nous* than men. "God is the form of the world's matter, he is the highest good in the world and the orderly arrangement of its parts" (Metaph.10, 1075 a 12-17).

Aristotle resolves the one-many problem through *ousia* and the composite. *Ousia* (the substratum or being) is that which underlies change or that upon which other things are predicated. One and being are together. Anything that is a being is a one. Substratum is the potentiality to have one quality or another. Every change (including change of place) implies the movement from potentiality to actuality. There are many substances (individuals and composites), each one having an underlying *ousia* (being) as substratum. Aristotle's categories of being are substance (Socrates) and figures of predication (accidental properties). The latter are: quality (pale), quantity (how much), time (when), place (where), relation (Socrates as a father), action (hitting someone), passion (being hit). Substance is what inheres in itself. All other categories of being inhere in substance. There is no science of the accidental. An accidental conjoinig of properties or events, (accident) is neither for the most part, nor always. Chance and spontaneity are types of accident. They are neither necessary, nor for the most part. The sophists did not differentiate between substance and accident. Their arguments dealt with the accidental. But, according to Aristotle, to know something, is to know why. Things are known through their causes. To know is to grasp the real principle contained in the thing. Prime matter is pure potentiality for form. Is nature matter or form? Nature (physis) is both, but fundamentally it is more form. For the Presocratics, matter is more fundamental.

Exercises. (Note: Metaphysical exercises are not meant to arrive at definite answers. They are meant only as reflections on the deeper meaning of things).

1. From time immemorial philosophers wondered about the "ultimate". What do you understand by the "ultimate"?
2. Is the ultimate a thing (air , water, fire, earth), is it mind (idea, form, thought), is it both or neither? Is it Love?
3. Is the truth hidden from the senses or does it reveal itself through the senses? Is there a realm of the supersensual, and what is it?
4. Epicurus says that all we can possibly know, is what we get through our senses. Do you agree or disagree? Explain why.
5. Why is there a question of one, and the many? Of unity in diversity? Are they opposed to each other, or can they be reconciled?

6. According to Parmenides, the difference between one and many is the difference between appearance and reality, truth and opinion, (episteme and doxa). How would you respond to this?

7. Diversity consists of beings, unity consists of Being. Is there Being within each being? Can there be beings without Being? Is Being that which is common to all beings?

8. All beings have in common that which means "to be". What can "to be" possibly mean?

9. Is "to be" a power inherent in each being? Is the power "to be" different for different beings? Could we call that power "to be" a possibility, a potential, and a reality?

10. Parmenides proves the One and the impossibility of the many by logical argument. Can the ultimate be deduced by Logic? Would that make the ultimate a logical category?

11. Democritus says that the universe consists of atoms and the void. Atoms whirl in the void without direction. There is no direction, and no up or down. Question: How does this relate to time? Can time be non-linear and without direction? Furthermore, if the notion of up and down does not signify direction, can there also be non-direction in time?

12. Is the non-direction of time related to the notion of eternity?

13. What is an absolute void? Scientists can construct an absolute void in the laboratory. Can an absolute void exist by itself?

14. Do things come to be from other things, or can there be creation from nothing?

Workshop 34. Some Aspects of Aristotelian Metaphysics.

Science studies first principles. First principles are definite and unchanging. Metaphysics is a quest for principles of Being as such. The question of Being, what is it to be? Being is an entity. A non-entity has no Being. Metaphysics is the quest for first causes, first causes of the sensible universe. Philosophy begins in wonder.

What is Substance?

Substance can exist by itself, (it is "a this"). There are substance and accidents (accidental qualities of a thing). Accidents depend on substance for their being. Substance is definite, it has form. Form is the principal sense of being. Every thing ("a this") has form. The form of a fly is higher than the form of a rock. In plants and animals, the soul is form. The form is a principle of organization. In plants, the soul is the power of life, and reproduction. In animals, the soul is what gives growth, reproduction, and perception. For humans, the soul is the rational part of man, it is man as a thinking animal.

Substance points to matter. If we strip away features, we are left with amorphous matter, perhaps prime matter. There must be something (not determinate) behind air, fire, earth, and water. Prime matter is totally amorphous, pure potentiality, and no intelligibility. What underlies fire is prime matter. The same for the other elements. We don't experience prime matter.

What is Essence?

Essence is defined as what the thing is in virtue of itself. Accident is what is neither necessary, nor for the most part. The essence of a thing is that what the thing truly is, the composite of form and matter. All its other qualities (categories of being) are accidental. History, for Aristotle, is filled with accidents. Therefore, there cannot be a science of history.

Form is the essence of a thing. Form is what makes something definite. It defines the thing. Form individualizes matter, the substratum. To lose form is to perish. The form does not come to be. Only the composite comes to be, (dog begets dog, etc.). Form or matter can exist by themselves only potentially, not actually.

The form is not a universal. The form of a dog is an actual living dog, not a universal. Form is universal only in our intellect, not in the way it actualizes the dog. The species dog is only in our intellect. What is particular is the composite. (Those that see universals as substances are Platonists). The form or soul that organizes the material component is not a material component.

For Aristotle, to know a thing is to know its cause. We know things by their causes. The four causes of change, (why a thing comes to be what it is) are : material, formal, final, and efficient causes. The material cause is the material substrate of the thing, (gold of the gold coin). The formal cause is the shape of the coin. The final cause is the end for the sake of which the coin was made (minted). The efficient cause is that which brought the process of making the coin into being. The essence of a thing is the thing's true identity, it is the thing's actual, realized form. Its final cause is identical with its formal cause.

Categories of being:

Substance, quality, quantity, time, place, relation, action, (actual action = motion), passion (suffering motion). Substratum is the potentiality to have one or the other categories.

Aristotle distinguishes four kinds of motion and change: change in quantity, quality, place, and substance. Motion is described as *kinesis* (the end is beyond itself), and *energeia* or activity (the end is in itself). Plant form or plant nature is to grow, and reproduce. They exhibit only motion. Animals grow, reproduce, and have sense perception. They manifest activity as opposed to motion. Man senses, perceives, and thinks. Every organism attempts to approach God at whatever level they can. The soul of a substance is either motion (plant) or activity. For man, it is activity. Motion in a circle is as close as we can get to activity. It is completed every moment. Heavenly motions are as close to the divine mind as one can get. The heavens move in circles. They are moved movers. In order to avoid infinite regress, a first cause is necessary. To arrive at a first cause of motion, there has to be an unmoved mover. The unmoved mover attracts the heavenly bodies. Locomotion is stimulated by a desire to move. Aristotle wants God to be a moving cause, but God is not doing anything to the universe. He just thinks. There is nothing higher than thinking. Thinking is the least dependent of activities. Sense requires other objects, thinking does not. The object of thought needs to be eternal, actual, and thinking itself. God is thought contemplating itself. It moves the universe by attraction (object of desire). Does God think of us? This goes beyond what Aristotle says. All substances aim at activity (to be like God).

Exercises.

1. Do Aristotle's categories denote aspects of being (reality), or are they merely logical terms?

2. Substance can exist by itself, the other categories depend on substance for their being. Discuss and give examples.

3. Aristotle: To know a thing is to know its causes. Discuss.

4. Change may be defined as why a thing comes to be what it is. What are Aristotle's four causes of change?

5. Are Aristotle's four causes reducible to the formal cause? In what sense, and how?

6. What is, according to Aristotle, the essence of a thing? Can we say that it is the same as the Aristotelian substance?

7. What is the source of motion in nature? Is it within itself (within nature), or outside of itself (outside nature)?

8. Theology concerns itself with Being as such. Science studies particular kinds of being. Comment.

Workshop 35.   St. Augustine's Discourse on Time.[1]

To understand time, it is necessary to conceive what transcends time. In order to understand something, it is necessary to get outside of it. We need to have a framework to which we can relate time. Eternity transcends time. What was God doing before he made heaven and earth? God is there for all eternity. What made God suddenly decide to create the world? God's words and man's words: man's words are characterized by succession. God's words are eternal. If there is sequential movement, it represents man's nature, not God's. The ten commandments are anthropomorphic projections of God's words, so that man can understand Him. The notion of creation (of the world) is created by creatures, by humans. God's nature is independent of creation.

St. Augustine (354-430) asks, what is time? He says, if no one asks me what it is, then I know, but if I have to explain it, I don't know. Time is a mystery. Because, if nothing was passing away, there would be no past time, if nothing exists, there is no present time, and if there is nothing to come, there is no future time. But the most real is the present, the past exists no more, and the future does not yet exist. Now, what is time? Is time just the present? If time was only the present, then the present is an eternity, an eternal present. But time is something coming to something which is not yet. It is a present coming from the past, and going into the future.

Some people confuse the notion of eternity with time. Time is not an eternity without end. Eternity is an eternal present. There is a radical difference between a prolongation of time into eternity, and a pure present with no succession. We cannot conceive of succession in eternity. If we conceive of succession, we talk about infinite time, not of eternity. Infinite time is not eternity. When we talk about God foreseeing anything, we project God into time. But God is not in time, God is in eternity.

A basic characteristic of time is necessary succession, past-present-future. Augustine asks: Are there other characteristics of time that we know? If the past is no more, what is the difference between long and short? How can something non-existent be long or short? What is the difference between one hundred years and one million years in the past? Neither one exists any more. Similarly, how can the future be called long or short? Long or short can only apply to the present. For example, we say, we live in the 20th century, but in 1994, we have one year, today we have one day, one hour, one instant, etc. That one hour consists of fleeting moments that cannot be divided or extended. The present moment cannot be extended. The minute I try to extend the present moment, it becomes the past. Isn't this a paradox? Why then is it that we call some moments short or long? We perceive time as if it were made up of intervals that are related to one another in such a way that some are shorter or longer than others. We do somehow measure time. We are measuring passing times, and we measure them as they are passing.

Augustine radically questions "clock" time. Time is not to be equated with measuring the movement of bodies. The clocks that measure time are not time, it is motion. Time is not the movement of planets, or the clock. A measure of time is not time. Time would go on even if the movement stopped. But is it genuine time if it is not measured? For Augustine, the answer is no. Without a mind, there would be no time.

If future and past do not exist, we cannot measure them, but we cannot deny common sense. We know that there is a past, it is an unquestionable fact. The same with the future. But if they are, where are they? The answer is, they are in the present. The past is present in my memory. The past leaves its input in my memory, those events that are present in my memory, and those things that are there as traces and images, (past things that are no longer present in my memory.) My childhood exists in my memory not in the way it really was, but in the vestiges it left behind. I measure the impressions in the mind made by passing things after they have passed. They become memory. The present goes by, and it remains in the memory. The same with the future. The future exists causally in those things that will bring them about. (My grandchildren are causally in my children, etc.) There are three different kinds of present: of things past, (memory), of things present, and of things in the future. All these things are in the soul or mind.

For Augustine, time is a *distentio,* being stretched out. Time is a relation of the mind, a *distentio* of the mind itself. Distention is a non-simultaneity of events, a succession of events identified by the mind. If there is no creature that admits of succession, there cannot be any time at all. Without the mutable creatures, without temporal beings, there is no time. Spiritual mutability is also in time, we have a succession of thoughts. Our thoughts are subject to successiveness. We cannot have more than one idea at a time. We are stretched out over time. I cannot have all my life all at once. The same holds for history. We only have a part of our life at one time, that is a shortcoming, a dissipation. Human beings can make up for this shortcoming, they can overcome this dissipation, by becoming one with eternity, one with God. St. Augustine: "What am I left to myself, I am stretched out, until I am purged by the fire of love and melted onto You. I take my temporality, my sinfulness, my successiveness, and become one with God". By being one with God I become one with myself. Man needs God to be one. Man is the only being that has for his major task in life to make himself one.

The Greeks and the Hindus have a cyclical view of time. Everything keeps repeating itself into infinity. The circle goes on forever. History is unimportant. The elusiveness of time is minimized. The Christian view of time is linear. There was a beginning and there will be an end. History is important. The elusiveness of time is maximized. Each moment is incapable of being repeated. Time is an occasion for qualitative enrichment.

Exercises.

1. "Time is an occasion for qualitative enrichment". Comment.
2. What is the difference between eternity and infinite time?
3. Why is eternity an eternal present?
4. How do you understand the meaning of God in eternity?
5. Are the past and future in the present?
6. Time is a relation of the mind, a distentio, a stretching out. What does St. Augustine mean by that? Can there be time without a mind?

Note

1. *The Confessions of St. Augustine.* Transl. by John K. Ryan, New York: Doubleday, 1960. Book XI.

Workshop 36.   Descartes' Discourse on Method and Meditations on First Philosophy.

Rene Descartes (1596 - 1650) was born in a small town in northern France. When he was 22 years old, he had a dream in which he saw the physical universe entirely explainable in mathematical terms.   He interpreted the dream to mean that he was destined to found a unified science of nature. He had absolute faith in the scientific method, and in the possibilities inherent in science for the improvement of the human condition. Mathematical physics, associated with Galileo, has come into the fore.   Galileo, the father of modern physics, introduced the invariable world of mathematics into the changeable world of nature. The book of nature is written in geometric characters. Nature is mathematical in its core. It is accessible to man not through his senses, but through his thinking capacity. A rational account of nature is a true account. Mathematical physics was in sharp contrast to the old Aristotelian Physics. Aristotelian physics is based on sense-perception. It is descriptive and non-mathematical. Aristotle's view of the sciences is ontological. The sciences deal with different kinds of beings. The different ways of being determine the different sciences. The new physics of Galileo (Galileo Galilei, 1564-1642) met strong resistance from the established ecclesiastic authorities of the Church. It needed a firm foundation and absolute justification. The young Descartes decided to dedicate his life to this task. He was determined to erect an absolutely certain and indubitable foundation for the new science of nature.

1.   The Method.

In Part II of the *Discourse on Method* Descartes lays out certain rules to be followed in any philosophical or scientific inquiry. These rules are: (1). ..."to accept nothing as true which I did not clearly recognize to be so: that is to say, carefully to avoid precipitation and prejudice in judgments, and to accept in them nothing more than what was presented to my mind so clearly and distinctly that I could have no occasion to doubt it. (2). ...to divide up each of the difficulties which I examined into as many parts as possible, and as seemed requisite in order that it might be resolved in the best manner possible. (3). ...to carry on my reflections in due order, commencing with objects that were the most simple and easy to understand, in order to rise little by little, or by degrees, to knowledge of the most complex, assuming an order, even if a fictitious one, among those which do not follow a natural sequence relatively to one another. (4). ....in all cases to make enumerations so complete and reviews so general that I should be certain of having omitted nothing."[1]

We have in these rules the gist of Descartes' theory of knowledge and rational inquiry. Any investigation must be approached with an open mind, without any preconceived notions or prejudices. Judgments should be made only on the basis of evidence discovered in the process of the investigation. Only what presents itself as clear and distinct, and what cannot be doubted, can be accepted as true. Complex problems should be broken down into the simplest constitutive elements, in order to find the best possible solution. It is necessary to proceed in an orderly fashion, in a natural sequence from the most simple to the most complex. And, it is important to make sure that nothing is omitted from the investigation. The Cartesian method is analytical (breaking down a complex problem into its constitutive parts), and also a method of discovery (to find the possible outcome). Cartesian logic presumes to discover the new instead of merely understand what has been known already. Truth is a matter of clarity and distinctness of perception. "Only what is clear and distinct will be accepted as true. ...a perception may be clear without being distinct, but it cannot be distinct unless it is clear."[2] The perception of pain is a clear perception but not distinct. Numbers are distinct units. For Descartes, clear and distinct ideas are for the most part mathematical ideas.

In the Authors Letter to the Translator of his book,[3] Descartes enumerates the two basic conditions underlying his new conception of Philosophy as the study of wisdom: First principles should be absolutely clear and self evident so that the mind cannot doubt their truth. The knowledge of other things depends on first principles. Without them, other things cannot be known. These conditions are articulated in the first two rules of the *Reguli* (1)."*The end of study should be to direct the mind towards the enunciation of sound and correct judgments on all matters that come before it. (2). Only those objects should engage our attention, to the sure and indubitable knowledge of which our mental powers seem to be adequate.* "[4] Human wisdom lies in clear and distinct cognition. Mathematical principles are clear and distinct. They should serve as the basis of our understanding of nature. Everything that is susceptible to true knowing is susceptible to mathematical knowledge. The power of knowing lies in the human mind. We can know the truth by the natural light of reason. Descartes seeks a rational, mathematical account of nature. It is a search of truth by the power of knowing (*lumen naturalis*, the natural light of reason). Nature, the world, is what the mathematical physicist constructs. The ideal of objectivity is oriented toward mathematical validity and exactitude. Scientific objectivity excludes all reference to human purpose and teleology in general. There are no final causes in nature.

The ideal of objectivity requires the thinking subject. Subjectivity becomes the foundation of the new ideal of objective science.

The intellect is pure spirit. It alone is capable of grasping the real truth. Philosophical reasoning must employ the same kind of method as mathematics. Philosophical problems can be resolved through the application of the mathematical method as the basis for a universal science, *mathesis universalis*. First principles are its starting points. The philosopher needs to show how the first principles are arrived at. Intuition and deduction are the only methodic ways of arriving at the truth of things. Intuition is intellectual cognition that is most simple and direct. *Intuere* means to see, gaze at, or look upon. Understanding is compared to seeing (Plato, Plotinus (205-270), Augustine (354-430), Husserl, Edmund, (1859-1938)). Intuition is "the undoubting conception of an unclouded and attentive mind, and springs from the light of reason alone."[5] Clarity and distinctness are the criteria for truth. Innate ideas, (mind, matter, substance, God) are clear and distinct. They are simple natures. Complex data are to be resolved into their simple elements. The simple natures are "analytically irreducible elements of intelligibility." They are grasped intuitively. There are three classes of simple natures:

1. Purely spiritual (knowing , doubting , willing).

2. Purely material: (extension, figure, motion).

3. Common to both, spiritual and corporeal things (existence, unity, duration, causality, logic, common notions, and axioms). They enable us to make deductions. The first principle of knowing is the finite thinking self. The order of thinking (soul), and the order of the material world (body), are distinct and independent of each other.

One identical method pertains to all human problems. The method consists in the correct application of the power of knowing. The power of knowing is a purely spiritual power. It is radically separated from all the bodily functions. All sciences are interconnected and form a unity.

Thus philosophy as a whole is like a tree whose roots are metaphysics, whose trunk is physics, and whose branches, which issue from this trunk, are all the other sciences. These reduce themselves to three principal ones, viz. medicine, mechanics and morals - I mean the highest and most perfect moral science, which presupposing a complete knowledge of the other sciences, is the last degree of wisdom.
(*Discourse on the Method. The Philosophical works of Descartes,* Renderd into English by Elizabeth S. Haldane, C.H., LL.D. and G.R.T. Ross, M.A., D. Phil. Cambridge: The University Press, 1970. p.211.)

The chief use of wisdom lies in man's mastery over the passions.The sciences reside in the mind. The mind (the subject) is the foundation of all knowledge. The end of knowledge is the improvement of the human condition. (Descartes, in his absolute faith in science, did not foresee that science could be morally neutral, and therefore can be put to any possible use, whether good or bad.)

2.   Meditations on First Philosophy.

In order to establish an absolutely indubitable foundation for all human knowledge, Descartes will rid himself of all opinion he previously held. He will subject everything to radical doubt. Whatever can be subject to the slightest doubt, he will consider as false. The methodical doubt is a free act of the mind whose purpose is to eliminate all doubt. The methodical doubt engulfes the external world of sense experience, including his own body. The awareness of his body comes through the senses. There is no absolute way to distinguish between waking life and dream life. All reality is open to possible doubt. Even mathematics itself is open to doubt, for "we can be mistaken in what we hold most certain." Mathematical principles become doubtful by employing the device of the evil demon, and the hyperbolic doubt. Perhaps "some evil genius not less powerful than deceitful, has employed his whole energies in deceiving me;"[6] Descartes systematically and rigorously pushes doubt to the utmost limit in order to establish the ground for the structure of the sciences. He has doubted traditional knowledge, sense experience, the sciences, metaphysical phantasies, and mathematical knowledge. He seeks one absolutely certain principle that will escape the methodical doubt, and which will serve as the foundation for the indubitable truth. In the second Meditation, he finds such principle. The act of doubting cannot be doubted. After all the doubting, what remains is the doubting itself. The reflecting philosopher survives all the doubting. The meditating philosopher undoubtedly exists. *Ego cogito, ego sum.* Thinking, consciousness implies being. The "I think" implies the "I am". The "I am" presupposes the "I think".   Consciousness for Descartes, is primarily self-consciousness. *Cogitatio* include all mental acts, thinking, volition, feeling, judging, and perceiving, These are all different forms of consciousness. The methodical doubt concludes with the discovery of consciousness - subjectivity, as the most fundamental and indubitable truth of all philosophy. By discovering what survives even the most extreme and exaggerated doubts, we can establish an unshakable and firm foundation for philosophy. Descartes has discovered the Archimedean point upon which the whole science of demonstrable knowledge can be based. Consciousness or subjectivity becomes the proper subject matter of philosophical discourse. The doubting and the doubting philosopher, both exist. He can now escape the state of doubt that he is in. He invokes God to rescue him from the evil demon. Mathematical truths are of divine creation, and God in his infinite wisdom would not allow an evil demon to deceive him.

The principal goal of the third Meditation is to establish the validity of the representational function of clear and distinct ideas. There is an external world beyond the "I think", but it is one that we know only in terms of mathematical construction. It is not at all similar in truth to our sense perception. In the fourth Meditation, Decartes is concerned with the qustion of cognitive truth and falsity. God's veracity gives validity to all clear and distinct ideas. It gives certitude to mathematical truths. The act of judgment involves a passive recognition of content (ideas), and an affirmation or denial of the passive apprehension. The passive assent is attributed to the understanding. The active assent is attributed to the will. There are two modes of the "I think": *intellectus* (understanding) and the will. The understanding includes the totality of all clear and distinct ideas. Will is wider than intellect. Understanding is a passion. Volition is an action. An assent is an act of will. Both faculties of the mind, the understanding and the will, are dependent on God. The natural perfection of the will is that it should extend beyond its limits. The principle perfection of man is the power to act freely. If our actions (of the will) were limited to clear and distinct ideas, we would not be acting freely. Clear and distinct ideas are limited in number. The will is unlimited. Therefore, our will can decide to assent to matters that are not clearly and distinctly perceived. If clear ideas are absent, we should ideally suspend judgment. The understanding, by its nature, is potentiality for truth. The connection of mind and body leads to the production of ideas that are different from clear and distinct ideas. Adventitious ideas come from the outside. Sensation can arise only in the mind-body context. Throughout the entire fourth Meditation, Descartes underlines the separatedness of the of the mode of the will from the understanding, although both are included in the "I think". If I assent wrongly, I err. The union of body with the mind gives rise to all those natural instincts and animal appetites by which we are inclined to make overhasty judgments. Error or falsehood is a deficient way of acting. As long as we are using our capacity for understanding in line with our will, we are not subject to error.

In the fifth Meditation, after proving the existence of God, [which we will not discuss here, except to say, that it rests on Anselm's (Anselm, St. 1033-1109) ontological argument], Descartes restores the validity of the mathematical ideas. Divine veracity eliminates the doubt with respect to mathematical ideas. But sensible things remain dubious even with a truthful God. Mathematical ideas are not dubious in themselves. External things are dubious in themselves. God's veracity is not sufficient for our attribution of objective reality (knowledge) to the external world. The existence of material and perceptible things is established in the sixth meditation, on the proposition that God is not a deceiver. God has given us a very great inclination to believe that ideas of sensible things are conveyed to us by corporeal objects. ..."if these ideas were produced by causes other than corporeal objects, He could be accused of deceit. Hence we must allow that corporeal things exist."[7] The existence of God is required to give us a foundation for our cognition of the external world and for the principle of distinctness and clarity as the criteria for true ideas. Without God, I cannot be certain of anything. The proof of the existence of God is the solution to this problem.

3.   The Cartesian Theory of Ideas.

In modern philosophy, ideas are effects of causes that are not ideas. My idea of the sun is the result of the sun being out there. In pre-modern thought, the meaning of idea was not understood as a structural part of the human intellect. For Descartes, ideas are forms that our acts of thinking take on. Ideas belong to the sphere of subjectivity. They are modes of consciousness. My idea of the sun is related to the real sun in various ways. We may have different ideas of the sun: visual (from perception), astronomical (from books), aesthetic (sunset), etc. The visual sun is very different from the astronomical sun. The Cartesian theory of ideas is a representative theory of ideas. My idea of the sun is precisely my idea, a modification of my consciousness. I relate to the external world through my consciousness.   We have no knowledge of what is outside us except through the medium of ideas within us. Ideas are conscious occurrences in the mind. They are images of things. What has hitherto been called objective has come to acquire a new meaning. Objective comes to mean not the object in itself but what I take to be objective. Objectivity means that which is meant to be objective. If the universe is not as it looks but as it has been constructed, it involves elements of consciousness necessary to construct it. This is the true objective account of the universe.

4.   Mind   and   Body.

The mind is an immaterial (unextended) substance whose principal attribute is thought (thinking , willing, feeling, perceiving, doubting). The essence of the mind is to think. As such it is truly distinct from the physical body. The self consists of the mind alone, and it is intrinsically independent of the body. The thinking part of us is entirely non-material, a separable spirit created by God. Mind is by nature indivisible. Thinking is reflexive. When I think, I know that I think. I am a thinking thing, *res cogitans.* ..."my essence consists in that I am a thinking thing." Mind and body are separate substances, distinct from each other. ..."this I [that is to say, my soul by which I am what I am], is entirely and absolutely distinct from my body, and can exist without it."[8] This is the famous Cartesian dualism.

Extension, (sheer three dimensionality or empty space), underlies the material universe. It is the essence of corporeal substance. (A substance is the bearer of attributes, also that which can exist by itself.) Individual items (planets, horses, trees, etc.) are modifications of the single extended substance. Matter, is a pure idea of reason. Pure matter is homogeneous, featureless extension. The conception of matter as extension is not derived from the senses. It is innate. Extension or space has no limits. Extension is a contiguous plenum, without void. The notion of an empty space is incoherent, for "the extension constituting the nature of a body is the same as that constituting the nature of space." Matter is infinitely divisible. God introduced a conservable quantity of motion into the plenum. Parts of matter (bodies) are distinguished by different parts of motion. Figure and motion are the modes of extension. Motion is the principle of differentiation between bodies. Laws of matter and motion are uniform throughout the universe. There are two worlds: the world of sense experience, and the mathematically constructed world. The mathematical account of the world is the true one. The scientific method consist in the application of the universal science of relation and proportion to physical bodies. We can know nothing in nature except what is susceptible to relation and proportion. There is the complete separation between the true reality of mathematical physics, and the false reality of the experienced world. Descartes' Meditations are to justify this thesis.

The Cartesian split between mind and body led to a mechanistic concept of nature, and a spiritualistic concept of mind. The body is compared to a machine (animals are like machines, purely mechanical automata, without soul or mind.) For Aristotle, animals and plants have souls. There are degrees of souls, plant soul, animal soul, and human soul. Descartes rejected the notion of grades of soul. Man is the composite of two independent substances, mind and body. These are united in composition, not in their essence. Life is found only at the level of mind. Mind and body act on each other mechanically, by way of efficient causality. The mind controls the body through the pineal gland. The mind interacts with other bodies and thus forms particular ideas of them. Ideas are modifications of mind just as bodies are modifications of matter. The representational content of an idea is called objective reality. Innate ideas, such as, God, substance, mind, extension, are those of the mind itself.

5. The Dual Theory of Perception.

Imagination refers to to the contemplation of external things. Imagination is our consciousness of externality. The interiority of consciousness is not disclosed to the imagination. The certainty of my existence does not reveal to me the meaning of the "I". I can be certain that I am, but uncertain of what I am. Sense perception belongs to the body. The experience of sense perception are acts of consciousness. Consciousness is a necessary but insufficient reason for the experience of sense perception. The reverse does not hold. Sense perception is not necessary for a conscious being. The soul is entirely distinct from the conception of the body. The example with the wax in the second Meditation: The stripping of the wax from all its sensible properties has not removed the identity of the wax. To the extent that the wax possesses distinctness, it is not through the senses. The knowledge of the material world cannot be gotten through sense perception. We must distinguish between the (geometric) properties that properly belong to a body, and the secondary qualities that don't. Wax near the fire is susceptible to indefinite variation of primary qualities (shapes and forms) that is beyond our imagination. The perceptual apprehension of an identical thing in light of the variation of its properties requires more than the sense data. This is Descartes' dual theory of perception. The sense (seeing, touching, smelling, etc.) involves consciousness, the cogito, the "I". The true being of a bodily object (extension) can only be grasped by the mind. Consciousness is a medium of access to itself and to everything outside the self. It is a universal medium of accessibility. The entities present themselves to us as they involve our consciousness. Modern philosophy deals with our experience and our consciousness, and it has absolute priority over what we are conscious of. In the order of ideas it is more easy to know the mind than the outside world.

The imagination cannot be a source of knowledge of the external world. In pre-modern thought, imagination was a rich source of knowledge. In modern thought, imagination loses its universality, and retains its aesthetic significance only. The faculties of imagination and sensation are not like understanding. They require a physical activity in the brain. Psychophysical phenomena (vision) cannot be clasified as purely mental or purely physical. They are both. Sensory experiences are absolutely fundamental to what makes a human being. Descartes (and Spinoza) start from original ideas (axioms), such as, substance, mode, extension, etc. These original ideas are not verified. The mind can acquire philosophical truth only after it frees itself from prejudice. The avoidance of error entails both understanding (the clarity and distinctness of ideas), and the will. Our understanding is limited, but the human will is unlimited. Belief is a matter of assent. Assent depends on the will. The latter is the source of prejudice and error.

Descartes' view is subjective and epistemological, not ontological. With Descartes, subjectivity becomes the foundation of objectvity. The human mind determines the subject matter. Numbers are creations of the mind, but space is a creation of God. A body can be conceived as extended in length, depth and breadth. Whatever is spatially represented becomes the subject matter of science.

Exercises.

1. How does the Cartesian view of objectivity differ from the correspondence theory of truth?
2. What role do "innate ideas" play in Decartes' theory of cognitive truth?
3. Discuss the notions of clarity and distinctness as criteria of truth.
4. What are Descartes' simple natures? Give examples.
5. Descartes sought to establish an absolutely certain starting point for all science. What is this starting point?
5. For Descartes, the subject, (the ego) is the foundation for all knowledge. Knowledge is to be sought in the subject, instead of, in the outside world. How is this different from Aristotle?
6. Hegel calls Descartes the father of modern philosophy. Why?
7. Do you agree that nature is inherently mathematical? Does nature follow mathematical rules? Discuss.
8. What are the Cartesian substances? Why are they called substances?
9. Is the knowledge (idea) of a thing the same as the thing?
10. For Descartes, pure intellect is independent of the senses. Explain.
11. The mathematization of science is one of the great legacies of Descartes. In physics, it led to great scientific discoveries. Is the same true of the biological sciences?
12. What about the social sciences? Can the social universe be captured through mathematics?
13. What have been the consequences of Descartes' dualism, the separation of mind and body? Discuss both the positive and negative aspects.
14. What is the meaning of wisdom for Descartes?

Notes

1. *Discourse on the Method.   The Philosophical works of Descartes,* Renderd into English by Elizabeth S. Haldane, C.H., LL.D. and G.R.T. Ross, M.A., D. Phil. Cambridge: The University Press, 1970. p.92.
2. *Principles of Philosophy.*   Ibid. p. 237.

3. *Author's Letter*. Ibid. pp. 203-215.
4. *Rules for the Direction of the Mind*. Ibid. vol.1. pp. 1-3.
5. Ibid. vol.1. p.7.
6. *Meditations on First Philosophy*.   Ibid. p. 148.
7. Ibid. p. 191.
8. Ibid. p. 191.

Workshop 37. Modern and Premodern Philosophy: Continuity or Radical Break?

1. The New Physics of Galileo.

The new physics of Galileo represents a radical break from Aristotelian physics. Galileo, the father of the new physics, conceived it as a mathematical science. Nature was understood to be mathematical in its core. The invariant world of mathematics was introduced and applied to the variant world of nature. A mathematical science of nature is in many ways at odds with human experience. Aristotelian physics is based on sense perception, and it is non- mathematical. It is a common sense view of nature without mathematical abstractions. It is compatible with human experience. It is as nature presents itself to us.

Modern physics derives its inspiration from Plato. In Plato, mathematics belongs to one level of the invariant world of ideas, (the divided line in the Republic). The Platonists and the Pythagoreans developed a mathematical physics and astronomy. There is a fundamental opposition between Plato and Aristotle. Aristotle understood nature as movement and process. The subject of physics is motion (change and process). "Motion (kinesis) is a process in which something which has the power to become a definite something else becomes that something else. It is thus the continuous actualization of what is potential" (Physics III, Chpt. I, 201 a 10-12.). Physics included biology where change is peculiar to living organisms. Process and function are fundamental ideas in biology. Aristotelian physics is descriptive, qualitative, and non-mathematical. It is teleological and functional, not purely mechanical.

The mathematical abstractions of the new physics are removed from nature. They are accessible to reason without any reference to nature. Mathematical principles are not accountable to the senses. They are accessible to man in his capacity to think. It is a rational rather than a natural account of the external world.

2. The Cartesian Revolution.

To justify the new science of physics, Descartes had to develop a new first philosophy, a new metaphysics that will serve as an absolute, certain foundation for the new physics. The true science of nature is mathematical. A rational account of nature claims to be the true account. What is not rational is relegated to mere experiences or phenomena, and is viewed as false. The gap between the scientific account of experience, and ordinary human experience had to be dealt with. The new science of physics had to be based on absolute certainty.

That absolute certainty was to be based on human consciousness or subjectivity. Descartes discovered consciousness when he pursued the foundation for all physics. A metaphysics of subjectivity became the foundation of objectivity, an absolute foundation of all science. This is the Cartesian revolution. It radically altered man's understanding of science, religion, and his conception of knowledge.

3. A New Conception of Philosophy and Science: Epistemology Versus Ontology.

Aristotelianism emphasizes the primacy of subject matter, the experienced world as encountered. Thus, the primacy of ontology. Man can grasp the structure, and relation of things, and expresses them in logos. ("Things are what they can be said to be.") Knowledge is how we can best state in language what we have found out. Inquiry starts with reality or being, and with what is given in nature *(to on.)* The premodern *eidos* (idea) is a datum, an object (it is ontological). In premodern thought, an image is derivative of the original (object). (Plato's things are images of ideas or the forms.)

For Descartes, knowledge of material things cannot be gotten through sense perception. He gives the example of the wax. Wax changes its color and texture under various conditions of heat. Descartes wants to distinguish between what properly belongs to the body, namely extension, and all the other properties. In modern philosophy, the power of the human mind, the "I", becomes the ultimate foundation of all knowledge. Our own consciousness has absolute priority over what we are conscious about. Knowledge is to be utilitarian. It has to serve human needs and purposes. The conquest of nature for the improvement of the human condition, is the ideal. For the Ancients, knowledge was for its own sake. (Philosophy begins with wonder.) Descartes substituted the quest for useful knowledge instead of knowledge for its own sake. His new metaphysics, whose core was the discovery of subjectivity upon which the new science was to be grounded, will culminate in a moral science. Descartes could not foresee that this new science will be morally neutral, and therefore amenable to any possible use. For the Ancients, knowledge and goodness go together, (virtue is knowledge, in the Meno.) In so far, as Descartes conceived of philosophy as the ultimate of human possibilities, it is the same as the Greeks formal definition of philosophy. But he differs from the Ancients in the utilitarian character of his philosophy. For Descartes it was the quest for useful knowledge, "the opening up of undreamed of possibilities" that served as the motive power for knowing.

4. The Unity of Science and the Singularity of Method.

Aristotle classified the sciences into: theoretical (first philosophy, physics and mathematics), practical (ethics, politics), and productive (medicine, architecture, etc.) (Metaphysics, Book VI, 1025 b3 -1026 a 32). This classification covers the whole of man's intellectual activity. The activity of mankind (man as a rational animal) was divided into: *noesis* - thinking (theoretical sciences), *praxis* - action (practical sciences), and *poiesis* - making (productive sciences). In so far as all of the above is alive with logos, he calls it philosophy or science. Science is determined by what it is, namely, by its object. The object is prior to the faculty *(dynamis)* of science.   There is thus an ontologicaal priority to science. The different ways of being determine the different possibilities for the different sciences. This is what Descartes rejects.

For Descartes, the distinction between the theoretical and the practical science breaks down. For him, there is a unity of all sciences. There is one philosophy, and one identical method pertinent to all human problems. "Thus philosophy as a whole is like a tree whose roots are metaphysics, whose trunk is physics and whose branches.... are all the other sciences (...medicine, mechanics and morals).[1] Each part is an articulation of the unified science, i.e. philosophy. Science is entirely constituted by clear cognition and distinct propositions that are true and evident, (Rule two of the Regulae). Mathematics alone has such a character (universal mathematics). Descartes' view is subjective or epistemological, not ontological. One identical method determines all objects of human knowledge. It is not the objects which determine the character of the sciences (philosophy), but the very acts of the human mind (subjectivity, consciousness), by linking objects together, relating, measuring, etc., that lead to their knowledge. It is a dynamic production instead of an order of classification. (Aristotelian logic is a logic of classification, genera and species, a lower kind of logic.) For Descartes, the faculty of knowing, the human mind *(vis cognoscens)* is the foundation of all rational knowledge.   His methodical doubt concludes with the discovery of consciousness or subjectivity as the most fundamental, indubitable truth of all philosophy. With this, consciousness takes on a privileged position in philosophy. With Descartes', *"ego cogito, ego sum"*, philosophy was transplanted to the sphere of subjectivity as with one stroke (Hegel). For Descartes, the search for truth is the cultivation and the perfection of the power of knowing, the natural light of reason.

5.   Continuity   and   Difference   with   the   Ancients   in Leibniz.

Leibniz praises the Schoolmen for allowing us to understand the universe through the substantial forms, but he also accuses them for using these forms to explain phenomena.   The latter leads to tautological reasoning.   Contrary to Aristotle, Leibniz affirms that final causes can only be seen in the essences of God's creation, and not in the existence of individual things.   Leibniz affirms his intellectual debt to Plato's immutable essences, (i.e. his theory of Forms) partaking in the mutable existencies.[2] God seeks the greatest perfection.   There are truths of reason and truths of fact.   Truths of reason are necessary truths since their opposite involves contradiction.   Truths of fact are contingent truths, their opposite does not involve a contradiction. God is free to choose why things are thus, and not otherwise. This is what is behind the principle of sufficient reason.   All phenomena agree because they all relate to God. This is the meaning of concomitance.   In the world, there is maximum   compossible perfection.   God is the principle of harmony.   All substances (monads) although independent, agree with each other perfectly.   This concomitance explains the union of mind and body. Mind and body are perfectly synchronized. There is no interaction between mind and body.   Body and soul follow independent laws, but there is perfect synchronization betweem them.
The monad is a metaphysical atom without parts and without extension. It is a simple substance, a primitive and unified center of force. The monad is indivisible and immaterial. It can only be created (or annihilated) by God. It has no windows, and does not communicate with other monads. A monad is a world by itself. It has no direct interaction with other monads. Each monad contains some intrinsic affection, otherwise they would all be the same. The monad has two main (immaterial) activities: perception (of the outside), and appetition (the striving for greater clarity of perception). The monad is a complete being. It is essentially a force, not a quantity. The force appears as perception and appetition. Perception is representative of the whole. Apperception or self-consciousness is conscious perception. Appetition - it is an internal principle that produces change. Change signifies a transition from one perception to another.   Through appetiton, the whole is realized in the part.   The monads are real ultimate elements. They cannot be dissolved, since they have no parts.   Each monad represents the whole from a special perspective. The totality of the monads represent the universe from every possible perspective. There is continuity of perception. Each monad differs from another in the least possible way.   No two monads are exactly alike. Everything in the universe is closely connected in perfect order, there are no breaks in the chain, there is infinite gradation in intension (perception and

appetition). Nature is a plenum filled with monads. The universe is not an infinite mass occupying space, but an infinite gradation of monadic differences, each one containing within it the principle of change (appetition). The universe is thus an intensive continuum of force or life.

Matter is ruled by the laws of motion. Spirit is ruled by the laws of justice. Motion is a derivative of force. Force is measured by the quantity of the effect. There are no motionless bodies. The force is in the corporeal mass. There is an infinite number and variety of substances: substances that think, and substances that dont think. An individual substance is a center of force. A substance is capable of action. Principle of individuation: no two substances are entirely alike, (identity of indiscernibles). Substances share perception but differ in their capacities for perceptual operations. There are gradations of beings. The world is a true plenum of individual substances. There are no empty spaces, no leaps, and no vacuum in nature. There is also temporal continuity: the present contains the past and is pregnant with the future. There is no real causality between substances, there is no causal connection between thought and motion, there is only concomittance. Cause - effect are equivalent. In substance, evidences of the future are traces of the past. Outside substance, there are only phenomena, relations and abstractions. Matter is infinitely divisible. There are no indivisible atoms in matter, the smallest part still has parts. Extended mass is pure phenomenon. There is only being by aggregation, no real being. Compound substances perceived by our senses are *phenomena bene fundata,* well founded phenomena. Although things don't have a true unity, this does not make them unreal. The dominant monad in the aggregate (the body compound) with the clearest perception, is the organizing principle - *entelechy.* Every finite *entelechy* is embodied. The body is the finite perspective of the immortal soul. Space and time are abstractions. A-priori truths, such as, perception, cause, substance, identity, are truths of reason. They express divine understanding, (logic, geometry, number). Contingent truths are truths of fact, they express divine will, (their opposite does not imply contradiction). The principle of sufficient reason is behind all existence. Necessary truths (God's decrees) are founded on God's understanding. The identity of indiscernibles (the indiscernible differences between the monads) demonstrates the plurality of substances. God produces substances through emanation (sudden flashings). Recognition always presupposes precognition. Laws of mechanics explain nature, but these laws must be explained metaphysically.

Lebniz sees Aristotle as a philosopher of particularity, while with Plato, the particular always leads to universal content. This makes Plato the greater philosopher of the two. Ideas, according to Leibniz, are stored in us. We have the power to represent to us the essence, nature, or the form of a thing. This is what is called the idea of a thing. "This is in us, and is always in us, whether we are thinking of it or no." Also, "nothing can be taught us of which we have not already in our minds the idea....This is what Plato has excellently brought out in his doctrine of reminiscence."[3] Leibniz explicitly connects his theory of knowledge to that of Plato.

For Leibniz, all cognition presupposes precognition. An idea is what is always already in the soul, whereby a conception is what is constructed by us. For Aristotle, our souls are like blank tablets, and all our understanding is based on sense perception. This is in accord with ordinary usage (naive realism). Such ordinary usage is not necessarily wrong, but it is not thorough enough. Leibniz thinks that Aristotle's position is more in accord with popular conceptions. But Plato, is the more profound thinker of the two. When we deal with metaphysical truths, we must look to what "extends infinitely further than is commonly supposed."[4] Conceptions that we have of ourselves and of our thoughts, such as our ideas of being, substance, action, identity, etc., have their roots in us, and are not derived from the outside. They come from our inner experience, not from the outside (the senses). The soul expresses the body, and the universe.

Leibniz wants to reconcile the language of metaphysics with practical life, that is, with ordinary speech. He wants to recover the Platonic theory of reminiscence when purged of transmigration of souls. For Plato, knowledge is recollection, i.e. preservation of the past. If one is thinking metaphysically, that is, against common sense, then only God is the external object of perception. "I see everything in the divine Light".

St Augustine expresses the same thought in his "Concerning the Teacher". We have in us the power to affirm or deny the validity of any statement. We can differentiate fiction from fact, truth from falsity, when the neccessary conditions for these distinctions are present.

For **Spinoza**, the best way to compare him with the Ancients is to quote him directly: "The Authority of Plato, Aristotle, and Socrates does not carry much weight with me. I should have been astonished, if you had brought forward Epicurus, Democritus, Lucretius or any of the atomists or upholders of the atomic theory. It is no wonder that persons, who have invented occult qualities, intentional species, substantial forms, and a thousand other trifles, should also have devised spectres and ghosts, and given credence to old wive's tales, in order to take away the reputation of Democritus, whom they were so jealous of, that they burnt all the books which he had published amid so much eulogy."[5] Spinoza acknowledges his intellectual debt to Democritus and the atomists. There is indeed, a direct continuity betwen Spinoza's world view and that of the atomists. The atomists may be seen as a response to Parmenides, (that being or matter is One, an unchanging unity of one reality), and as a way to reconcile the One with the perceptible many. The fundamental unity and immutability of all underlying (physical) matter and being (reality), is a necessary prerequisite for the operation of the laws of nature. The latter are unchanging and eternal. Points of similarities between Spinoza and the atomists can be seen in the unity of substance and the multiplicity of modes. Nature is conceived as a single individual "(the face of the universe"), whose parts change in infinite ways but whose nature remains the same. Physical bodies consist of different configurations of motion and rest, and change consists in an alteration of their proportion. This is similar to the atomists position which explains change by the variability of arrangement, size and position of the atoms.

Exercises.

1. Modern philosophy begins with Galileo and Descartes. Explain why.
2. Plato and the Pythagoreans developed a mathematical view of nature. Aristotle saw nature as movement and process. Discuss the meaning of each.
3. What is the Cartesian revolution?
4. Can sense perception give us knowledge of the world around us?
5. Is the physical universe the basis of our knowledge?
6. Is knowledge to be gotten for its own sake (as the Ancients thought), or is knowledge to be gotten because it is useful (as Descartes thought)? What is your view on this?
7. What is Plato's doctrine of reminiscence? Is all coginition pre-cognition? What is Leibniz's view? St. Augustine: "We have in our power to affirm or deny the validity of any statement". Is this the same as the theory of reminiscence?
8. What does Spinoza think of Plato's substantial forms? What does Spinoza think of Democritus and Epicurus?

Notes

1. Rene Descartes, *The Preface to the Principles of Philosophy,* Author's Letter, Haldane & Ross trans. vol. I, p.211.).
2. Leibniz, *Discourse on Metaphysics,* Prop. XX.
3. Ibid. Prop. XXVI.
4. Ibid. Prop. XXVII.
5. Benedict De Spinoza, *On the Improvement of the Understanding, The Ethics, Correspondence.* R.H.M. Elwes transl. Spinoza's Letter to Hugo Boxel, Letter LX. New York: Dover Publications, Inc. 1955. p. 388.

Workshop 38. Proofs of the Existence of God.

Proofs for the existence of God go back to the Old Testament. The Book of Wisdom: "All men are vain in whom there is not an understanding of God." The Creator is known through the beauty of nature. It is a proof from the effect to the cause. Cause must precede and contain at least as much power as the effect. St. Augustine: "Who made heaven and earth? God is the Creator." Augustine also refers to God as the truth. To possess God is to possess the truth. In Book 2. On the Free Choice of the will, Augustine gives a formal proof of the existence of God. It is a proof from the life of the mind, and from the awareness of truth. Existence, life, and understanding, *(esse, vivere , intelligere)* constitute the three levels of reality. (We know that we exist, that we have life, and that we have understanding.) The three levels of reality are hierarchical: existence is the lowest, life is the middle level, and understanding is the highest level. The higher level always involves the lower. We start from the awareness of the life of the mind. Augustine asks: What is higher than understanding? Objective truth, truth that is common to each mind, is higher than understanding. Unchangeable truth (laws of nature) exists, and such truth is independent of the individual mind. Objective and common truth is transcendent to the mind perceiving it. Can we judge the truth or does it judge us? All we can do to the truth is bear witness to it. God is the ultimate truth, the supreme measure. Truth is higher than I am. Truth itself is God. It is eternal, common, objective, and independent of me. It measures me, and I don't measure it. Truth is the highest reality. This, Augustine claims, is all we need to say that God exists.

Aristotle saw God as the world's "prime mover". He is incorporeal, and the heavens move by the force of His attraction. God is Thought reflecting on itself, (on Thought). The heavenly bodies move by the love of god.

The ontological proof for the existence of God was first formulated by St. Anselm and afterwards used by Descartes. This proof is based on the a-priori reasoning of God's essence. A more perfect being then God is not even conceivable. Since nothing greater than God can be conceived, there must be something that corresponds to it in reality. For Descartes, the idea of a supremely perfect being must necessarily include existence as one of its attributes. It would be a contradiction to think of a supremely perfect being which did not include the attribute of existence. The latter would deny its supreme perfection.

Cosmological arguments for the existence of God are given by St. Thomas Aquinas. They are arguments from motion, from efficient causality, and from contingency. The argument from motion runs like this: Whatever is moved, must be moved by another. Motion is the reduction of potency to act. Nothing can be reduced from potency to act except by act. If infinite regress is to be ruled out, there must be a first mover who is pure Act (God). God is the cause of all cosmic motion. (Aristotle: The first mover moves itself and thereby causes motion in the entire universe.) Proof from efficient cause: A being cannot be its own efficient cause, since it would have to be prior to itself, which is not possible. There cannot be an infinite regress of causes, for without a first efficient cause there would not be any intermediate cause. Therefore, there must be a first efficient cause for the existence of things, (God).

Proof from the necessary being: There is a difference between the possible and the necessary. The possible (contingent) can either be or not be. The possible derives ts existence not from itself but from a necessary being, namely, God. Descartes in the Third Meditation says, that God is the cause not only of our creation but of our continued existence, ("...from whom could I.... derive my existence") if there were no God.

Kant's Refutation of the Proofs for the Existence of God.

The concept of an absolutely necessary Being is a concept of reason, not of fact. The necessity of judgment is not the same as the necessity of things. Surely, the idea of the most perfect being must contain existence as one of its predicates. If I reject the predicate (existence) and retain the subject (the concept of the highest, perfect being), there is a contradiction. However, if I reject the subject as well as the predicate, then there is no contradiction. The concept of all reality, (of the most real thing *ens reallissimum)* necessarily contains existence as one of its attributes. But the absence of a contradiction in a concept does not prove the actual existence of the object. The error lies in the failure to differentiate between a logical predicate and a real predicate. If the proposition is an analytical one, (i.e. reality includes existence), then it is tautological. If the proposition is synthetical, (i.e. it is added to the subject), then it can be removed without contradiction. The concept of God, Kant says, is a useful idea, but we cannot conclude from it that God exists.

The refutation of the cosmological proof:

The cosmological argument for the existence of God is demonstrated from the existence of contingent beings. The principle that everything contingent has a necessary cause is valid only in the world of sense. It does not apply to the supersensible. The existence of a first cause (God) is an inference beyond experience, and cannot therefore be subject of possible knowledge. Many powers of nature remain unknown to us, (a reference to the infinite attributes of Spinoza's substance?), because they are not subject to our possible experience of them, i.e. the nouminal world. The principle of the greatest possible unity of all phenomena cannot be experienced itself. It may serve as a regulative principle but not as a constitutive principle.

The idea of God is beyond possible experience. The conditioned cannot experience the unconditioned (a supreme Being). Knowledge can only relate to possible experience. The concept of a supreme Being as the original cause of all empirical reality satisfies reason's need for unity, order, and system in nature, but its principle must be outside nature. While the idea of a supreme Being, as the author of the universe with all the splendor and majesty of nature is a worthwhile idea in itself, it cannot be raised to apodictic certainty. We may accept it as an article of faith, but we cannot dogmatically assert it, based on supposed proof. The existence of God is a matter of faith, and not of possible knowledge. Faith must however be based on reason. It is reasonable to suppose the existence of God, and the immortality of the soul.

The concept of freedom under the moral law bridges the gap between the real, and the supersensible. We may account for the existence of the moral law by attributing it to the author of the universe, who instilled in us a final purpose, namely, the adherence to the moral law. The reason for the existence of morality, and the possibility of carrying it out, is given to man by God. Freedom (the basis of the moral law) connects the idea of God, and the immortality of the soul. From a merely practical point of view that is based on faith, we can prove the existence of God from the moral argument. The principle of freedom determines the idea of the supersensible both within us, and outside us.

Moral purposiveness (teleology) gives us the concept of God (a single author of the universe) that is suitable for religion. The concept of God is used here merely from a practical, not a theoretical point of view. The categories (causation, etc.) apply to objects of possible experience as a condition for their theoretical cognition. I can think of a supersensible being without trying to cognize it. This causality (of thought to being)   pertains to the universe of moral aims and not to the sensual world. We can reason by analogy (with our categories from the sensual world), and derive a cognition of the existence of a supreme being from a practical point of view.

The ontological and cosmological proofs of the existence of God and their refutation still leave open the proposition that God may be the immanent cause of the universe, and not its transient cause. This presupposes the identity of God and nature, or that God's substance is contained in the whole of nature. This is not a pantheistic identification of nature (as we experience it) with God. It is not pantheism, but panentheism, namely, that God is not of empirical nature but is in empirical nature. (Thus, God is not me but God is in me, God is not the mountain, the river, etc., but God is in the mountain, the river, etc.) This is the essence of Spinoza'a metaphysics. The whole of nature is the single substance which is called God. God is the all inclusive totality of nature.

Substance is defined as that which is in itself, and conceived through itself (Spinoza, Ethics I, Prop. III.). There can only be one such substance. For suppose that there were more than one, then each would have to be conceived through the other (or others), and not by itself. Therefore, there can only be one substance, one nature, one God. Since there is only one substance, all its attributes and modifications must be derived from its essential nature. Nothing exists outside substance, and no modification or change could be caused from the outside. Substance is therefore self caused *(causa sui)*. Rational understanding consists in the knowledge of causes of things. If there was more than one substance, then the cause of each would lie in, or necessitate the other. They could not be self- caused. Or again, suppose that there were many self-caused substances. If all change and modification are to be derived from within (according to their essential nature as per definition of substance), then the universe would be arbitrary, and could not exhibit regularity. This would make rational knowledge impossible. It follows, that there can only be one substance (God) which comprises the whole of the universe. Substance is the cause of itself *(causa sui)*, and the ultimate cause of everything that is in nature. This makes nature an intelligible whole. It is intelligible, because we can understand, and grasp the system of causes in nature, and nature itself, as being the ground of these causes. Nature (or God) is infinite, because if it was finite, there would be something outside it, that would limit it . This is inconsistent with the singularity and unity of substance.

God is "the immanent and not the transient cause of all things" means, that everything in the universe must be explained within the single and all inclusive system of nature. Nothing can be explained outside the order of nature. The conception of God as a transient cause or, the doctrine of a transcendental God, involves God as the Creator, and the act of creation ocurring outside nature. This is not explainable on rational grounds.

If God were a transcendental Creator, then either he was free to create any world or none at all. Thus, there could not be an absolutely immutable essence in nature and a rational system of causes within it. Causes in nature would depend on God's arbitrary choice, and not on rational or logical analysis. The basic question is whether everything in nature is ultimately intelligible within nature itself, or whether there are things, that cannot be explained within the system of causes in nature. The latter would make it necessary to appeal to revelation. The doctrine of immanent causality presupposes that nature is intelligible within itself. God (nature) is the eternal cause of itself, and of all things. Nature (God) is self creating. All of nature's acts are solely determined from within, and therefore are absolutely free. Nature actively creating itself (i.e. substance and attributes) is called *natura naturans*. All that is created in nature (the system of modes) is called *natura naturata*. The creating and the created cannot exist apart from each other. Everything within the universe falls within a single system of causes. A complete explanation of anything in the Universe, would involve the knowledge of the entire chain of causation within nature (God).

Exercises.

1. In the late Roman Empire, many people converted from Paganism to Christianity. Is that the reason why St. Augustine provided proofs for the existence of God?
2. Does religion try to prove the existence of God? Religion knows that God exists. Discuss.
3. Can the existence of God be proven by logical argument?
4. The proof from design of the existence of God is a creationist argument. Is the theory of evolution contrary to the existence of God?
5. What do you mean by God? Is God corporeal or not-corporeal?
6. What are the ontological and cosmological proofs of the existence of God?
7. Kant: The existence of God is a matter of faith and not of posssible knowledge. Discuss.
8. Is St. Augustine's God as the ultimate truth, within nature or outside nature?

Workshop 39. Spinoza's God.

Spinoza (1623-1677) uses God, Nature, or Substance as equivalent terms. For the purpose of exposition, we will use the term Nature, (except when quoting Spinoza's text), remembering that Nature or Substance are alternative designations of Spinoza's God. Nature is the cause of itself *(causa sui)* and of everything else. *Causa sui* means eternity. Nature is not temporal. From a temporal order it is not possible to see how anything can be a cause of itself. Nature's being is eternal. Nature is eternal and absolutely infinite. Existence is eternity. "By eternity I mean existence itself..." (EI, 7). It also means freedom. Nature is freedom. Nature is presence. It is here. It is not a transcendent reality. Nature is immanent, concrete, dynamic, an eternally acting, and creating power. There is nothing beyond Nature. "Whatever is, is in God, and without God, nothing can be, or be conceived"(EI, 15). Nature is the ultimate and highest reality. Human beings are in Nature. When we are intimate with Nature, we share in Nature's eternity, in its powers, and creativity. Intimacy with Nature, also means an intimacy with our own nature. Intimacy with Nature is a source of great joy. Love is joy. We derive the greatest pleasure from the experience of Nature. The intellectual love of God is precisely this intimacy with nature. When human beings lack intimacy with Nature, they are confused. Spinoza focuses on that which promotes our own being, our power to be, to exist, to create, and to have joy. The source of our being, our power, and creativity lies in Nature.

Nature is one and identical with itself. *Natura naturans,* the presence which is identical with itself. The presence necessarily exists. World is time. The world exists in Nature, not in the subject. Nature is not time. It is ever itself. Nature is that which is in itself, *in se*, and which can be conceived through itself, *per se.* Everything else depends on Nature for its formation. Particular things cannot be conceived without Nature. "Everything which exists, exists either in itself or in something else" (EI, Axiom 1). The knowledge of every particular thing is rooted in Nature. (The world is seen entirely through the eyes of Nature.) Nature is the most important relation in all things. Spinoza collapses the duality of the physical and the mental, body and mind, subject and object. Spinoza's philosophy is a philosophy of identity, not of duality. The nature of the mind is in the human body. *Conatus,* the force that brings thinking and being together, is the human desire for self-preservation and self-elevation. The human body signifies the possibilities for knowing the world. Spinoza radically deconstructs the Cartesian philosophy of subjectivity. *Ego cogito* is not the ground. The subject or consciousness, does not take on the primary position as in Descartes. The subject is not foundational.   Certainty is based on Nature not on the subject. Spinoza's Absolute is not a personality, a subject (or object). Spinoza liberates Nature from personhood.   There is only infinite power.   This power is not constituted in the subject. If there is no subject, there is no intentionality. Nature's power is not intentional. Nature does not possess a will.   The essence of the human being is appetite, desire, longing, striving, drive. It is not reason, as for Aristotle. Human reason tells us that we desire to be free. Happiness lies in human freedom. The human being can attain happiness by its knowledge of the Absolute.   When the human mind is directed to *Natura naturans,* it experiences bliss. Nature is identified as joy, pleasure, love.

Nature is qualitatively different from anything in Nature. *Natura naturans* and *Natura naturata:*   Nature and modes.   Modes are *affectiones*, determinations of Nature. The origin of the modes is in Nature.   That which is *in se* (in self), and that which is *in alio*   (in another). Nature is *in se,* the modes are *in alio.* "The essence of things produced by God does not involve existence"(EI, 24).   Not all modes exist. Non-existing modes are those that could exist, but don't. All modes (in the past and future) that do not violate the laws of Nature could exist. The proposition of non-existing modes together with the infinity of Nature's attributes opens up infinite possibilities for human genius and creativity.

It is necessary to distinguish between the ground and the grounded, between Nature and the things themselves. Nature and its modes are distinctly different. There is an eternally dynamic, active, and creative power flowing from Nature to things in Nature. Science seeks to reveal the secrets of Nature, but Nature is infinite, its secrets can never be exhausted.   Nature cannot be appropriated by the human subject. Nature's presence signifies the dynamic possibilities of what is alive. Nature expresses itself through its attributes. Attributes express difference in identity. They are dynamic expressions of Nature. Attributes open up Nature to the human mind. The intellect perceives what Nature shows.   The intellect perceives the attributes as constituting the essence of Nature. The human mind is a mode in the attribute of thought. Without the attributes there is no intellect to perceive them.

The human mind can conceive two of Nature's attributes: the attribute of thought and the attribute of extension.   Nature is not beyond the universe. Nature (God) is an extended thing. Nature (God) is also a thinking thing.   Nature is to be understood from the immanence of things. Spinoza wanted to distance himself from Descartes. *Res cogitans* and *res extensa* are not Cartesian substances. They are equivalent expressions of one substance (Nature).   Nature manifests itself in infinite ways. Nature's attributes (expressions) are infinite. Each attribute is infinite after its kind. Nature is absolutely infinite. Nature cannot be constrained or conditioned by anything. Nature is all. There is nothing beyond it. Nature is infinitely free. "That thing is called free, which exists solely by the neccessity of its own nature"... Nature is not constrained by anything (EI, Def. 7). Absolute freedom is absolute necessity. Nature's freedom is its power of self-determination. Our connectedness to Nature, our freedom, is in accordance with what is necessary. Freedom is understood from the perspective of power. It is a power without a subject, a power that does not depend on subjectivity. There is no subject, no will, but pure necessity. That is the power of Nature.   There is no intentionality inherent in this power.   The power is pure freedom, and pure necessity.   There is an intriguing relation between freedom, power, and necessity. *Natura naturata* highlights the intensity of the power of Nature. "Whatsoever is, is in God, and without God nothing can be, or be conceived" (EI.P15). An awareness of *Natura naturans* in *Natura naturata* that is not rooted in the subject.   Nature (God) signifies necessity. God does not emerge as master. The task of philosophy is to understand Nature, God. Spinoza's philosophy is rooted in expression, not in presentation or representation. German Idealism subjectivised Nature.   In Spinoza, will and intellect are the same. Will is a finite mode of thinking. It exists conditionally. It is always determined by other causes. Will is not part of Nature. ..."God does not act according to freedom of the will" (EI, 32. Coroll.1). Free will is the same as free necessity. Free necessity is Nature's perfection. Nature's perfection is not "what is serviceable or repugnant to mankind"(EI, App). It is not the same as human perfection.

Let Us Now Consider Spinoza's God (Philosophy of Nature) in a Somewhat More Systematic Way:

1. The most important distinction betwen Spinoza's God and the God of religion is the following: " *God is the indwelling and not the transient cause of all things.*" (EI, 18). Spinoza's God is not prior to creation or prior to nature. God or Nature, Deus sive natura. God, nature, or substance are alternative terms. Substance expresses itself through its attributes. Attributes are indivisible, they are pure essence. Each attribute has the power of substance. Attribute is that which the intellect judges to be the essence of substance. Intellect is the faculty of judgment. Intellect is the immediate, infinite mode of substance in the attribute of thought. Thought is Spirit.   Intellect is reflection, understanding, reason. Thought makes the thinking of the intellect possible. Both dimensions are infinite.

Natura naturans and *natura naturata:* Substance, attributes, and modes. The infinite modes bridge *natura naturans* and *natura naturata.*

Things are modes of substance. (God is a thinking thing.) By stressing *res* - thing, Spinoza emphasizes nature, not the ego. Nature is seen as *res* thing. Spinoza wants to distance himself from the Cartesian ego. Nature in its essence is infinite power, absolute perfection. Modes are divisible, attributes are not. Spinoza's God is immanent in nature. He is both creator and created. Existence is eternity. Only substance exists. Substance - a dynamic ground, full of movement. The modes exist only because of substance. God acts by the necessity of his nature. He is not compelled to act by anything external to him. He is the only free cause. (EI,17). And, *"neither intellect nor will appertain to God's nature"*. Will and *intellectus* are one and the same. As affirmation or negation, will is present within an idea. Volition is nothing but an idea. When the will affirms an idea it expresses the knowledge of a necessary cause. The cognitive nature of the will is to be understood as a necessary cause. The will is only a particular mode of thinking, not a free cause. God is not conscious of himself (of being God).

2. God is an infinitely and eternally creating power. He is absolutely infinite, (EI, Def. 6), and involves no negation. He cannot be determined in any way. *(All determination is negation)*. God's essence is his existence. Substance is self-caused, *causa sui*. God, nature or substance are one, indivisible, eternally creating, and infinitely active. God's existence equals God's power and activity. God's power is complete in itself, and encompasses all reality. Nature reverberates with God's power and activity. Essence is immanent, absolute being. God is not external to being. Nature is supreme Being. The understanding of Being and Nature is connected to eternity, not time. Whatsoever is, is in nature.

3. God, nature or substance. Formal definitions:
    Definition of Substance: (EI, Def. 3). *"that which is in itself and can be conceived by itself."*
    Definition of Attribute: (EI, Def. 4). *" that which the intellect perceives to be the essence of substance."*
    Definition of Mode: (EI, Def. 5). *"that which exists in, and is conceived through, something other than itself."*
    God expresses his essence through an infinity of attributes. God is all reality *(ens realissimum)* (EI. Def. 6). The human intellect can perceive only two of God's attributes: thought and extension.

4. Substance and modes: *Natura naturans* and *natura naturata*. They pertain to the creating and the created aspects of nature. Substance and its modifications do not form a sequential order but stand in a logical order of causation. Substance and modes cannot be separated from each

other.   God eternally embraces and involves both.   The relation between nature and modes are those of ground and grounded or ground and consequent. Without ground there is no grounded, and no consequent. God as the ground of Being *(natura naturans)* and the infinite diversity of beings, *(natura naturata)*. The one cannot be without the other. Each mode (each individual thing) contains within itself the essence of the whole. God connects all things in nature to his essence. Substance is not outside nature but outside the modal system of nature.

5.   God's attribute of extension: It is the ground of all physical things. Extension is not material space, it is not matter. Matter exists in extension. Extension like thinking is an infinite attribute. It cannot be divisible, and cannot consist of parts. It is a dynamic essence of substance, it is not physical in nature. It is the ground for the material world.   Extension expresses God's power to produce motion and rest (physical energy).   Motion and rest is an inmmediate and eternal modification of substance. The laws of nature are inscribed in the Face of the universe *(Facies totius universi)*. This is the mediate, infinite, and eternal modification of substance. It is accordindg to these laws of nature that motion and rest (physical energy) and the finite modes (things or bodies) interact. Everything is determined by causal necessity,   a complete determination of everything that is finite. Substance is a necessary cause. The cause of existence is contained in nature. *Natura naturata* - the universe of modes, it is nature disclosed as negation. Modes do not have a necesssary existence. Their existence is entirely conditional, dependent on *natura naturans*. *Natura naturata* is in *natura naturans*. Together they are nature. The division of *natura naturans* and *natura naturata* should not be seen as as subject-object division.

Bodies continuously interact with respect to motion and rest. There is a constant interchange of energy betwen them. Here duration (temporality) arises, since changes in motion and rest follow sequentially. Eternity is outside time. God and his immediate and mediate infinite modifications (i. e. motion and rest and the laws of nature inscribed in the Face of the universe), are eternal. The relation between substance and infinite modes is of a logical, not sequential order of causation. Infinite modes exist for all eternity. They are not in time. Duration (time, temporality) arises with the advent of finite modes, the beginning of the universe. The question to be answered is how did the universe of finite modes evolve from the immediate and the mediate infinite modes? Both the Big Bang theory and Fred Hoyle's continuous creation theory, (Fred Hoyle, The Nature of the Universe), can be reconciled and made consistent with Spinoza's metaphysics.

6. The attribute of thought: God's attribute of thought is the ground of all possible knowledge, and of everything conceivable. Substance has an idea of everything. The attribute of thought expresses God's activity flowing into the infinite intellect. The infinite intellect is the immediate infinite modification of substance in the atttribute of thought. *Natura naturans* has an idea of intellect in *natura naturata*. Neither intellect nor the will are part of God. The intellect perceives (comprehends, judges) God's attribute as the essence of substance. The infinite intellect comprehends all reality, all possible knowledge, everything conceivable. The infinite intellect in the attribute of thought corresponds to physical energy in the attribute of extension. Thinking is derived from nature, not only present in nature.

The idea of God *(Idea dei)* is the mediate, infinite modification of substance in the attribute of thought. It corresponds to the laws of nature as inscribed in the face of the universe, in the attribute of extension. The *idea dei* represents the thought side of all things. God's power of thinking is equal to his power of acting. In God, there is an idea of every external thing. Every external thing has its mental counterpart. The mental counterpart of things is what we call life. Thus everything in the universe is imbued with life. The universe is animated in various degrees. The degree of animation is compounded vertically (from so called inanimate to the animate). Our body is part of the infinite and eternal modification of substance in the attribute of extension. Our mind is part of the infinite and eternal modification of substance in the attribute of thought. It is a part of the *idea dei,* God's intelligence, and his infinite intellect.

7. Nature alone is a free cause. Nature is self caused *(causa sui)*. Substance is a free and necessary cause. The cause of existence is contained in nature. Spinoza limits the idea of freedom to causal necessity. Free will is incompatible with causal necessity. Will is a finite mode of thinking. It exists conditionally. It is always determined by other causes. All finite modes are determined. Nothing in nature is contingent. Everything in nature occurs in accordance with nature's necessary laws. The laws of nature are eternal, the occurrences are temporal. The universe is orderly, rational and intelligible. The same causal order prevails in nature as in thought. God cannot be other than he is, and nature cannot be other than it is.

8. Infinite modes derive from substance. Finite modes (all particular things) derive from other finite modes. All modes exhibit the eternal order of nature. Each of God's attributes expresses the eternal order of nature. Thus, "the order and connection of ideas is the same as the order and connection of things" (EII, 7). All reality constitutes the same, all inclusive logical system, and causal order. Whatever occurs in nature,

occurs by necessity. Everything has a cause (or convergence of causes). A particular thing or event must be understood, or made intelligible within the logical system of causes in nature. Its existence cannot however be deduced from it. Since, "every individual thing, or everything which is finite and has a conditioned existence, cannot exist or be conditioned to act, unless it be conditioned for existence and action by a cause other than itself, which is also finite, and has a conditioned existence; and likewise this cause cannot in its turn exist, or be conditioned to act, unless it be conditioned for existence and action by another cause, which is also finite, and has a conditioned existence, and so on to infinity" (EI, 28). Thus, each thing can be made intelligible only within the general system of causes in nature and not outside it. Things exist in God but they are not of God. Spinoza's metaphysics is panentheistic, not pantheistic. Everything in nature must be understood in terms of nature's general order. The latter must be understood in terms of itself. Thus, "without God, nothing can be, or be conceived" (EI, 15). Spinoza's God reveals himself in the orderly harmony of what exists. He does not concern himself with fates and actions of human beings (Einstein, in Hans Kung, *Does God Exist?*, p. 62).

Identity of mind and body: We perceive ourselves through our senses. The human mind is the idea of the body as actually existing. The human mind perceives the ideas of the modifications of the body. The ideas of bodily manifestations are confused. As long as perception is determined from without, it will be confused. The task of the mode is to discern the truth. As long as we see things through our feelings, images (imagings or imprints), we see them confusedly, we cannot see them clearly. Imagination is the only source of error. Spinoza is not against the playfulness of imagination. He is against imagination only when it is for the sake of the irrational. Spinoza is a rationalist. Imagination works in our favor when it is connected to *natura naturans*. Spinoza does not accept the Kantian noumenon-phenomenon distinction. The only object of knowledge is substance. The human mind can understand the necessary cause relation between attribute and mode. Time is perceived as a mode of imagination, as limited duration. Duration is only related to modes whose existence is indefinite, not certain. Spinoza deemphasizes time. Time is an abstraction, not a reality. Time is a submode of the human mind.

Exercises.

1. How do you understand the "whole of nature"? Is the whole of nature accessible to the senses? to the intellect?
2. What is the relation between a single flower and the whole of nature? Can you say that a flower is a modification of nature? What

about a rock, a mountain, a star, a man? Are they all modifications of
nature?

3. Are   processes of composition and decomposition, growth and
decay, part of nature's system of causes?

4. Life is the mental counter-part of things, and everything in the
universe is animated in various degrees. Comment.

5. Does the infinity of God's attributes allow for the possibility of
supernatural phenomena?

6. What is the difference betwen infinity after its kind and absolute
infinity?

7. Is there a reality outside nature? Why does Spinoza identify nature
with God?

8. If one of your ancestors were a different person, would you still be
the identical individual that you are? Or would you be a non-existent
mode? Think of the possible implications of non-existent modes. Are
non-existent modes part of nature's system of causes? What about a
flying horse? Is a flying horse also part of nature's system of causes?

9. Is it possible that ESP is subject to nature's system of causes which
are not yet known to us?

10. Can Spinoza's God go against science? Is he confined to science?

Workshop 40.   Hegel's Phenomenology of Spirit.

In the Introduction to the Phenomenology of Spirit, Hegel (1770-1831) refers to it as the science of the experience of consciousness. The German word *Wissenschaft* can be translated both as science and study. It means a systematic investigation leading to a disciplined grasp of the organic whole of the object. Phenomenology (from the Greek *phainomenon*, what appears) is the study of phenomena (appearances) as they present themselves to our consciousness. Hegel's phenomenology is the science of true appearances. Hegel rejects Kant's distinction between phenomena (appearances) and noumena (the things in themselves). The latter presupposes a distinction between what is true, (the noumenon or the thing in itself), and what only appears as true (the phenomenon). Since we cannot know the thing in itself, knowledge for Kant, is of appearance only. We cannot experience the thing in itself. Hegel argues that the appearance itself is true, that the phenomenon is the only source of truth. He rejects Kant's a-priori conditions for the possibility of experience, (the transcendental categories of understanding). For Hegel the way to knowledge is already part of knowledge. The way to truth is part of the truth. Phenomenal knowledge (the whole range of thoughts, opinions, and ideas) leads to true knowledge.

The exposition of untruth (opinions and ideas) is a necessary step towards truth. The way to science (the dialectic) is already science itself, the science of the experience of consciousness. Knowledge develops dialectically along a progression of stages. Each stage in the process negates the one before it, but at the same time it also preserves it. Determinate nothing and its supersession, they have a double meaning of preserving and destroying, (*Aufhebung* or sublation). What we negate, we also preserve. Untrue knowledge is a nothingness with content, it is a determinate nothingness. The determinate negation leads to new forms, and to new knowledge replacing the old. The path of science provides numerous examples of dialectical progression. Let us give an example from Economics. Classical economists assumed that there cannot be a deficiency in aggregate demand for goods and services ("Say's law of markets)." Modern theory, associated with John Maynard Keynes (1883-1946), and Karl Marx (1818-1883) before him, proved the opposite. Applying it to a somewhat different context, we may find, in human relationships, that we are mistaken about a certain character quality of a person. We negate (correct) our previous assumption, but we preserve the person.

Knowledge is a process. Truth is the essence of consciousness. Consciousness seeks its own essence, true knowledge. The evolution of knowledge proceeds through a series of transitions, each successive essence (or the "in itself") is different from the preceeding one, until truth is reached. The process of successive stages of knowledge involves at each stage negation as a condition for movement and change. ..."negation .... covers difference, opposition, and reflection or relation, (it) is essential to conception and being:"[1] The dialectical movement of knowledge and its object (the object of knowledge) is what is called experience. Experience consists of a series of interactions: as my view of the object changes, the object changes. To know an object means that the object and the concept coincide within consciousness. When there is no correspondence, consciousness must change the object of consciousness. Dialectic is a process by which consciousness goes from stage to stage. Phenomenology is the science of the experience of consciousness, when consciousness grasps its own essence. Stages of the evolution of consciousness are: self-consciousness, reason, spirit, religion, absolute knowledge.

Logic is the method that articulates the organic whole. For Hegel, logic does not mean formal Aristotelian logic, (the syllogism, deduction, the principle of identity, contradiction, and the excluded middle). Rather it means, to overcome the subject-object distinction, and grasp the organic whole. Logic is dialectical, it includes movement and contradiction. Contradiction is at the root of all movement and vitality. The law of the excluded middle (a statement is either true or false), is suspended. The logical method discovers the fundamental categories of thought and being. Hegel's logic is dynamic, it is both method, and part of the content of philosophy, i. e. ontology.

Hegel discusses the progression of stages of consciousness throughout human history. Let us take a brief look at the highly complex structure of the Phenomenology.[2] The Preface: On Scientific Cognition, was written after the book was completed. The Introduction gives a preliminary conception of what the book is about. It is very dense and needs to be read vey carefully. The chief divisions of the text are: A. Consciousness: B. Self-Consciousness: C. (AA.) Reason. (BB.) Spirit. (CC.) Religion (DD.) Absolute Knowing.

Consciousnes is divided into: Self-Certainty, Perception, and Force and Understanding.

Self-Consciousness and The Truth of Self Certainty include: Lordship and Bondage, Stoicism, Scepticism, and the Unhappy Consciousness.

Reason include: Logical and Psychological Laws, Physiognomy and Phrenology. Pleasure and necessity. The law of the heart and the frenzy of self-conceit. Virtue and the way of the world. Reason as lawgiver, reason as testing laws.

Spirit is divided into: A. The *true* Spirit; The ethical order. B. Self alienated Spirit; Culture. C. Spirit that is certain of itself; Morality.

Ethical order is subdivided into: The ethical world. Human and divine law: Man and Woman, Ethical action, Human and Divine knowledge, Guilt and Destiny, Legal status.

Culture (Self alienated Spirit) is subdivided into: Culture and its realm of actuality. Faith and pure insight. The Enlightenment: The struggle of the Enlightenment with Superstition. The truth of Enlightenment. Absolute Freedom and Terror.

Spirit that is certain of itself; Morality. It includes: The moral view of the world. Dissemblance or duplicity. Conscience. The beautiful soul, evil and its forgiveness.

The divisions in religion are: Natural religion. (God as Light, Plant and animal, The artificer.) Religion in the form of Art. (The abstract work of art. The living work of art. The spiritual work of art.) The revealed religion. The last section, SectionVIII. is entitled, Absolute Knowing .

Let us briefly discuss some of the headings. Sense certainty sees the object as existing, without making qualitative distinctions. Perception distinguishes properties of the object, but fails to integrate them. Understanding penetrates behind the surface, and defines patterns of mutual interrelationships. The essence of sense certainty is neither in the object, nor in the subject, but in the interaction of the two. We comprehend the object as a unity. Perception is the process of the dissolution of the unity into a diversity, a myriad of qualities. Perception qualifies the object. Understanding comprehends the unity in diversity, and the interrelation between the parts. There is the movement from an initial unity through diversity, and back to unity at a higher stage. The particular arises at the level of understanding. *Verstand* (understanding) is the most abstract grasp of the object. Our initial understanding of a concept is intrinsically analytical in nature. We see its characteristics in their fixity, not in relation to each other. The dialectic unfreezes the initial fixity. The power of negation gets things moving. (Getting stuck in the negation is to be a sceptic. This can also lead to sophistry, or a lack of concern with truth. These are the things that can go wrong with the dialectic). A speculative grasp of the object is to grasp the most concrete side of the object. (Speculative means more concrete.) It is to apprehend the unity in the opposition.

Consciousness of the external world (the world of objects) preceeds self-consciousness. Self-consciousness derives from consciousness. Self-consciousness is identified as desire. (Connection to Spinoza?) It is the beginning of individuality. Desire *(Begierde)* is now taking center stage. (For Spinoza, desire is the essence of man.) Individuals want to be recognized by others as being superior. A struggle for life

and death ensues. Hegel now develops his most celebrated section on
the master and the slave. He who is willing to risk all, including his
life, becomes the master. He who is attached to his existence and is
afraid of death, becomes the slave. The slave works for the master. The
slave produces, and the master consumes. The master cannot exist
without the slave, but the slave can exist without the master.
Eventually, it leads to a reversion of the relation. The master does not
work. He gets soft and dependent. The slave works, he learns to
conquer desire, and to delay gratification. As a result, the slave gets
strong and independent. Thus begins the process of the liberation of
the slave, and the enslavement of the master. As the slave becomes
conscious of his own liberation, he rises to a universality that includes
the liberation of the master. (In Marxian terms, the historical mission
of the proletariat is to free mankind from individual exploitation. By
this act, it liberates itself and the bourgeoisie. A new, classless
society is established.)

     Man develops and makes himself by transforming nature through
his labor. The slave, by mastering nature, gains freedom through his
work. The Stoa seek freedom in the mind itself. The Stoic withdraws
from the world. The Sceptic negates any rational claim for knowing
the external world. Stoicism found its completion in Scepticism. Both
Stoic and Sceptic are found in the subject-object relation. The Stoic
regards the object as insignificant. The Sceptic denies that there is any
kind of knowledge to be had. The result is the same. There is internal
tension.   Both Scepticism and Stoicism are ultimately self-
contradictory.

     The next stage in the evolution of consciousness is the unhappy
consciousness. Consciousness has a dual nature. I am a part of the
world, and I am also all the world. The self is divided against itself.
The tension between what is denied and affirmed is recognized. The
opposition between subject and the world, is within consciousness.
This is the stage of the unhappy consciousness. Hegel's way to
overcome the duality (of self and other) within oneself is to relativize
the opposing dualities, by making the other to be oneself, or by seeing
oneself in the other. The unhappy consciousness represents the
transition from philosophy to religion. It is the transition from truth
to certainty. Merely to be certain is not to know. Religion does not
know what it claims to know, it is only certain about it. In religion,
man gains consciousness of the Absolute. After discussing the
historical stages of religion, primitive religion, worship of spirits in
nature, Hellenistic paganism, Greek temples and statues, and
Christianity which unites the divine with the human, Hegel concludes
with the Absolute Mind as the supreme form of knowledge. The
unfolding of the historical stages of Mind (freedom) proceeds

dialectically, through fluctuation and change, conflict and opposition, on its way to progressively higher levels of self-expression.

In order to develop as an individual, we have to go into the world of actuality, the world of desire and work. We actualize ourselves in what we do. Theory precedes practice. Hegel's concept of reason is developmental. He starts from the object and goes to the subject. Knowledge is derived from experience. Kant (also Descartes) starts from the subject and goes to the object. For Kant, the conditions of knowledge and the conditions of experience are the same. For Hegel, they are not. Reason is the cognitive tool that philosophers have. Reason is a synthetic faculty. It transforms sensual existence into notions. It comprehends sensuous existence intellectually. This intellectual interplay between the individual and the universal is the activity of reason. Philosophy turns reality into thought. Through this, it makes reality more real. Reason is the thinking activity of true (the Absolute) Spirit. Spirit (Geist) is what is common to every human consciousness. It is the universal consciousness. Spirit actualizes itself in human history.

Alienation is a separation between our identity and the objective world, the culture. It produces tension within us in terms of our own identity. The social rules and institutions created by man, alienate man and estrange him from himself. Man has to succumb, and conform to the cultural norms. Culture is the self alienated Spirit. Culture alienates the personality. The person splits off against itself. The culture restricts our action in certain ways. The world we created is different from the world we intended. Living in the cultural world is alienation. We cannot overcome this alienation. The real world is a soulless existence. Culture restricts our actions in certain ways, while allowing us to be concrete human beings. For Hegel, to be something, is to do something, (the priority of the deed, *die Tat*). True culture requires that we express ourselves (externalize ourselves) through deeds. Our cultural world is the world that we function in. We live in the cultural world. It is our creation, the creation of human beings. We cannot overcome this alienation.

Spirit is the ethical life of the nation, the higher level of reason. Culture is objective Spirit. Subjective spirit is personal. The ethical substance is spirit. Human law is the law that we make. The divine law is based on love. Perfect divine law proceeds from love only. The divine law is basic to the family. Human law concerns civil society. We live both in the sensible world (the world of our passions), and in the supersensible (the world of ethics). There is tension between the two worlds, the sensible (wealth, power), and the supersensible (good, bad). Neither can win against the other. True Spirit is a synthesis of the sensible and the supersensible worlds. It is the diversity and the unity of experience. Language has been debased. It has been put in the service of the state to impose its power over the individual.

Hegel is an idealist philosopher.   Hegel does not deny the existence of the physical world. The mind develops through individuals who are actively developing their minds (their potentialities). Infinite mind is the highest reality.   Hegel's looks for the essence of consciousness. Consciousness has to grasp its own essence. Consciousness seeks true knowledge. An experience is nothing other than what is present in the mind.   Being is nothing but the phenomenon of being.   Truth is many sided. The task of the science of Logic is to grasp all those sides. Self-identity is a criterion of truth. The concept of the object and the object must coincide (self-identity). When they fail to coincide, our perception of the object is not a true one. The object is objective, it possesses intrinsic being. The thing exhibits itself in consciousness, but it also reflects itself. Hegel uses the terms abstract and concrete in a special way. The abstract is the immediate experience.   The concrete is arrived at only through conceptual mediation.   When the abstract is fully mediated it is knowledge. Knowledge is always concrete. Understanding is the faculty that produces distinctions and unity. The test of understanding is to create unity from diversity. Reason is the faculty that synthtizes distinctions. Understanding is an analytic faculty, reason is a synthetic faculty. Our experience of an object is the experience of an object that is changing.   Pure insight is noble consciousness that has itself as subject. Noble consciousness is the essence of universal substance.

Hegel differentiates between good and bad infinity. A bad infinity is an infinite regress. A good infinity is like infinite knowledge. It is open-ended.   A subject is only given with respect to an object, and vice versa. Subject and object have to be relativized. Life is the object of desire. It consists of permanency (the essence), and transitoriness (appearance). Life is a circular process. Knowledge is a process of arriving at a totality of a whole, a totality that relates together all particular differences in a structured whole. This structured whole is Spirit-*Geist*.

Exercises.

1. Why would you classify Hegel as an objective idealist?
2. As we penetrate into the nature of external things, we penetrate more into ourselves. Knowledge of the physical world leads to self-knowledge. Discuss.
3. Is contradiction a necessary part of our life experiences and attitudes?
4. How does Hegel view human labor in the historical process?
5. Man creates himself by transforming nature and creating items of use. Discuss.

6. "Religion doesn't know what it claims to know. It is only certain about it." How does this relate to proofs of the existence of God?
7. What does Hegel mean by alienation? Why is culture alienating?
8. What is Hegel's Absolute Mind?
9. How do you understand Hegel's notion of progress in history?

Notes

1. *Hegel's Phenomenology of Spirit.* Translated by A. V. Miller with Analysis of the Text and Foreword by J. N. Findlay, F.B.A., F.A.A.A.S. New York: Oxford University Press, 1977. p. ix.
2. Ibid.

Workshop 41. The Question of Being: Heidegger's Being and Time.

Heidegger (1889-1976) poses the question of the meaning of Being, *(Der sinn des Daseins)*. The problem of Being, *(Die Seinsfrage)* is the primary question. Every other question is subordinate to the above. Heidegger interprets Being not as something that exists, or as a category of logic (one of Aristotle's categories). We cannot ask what is Being, for this would imply that Being is something. While all beings (akin to Spinoza's modes or Aristotle's substances) share in Being, the asking of the question of the meaning of Being is restricted to Dasein as a human being. Rivers, rocks, and animals are, but only humans exist in the sense, that their very existence is an issue for them. Dasein is "ontically distinguished by the fact, that in its very Being, that Being is an issue for it."[1] Our access to Being is through Dasein, an entity that is ourselves. Dasein, the human being, is always a Being-in-the-world. Dasein finds itself in a world. It understands itself in terms of existence. It is through Being-in-the world, through existence, that we ask the question of the meaning of Being. The essence of Dasein lies therefore in what it means "to be". Heidegger uses Dasein, the human being, as a way to inquire into questions of fundamental ontology, namely, the meaning of Being in general.

Heidegger differentiates between problems pertaining to individual existence which he refers to as "existentiell", and an inquiry into the nature of (human) existence in general, called the "existential" question. People deal with questions pertaining to their own existence, but they rarely if ever, ask the question of the meaning of human existence in general. It is not possible however, to answer the question of one's existence, without considering the existential question of what it means "to exist, or to be". Heidegger's "existential analytic" maps out the basic structures of human existence. Heidegger views things from a phenomenological perspective, he has a phenomenological view of spatiality. He explains that the term phenomenon must be understood as "that which shows itself in itself,"[2] and not just as appearance or mere semblance. Phenomenology sees things as they appear to consciousness. Truth is that which shows itself. Space is relative, dependent on Dasein. *Phainomenon - Phainestai-* to show itself. The light *(pha)* is that wherein something becomes manifest, that which shows itself in itself.

Signs indicate where our concern dwells. Signs orient us to the environment. Establishing a sign requires circumspective forsight *(Vorsicht)*. A sign lets something ready at hand become conspicuous. Logos primordialy is *Rede* (discourse). *Rede* is the articulation of understanding. *Phainestai*, to see what the discourse is about. *Logos* allows something be seen by pointing it out. *Logos* can acquire the sense of truth. It lets something be seen by disclosing it, by taking it out of its hiddenness. To disclose, to discover, is a fundamental condition of Dasein. (*Entdecken* =to unhide, to discover). Truth - *a-lethea* is unforgetting. *Lethea* is forgetfullness. *Logos* is also perception. It uncovers the (empirical) properties of things by letting us see them. By letting entities be perceived, *logos* becomes reason. The counter-concept to *phainomenon* is "covered-upness", the covering up or the disguising of the truth. Disclosure is *Lichtung* , clearing. Disclosure lets light come in. The disclosure discloses clearing.

To exist (to be) is to anticipate one's possibility. Possibility is Dasein's existentiality or transcendence. Within the limits of our being in-the-world, we always reach beyond us, we reach for that which is not yet. To exist is to transcend the actual, and to make the world ours. It is for Dasein to appropriate its world. Dasein's existence must be understood in terms of possibilities, not properties. Properties describe objects, (honey is sweet, an airplane flies, iron does not bend, etc.). Objects don't exist, they just are. Only Dasein exists. *"The essence of Dasein lies in its existence."* [3]   The temporal significance of existence is Dasein's futurity.   Dasein is its possibilities. "To be" is the essence of Dasein. The person exists only as intended action. (The Greek notion of being is activity, *to-on, energeia* -action.) Dasein's existence is uniquely my own. It cannot be exchanged for another. This "mineness" is an essential characteristic of Dasein. The question of existence of Dasein turns on the question of considering the possibilities inherent in concrete existence, namely, to elucidate the "existential" for the sake of the "existentiell". Dasein's existence is always Being-in-the-world. It is an embodied existence. Dasein, the human being, can comport itself to its possibilities in two ways: authentic or inauthentic. These are the two choices. Existence can either be authentic or inauthentic. Authentic existence is Dasein's awareness of its inherent possibilities. Inauthentic existence is the suppression of Dasein's ownmost possibilities. Being-in-the-world encompasses all of Dasein's ties to the world around it, (work, relationships, interests, etc.). Heidegger denotes our normal, everyday connection to the environment, (the world around us), as "concern." The "world" consists of all kinds of things, rivers, mountains, cars, tables, etc. Dasein is surrounded by objects, things. Things are not independent of Dasein. Things are there to the extent that they are accessible to Dasein. (For Descartes things or *res extensae* are independent entities.) For Heidegger, things in the world exist for Dasein. A basic way of being is being with entities.

Things in the world are either just there, "present at hand", or they are there to be used by us, as "ready to hand". The latter indicates a practical concern on our part. Our connection to the world consists of a highly interrelated and integrated system of relations. Only when something breaks down, do we become aware of how closely we depend on the "world" around us. For example, we take it for granted that when we go to the store we can buy whatever we want. We take the market system for granted. Only when we cannot get what we need, do we become aware of the intricacy of the market system, and of our dependence on its smooth functioning. A simpler example would be the car. Only when the car breaks down are we aware of the distinction between present at hand and ready to hand. A stalled car is present at hand, but not ready to hand. Our everyday existence centers on routine functioning, with objects (of use) being ready to hand for us. This is what "Being-in" means. However, the world also consists of other people, other existents, other Daseins. We necessarily exist in community with others. This is what "Being-with" means. We can neither exist without objects, nor can we exist without other people.

"Being with" is a basic *existentiale* for Dasein. Dasein's concern for other existents (co-Daseins), Heidegger calls solicitude. Solicitude signifies authentic concern for the spiritual growth of other human beings. It means helping another actualize his or her ownmost possibilities. People however, are ruled for the most part, by convention. They hardly think for themselves, they mostly follow others. The others are the anonymous mass, *das Man.* Therefore, there is no authentic Being-with, or Being-with one another. "The Self of everyday Dasein is the *they self,* which we distinguish from the *authentic Self.* "[4] For Heidegger to exist, means to stand out, to ex-sist.[5] Existence involves selfhood. For me to exist, (to stand out), means to be my unique and distinct self. It means not to be totally submerged in the practicalities of life, (routine chores). It also means not to be entirely determined by the outside, by convention. Only thus do I exist authentically, as the unique person that I am. To be totally absorbed in practical aspects of existence, or to be wholly determined by convention, is to lead an inauthentic existence. Dasein must be aware of its possibilities and responsibilities to itself, and to others, in order for it to stand out, and ex-sist. For Heidegger, potentiality is higher than actuality. The actual is ontical. The potential is the possible. Understanding is the way a person understands his possibilities. Keeping silent is a more authentic way of making oneself understood. For Husserl, truth is intuited by the transcendental ego. For Heidegger, truth appears to Dasein, truth comes to Dasein by disclosure. Alienation is defined as the hiddenness of being, it is Dasein's hiddenness from its ownmost possibilities. (For Kant, our access to ourselves is not different from our access to the outside world.)

The "there" in Being-there is indispensible to Dasein's existence. Only thus, can Being-with be a true dwelling. This awareness of the "there", its disclosedness, comes to us from our inner light, *lumen naturale. "Dasein is its disclosedness".* [6] Disclosure is a clearing *(Lichtung)*. The disclosure discloses clearing. The "clearness" *(Lichtung)* opens itself up to us in two basic ways, through the affects, and through the understanding. Our moods (our affects) light up the "there" for us. These affective states, (fear, joy, disgust, boredom, anxiety, etc.) are a fundamental *existentiale* for Dasein. They light up the place for us. They remind us where we are. What our affects disclose to us, Heidegger refers to as 'facticity'. The latter includes the "givens" (our heredity, personal history, etc.) of our situation. Dasein comes into a world that is not of its making. This is its facticity. Dasein has to appropriate and assimilate its world. Dasein's essence, its existence, is transcendence (existentiality). Dasein appropriates and assimilates its world within limits. Dasein cannot separate itself from its world. The world of objects consist in their being present at hand or ready to hand. Traditional ontology understands being as present at hand, *(vorhanden)*. For Heidegger, things exist for us. They are the equipment that we make use of, in our being in-the-world. They are ready to hand *(zuhanden)*. Objects (*Zeug,* equipment) ready to hand are more basic than present at hand. Fundamental ontology sees being as "to be", for which things are ready to hand. Traditional ontology takes things as existing, as present at hand. In this lies the difference between Heidegger's fundamental ontology and traditional ontology.

Dasein's moods reveal its "thrownness". Dasein is thrown into the "there". Dasein's possibilities are conditioned by its facticity. Facticity, existentiality, and fallenness are Dasein's three most basic existentials. Facticity relates to the world as given to us. We have no choice in determining how, when, and where we were born and raised. Existentiality relates to our ability to transcend our facticity, the world as given to us. By fallenness, Heidegger is telling us that we forfeit our essential self (our self as a possibility) for the sake of every-day being, for the sake of the public self. Dasein"finds itself in its thrownness...it finds itself in the mood that it has."[7] Heidegger somewhat contemptuously refers to this public or every-day self in a neutral prefix, "das Man".

Where moods disclose facticity, understanding discloses possibilities. Understanding involves interpretation. There are two levels to interpretation, an informal one, and the active act of interpreting. The latter involves the assignment of meaning. The formal act of interpreting is not entirely free from the informal, habitual or the unconscious one. Interpretation is never without presuppositions. Interpretation is conditioned by the fore-structure, (prior understanding or frame of reference), and the as-structure, "we interpret something as something". Only thus can we say we understand it. "We see it *as* a table, a door, a carriage or a bridge;[8] Our fore-structures (fore-having, fore-sight, and fore-conception), would seem to put us in a hermeneutical circle. "What is decisive is not to get out of the circle but to come to it in the right way....to make the scientific theme secure by working out these fore-structures in terms of the things themselves."[9] Interpretation leads to discourse. This involves language. Discourse is another *existentiale* of Dasein. It is the living language that expresses our Being-in-the-world. Through it, truth gets to be communicated and illuminated. Truth is a-lethea, it lies in making un-hidden of the thing itself. "Truth is also letting be, letting something be what it really is."[10] In everyday existence however, discourse degenerates into idle talk. There is no genuine communication. There is only repetition and the uncritical acceptance of the official line, however that line is communicated, whether through the mass media or custom. This repetitive, thoughtless chatter, and idle talk does not reveal the truth for us. Rather, it hides it. The possibilities of Dasein are thus perverted in everyday existence. Heidegger calls it Dasein's "fallenness". Man's falling consists in his absorption in the practicalities of everyday existence, and in his being submerged in the anonymous mass culture. The submergence in the mass weakens man's capacty to have true emotions, it reduces the level of his anxiety, it desensitizes him to his genuine needs, and it makes him insensitive to others. It alienates Dasein from its own self. Since, in this situation, Dasein's possibilities are determined not by himself but by others (from the outside), it is also a scattering of the self. The self lacks cohesion and unity. Spiritual strength can only come from the person's inner self, not from the outside.

Let us briefly recapitulate the threefold structure of Dasein's existence: (1) Dasein is always ahead of itself, through its understanding and projecting plans and possibilities. (2) Dasein is a being who is already-in-a-world. Dasein's thrownness and facticity prevent it from having a clear start in life, at any time. (3) Dasein scatters its ownmost possibilities by its complete absorption in the mass culture, in the "they" world. Heidegger designates this threefold structure of Dasein as "care". "Care" is a general characteristic of human existence. Animals don't care. Animal existence is carefree.

Man is bound by heredity and by history, but he is also free to assert himself and to make himself. The every-day chores, and work routines that consume me are not the essential me. People can break out from their stultifying existence, by tuning in to their true-selves, by breaking out from the little creature comforts that hold sway over them, and by freeing themselves from the grip of convention and mass culture that rule their life. They can thus become less fragmented within themselves, and be more whole. They can become more authentic. My essence is my existence. Dasein is its possibilities. My every-day existence, my public self is my inauthentic self. The essential me, what I truly am, is my possibility. My possibility is

hidden from me. It is buried in my every-day existence.   I am
determined by history and by my inauthentic every-day existence, but I
can transcend them, discover my real self, and become more free in
both.

Heidegger asks now, the most important question of, how this
return to authenticity, is about to happen? He points to two ways:
anxiety and the call of conscience. Heidegger's anxiety is not the
anxiety of the everyday life. It is an anxiety that requires great moral
and spiritual strength. It is the anxiety of facing up to the realization of
the finitude of our existence, an anxiety that comes when we
contemplate our own death.   Anxiety related to our death forces us to
look at the whole of our existence. It awakens the call of conscience
within ourselves. It asks us to accept responsibility for our life and
deeds. It makes us aware of a sense of urgency, that we cannot
continue wasting our limited talents and energies.   The call of
conscience bring us closer to our authentic, inner self. We realize that
we must turn away from the "they" world, and pursue our inner calling.
This is the authentic resoluteness that accompanies the call of
conscience. Heidegger's call of conscience can be interpreted as a
rebellion against conventional morality, and as an assertion of the
individual against the community. However, since Being-with is a
primary *existentiale* for Dasein, such interpretation should be discarded.
Rather, it is a calling that harmonizes our individual creative needs with
those of the community. Heidegger however, leaves the question with
regard to the nature of the community open. Is it a community of
Daseins, of certain self elected individuals, of people belonging to a
certain group characterized by the community of race, color,
nationhood, common past, and common destiny? He does not address
himself to this question.   The call of conscience is a summons for
Dasein to resoluteness, to take matters into its own hand.   It is a call
to do away with the illusions and soft living of the past, to break away
from the "they" world, and be free. Even as I am determined by history
and by my inauthentic every-day existence, I can transcend them,
discover my real self, and become free. The call of conscience is a call
to authenticity, and to transcendence. (Conscience is the call of itself to
itself.) It is a call to my freedom and my possibility. I can return from
my inauthentic life, from my public image of myself, from the "they"
world, and from my every-day existence, to become my real self. I owe
it to myself to be my true (authentic) self. This inner liberation
brings with it an overwhelming feeling of joy.

Heidegger then turns to the discussion of temporality. The
dimensions of temporality, past, present, and future, correspond to
"care" as the threefold structure of human existence. As we have
already pointed out, "care" consists in projecting of what is to come
(future), in the "facticity" of what has been (the past), and in falling (the

concern with the present). Authentic existence unifies all three dimensions of temporality, and give true meaning and purpose to life. ..."it has the unity of a future which makes present in the process of having been; we designate it as temporality."[11]

The meaning of what it is "to be", of our possibility, comes to us through dread. Heidegger's dread *(Angst)* makes us aware of ourselves as "being to death". Through death we confront life in its wholeness, as a totality. Dread frees us from the illusion of the "they", from the illusion of our every-day existence. Dread takes us back to our authentic self. It opens us up to the totality of our life and existence. In this sense, it may be said that authentic being is being-to-death. My life as a whole will end by death. The "they" don't matter anymore, since my death is mine alone. Time is the ontological ground of my being. My existential time is finite. My time is the future. My future reaches to the past and together they constitute the present.

Exercises.

1. Heidegger nowhere identifies Dasein as the human being. Can it be that Dasein, as the fundamental aspect of "Being there", refers to a mode (i.e. Spinoza's modes of substance), or "a this" (the Aristotelian substance)?

2. Subsequently, Heidegger speaks of "Dasein" as a person. Is there a reason why Heidegger hides the person behind Dasein? Is it a way of avoiding moral concerns, while retaining the claim to a universality of Dasein?

3. Fundamental ontology deals with being as "to be", while traditional ontology deals with being as existing. The essence of Aristotelian substance "a this", or Spinoza's "mode", is the mode's inner *telos* , the striving to realize its being, to actualize its potential. Essence comes from the Latin *"esse"* to be. It is both a noun and a verb. If this is the case, do you still think that Heidegger's "fundamental" ontology is really fundamental, that is, original with Heidegger? Or did he borrow from his predecessors, primarily from Spinoza, without acknowledging it?

4. What does Heidegger mean by possibility? What Do I mean by possibility? Can I know my possibility without knowing myself? Doesn't self-knowledge precede possibility? If I don't know myself, how do I know my possibility?

5. To know myself as possibility is to know my real me. Is the real me fixed, or is it evolving? Can I be wrong in assessing my real me?

6. Heidegger's dread is a coming face to face with my own finitude, my "being onto death". This dread will make me face myself.

Will the recognition and my pre-occupation with death necessarily reveal myself to myself? Can it not force me to act wrongly and be mistaken about myself?

7. Is Heidegger's dread the dread of not having made my imprint on the world before I die? Is this dread a recognition that my time on this earth is limited, and that I cannot go on procrastinating? Does dread imply compulsion and force?

8. Heidegger's dread brings out the call of conscience. What does Heidegger mean by conscience? Does he mean the conscience of humanity in me? Or, is Heidegger's conscience a call to be myself, to make myself, to become my possibility, while there is still time?

9. How do other Daseins and other consciousnesses figure in this my conscience? Do they matter only in terms of my possibility, i.e. to consider them or to ignore them?

10. When Heidegger speaks of things as ready to hand, as *Zeug* or equipment, does this apply only to objects, or could it also include people as ready to hand i.e. to be used by Dasein? What does Heidegger say about that? Is he clear about it? Is it posssible that Heidegger's philosophy is anti-human, amoral and unethical?

11. What does Heidegger mean by "care"?

12. Heidegger never mentions love. Why?

13. If Dasein sees itself (through arrogance or character weakness), as superior to others, may its responsibility to itself, i.e. its possibility, dictate the conquest or the oppression of the other or others?

14. Is the Heidegarian concept of "Dasein" restricted to the individual, or can it apply also to a collectivity, the nation or *Volk* ?

15. If a *Volk* (nation) sees itself superior, does its possibility (its responsibility to itself) dictate the conquest and oppression of other nations? Can it use other nations and peoples as means to its ends, as "ready at hand"?

16. Can you see how Heidegger's philosophy may lead to extreme nationalism, and to nazism?

17. Heidegger's dread is the call of conscience. Can the call of conscience disclose itself to a maniac and a diabolic leader, "the Fuhrer" who sees his destiny in saving his nation by unleashing a war and terror against all those who stand in his way?

18. Would Heidegger's philosophy idealize and uphold such a great "Fuhrer"? The Fuhrer does not have to answer to anyone but to God and history. He sees his destiny as the destiny of the nation. Can the "Great Fuhrer" be wrong?

Notes

1. Martin Heidegger, *Being and Time*. Translated by John Macquarrie & Edward Robinson. New York: Harper @ Row, Publishers, 1962. p. 32.

2. Ibid. p. 54.
3. Ibid. p. 67.
4. Ibid. p. 167
5. John Macquarrie, *Martin Heidegger*.   Richmond, Virginia: John Knox Press, 1969. p. 8.
6. *Being and Time,* p. 171.
7. Ibid. p. 174. (Cited in Macquarrie, p.21.)
8. Ibid. p. 189.
9. Ibid. p. 195. (Cited in Macquarrie, p.24.)
10. John Macquarrie, *Martin Heidegger*. p. 26.
11. *Being and Time.* p. 374.

SECTION VI.   ETHICS

Workshop 42.   Presocratic and Platonic Views on Justice and Ethics.

Anaximander considered justice in Nature. The question was whether nature was just or not. He maintained that the cosmos is just. For, opposites.... "pay penalty and retribution to each other for their injustice according to the assessment of time". Justice is built-in in nature, for the excess of one of the opposites (hot-cold, winter -summer, etc.) is balanced out by a corresponding excess in the other. Penalty and retribution is built-in in the natural rhytm of change, according to justice, (i.e. the assessment of Time). Time is the limit for how long the retribution is to be made. Change itself (things changing into their opposites) is seen as a compensation or reparation for injustice. Cosmic stability requires that opposing substances recompense only to each other (hot to cold, etc.,) and not to any one else (such as hot to heavy, etc.) The natural rhytm is a just one. Anaximander viewed justice in the context of nature, and not in the context of society. Justice is nature's way of balance, and compensation for excess.

Heraclitus proclaimed that strife itself is justice, since it is a necessary part of the operation of the cosmos. "In the eyes of God justice and injustice are the same." God is the unity of being and non-being. Justice and injustice are the same components of truth or the logos. "Sun will not overstep its measure: Otherwise the Erinyes, ministers of Justice will find him out". (Fragm. 226). Measure (nature's balance and rhythm) is justice. It is contained in nature's strife and in the unity of the opposites. Heraclitus, like Anaximander, considers nature's rhythm and balance to represent justice. The difference between them is this: For Anaximander, Justice is the reciprocal compensation for nature's excess. For Heraclitus, justice is Nature itself. In nature (God?), there is no difference between justice and injustice. Everything that accords with nature is just. In this sense, nature's rhytm is the standard by which justice can be measured.

The Pythagoreans look for formal causes of things in numbers. Everything is numbered and everything is countable. Numbers represent the essence of things. The number 4 represent justice, since it is a square, and each side treats the other equitably. Number 5 stands for marriage, (the lowest junction of odd and even, (3+2). Ten is considered to be the perfect number (i.e. ten fingers, the number base, the sum of 1+2+3+4). One represents a point, 2 a line, 3 a plane, and 4 a solid. Also, one equals intuition (or cognition), two is demonstration (from premise to conclusion), three is opinion (superficial), and four is sense perception. The Pythagoreans came up with the principle of the limited (formal cause) and the unlimited (material cause). The ultimate principle is one. It is the principle of limitidness. Out of the one, numbers are generated. (The one and the indefinite dyad).

Empedocles was important to the medical tradition. The four roots, (earth, fire, air, and water) are identified with the four seasons, and they are linked with the four humors (phlegm, yellow bile, black bile) in blood. These also affect one's character, (sanguine, melancholic, phlegmatic, etc.). There is a cosmic cycle, which consists of Love, (the unity of the four roots), and of Strife, (separation of the four roots). Love and Strife alternate in the cosmic cycle. Blood is composed of a ratio of the four elements. (One should therefore not spill blood, one should not kill, etc.) Love imbues the world with value. It is the principle of coherence and synthesis. Strife is the principle of stress. Nothing wants to stay in its place. Things want to separate. A living organism is ruled by love, (is coherent). Strife is not necessarily negative. It leads to renewed composition (love).

Leucippus and **Democritus** hold that the elements of nature are the atom (the full), and the void. They are the material causes of things. Atoms are small, invisible, and infinite in number. They differ by shape, arrangement and position. They are also indivisible, but can aggregate into compound bodies. The latter are divisible due to the void that exists between the atoms. Democritus conceived of the possibility of an atom as big as the universe. He also postulated the existence of innumerable universes.

Democritus based his ethical theories on his physics, (Fr. 594, On Good Spirits). He advocates temperance and moderation in judgment and desire. Envy, jealousy, and malice are the chief curses in life. One should stay within the limits of one's natural ability, and not depend on good luck. (Fr. 593). However, one's nature is not fixed. One can extend one's natural abilities by learning, as for example, one learns how to swim. Right conduct is based on "conviction, understanding, and knowledge" (Fr. 181).

Epicurus accepted the atomic theory of Leucippus and Democritus, but he modified it by the doctrine of the "slight swerve". It assumes that an atom may slightly deviate from its path. This brings about collisions with other atoms, and gives rise to complex motion of which the universe is made. The doctrine of the swerve was to explain the existence of free will (the non-dependence on fate). Epicurus (according to Lucretius) freed men from the fear of death. When one knows what happens after death, one is not afraid of it any more. The soul has a corporeal structure and it does not exist after death. The Gods reside in "spaces between the worlds", and they do not worry about humans. Man has to decide how best to live his life. Pleasure is the end of life and the measure of the good. A man should be virtuous, seek simple pleasures, and avoid pain. Virtue is seen as instrumental to the end, which is pleasure.

For **Plato** "the good" is the *arche,* the measure or fundamental principle. Virtues are both instruments and components of the "good". Plato compares the good to the sun. As the sun is to the visible, so is the good to the intelligible. The knowledge of the good activates the soul. One cannot stare at the sun or the good. Staring at the sun (or the good) causes pain. The idea of the good is the highest among all the ideas. The knowledge of the good is dialectic in a higher sense. Unlike science, dialectics does not rest only on hypotheses, or insecure starting points. Dialectics tests its starting points, and thus makes them more secure. Philosophy (dialectics) tries to justify its hypotheses or come up with higher hypotheses to justify the lower ones. In order to avoid infinite regress, we assume that there is an ultimate principle, the good. Plato identifies the idea of the good with the supreme deity. It is immutable, eternal, and perfect in its kind.

In the *Phaedrus,* Plato presents the ideas of justice, temperance, and science as being enthroned in heaven, (the myth of Phaedrus). They are accessible only to the contemplative view of reason *(nous).* There are two realms of reality; the realm of ideas, and the realm of objects. Ideas are immutable, eternal, and wholly self-subsistent. They do not come into being or pass away. Individual objects come into being at definite places and times, and are always in motion. The two realms represent the difference between knowledge *(nous)* and opinion (sense perception). In discussing the education of the warrior class (Republic, book II), Plato asserts that the gods are good, they do not cheat, lie, deceive or betray. By connecting the gods with the good, Plato reaffirms that the good is the ruling principle of the universe. The gods are the embodiment of the ideas. They are eternal, immutable, and are not moved by sensual desires. The warrior class will learn to be pious, and honor the gods. They will respect the community, and their ancestors.

With Plato, there is a fundamental shift in the concept of justice. Justice and virtue are not concerns of nature. They are human concerns. They deal with actions of individuals and society. Justice is the main theme of Plato's Republic. Plato refutes several of the sophist views on justice: That justice benefits friends and harms enemies (Polemarchus). That justice is the advantage of the stronger, meaning that it is just to follow the ruler and to obey the law (Thrasymachus). And, that injustice is natural to man, since man is by nature plenoxic, he always wants more of everything, power, money, etc. (Glaucon). Money, honor and knowledge are the primary driving forces in man. In each one of these, people tend to overreach themselves.

For Socrates, justice is beyond the law. Where wisdom rules, the law is not necessary. The just man profits both himself and the community. Life is not mere *plenoxia*. Justice is a virtue, and it is good in itself. In a just community, everybody follows his calling, and performs the work for which he is most suited. Each contributes according to his ability and receives according to his needs. There is no conflict between private needs, and the common good. Men form communities because they need each other. Men are unequal in their abilities, and are not self- sufficient. In order for the commmunity to function optimally and justly, a division of labor and a specialization of tasks according to natural endowment of each, is necessary. In a just society, each man performs the work for which he is most suited by nature. The just man does not seek his own advantage at the expense of another.

For Plato, the constitution of the human soul parallels that of the ideal state. There are three parts to the human soul: the rational (reason), the appetitive (bodily desires), and the spirited (passion). Correspondingly, there are three classes in the city: The warrior class, motivated by the desire for honor, and whose primary virtue is courage. The class of artisans, motivated by bodily desire and money. Its primary virtue is moderation. And the class of the rulers, who are motivated by the love of knowledge (philosophy). Its primary virtues are wisdom and justice. The three parts of the soul match the three classes of the state. The state is just when each of the three classes do the work of their own class. When the trader, the auxiliary, and the guardian perform their respective duties each, it will make the city just. Similarly, with the soul. Each part of the soul performs its function. The bodily appetites are restrained by reason. Courage is reason ruling and restaining the passions. Reason's virtue is sophia (wisdom). It alone can discern justice, beauty, and the form of the good. Justice is allocating to each part of the soul its specific function. The individual is just when the various parts of his soul perform their respective functions. The rational principle has to rule, and the spirited principle has to be subjected to it. The two will rule over the appetitive part.

The latter is the largest part of the soul. The higher virtues (the rational and the spirited) must keep guard over it. Together, they will defend the whole body against an attack from without.

Likewise in the state, each class exhibits its own virtue. Courage is the virtue of the class of warriors. It deals with the knowledge of what to fear, and what not to fear. Moderation is the virtue of the the artisan class. To be temperate is to accept the rule of reason, and to harmonize the three elements in the soul. Wisdom and justice is the virtue of the rulers. They rule for the interest of the community, and know how to harmonize the interest of each class with the interest of the state. "The just man does not permit the several elements in him to interfere with one another, or any of them do the work of the other". The action that preserves harmony (between the various parts of the soul and the various classes of the state) is good. The knowledge which leads to it is called wisdom. The opposite is called ignorance. When the various parts in the soul or in the state are not in harmony, there is conflict. Conflict is the enemy of virtue. For Plato, all virtues are compatible, and each requires the presence of the others. There is a unity of virtues. This is also reiterated by Aristotle. There is a cosmic order in the Universe which makes morality, and the moral order conform to it.

In Plato's *Republic*, perfect justice requires the common ownership of everything, including women and children (full communism). The community of women and children will emancipate men from selfishness, and make them desire the good. The just State will be ruled by philosophers, who have to be enticed to rule. Plato is trying to show that perfect justice is not only not possible, but that it is also against human nature. Such a city would not be natural. Man is by nature attached to family and property. Plato's Republic is a disguised argument against perfect justice. Perfect justice is possible only on the level of speech, not in actuality.

For **Aristotle,** justice is a state of character that predisposes man to do what is just. The laws are just because they aim at the common advantage. Justice is complete virtue. It concerns the actions of man with respect to what is good to himself, and to his neighbors, (i.e. not to harm or exploit others). "Justice is what is in the common interest" (Politics III, 1282 b 18.). What is just accords with a sense of proporton. The unjust man violates the sense of proportion. He takes too much for himself, and the man who is treated unjustly gets too little. When equals are awarded unequal shares or when unequals are awarded equal shares, injustice prevails and quarrels arise.

"What is just and right is to be interpreted in the sense of "what is equal"...with reference to the advantage of the State and the common good of the citizens.... In the best state all citizens are willing to rule and be ruled with a view to the life of virtue" (Politics III, 1283 b 40.).

The just man will not claim more than his share, which is proportionate to his merit. He will not take more for himself and leave less for the other. To know what is just or unjust requires a great deal of wisdom, and it is a distinct achievement of a man's character. The equitable is just in the sense that it corrects what is often only legally just. The law deals with universals, and when applied in actual situations, the result might be inequitable. The city-state is the best political forum whereby man can exercise moral virtues. The Polis aims towards man's good as such. It is concerned with man's life as a whole. Aristotle's belief in the unity of virtues is the same as that of Plato's. In the good man as in the good state the virtues are all in harmony with each other. However, the absence of conflict is not entirely good, since it is through conflict that man learns his aims and purposes in life.[1] For Aristotle, the exercise of moral virtues is synonymous with happiness. *Phronesis* (the ability to exercise right judgment) is an intellectual virtue. It is acquired through teaching, and it underlies the exercise of the character virtues. Character virtues are acquired through practice, by letting virtues become habitual. Practical intelligence requires the virtues of character. Otherwise, they will deteriorate into cunning or cleverness. Moral excellence results from good upbringing and good education. The moral man delights in doing good, and is pained by meanness. He seeks the noble, the advantageous, and the pleasant. He avoids the base, the injurious, and the painful. His virtue *(hexis)* is reinforced by his actions.

When we strive for excellence in our activity (work, projects, etc.), we derive enjoyment and pleasure. Life is an activity, and "every activity is completed by the attendant pleasure" (NE,1175 a22.). Pleasure accompanies activity *(praxis)*. Each activity is intensified and improved by pleasure. Activity *(praxis)* is at the very center of happiness. Happiness is an "activity *(energeia)* of the soul in accordance with perfect virtue" (NE 1099a23-24). Moral excellence is its own justification.

Exercises.

1. Heraclitus: "Everything that accords with nature is just." Discuss.
2. Epicurus freed men from the fear of death. How?
3. Which is the higher principle for Epicurus, virtue or pleasure? Is virtue good in itself or is it only instrumentally good?
4. What is the difference between Pre-Socratic and Socratic views on justice?
5. Plato: Money, honor, and knowledge are the primary driving forces in man. Do you agree? Examine your own primary drives.

6. Aristotle: Practical intelligence has to be combined with character virtues, if it is not to deteriorate into sheer cleverness or cunning. Comment.

Note

1. Alasdair C. Mac Intyre, *After Virtue: A Study in Moral Theory.* Notre Dame, Ind.: University of Noter Dame press, 1984.

Workshop 43.   Ethics and Politics: Aristotle's Philosophy of Action.

Action or *praxis* is what we do, not what we suffer. For example, when we get hit, we are passive, we suffer. Action and passion are opposites. Passion is connected with "to suffer". It is however a principal cause of action. We move or are being moved. The outcome (or completion) of one is action, of the other passion. A movement for which the end is present, for example, I live - I have lived, I see - I have seen, I enjoy - I have enjoyed, is an action or actuality. The action is complete in each moment (seeing is complete in each moment, so is pleasure, etc.). In acting or doing, the end is in itself, (seeing. hearing, etc.)   This is what Aristotle means by *energeia* or activity. The activity is completed at every moment. Man is a composite of matter and form. Matter is potentiality, the form is actuality. In a bronze statue for example, the bronze (matter) is potentiality, the statue (form) is actuality. Nature strives to fulfill itself. The form is more nature than the matter, because a thing is more in fulfillment in its actuality (form) than in its potentiality (matter).   The inner striving of a thing toward the fulfillment of its nature, *entelechia* , is its power, *dynamis* or capacity. Nature acts for the sake of an end *(entelechia)*. Intelligent action is for the sake of an end.

The undeveloped potentiality of a thing lies in its disposition, *hexis* or habit. *Hexis* or disposition is the thing's potential to act. We need to differentiate between action and motion, between doing *(praxis)* and making *(poiesis)*. Making and motion has an external end, an end outside of itself. In doing, (seeing, hearing, etc.) the end is in itself. The activity is completed every moment.

This rule is behind Aristotle's division of the sciences into theoretical, practical and productive. Theoretical sciences (physics, theology-metaphysics, mathematics) have the principles in themselves, the principles are in the object, (to comprehend things as they are). In the practical and productive sciences, (ethics, politics, arts and crafts), the principles are in us. We make the choices, we decide what we want to make or do. The practical sciences (ethics, politics) reflect the intellectual side of doing (activity). The end is internal to the activity. The productive sciences (art-techne, arts and crafts, medicine, etc.) reflect the intellectual side of making. The end is external to the making, to build a ship, for example.   Art represents the intellectual capacity to make things. Practical wisdom is the intellectual capacity for doing things. The using of art is higher than the making of art. The user judges the product of the maker.   The user also makes specifications for the kind of product he wants to have produced. The Statesman is the ultimate user of all Art.

Hanna Arendt (1906-1975), in her book *The human Condition* [1] states that we, as human beings, disclose our uniqueness in action. Every action is a new beginning. The private realm is that of the supplying and making of necessities. The public realm is the realm of freedom. It is the realm of true action, of what life is supposed to be. By making our private concerns the predominant ones, we have basically lost the public realm. We have lost our freedom to disclose ourselves in action, and the possibility of becoming what we really are, true human beings. For the Ancients, politics and ethics were always together, action always meant political activity *(energeia)*.

For Aristotle, the principle human function is thoughtful action. To act thoughtfully is to be human. Happiness is to do thoughtful action well. Action is the exercise of moral virtues or moral habit. It involves choice which involves thought and desire. A distinction is to be made between the free life and compulsory life (a life for money). When you are entirely motivated by money, you are not free to contemplate *sophia* (wisdom), and pursue the things that matter most in life, the good, the just, and the beautiful. Vulgar people and tyrants identify happiness with pleasure. Others identify happiness with honor. The identification of happiness with honor is too superficial. Honor depends on others. Human beings act for ends. Human actions exhibit rationality, they are guided by thought and reason. Humans act thoughtfully. Virtue and excellence is to do that (thought) well. What underlies human action is thought. Choice is the moving cause of *praxis* (action). The origin of action is choice. Choice creates our moral character. (Children don't choose.) Bad people see opportunities to do bad things, and they think that they are doing good. Good people (people of good character) are inclined to do good things. True statesmen are both clever (practically wise), and good (have moral virtue).

The practical life is perverted if it does not have something above it, some higher aim or reason. Action itself is good, but it needs to be in the service of a higher life. Practical wisdom *(phronesis)* deals with changeable things. Philosophical wisdom *(sophia)* deals with unchangeable things. For Aristotle, political skill and philosophic wisdom need to come together. Good statesmen ought to appreciate philosophy, the contemplative life. Goods of the soul have to come together with the goods of the body. All external goods have a limit. Goods of the soul are without limit. The more you have them, the more are they useful. Contemplation is the actualization of our highest capability.

For Aristotle, citizenship is participation in rule, in collective decision making, which means engaging in action. *Politeia* is the arrangement (constitution or regime) of the *polis* (the City-State). The arrangements of the citizens, of those that act and participate in rule, is the *politeia*. The *politeia* determines what is just. Action is the exercise of moral virtue. The *Polis* is taken as collective action, that is, the citizenry being organized in a certain way. Aristotle accepted slavery, but he distinguished between natural and unnatural slavery. Unnatural slavery may be thought of as an argument against slavery. Aristotle viewed slavery as an economic necessity. (Hanna Arendt: Everybody is capable of action. There are no natural slaves.)

In a good regime, the rulers should have practical wisdom. Therefore they should be good men. Political freedom means access to rulership, the freedom to participate in politics. The political meaning of freedom is equality. For Plato, freedom is escaping the cave, to be free from prejudice. "The State exists for the sake of the good life and of life only" (Politics III, Chpt.9. 1280 a 32). A common place, internal and external security, prevention of crime and facilitation of exchange (contractual obligations) are necessary but insufficient ends of a state. The *Polis* is not for the sake of mere life. The state is a community of families, it functions for their well-being. The end of the state is the good life, reflected in bonds of friendship (Politics 1189, 35-40). A political society exists for noble actions. Justice is the common interest. Merit is the basic principle of distributive justice. Perception of injustice is the most general cause for political change. "A citizen is one who shares in governing and in being governed... with a view to a life of virtue in the best state" (Politics 1282b15). The law is the embodiment of practical wisdom. Man is a political (social) animal by nature. Moral virtue deals with ends. Practical wisdom deals with means. Action is the exercise of character. Character sets our ends. It reveals choice.

Exercises.

1. Explain Aristotle's notion of activity *(energeia)* .
2. Is Aristotelian activity restricted to the public domain only? Why?
3. What is Hanna Arendt's view of human activity? How is this related to human freedom?
4. What is the difference between activity and work? What is Aristotle's view of slavery? Can slaves act?
5. What did Aristotle mean by natural slaves?
6. What is according to Aristotle the function of the *Polis?*
7. Why is moral virtue a necesary part of action?
8. What is according to Aristotle the supreme aim in life, and how does the state fit in to this?
9. How can the the notion of "natural slaves " be turned into an argument against slavery? Can humans be turned into mechanical robots?

10.   With the advanced sophistication of modern electronics and cybernetics, is it conceivable to turn robots into humans?

Note

1. Hannah Arendt, *The Human Condition.*   Garden City, N. Y.: Doubleday, 1958.

Workshop 44.   Plato and Aristotle: Can Virtue be Taught?

Socrates says in the Meno that virtue is not many but one. Virtue is the proper functioning of the soul.   The soul has three parts: appetitive, spirited (emotions or passions), and a rational part. To these correspond reasoning, feeling, and desiring. Each of these has its own particular objective, such as, knowledge, honor, and money. Plato thinks of three kinds of life: the philosophical life (goods of the soul), the public life (external goods), and the private life (the goods of the body.) The corresponding virtues are: temperance, courage, and wisdom. Justice is the proper balance between these parts under the guidance of reason. Just as health requires the proper balance of all the parts in the body, so does justice. Health is to the body what justice is to the soul. Appetite (the desire for acquisitions) should be checked by temperance, which is to be guided by reason. Otherwise it might lead to narrow-mindedness or self-righteuousness.   Passions need to be checked by courage, and courage must be guided by reason. Otherwise it will lead to arrogance or brutality. Virtue is the safeguarding of the right proportion between the various parts (faculties) of the soul so that none is destructive of the other. Now, can it be taught?

For Plato, early training should prepare the young to view reason as a friend, and accept it as a guide when they reach adulthood. The second (higher) level of education deals with the question of means and ends, that is, with the cultivation of intellectual activity. Proper early education (which for the Greeks meant gymnastic and music) will lead to the acquisition of a balanced character (i.e. virtue). The purpose of gymnastic is to shape the body, that of music is to discipline the soul. For Plato, human conduct is chiefly based on habit, and moral character is a *hexis* (habit). That is why early training is important. With respect to higher education, the teacher can only bring out what the soul inherently contains. We cannot go beyond the limitations of our nature. For Plato, knowledge is recovered through recollection, as is shown by the example of the slave boy in the Meno. (Plato uses learning as recollection as an argument for the immortality of the soul). Plato concludes the Meno with the statement that virtue comes to the virtuous as a gift from God. We can teach what virtue is, but we cannot teach virtue itself.

For Aristotle, as for Plato, early education is the basis for the acquisition of virtue, (a good moral character). Parents should instruct their children with a view towards the noble rather than the useful. True courage is not exhibited in what is brutal (like animals) but in what is noble. Music habituates the soul to true intellectual pleasures, and is conducive to virtue. Good music influences character, and shapes the soul of man. Virtue is a state of character. Moral virtue is a mean between excess and defect in passions and in actions. If happiness is an activity in accordance with virtue, it should be in accordance with the highest virtue, that is, with that which is best in us. (The rational element in the soul should be our guide and ruler.)

Our character is determined by our actions. We become just by doing just things, etc. We become courageous with our reactions to danger, and become moral in the way we deal with others. States of character arise from our activities. Moral virtue is a mean between excess and deficiency, (the only exception being excellence in wisdom). We have the power to act or not to act, to be good or bad, virtuous or vicious. Tact or good taste is a middle between the excess of humor and the complete lack of humor. The one becomes vulgar, the other uncouth and unpolished.

In the soul, there is the rational and the irrational part. A man can be unjust to himself if there is no right proportion between the rational and the irrational parts in his soul. Within the rational part, there is the part with which we contemplate the invariable, (i.e. object of knowledge), and the part whereby we contemplate the variable or the practical. Practical wisdom is to deliberate well on what is conducive to the good life. Practical wisdom is a virtue, not an art. It has the power of foresight. Philosophic wisdom deals with the knowing of things that are "remarkable, admirable, difficult and divine, but useless, because it is not human goods that they seek" (NE, 1141b 8-10). Virtue makes us aim at the right ends, and practical wisdom makes us use the right means. Cleverness is good if the aim is noble. It is mere smartness if the aim is bad. It is not enough to know virtue, but we must use it, in order to be good. Happiness is excellence of character. External goods have a limit. The goods of the soul are without limit.

Exercises.

1. What is Socratic virtue?
2. Appetite needs to be checked by temperance, passion by courage, and courage has to be guided by reason. Discuss.
3. What is Plato's recollection theory of knowledge?
4. Our character is determined by what we do (our actions), and not by what we say. Comment.
5. What is the Aristotelian distinction betwen practical and philosophic wisdom?
6. The aim of education is nobility of character. Discuss.

Workshop 45. Kant's Categorical Imperative and Hegel's Criticism of it. (Kant's Groundwork of the Metaphysic of Morals, and Hegel's Phenomenology of Spirit, #598-#671).

1. Kant's Categorical Imperative.

Kant's Categorical Imperative states the following: *"Act only on that maxim through which you can at the same time will that it should become a universal law."* The same expressed in terms of ends, leads to the following formulation: *"Act in such a way that you always treat humanity whether in your own person or in the person of any other, never simply as a means, but always at the same time as an end."* [1] The above constitues the *"supreme principle of morality."* [2] The Categorical Imperative is the essence of Kant's ethics. We may note that each statement of the Categorical Imperative starts with "act". It is action that underlies Kant's ethics. Behind each act, there is a will. The question of ethics comes down to the question of the nature of the will to act. An action can be good or bad, but only the will alone can be good per se. The true function of reason lies in affecting a *will* that is good in itself, and not as a means to some further end (i.e. a self serving end). A will that is good in itself is best reflected in the concept of duty. If the action is based on duty, it is genuinely moral. If it is based on inclination, the question of morality is left open.

Kant defines duty as *"the necessity to act out of reverence for the law."* [3] Reverence for the law means obeying it, even if it is against one's inclinations. This universal law applies to all rational beings (men). It is a maxim to guide all our actions. I ought always to act in such a way *"that I can also will that my maxim should become a universal law."* [4] It is not possible on the basis of experience alone to establish whether an action has been performed solely from duty, or whether it has been tainted with self interest. The Categorical Imperative cannot be empirically verified. For Kant however, this is entirely irrelevant. Even, if there were not a single action based on moral duty, the Categorical Imperative would still hold, since its origin lies *"in reason completely a priori."* [5] The command of reason is called an Imperative. All Imperatives express an "ought" rather than an "is" (fact). A Categorical Imperative makes an action necessary regardless of the end. A hypothetical imperative links an action to a desired end. The latter is called prudence or practical wisdom. Only the command of the moral law makes an action totally unconditioned and universally valid. It makes it both objective and necessary, even if it is against one's inclinations.

The meaning of *duty* is that it holds *equally* and *unconditionally* for all human beings. It is a purely objective principle underlying the will to act, irrespective of any subjective motives or contingent grounds. It is based on the proposition that man exists necessarily as an end, and not as a means. This idea, that each person is an end in himself, forms an objective principle of the will, which can serve as a practical law. This principle, "rational nature exists as an end in itself"[6] is both subjective (it is valid for me), and objective (it is valid for everyone else). That is all that is necessary to establish its claim to equality under the moral law. The principle is not based on any accident of nature or fortune, but on my *humanity*.

Man's dignity is based on his humanity. Man as a rational being is subject to laws made by himself and valid for all. That is what Kant means by the autonomy of the will. In this autonomy of the will lies the freedom of man and his worthiness as a human being. This will is free of any interested (subjective) motives. A will whose maxims accord with the laws of its autonomy is a holy, and an absolutely good will. A will that is not perfect (meaning holy), will depend on the principle of autonomy (freedom) as an obligation or moral necessitation. The necessity to act from obligation is called duty. Thus, the concept of duty entails the concept of freedom, since the rational being is the author of the law (made universal), that he is subject to. What imputes our actions with moral worth is not fear or interest (i.e. inclination), but reverence for the law that we both make and are subject to. The principle of the autonomy of the moral will is entirely a priori. This (the Categorical Imperative) is the sole principle of ethics. No other principle (such as personal happiness, etc.) can serve as a basis for morality. The latter would put morality on a calculative basis.

The autonomy of the will and the Categorical Imperative rest on the concept of freedom. Necessity means necessary causality. The freedom of the will is not bound by necessary causality (i.e. by the laws of nature), but by its own laws, expressed through the autonomy of the will, and the Categorical Imperative. In other words, man is free to follow the Categorical Imperative. Since morality is based on freedom, it is necessary to show that freedom is a property of all rational beings. The demonstration is a priori, and it proceeds as follows: A rational being must have reason for each of its actions. The reason cannot come from the outside, since in such a case, the action would be based on impulse rather than on rational judgment. The reason must be free from outside determinations. Only then, as practical reason or as a will to act, will it be regarded as free. Thus, the will of rational beings can be autonomous only under the idea of freedom.

A free will is not subject to efficient causation of nature. It is subject to its own, immutable moral law that rules in the realm of the intelligible world (i.e. the noumenal world of the self in itself). However, since freedom and autonomy are reciprocal concepts, one cannot use the one to explain the other. Kant points the following as the way out of this circle: Man belongs both to the sensible world of nature (the phenomenal world), and to the intelligible world of reason (the noumenal world). In the sensible world, man is subject to all a priori rules and categories of understanding (causal laws) that condition his experience and knowledge. Reason however goes beyond understanding. It marks out the limits of understanding. In the intelligible world of reason (as a rational being), man is not subject to the causality of the sensible world. In the noumenal world, man is free. This freedom is the basis of morality. When we think of ourselves as free, we operate in the noumenal world. When we think of ourselves as determined, we operate in the phenomenal world. In the intelligible realm, actions are grounded on freedom (morality). In the phenomenal world, actions are grounded on causality (happiness).

"But the intelligible world contains the ground of the sensible world and therefore also of its laws." [7] The intelligible must guide the actions in the sensible world in accordance with duty. If man belonged only to the intelligible world, his actions would always conform with duty. Since he also belongs to the sensible world, his actions ought to accord with duty. The categorical "ought" is a synthetic, a priori proposition, since it is added to the sensuous will in the natural world. (A synthetic judgment is one where the predicate is added to the subject, as in "all bodies have weight". In a analytic judgment, the predicate is contained in the subject, as in "all bodies are extended.") That the categorical "ought" is a synthetic a-priori judgment is proven by the general observation that all men strife to be right in whatever they do. They strife to morally justify their actions.

2.   Hegel's Criticism of Kant's Categorical Imperative.

The Kantian moral view is based on an absolute morality (i.e. consciousness of duty) as opposed to Nature which is indifferent to moral purpose. Moral consciousness may not be rewarded, while the non-moral consciousness may actually enjoy the action. Yet, morality cannot leave out happiness altogether. One must therefore assume that a moral consciousness is joyous in its fulfillment of duty. It is conscious of its unity and harmony with nature. The latter can only be achieved by suppressing sensuousness. It is done in the belief, that ultimately, in a distant future, reason will come to be in harmony with sensuousness. Such harmony must however be projected into a future that can never become real, since actual morality depends on its absence. This is so because, when the (sensuous) will and duty are in perfect harmony, morality is irrelevant. And, if there is complete disharmony between them, morality is not possible.

The moral individual tries to unite the sensuous will with moral duty in his actual conduct. This is how he resolves the conflict between them. Here however, another conflict arises. It is the conflict between the notion of pure duty (which is devoid of specific content), and the consciousness of many duties, each with specific content. Since actual living and doing is obviously specific, pure duty is relegated to a higher consciousness, while the consciousness that acts (actual consciousness) will be considered an imperfect one. Thus it can expect happiness not as a reward, but as an act of grace.

Moral consciousness rationalizes its action by relegating pure duty to the realm of thought. Will and duty can be perfectly united in thought, and the person will expect Grace from a Superior Being. This however brings in an element of insincerity and duplicity, since the moral individual both affirms and negates his own morality. Thus, the Kantian moral world is full of contradiction.

The assertion of ultimate harmony between morality and nature or that betwen inclination and duty are revealed as untenable, since they yield results that make morality either unnecessary or impossible. The same contradiction arises between pure duty (i.e. sacred lawgiver or universal consciousness), and a particular consciousness that is faced with conflicting duties. If God sanctions a particular act, there is no reason why he could't sanction any of the other conflicting acts and deem them equally moral. (One can easily cite any number of conflicting duties). This makes the actual act less than moral, and the underlying justification less than sincere. There is no way out of this (Kantian) dilemma. The Kantian moral view collapses by its own contradictions.

Hegel reconciles these contradictions in conscience *(Gewissen)*. The latter is a higher moral consciousness. Conscience is absolutely aware of its true self, namely, of its Spirit. This higher Spirit actualizes its being. As a result, its actions become concretely moral. The individual acting from conscience is convinced of his own truth. This truth is his duty. This is his being "for self". This duty as conviction also represents "being in itself". The lattter appears as being for another, which is indeed objectively and universally recognized. This "in itself" is embodied in the individual act. It carries the conviction that in this act, both individual duty ("for itself") and universal duty ("in itself") are equally realized. The individual acting from conscience is convinced of the rightness of his act. He must proclaim that he speaks the truth. For it is "the self which declares that it acts on truth and is acknowledged by others."[8] By doing so, the self acquires moral validity, which makes its act into an effective deed.

Exercises.

1. Reason concerns itself with ends, understanding with means. Comment.
2. A human being is an end in itself, not a means to an end. Elaborate.
3. Explain Kant's distinction between the phenomenal and the noumenal realm.
4. As a sensuous being, man underlies causal necessity, as a rational being man is not bound by the causality of nature. Discuss.
5. State in your own words Kant's Categorical Imperative.
6. Man as a moral being is free to follow the commands of reason. Discuss.
7. A moral act is judged by its intention, not by the outcome. Discuss.
8. Kant's morality is connected to duty, not to voluntary choice. Discuss.
9. Do you, as a rule, feel the need to justify your actions on moral grounds? Give examples.
10. Does Hegel maintain that morality needs to be rewarded by happiness?
11. Give examples of possible conflict between universal duty and particular duty.
12. Can the Kantian Categorical Imperative resolve this contradiction?
13. For Hegel, conscience is the ground for morality. Do you agree or disagree? Why?
14. If conscience is the determinant of morality, what determines the morality of conscience?

Notes

1. Immanuel Kant, *Groundwork of he Metaphysic of Morals,*   New York: Harper & Row, 1954. p. 96.
2. Ibid. p. 60.
3. Ibid. p. 68.
4. Ibid. p. 70.
5. Ibid. p. 79.
6. Ibid. p. 96.
7. Ibid, p. 12.
8. Hegel, *Phenomenology of Spirit.* #655.

Workshop 46. Aristotle and Marx: The Relation of Theory and Practice.

Aristotle makes a distinction between the practical and the theoretical life. The practical pertains to the politically active life (i.e. the citizen participating in the affairs of the Polis.) The theoretical life refers to the active contemplation of eternal truths. It is the life of the philosopher, the lover of wisdom, whereby wisdom is defined as the knowledge of things beautiful, divine, and eternal.

For the Greeks practice (or praxis) was synonymous with political activity. The relation of theory and practice is viewed from the perspective of human happiness. For Aristotle, happiness is the final end, the highest good, and it is the end of action" (NE 1097b 22). Praxis (activity) is placed at the very center of human happiness. The latter is defined as an activity of the soul in accordance with perfect virtue (NE 1102b5). Virtue is a state of character that inclines man to do his work, and to be good. It is a *"hexis"*, a character disposition, which is reinforced by virtuous conduct and right action. Action originates from choice as the efficient cause (one chooses to act), and one acts for the good as the final cause. A choice is moral when both the thought and the desire are based on reason.

Wisdom is seen as an intellectual virtue. *Theoria* or contemplation is its exercise. Practical wisdom deals with what is changeable. Philosophical wisdom deals with the unchangeable. The changeable includes both "making" and "doing". In doing or acting, the end is contained in the act itself. Doing *(praxis, energeia)* is its own end. In making, the end lies in the completion, (building a house, etc.). *Poesis* or making is for the sake of some end. Life is more like *praxis,* the end being contained in (the activity of) life itself. A life of inactivity cannot be a happy life. The Greeks did not consider mere making (working for a living) or pure reflecting (that is reflecting without acting) as *praxis* or *energeia.*

Practical wisdom requires deliberation and action. Deliberation without action is sterile, and action without deliberation is futile. The practically wise man will pursue moral ends because they express his moral character. Therefore his actions will always be for the good. *Phronesis* or practical wisdom is a virtue. It means the ability to form right opinions, and make right choices in life situations. When we act in accordance with our nature, we derive pleasure from our actions. Philosophic wisdom *(sophia)* is an activity that consists in contemplation of the eternal and unchangeable truth. This brings with it the highest pleasures.

The relation of theory and practice was conceived for the Greeks, in terms of the relation of the philosophical and the political life. It is life itself that unites the practical with the theoretical. Practical life is enhanced by contemplation, and theoria "completes and perfects" the practical side of life. Men like Pericles were practically wise because they had a philosophic understanding of what is good. The good statesman must unite within himself the practical and the philosophic. Politics deals with creating the necessary conditions (in the City-State or Polis) for the exercise of man's capacities, and the realization of his potential. The contemplation of the divine and the unchanging *(sophia)*, also includes the contemplation on humanity, since the species man is part of the unchanging. The good *politea* (republic) would provide the necessary conditions where human potential can be realized in its practical and contemplative dimensions.

Praxis in its modern usage differs from the Greek in that that it includes "making" or human activity that is productive in a broad sense. The latter means human labor in general. The foremost expression of the philosophy of praxis is to be found in Marx. Marxism is the philosophy of praxis. Praxis is viewed as human activity that aims at transformation of society and nature. Theory is the consciousness of this activity. Theory and practice are united in the sense that theory is a guide to practice, and practice is the expression of theory. Marx was primarily concerned with changing society towards actualization of human potential. In this, he continues the Greek tradition. Similarly, human activity or praxis is seen from the perspective of the transformation of the State toward this end. In this sense, praxis means revolutionary activity.

Marx's views on the relation of theory and practice are contained in his Theses on Feuerbach.[1] In the first thesis, Marx criticizes both materialism and idealism in terms of the cognitive relation between subject and object. In traditional materialism (meaning Feuerbach), the subject is passive relative to the cognition of the object. The sensuous image of the object imprints itself on the consciousness of the subject. The object exists by itself, and is not a product of human action in the cognitive process. It means that man is passive relative to the existence and recognition of the external world (objects) around him. In idealism, the subject grasps the object as a product of his activity. Idealism stresses the active role of the subject in the subject-object relation. The problem with this view is that it regards cognition as pure activity of consciousness, and it does not take into account real sensuous activity.

Marx conceived cognition of the object as the product of practical (sensuous, material, and real) activity, which is inseparable from the thinking activity of consciousness. True activity is neither contemplative of reality (as in Feuerbach), nor is it purely speculative (as in idealism), but an overcoming of both. True activity is revolutionary, since its aim is the transformation of reality. In the latter, theory and action are united as they both complement each other.

Action (praxis) is at the root of knowledge. Man's knowledge of nature is seen only in conjunction with praxis. The object is a product of human activity which is real, sensuous, and objective. In the second thesis, Marx discusses the relation of objective truth to practice. For thought (theory) to be objectively true, it must be tested (proven) in practice. Objective truth is not a matter of theory alone. It is both a theoretical and a practical question. The truth of a theory can only be judged as it is realized in practice. Truth cannot exist outside of, and independently from, practice. Truth or falseness of thought (i.e. reality and unreality) that is isolated from practice, is for Marx a "purely scholastic question".

Praxis is an activity whose aim is to change reality. Transformation of reality is its very definition. However, praxis itself is a function of the reality that is to be transformed. The awareness of the latter is an aspect of knowledge (theory). Theory and praxis are two sides of the activity that is designed to transform reality. If our knowledge of the nature of reality is false, our ends will not be realized. On the other hand, if our ends are realized through practice, the knowledge that guided it, was true knowledge. It is necessary, however, to guard against a simplistic or pragmatic interpretation of the relation between theory and practice. It is wrong and dangerous to interpret objective truth or falsehood in terms of success or failure of intended objectives. A true understanding of reality (in its complexity) will have a greater chance of bringing about positive results than a theory that is flawed. Success however, is not the same as truth. It is merely a measure of the extent to which thought (theory) was able to reproduce reality.

In Thesis III, Marx discusses revolutionary praxis as leading to change in man, as well as, to change in his circumstances. The third thesis is a clear cut and forceful statement against a crude, materialist conception of history, which sees man primarily as a product of his circumstances. Marx disputes the utopian socialist notion that man is a product of the environment whose influence can be mitigated only through education. Marx was reacting to German Enlightenment which greatly stressed the role of education in the proces of social change and social transformation. Society was seen as divided between the educators (enlightened philosophers ruled by reason rather than prejudice), and the great mass of people that are ruled by prejudice instead of reason. It was the function of education to free man from prejudice and superstition, and to let him see the light of reason. German Enlightenment saw the question of changing social reality primarily in terms of education.

Marx completely rejected this notion of a society whereby the educators need only to better educate others in order to bring about social change.   The implicit assumption was that the educators need not educate and change (trasform) themselves. This was characteristic of the 18th century revolutionary bourgeoisie which considered itself to be the carrier of social development, without the need of changing itself. This view of society, divided into small (active) and large (passive) segments, a subject- object division of society, was rejected by Marx. The process of social transformation necessitates continuous practice of both subject (the educators) and object (the masses).

By changing the circumstances, man also changes himself. The circumstances that shape man are themselves shaped by man. Man and his reality (circumstances) stand in a reciprocal relation to one another. The essence of this reciprocity between man and his circumstances lies in revolutionary practice. Only through revolutionary practice, can man transform himself and his environment.   Neither education nor technological and environmental changes are sufficient on their own to bring about social transformation. The latter can only be brought about through revolutionary practice. This is the chief content of Marx's famous eleventh thesis: "The philosophers have only interpreted the world in various ways; the point, however, is to change it".

The world is the object of knowledge (philosophy), and the object of change. If philosophy is to relate to the world, it cannot be reduced to mere interpretation, that is, to a mere object of knowledge. Moreover, as we have seen (Theses I and II), the world cannot be known without practice. Man knows the world to the extent that he acts upon it. Philosophy cannot isolate itself from practice if it is to be relevant to social change.

The philosophers "who have only interpreted the world" always remained within the political framework of the status quo. They have justified its existence, and served as a bulwark for its continuation. For Hegel, the task of philosophy was to reduce the world to the level of thought. What could not be reduced to thought, did not exist. When the world was fully conceived in thought, then it was as it ought to be. Theory, for Hegel, had primacy over praxis, and ideas once formulated would tend to realize themselves.

Marx accused Hegel of wanting to change reality on the level of thought alone. For Marx, the proper object of philosophy is praxis. It is the kind of philosophy that not only seeks to interpret the world, but also to change it. Such a philosophy will necessarily provide a critique of the status quo and of the philosophical doctrines that justify it. On the level of theory, this philosophy will point to the conditions and the possibilities of action (praxis) directed towards humanizing and transforming the world.

Exercises.

1. What do you understand by theory and practice?
2. Why is practice or praxis for the Greeks restricted to the public domain? What constitutes for the Greeks practical intelligence? Explain how *phronesis* and *sophia,* are to guide the public and private citizen.
3. How did the understanding of practice change in modernity? As the meaning of the term shifted from antiquity to modernity, did the public part of the term recede? What are the implication of this for the question of human freedom?
4. Is there a schism between theory and practice in an alienated culture?
5. How do you combine theory and practice in your own life?
6. What is Marx's view of the relation of theory and practice? How does Marx's view of practice differ from that of Aristotle?
7. Why is practice for Marx revolutionary activity?
8. What is the difference betwen Marx and Hegels view of history?
9. What is according to Marx, the proper function of philosophy? Is it merely a guide to action?
10 In the eleventh thesis (Theses on Feuerbach) Marx raises the question of interpretation vs. action. Discuss the eleventh thesis.

Note

Karl Marx and Frederick Engels. *The German Ideology.* Appendix: Marx, *Theses on Feruerbach.* New York: International Publishers, 1969. pp. 197-199.

SECTION VII. THEORIES OF KNOWLEDGE

Workshop 47. Skepticism as a Philosophical Issue.

The Sophists of ancient Greece may be considered as the first skeptics. The Sophist (derived from *Sophia* =wisdom) were principally teachers of Rhetoric, the art of persuasion. They taught aspiring young, and wealthy Athenians how to become successful in politics. They earned a living by teaching. (The Sophists taught for money, not for truth). In ancient Greece, success in life meant success in politics, (in the art of rhetoric and persuasion). In modern times success means success in business, (in the art of making money.) In this sense, the Rhetoric of the Sophists can be compared to modern-day advertising, where the outcome matters more than the truth. A skillful rhetoritician was one who could develop strong and opposing arguments on any topic. The art of persuasion was based on the ability of the speaker to make the weaker argument appear to be the stronger one. There was no inherent truth upon which an argument had to be based. Truth was relative to the perceiver. The Sophists held that virtue *(arete)* can be acquired and taught. (The latter is a skill, not unlike *techne*, the art of making).

The two most prominent Sophists were Protagoras and Gorgias. Protagoras (490-420 BC.) was teaching his pupils how to become successful politicians. He taught the art of persuasion. There are two arguments to each question, and good rhetoric meant the ability to make the weaker argument appear the stronger. His most famous quote is: "Man is the measure of all things, of the things that are that they are, and of the things that are not that they are not." (Plato, Theaetetus, 152a.) Truth is in appearance only. The wind feels warm to one and cold to another. Is the wind warm or cold? It is both. Things are made of opposites, and they are what the senses reveal. Opposites coexist in things. Things (as properies) are what they appear to the individual perceiver. There is no one immutable reality (truth) behind appearances. Each judges the truth as it appears to him or to her. In Ethics, this would translate itself to extreme subjectivism, (cheating and lying would be justified on the basis of their value to the individual). Protagoras modified this however, by saying that some appearances are better than others, and the community may impose a higher stanard of behavior on its members. A relativistic Ethics would nevertheless hold for different communities in different times and places.

The other famous Sophist was Gorgias, a contemporary of Protagoras. Gorgias was born around 490 BC. and lived to be more that a hundred years old. According to Plato (Meno 95c), Gorgias was not concerned with teaching virtue. He wanted to make his pupils become clever speakers. Skill in argumentation is seen as the best promise of success. Virtue is relative. (The virtue of the freeman is not the same as the virtue of the slave.) The same skill can be used for good or bad purpose. The art of Rhetoric is morally neutral. In Politics, proper timing is crucial to success, (*kairos*, the right time or opportunity). The speaker should know how to adapt his words to his audience. As with Protagoras, truth is relative, there is only opinion. Rhetoreticians need to persuade their audiences of the truth of their views (opinions). Rhetoric is the essence of politics and the art of government. The Sophists used language for persuasion rather than for the discovery of truth. They were the precursors of the later Skeptics.

Skepticism dates back to Pyrrho of Elis (3rd-4th cent. BC.), and the Pyrrhonian school of the later period. Its most notable representatives were Aenesidemus and Sextus Empiricus (ca. 200 AD.). They developed ways of skeptical argument, so called Tropes (turning or balancing modes). The basic principle of skepticism is the proposition that "to every argument an equal argument is opposed."[1] Through the application of the above principle, the skeptic learns not to be dogmatic. The opposition of equally plausible (or implausible) claims to knowledge makes the skeptic suspend judgment about the reality of sensible things. The skeptic neither denies nor asserts the truth of a knowledge claim. He simply withholds judgment. An assertion of truth or its denial are both considered to be dogmatic. The skeptic suspends judgment by pointing out the opposing sides of a metaphysical claim. He denies any decisive criterion of truth or falsity. The aim of the skeptic is to achieve peace of mind (*ataraxia* or a state of imperturbedness). Bertrand Russell (1872-1970) in his *Sceptical Essays* points out that people who have rational grounds for their opinions, argue calmly about them. Those who do not have good grounds for their opinions tend to argue with passion.

The Tropes of Sextus Empiricus (of whose the first ten are attributed to Aenesidemus), deal with the arguments that question the validity of our claims to knowledge. They show contradiction and inconsistencies in our perceptions of the external world. Men perceive things differently, and we may perceive the same object in various ways, depending on the angle of vision, location, circumstance, subjective state of mind, etc. (Recall Husserl's concept of adumbration which states the same thing but used for a different purpose, i.e. the *eidos* or idea). The Tropes are presented as a way to induce suspension of judgment. The argument runs as follows: The same object appears differently to different observers. There is no way to decide whose observation is correct and whose is not. No one can claim greater authority than any other. Should we decide on the basis of wisdom, namely, on the authority of the wise man, then how do we know whether the wise man is really wise, etc. Every point of view is partially distorted, since it is based on a particular state of mind and body. Thus, we can only say how things appear to be, and not how they are by nature, or how they are by themselves. (The argument is based on the undecidability of opposing or conflicting views.) A parallel argument has been held with respect to the possibility of objectivity in history. Some people claim that it is not possible to get an objective view of history, since historians tend to judge events from their respective particular (educational, cultural, political, temporal, national, etc.) backgrounds.

The force of the undecidability argument lies in the observation that different impressions contradict each other, (the honey is sweet or bitter, the wind blows hot or cold, etc.) The skeptics do not deny appearances, but they question the truth of these. Neither do the skeptics deny the existence of empirical objects. The question is not, is it a man or a statue? The question is, what is man? To this they suspend judgment. Given the widely differing views of philosophers about man's nature, they say that man is unknowable. The Tropes are arguments against the (dogmatic) thesis that we can know how things really are instead of how they appear to different observers.

Another type of argument in the Tropes deals with the relativity of things. Things are relative either to the observer or to other things. The argument runs as follows: (1). Each thing is whatever it is (or more precisely, what it appears to be), always in relation to some other thing, and (2) "what a thing is relatively, it is not absolutely or by nature". Therefore the skeptic will suspend judgment as to what a thing is absolutely or by its nature. Pyrrhonism is based on the equal force of opposing propositions. This makes the skeptic suspend judgment in order to achieve peace of mind *(ataraxia)*. The Skeptics do not deny the possibility of knowledge without direct evidence. Such a denial would also amount to a dogmatic assertion. They simply suspend judgment.

St. Augustine (354-430) was very much concerned with the problem of skepticism. He refuted the Skeptics. ("If the Skeptics are right, my life is worth nothing".) According to St. Augustine, the error is not in the senses. The senses are correct to the vigilant and the fair. When I see the stick bent in the water, the error is not in my senses, but in my judgment. I assent to something that is false. It is possible that the senses are defective but I must intellectually compensate for that. The soul can know things directly, without recourse to the senses. We know that we exist *(esse, vivere, cogitare, intelligere)*, and we know that we think. We can doubt the physical, but we cannot doubt our own existence.

St. Augustine's refutation of the Skeptics extends also to the moral sphere. In the moral sphere we must pertain to the truth, since we have to act, and we normally cannot postpone moral action. Think of a man drowning: should I first ascertain whether the man is actually drowning or only appears to be drowning before I jump in to save him? People resort to skeptic positions because it is difficult to attain the truth. The latter requires a sustained effort, and it may take a long time. For St. Augustine, skepticism can be overcome by faith. Faith is not contrary to or apart from reason. Faith and reason complement each other, *(crede ut intelligas;* believe that you may understand.)

St. Thomas Aquinas (1225 -1274) also denied the validity of the skeptics. For him the question of subjectivism, skepticism, and objectivism of the outer world are all false problems. We get an idea of what a dog is from all the perceptions that we get of dogs. When we abstract the immaterial nature (idea) from the object (the individual), we only get one essence. The intelligible species (idea) that I abstract from the individual is not my own private impression. If this was so, there would be no basis for objective truth, and every one's opinion would be equally valid. The intelligible species (ideas) of the outside world are not that which I know, but that by which I know. This makes a monumental difference. I don't have the problem of going from my perception to the outside world. The outside reality is conveyed to me through the intelligible species (ideas). The sense impressions may differ for different people. The essence abstracts from all these differences. It therefore must be the same for everybody. (Consider the affinity of St. Thomas Aquinas intelligible species, idea or essence, with Spinoza's common notions, and the latter with Kant's transcendental rules. They all speak of the same a-priori given necessity by which one comes to know the external world.)

Descartes (1596-1650) used the method of radical doubt in order to overcome all doubt. The new science of Galileo's Physics had to be established on the basis of absolute certainty. Nature is ruled by mathematical principles. Mathematical principles are not accountable to the senses. They are accessible to man in his capacity to think. The absolute certainty of the new science of nature was to be based on human consciousness or subjectivity. A metaphysics of subjectivity became the foundation of objectivity, an absolute foundation for all science. The *cogito* was the indubitable truth. Clarity and distinctness were to be the criteria for the truth of any idea. Gassendi,

(Gassendi, Pierre 1592-1655) questioned the certainty of what is (or appears to be) clear and distinct. By questioning the ground for the criterion of truth, he takes us back to the skeptics.

Hume (1711-1776) radically questioned causality in nature. "One event follows another: but we can never observe any tie between them". We cannot therefore conclude that there is a necessary (cause-effect) connection between them. Events are conjoined but not connected. According to Hume, the assumption of causal connection, and of uniformity in nature cannot be justified. One cannot be sure that the future will resemble the past, and there is no way to demonstrate conclusively that that which is, cannot be otherwise. Science, for Hume, is not based on absolute truth, but on probable or most reasonable truth. One such (most reasonable) truth is the assumption of a causal connection between events in Nature.

Kant (1724-1804) was awakened from his dogmatic slumber by reading Hume. Kant sought to establish a middle ground between complete skepticism with regard to metaphysical knowledge, and complete certainty with respect to the conditions for the possibility of knowledge (i.e. experience) whatsoever. He assumed that knowledge is possible, and that extreme skepticism is false. Knowledge begins with experience but does not originate in it. The transcendental, a priori, categories of understanding (including space and time) make it possible to experience (to know) the external world. All experience must be ordered and organized according to the transcendental categories of understanding. This enables us to have a science of nature. What is not subject to experience, we cannot know. By transcendental analysis, we cannot discover that which transcends experience (i.e. the thing in itself or the supersensible). The conditions of experience cannot apply to that which is beyond the limits of all possible experience, namely, metaphysical knowledge.

For Hegel (1770-1831), skepticism is a stage in the process of understanding of events. Human knowledge is a historically developing process. At each stage of the process, our knowledge is contradictory and limited. It is partly true and partly false. These contradictions are overcome in the next, higher stage of the historical development of consciousness. Each stage in the process being a away to knowledge, is also in itself, part of knowledge. Absolute knowledge can only be reached in the final stage, where no more contradictions can be developed. For Hegel, philosophy entails neither skepticism alone, nor dogmatism alone, but both at once. Every genuine philosophy sublates the principle of contradiction (such as the one and the many, substance and attributes, cause and effect, etc.). It is possible to leave out the contradiction, and develop a skeptical attitude. Hegel cites Spinoza: "God is the immanent, not transient cause of the world". Here, cause and effect are one with each other (immanent), but a cause is a cause only as it is opposed to effect. In the Absolute, cause and effect are united and not opposed to each other. Every proposition of Reason admits the resolution of two contradictory assertions, such as, God is the cause and he is not the cause, he is one and not one, he is many and not many, etc. The skeptical principle of opposing arguments is readily seen, when one puts aside the contradictory aspects of the propositions of speculative philosophy.

Exercises.
1. Are all claims to knowledge equally valid or invalid? On what do you base the validity of a knowledge claim?
2. Honey tastes bitter to the sick and sweet to the healthy. Is honey sweet or bitter?
3. A skeptic always sees both sides of an argument, therefore he suspends judgment. Discuss.
4. Who were the first Skeptics? What are the Tropes?   Do Skeptics have first principles? Is *Ataraxia* a first principle?
5. What is St. Augustine's argument against the Skeptics?
6. What is St. Thomas Aquinas' argument against the skeptics?
7. According to Hume, there is no causality in nature, only a conjoining of events. Discuss.
8. God is immanent in nature. According to Hegel, what problem does this raise?
9. When your argument is rational you remain calm, when not, you get excited. Discuss and relate to your experience.

Note

1. Sextus Empiricus, *Selections from the Major Writings on Scepticism, Man and God.* Indianapolis, Indiana: Hacket Publishing Co. 1985. p. 35.

Workshop 48. St Augustin and Thomas Aquinas on Intellectual Cognition.

St. Augustine: There are two kinds of knowledge, knowledge derived from the senses and knowledge derived from the intellect. The senses are correct to the vigilant and the fair. The error is not in the senses but in my judgment (for example, a crooked stick in the water.)The soul knows directly, without recourse to the senses, that we are, that we are alive *(esse, vivere, cogitare, intelligere)*. This is similar to Descartes' *cogito*. We cannot doubt that we exist, that we are alive, and think, *(cogitare, vivere, esse.)*

Intellectual truths are known to the soul by divine illumination. The inner light lights up the truth just as the sun lights up the senses. However, a person must be ready for the inner light to be lit up. One must be receptive to the grasping of eternal truths. Words coming from others (the teacher) do not teach us anything. It is my inner truth that makes me judge what I am hearing. The truth is not created, it was already in our mind. For Augustine, understanding has the need of the light of God. There is an inner light unknown to the bodily senses which lights up the truth for us. However, a person must be ready for the inner light to be lit up. "One must purify the soul in order to see the light of truth" (On the Advantage of Believing). "God, the sun of our soul" is not an object which we see, but by which we are able to know. We know the truth by an inner light that is unknown to the body senses. (The number by which we number are not the things numbered). I can do nothing to alter the truth. All I can do is bear witness to it. God is what is most true of all truths. Truth is common, independent, objective, mind measuring reality. That is what St. Augustine means by God.

St. Thomas Aquinas: The intellect knows by abstraction from sense representation. There are three levels of abstraction:

1. We abstract from the individual sensible matter but not from the common sensible matter. At this level of abstraction, the object (say an elephant) can neither be thought of without matter, nor can it exist without matter. This is the level of abstraction used in ordinary speech, and in natural science.

2. We abstract from the individual sensible and the common sensible matter, but not from the common intelligible matter. This level of abstraction applies to mathematics, (points, lines, numbers, quantities, etc.) On this level, the object can be thought of without matter, but it cannot exist without matter. (You can think of a triangle without it occupying space, but if it is going to exist, it has to be physical.)

3. We abstract from all matter, from individual sensible, from the common sensible and from the intelligible matter. Here the object can exist without matter (i.e. act, being, unity, spirit, existence, substance, etc.) These concepts do not involve matter at all. This is the domain of Metaphysics (philosophy).

The intellect of man is given for the purpose of understandig *(nous)*. In order to understand, we have to proceed by steps (discursively). We start with principles, premises etc. and arrive at conclusions (understanding) based on *ratio* (reason). St. Thomas holds that we can control the emotions by reason. We can do this, by controlling the objects that bring about the emotion, by an overflow of spiritual love into the body, or by controlling the locomotive powers of the body. Reasoning *(ratio)* is for the sake of understanding (intellect). The essence of a thing must be the same for all of us. The sense impressions may differ for different people. The essence abstracts from all these differences. It therefore must be the same for everybody.

Exercises.

1. St. Augustine: The error is not in the senses but in my judgment. Discuss.
2. We know the truth by divine illumination. Explain.
3. The truth is not created, it is already in us. The teacher does not teach us, he only helps us know what is already in us. Discuss.
4. Discuss St. Thomas Aquinas' three levels of abstraction.
5. The intellect knows by abstraction from sense representation. Discuss.

Workshop 49. How Viable is the Common Distinction of the Tradition of Modern Philosophy into Empiricists and Rationalists?

Empiricists justify their beliefs by appeal to experience. Beliefs (and ideas) originate in experience, and have to be tested against their origin. The reliability, and certainty of knowledge is tested against the "data" upon which it is based. The evidence must come from the senses, ("seeing is believing"). Experience consists of observation of facts and generalizations based on them. There are no self- evident (a priori) truths. All truths must be justified by experience.

The rationalists hold that there are truths that are self-evident, and a-priori. Such truths are apart from, and independent of experience. In contrast to the empiricists, the rationalists claim that truth can be derived from thought itself. Yet, the opposition between empiricists and rationalists is not a basic one. The rationalists do not deny the importance of experience for the contents of our thoughts. They similarly refer to experience for the validation of truth. Empiricists, on the other hand, also use deductive reasoning to arrive at true statements. This narrows the difference betwen them to the proposition of, whether there is, or there is not, any general truth that is not derived from experience.

The Rationalists.

Descartes, Spinoza, and Leibniz are the chief rationalists. Bacon, Locke, and Hume are the chief representatives of empiricism. It is worth noting, that the division took place along geographic lines, the British tending towards empiricism, and the continental philosophers tending towards rationalism and abstract thought.

For Descartes (1596-1650), ideas are modes of thought or consciousness. They can be grouped into innate, adventitious, or factitious ideas. Innate ideas come from our own nature. They are given to us by God. They are eternal truths not bound by time and place. Substance, God, infinity, extension, etc. are innate ideas.

Adventitious ideas are derived from experience, as for example, the idea that the sun is hot. Factitious ideas are constructed by the mind, as for example, the astronomical properties of the sun. Thus, the heat of the sun is an adventitious idea, that the sun is of a certain size and distance from the earth, (astronomical idea of the sun) is factitious, and the idea of the mind, is innate. Innate ideas (mind, matter, etc.) cannot be derived from experience, since they are necessary to comprehend experience. They are pre-reflective and pre-experiential. They are given at birth. For Descartes, thought starts from thought and not from

anything outside it. I can be absolutely certain only of thought itself.
The "I" in the "I think, I am" is indubitably certain of its being. Even
if I doubt, it is still I that am doubting. I can abstract from everything,
but not from the thinking I. Only the *cogito* is indubitably certain of
itself. I do not have such indubitable certainty of my body. I can be
deceived by a feeling of pain in a limb that has been amputated before.
    Only the subjective "I" is absolutely certain of itself. It
(subjectivity) is the corner stone of philosophy. The truth of ideas lies
in their clarity and distinctness. The latter are the criteria of truth. The
mind has the notion of a most perfect Being, whose existence is a
necessary aspect of perfection. The mind concludes that such a Being
(God) exists. This reasoning is not based on experience. The idea of a
most perfect Being is innate in us. God as eternal truth is not made by
us but is contained in us.   God is the cause of all true ideas. The
mind has the power to acquire knowledge by the natural light of reason
(lumen naturalis).   What is perceived clearly and distinctly by the
natural light of reason is necessarily, and objectively true. The natural
light of reason is given to us by God. We err because we want to
overreach ourselves. If our will extends no further than what we clearly
and distinctly perceive, then there will be no error.
    Intuitive knowledge is for Spinoza (1632-1677) the highest kind of
knowledge. It is the knowledge that all things take their existence from
God or Substance. Innate ideas are conceived as true as soon as they are
understood. "I therefore thought it wiser to unravel the difficulty
through premises ascertained and thoroughly known by the natural
light of reason."[1]   A perfect character is attained in "the knowledge of
the union existing between the mind and the whole of nature."[2]   The
reasoning from true premises to their conclusions, (a deductive system
of thought) is seen as the highest form of knowing.
    Leibniz (1646-1716) along with Plato, held that knowledge is
innate and recollected. Every monad develops its own potentialities. It
has no windows, and it is not affected by the outside. The soul is a
monad with its own innate thoughts. Monads are incorporeal, they
have no extension. Matter itself is something ideal and supersensible.
Infinite divisibility of matter implies, that it either has no substantial
reality, or that it is reducible to unextended elements or monads. The
supersensible is the source of the sensible, and metaphysics is the
source of physics. Leibniz distinguished between "truths of reason" and
"truths of fact". Truths of reason are based on the principle of non-
contradiction. Truths of fact are based on the principle of sufficient
reason. Such truths are contingent, and their opposite does not violate
the principle of non-contradiction. The universe consists of a system of
dynamic forces that coexist harmoniously, and are regulated by God.
(The idea of pre-established harmony). The predominant element in this
system is force, and extension is seen as a mode of appearance of force.

Leibniz rejected Descartes' mechanical explanation of physical phenomena through motion. He looked for the inner causes of physics, represented by the monads.

The Empiricists: Bacon, Locke and Hume.

Francis Bacon (1561 -1626) devised the scientific method based on empirical investigation. The latter is the only true source of knowledge. It opposes experience to speculation (thought). Knowledge is to be derived from experience only. Science originates in empirical knowledge. "Empiricism is not merely an observing, hearing, feeling, etc., a perception of the individual; for it really sets to work to find the species, the universal, to discover laws."[3] Science requires a progression from the individual to the universal.

Bacon divides learning, and acquisition of knowledge according to the faculties of memory (history), imagination (poetry and art), and reason (philosophy). The study of nature must rest on the investigation of efficient causes. The preoccupation with ends or final causes is left to metaphysics. Thus he states in the *Novum Organum:* "Let the investigation of Forms which are eternal and immutable constitute metaphysics."

John Locke (1632 -1704) argues that truth and knowledge have to be based on observation and experience. The scientific method (analysis and generalization) are the ways of acquisition of knowledge. The mind at birth is a *tabula rasa.* It gets to be filled through experience. Locke disputes the adequacy of innate ideas. Savages and children do not possess the idea of God. This proves that there are no innate ideas. Locke distinguishes between primary and secondary qualities. Locke's primary qualities pertain to the objects themselves, for example, extension, figure, shape, size, movement, rest, etc. Secondary qualities, such as, color, sound, smell, taste, etc., are not real qualities, since they depend on the organ of sensation. Ideas like faith, judgment, doubt, etc., come from reflection. Simple ideas derive partly from outward and partly from inward experience. The mind actively combines simple ideas into complex ones. The latter are based on understanding. General conceptions (or general ideas) are deduced from the experience of objects of the outside world. These constitute our fund of knowledge. We start from individual conceptions, and proceed to universal notions. The latter represent the general development of our mind based on concrete experience. The universal is based on the concrete or the empirical.

For David Hume (1711 -1776) all ideas come from internal or external sense impressions. Hume radically questions causality in nature. "One event follows another: but we never can observe any tie between them." We cannot therefore conclude that there is a necessary connection between the first event (cause) and the second event (effect). These are not subject to our senses. Events are conjoined, but not connected. The connection that we assign to sequential events are merely a product of our thought, so that "when the mind is presented by one, it always expects the other.[4] The world is a succession of particular events that exhibit regularity. But the world could be different from what it is, for "whatever is, may not be."[5] , and "nothing we imagine is absolutely impossible."[6] The world is not a system of mathematical relations and properties. The relations of cause-effect mean observed succession, not logical necessity. There is no power in a cause to produce the necessary effect. Laws of nature are arbitrary, and there is no necessary reason that they should be what they are. Hume does not question the uniformity and regularity of nature, but he questions the existence of an intelligible source of order, namely, God. Hume is concerned with evidence for man's beliefs. The belief in constant conjunction is a justified belief. Its denial would make experience and inference impossible. The belief in a necessary, cause effect connection, is not justified.

Hume denied the existence of a permanent self. The self is a "bundle or collection of different perceptions, which succeed each other with an inconceivable rapidity, and are in perpetual flux."[7] The mind feigns a self. However, the self as a system of constantly conjoined perceptions, is a justified belief. Resemblance, contiguity, causation, and inference, are all operations of the mind, based on custom. In the objects themselves, there is only constant conjunction. This has led Kant (1724 -1804) to awake from his slumber, and the deduction of the transcendental categories. "I openly confess my recollection of David Hume was the very thing which many years ago first interrupted my dogmatic slumber and gave my investigations in the field of speculative philosophy a quite new direction."[8]

The main difference between rationalists and empiricists is, whether there can be any general truth which is not derived from experience. The empiricists deny it. For them all knowledge comes from experience. The rationalists hold that some of our most fundamental truths, (God, substance, extension, mind, etc.) are not subject to experience. These truths are necessary, pre-experiential and a-priori. They are outside the possibility of experience and yet, they are necessary in order to have experience. The self for the rationalist, is the source of our basic, general ideas. Our important beliefs are based on reason ("the natural light of reason".) These self- evident truths are at the base of all our inferential truths, as for example, that the law should treat all men as equals. For the empiricists, there are no self- evident truths. All truths must be justified and corroborated by experience. Experience consists in observation of facts, events, etc., and making generalizations by induction. General hypotheses need to be tested by experience. The cause-effect connection is considered to be not a necessary connection but a customary one. This applies also to the field of laws and morals. "The ideas of justice and morality rest upon an instinct, on a subjective, but very often deceptive moral feeling."[9] Hume disputes the absolute validity of morality, justice, religion, etc. Morals are not universal but relative to the practices and customs of peoples. Since knowledge arises from experience, morality will differ among nations, groups and historical periods.

It is true that experience is the most reliable source of information and knowledge. However the interpretation of information is more important than the facts. Facts by themselves do not teach us anything. It is what we make of them that is important. The latter requires intelligence and the use of reason. The ability to draw the right inferences, and the right lessons from experience is an innate ability. Intelligence is not experiential but an innate ability. This makes the distinction between rationalists and empiricists, however valid, not a fundamental or a wholly justifiable one.

Exercises.

1. Empiricists: All knowledge is derived from experience. Discuss.
2. Rationalists: Truth can be derived from thought. There are self-evident truths, such as, substance , God, infinity, extension. Such truth are innate and pre-experiential. They enable us to have experience. Discuss.
3.   All things take their existence from substance (God or Nature) is an intuitive truth that is not subject to experience. Discuss.
4.   Leibniz: Truth of reason are ruled by the principle of non-contradiction, truths of fact are ruled by the principle of sufficient reason. Discuss.
5. Hume: Events in nature are conjoined not connected (through cause and effect). The belief in constant conjunction is justified, the belief in causation is not justified. Constant conjunction is a justified belief because without it, experience based on observation would be impossible. Discuss.
6. Hume: The belief in an intelligible source of order in nature (God) is not justified. Discuss.
7. The self as a system of constantly conjoined perceptions is justified, the belief in a permanent self is not justified. Discuss.
8. What about intelligence? Is it innate or acquired (experiential)?

Notes

1. Benedict De Spinoza, *A Theologico-PoliticalTreatise*.   Transl. by R. H. M. Elwes. New York: Dover Publications, Inc. 1951. p.96.

2. On the Improvement of the Understanding, The Ethics, Correspondence. Transl. by R. H. M. Elwes. New York: Dover Publications, Inc. 1955. p. 6.
3. Quoted in: Hegel, *Lectures on the History of Philosophy.*   vol. III. p.176.
4. David Hume, *An Inquiry Concerning Human Understanding.*
5, Ibid, p.144.
6. Ibid. p. 22.
7. Treatise, p. 252.
8. Kant, *Prolegomena to Any Future Metaphysics.*   p. 8.
9. David Hume, *An Inquiry Concerning Human Morals.*

Workshop 50. Kant's Theory of Representation.

Kant's purpose is to explain the conditions for the possibility of knowledge whatsoever. The question is: how do we know the external world? For Marx, we know the external world through work. All knowledge is social in nature. Hegel looks at metaphysics epistemologically, that is, how a subject gets to know an object. Kant views metaphysics as a-priori knowledge, purely conceptual, not experiential. Leibniz distinguishes between truth of reason and truth of fact. For Hume, metaphysics is what is beyond experience, (abstract or obstruse reasoning). Metaphysics concerns itself with ultimate questions, such as, questions of God, freedom, and immortality. Philosophical truths cannot be experientially demonstrated. A-priori means prior to, and apart from experience. A-posteriori concerns knowledge derived from experience. A priori judgments are always universal, judgments from experience are not universal. Their truth is not necessary, but contingent.

Kant holds that it is possible to know the external world. We can prove that there is something outside of us which must correspond to our outer peception. To invent the world from the mind is to be a strict idealist. Kant is not a strict idealist. He refutes idealism. The external world must affect me in order to have an experience. Kant has an active theory of knowledge. Kant's transcendental philosophy deals with the a-priori conditions for the possibility of experiencing (i.e. knowing) objects, whatsoever. In the previous conceptual framework (transcendental realism), objects are the starting point, and their representations (i.e. sensory perceptions) are considered as representations of objects. For Kant, representations are the starting point, and objects are thought of as objects of representations or of consciousness. Kant calls this framework transcendental idealism. Kant does not deny the independent existence of objects. He only wants to conceptualize what it means to be an object. In the older framework, knowledge of an object means that our representations (i.e. consciousness) conform to the object. For Kant, to know an object means that the object conforms to our representations (or consciousness) of it. That is what the Kantian revolution signifies.

From our senses we get a manifold of sensory impressions. We synthetize this manifold impressions into an object. This synthesis is not given by the senses. It is given by the mind, (the "I think" or the unity of self consciousness). Kant calls this, the transcendental unity of consciousness, or the unity of apperception. Kant asks: what is it that makes representations of objects into knowledge of objects? Only when these representations conform to certain a-priori rules of synthesis in consciousness, can their knowledge be possible. Only when we apply these rules to the sensory manifold, do we come to experience (to know) the object. These a-priori rules, or transcendental categories of understanding, are the very condition for the possibility of experiencing (or knowing) objects (the world) whatsoever. "The principles of pure understanding.... contain nothing but... the pure schema of possible experience."[1] Kant defines nature as "the whole object of all possible experience". The understanding can apply its a-priori principles to objects of possible experience, that is, to phenomena (appearances) only. The distinction is made betwen nature as the object of possible experience (phenomenon), and nature as a thing in itself (noumenon). Kant's transcendental philosophy aplies to the phenomenal world only. It does not apply to the noumenal world.

Kant distinguishes between judgments of perception and judgments of experience.   All judgments of experience are empirical, but not all empirical judgments are judgments of experience, (knowledge). The empirical realm includes judgments of perception. Perception precedes experience. Judgments of experience are objectively valid. Judgments of perception are only subjectively valid.   Judgments of experience of the same objects must agree with each other. Judgments of experience depend in some sense on the object, (the way the object is), a correspondence between the object and perception. In judgments of perception, there is no pure concept of understanding under which the judgment is subsumed. In perception, the subject is passive.   In judgment of experience, the subject is active, you have to add the pure concept of understanding to the sensory intuition. There is sensory intuition from the outside, and the application of the categories, (i.e. a-priori rules of synthesis) from the inside. The pure category of understanding is the rule for connecting the contents of empirical (sensory) intuition under a concept. Thinking must proceed according to necessary rules. Cause and effect are by themselves not given in experience. They are supplied by the understanding. The concept of magnitude (length) is prior to the statement that a straight line is given by the shortest distance between two points. There must be a finite list of pure concepts of understanding. Pure concepts serve to unite the multiplicity of sensory intuition. A category is an a-priori rule or principle of possible experience. The a-priori, transcendental categories of understanding include concepts of quantity, quality, relation, modality, causation, etc.[2] Space and time are included in Kant's scheme as super-categories. Space and time, outer and inner sense, are conditions for the possibility of experience whatsoever. Space and time are only in the mind, not in the object. Cause and effect are not themselves given in experience. They are supplied by the understanding.

There are 12 basic ways that the mind functions, (12 categories of understanding plus space and time.) Space and time are forms of intuition, super-categories. Rules of understanding, categories or a-priori rules of synthesis, must be added to perception in order to yield knowledge. In perception, the subject is passive with respect to sensory inuition. In judgment of experience, the subject is active, he brings the sensory intuition under the categories. Sensory intuition (phenomena and the sensory manifold) comes from the outside, and the generation of the object comes from the inside. It is all a matter of judgment. All objects of experience reflect the objective criteria, (the categories, quantity, quality, relation, causality, modality). We put causality into experience because we cannot conceive anything without causality. Transcendental analysis deals with the possibility of experience. (A transcendental argument is an argument from the possibility of experience). The conditions of experience are not given in experience, they transcend experience.

Pure concepts of understanding concern appearances only. They do not apply to the noumena. Noumena stand outside of experience. What is given in experience has only phenomenal value. Any claim about noumena must be based on a transcendent use of reason. All representations are at first judgments of perception, that is, modifications of consciousness derived from sensory input. Only when they are subsumed under the a priori concepts of understanding, do they become judgments of experience. Noumena ("things in themselves") are outside of experience. Any claim about noumena is a transcendent of the mental faculties. Reason is transcendent of the mental faculties. Science is concerned with nature. Nature affects us in a material sense, by sensibility. Nature affects us in a formal way, by means of the constitution of the understanding. There are rules in nature. These are applied by the mind in order to arrive at objects of experience. Nature and its laws are rooted in understanding. Metaphysics is concerned with pure rational concepts that cannot be given in experience. It is concerned with the occupation of reason with itself. Reason tends to make general claims about the totality of experience, but the totality is never given. There is a tendency in the mind to reach out beyond possible limits. The right use of knowledge is in understanding. Reason attempts to expand knowledge beyond the sphere of experience. Reason gives us the possibility of knowledge. It does not give us the object of experience. We can call the "thing in itself" substance, but we cannot prove it because we have no experience of it. The concern with reason is an illicit use of knowledge. The ideas of reason (metaphysical ideas) are useless to the understanding with respect to necessary experience.

Kant is trying to specify the legitimate bonds of reason. He shows the bonds of reason through the antinomies. There are four pairs of contradictory metaphysical doctrines or antinomies. The two doctrines in each pair seem to contradict each other directly. The antinomies are rooted in reason itself. They cannot be resolved. In each pair of the antinomies, both the thesis and the anti-thesis can be demonstrated. The first pair of antinomies: The world has a beginning, it is finite in space and time. The world has no beginning, it is infinite in space and time. The second pair: Everything in the world consists of elements that are simple. There is nothing simple, everything is composite. The third antinomy pertains to the relation between freedom and determinism. Causality relates to the physical realm, the realm of appearance. Freedom is the capacity to initiate a series of causes. In the realm of morals, there is freedom. In nature there is determinism.

Representations are united in consciousness through thinking. For Kant, thinking is the same as judging. A judgment is either analytical or synthetic. A judgment is analytic if the predicate is included in the subject, for example, "All bodies are extended". Every analytic judgment is a-priori, since its truth does not depend on experience. Synthetic judgments are based on experience, for example, "all bodies have weight" can only be known from experience. All experiential judgments are synthetic a-posteriori. Synthetic judgments are either a-priori or a-posteriori. Synthetic a-priori judgments constitute philosophical knowledge. Non-experiential, a-priori judgments are analytic or synthetic. Mathematical judgments are synthetic a-priori, since we require an a-priori intuition in order to perform the operation. The same also holds for the principles of physics, as for example, in the statement, that the quantity of matter in all physical change remains unchanged. The latter is a synthetic a-priori judgment. All definitions are analytic a-priori judgments. Knowledge is always in the form of judgment. The judgment occurs in the form of these two pairs of a-priori and a- posteriori. Synthetic a-priori judgments give us access to philosophical knowledge. The rationalists seek to have knowledge a-priori. The empiricists try to have knowledge a-posteriori. Kant is combining the two.

Understanding is a faculty whereby the distinctions get to be united. Understanding forms unity out of diversity. It is a unifying principle. For Kant, the supersensible (the thing in itself) explains the sensible. We derive the appearance from the supersensible. (Appearance and the supersensible, the straight world and the inverted world, somehow, we have to put them together.) For Kant, a priori judgments, (judgments not derived from experience), are both necessary and universal. Whatever we know through the senses, including inner sense, is the realm of the phenomenal. We synthetize appearances according to rules (necessary laws). For Kant, necessary means according to rules. These rules, or categories of understanding, are universally valid. In addition to the understanding, we also have the intellectual faculty of reason.   Reason is the grasping of the unconditioned prior to the conditioned. It is not possible to experience the unconditioned. Reason regulates understanding, but one can never directly experience reason.   Reason is the transcendental idea. Understanding is based on experience. Understanding is empirical. For Kant, reason is subordinate to understanding. Reason consists merely in regulating understanding. Reason points to the possible in the actual. Understanding separates the possible from the actual. For Kant, truth is related to thinking, not to knowing. (For Hegel, truth is in knowing.)

Pure mathematics requires the construction of concepts.   In philosophy we analyze concepts. Both philosophy and mathematics are synthetic, a-priori. Pure intuition is a-priori. Sensory intuition is a-posteriori. It contains the contents of experience. The will is free, is an example of an a-priori synthetic judgment. Kant is concerned with the conditions for the possibility of metaphysics, not with actual metaphysics. How is metaphysics as a science possible? For Kant philosophy must be a science.   Mathematical knowledge is not empirical, it is a product of pure reasoning. It is based on pure, a-priori intuition. The contents of the objects in mathematics are space and time. Space and time are pure intuitions, time is a form of inner sense, and space is a form of outer sense. Everything that is given to us in experience must be in space. Geometry is the science of space. Appearances contain only what geometry prescribes to them. All external objects must conform to conditions of geometry. Anything understood in geometry a-priori must be demonstrated a-posteriori, in experience.

Physics deals with things as they appear to the senses. Metaphysics deals with things as they really are. Properties belong to appearance only. All properties are appearances, they don't inhere in the noumenon, the "thing in itself". The "thing in itself" we cannot know. Temporality and spatiality do not belong to the object, they belong to the condition of the experience the object. Objects are not in space and time.   Kant denies the so called container theory of space and time. Space and time are not objective, they do not possess objective existence. Space is a way that "I" (a subject) can experience an object. Space is only in the mind, not in the object. Our ideas about space and time are not derived from experience. They are the form, and not the content of our experience of the world.

The universal laws of nature are examples of pure a-priori concepts. The universal laws of nature give us the a-priori conditions for the possibility of experience of nature. The possibility of experience and the universal laws of nature are one and the same, they are both conditions of knowledge.   Nature and its laws are rooted in understanding. Metaphysics is concerned with pure rational concepts that cannot be given in experience.   Reason tends to make general

306 Introduction to Philosophy and Applied Psychology

claims about the totality of appearances, but the totality is not given to experience. One cannot draw conclusions with respect to the whole. Ideas of reason are inherent in the nature of reason itself. There is a tendency in the mind to reach out beyond any possible limits. Knowledge in the right sense, deals with understanding.

The origin of the idea of reason lies in the subject (psychology), the object (cosmology), and in the combination of the two. Reason attempts to extend knowledge beyond the sphere of appearance. The psychological idea of the subject is when you subtract all the accidents from substance. Pure reason requires us to see all possible subjects in every predicate. It leads to the ultimate subject (the ego), in all possible subjects. This ultimate subject is Kant's view of the soul. We can call it the thinking self, substance (or soul), but we cannot prove it because we have no experience of it. The self as subject (as noumenon) is never given to itself. The self is given as an object of thought, (an intersubjectivity and a comparison with other selves). We cannot make any statement concerning the permanence of the soul after death.

Exercises.

1. Kant defines nature as "the whole object of possible experience." Discuss.
2. Space and time do not have objective existence. They exist in the mind only (super-categories of understanding). Discuss.
3. Reason attempts to expand knowledge beyond the sphere of existence. Reason is transcendent to the mental faculties. Discuss.
4. For Kant, to know (experience) an object, we must start from the self. From the outside we get a manifold of sensations. When we subject this manifold to a-prori rules of understanding, we get to know the object. Comment.
5. Knowledge, for Kant, pertains to appearances (phenomena) only. The "things in themselves" (noumena) we cannot know. But if the noumenon is not knowable, how do we know that there is a noumenon?
6. Are the Kantian categories of understanding the same as Spinoza's common notions, (i.e. what is both in the part and in the whole)? Discuss.
7. Physics deals with things as they appear to consciousness. Metaphysics deals with things as they really are. Comment.
7. Why are the categories of understanding called transcendental?
8. What are the Kantian antinomies? Are they inherent in reason itself? Discuss.
9. Why is freedom important to morality?

Notes

1. Immanuel Kant, Critique of Pure Reason, Transl. by F. Max Muller. New York: Macmilan Company,1966. p. 187.

2. See, Kant, *Prolegomena to Any Future Metaphysics*. New York: Macmillan Publishing Company, 1989. Transcendental Table of the Concepts of the Understanding. (p. 51.)

Workshop   51.   Hegel's theory of Knowledge.

For Hegel, the way to knowledge is already a part of knowledge. The exposition of the untrue is a necessary step toward the true. The same holds with regard to self- knowledge. Self-examination is already a part of self-knowledge. Glossary of Hegelian terms: The "in itself" is the essence of the thing. The "being in itself" is the truth. "Being for itself" is being for another, i.e. relating. This corresponds to the object and the notion. The object is the "in itself" and the notion is the "for itself". As my knowledge of the object changes, the object also changes. The dialectical movement of the object and its knowledge (the notion), leads to new (higher) levels of truth. This is what we mean by experience. Since the object changes as my view of the object changes, experience means the arising of new objects. Hegel relativizes the two poles of appearance and essence. Neither is absolute in itself. The inessential is a necessary moment in the grasp of the essential. Experience is a movement in the subject -object relation, (appearance - essence, the in itself- for itself) or interaction. To tell a story is to exchange experiences. Our conception of the object and the object must coincide. The object possesses intrinsic being (it is objective), but this intrinsic being is ultimately in our consciousness. The essential object is the object perceived, (objectivity depends on subjectivity.) There cannot be any kind of experience outside the subject. The interplay of the singular and the universal is called commom sense. The dual nature of consciousness: I am part of the world and I am also all the world. We overcome this opposition (the split) in our consciousness through our actions. We actualize ourselves in what we do.

Hegel gives up the notion of certainty as a condition for truth. For Hegel, truth is in the whole. He is concerned with the framework of knowledge in general. There are many interpretations, some of them may be better than others. If we make a foundation a condition for the beginning of a theory, we can never begin. It leads to a bad infinity, (what is the foundation of the foundation, etc.).   There is no unassailable initial principle. Instead of an initial principle, we must have the notion of system or the whole.   Hegel is trying to create a structured identity of subject and object, where the differences are preserved through the category of the whole or the totality.   Hegel thinks that there must be many more categories in order to embrace all reality.   To deal with all objects of experience, we need to have categories on different levels, etc. (Categories explain the primary nature of appearance.) The explanation of presentations (or representations) requires sensory intuition (the object), intellectual intuition (the subject), and the unity of the two (subject and object united in the presentation). The development of consciousness proceeds in three stages: from (1) sensuous consciousness to (2) perceptive consciousness to (3) understanding.

In sensuous consciousness (or intuition), the object reaches me through the senses, whether internal or external. Its presence is immediate. The form of the object, namely, its occurrence in space and time, is grasped by intellectual intuition. By this intuition, the manifold of sensations coalesce into an object (unity). The single object cannot be confined to itself, since it relates to and involves the other. "The *proximate* truth of the *immediately singular* is......its being related to another". (Philosophy of Subjective Spirit, #419.) This truth (the object's relation to another) can be determined by reflection only, that is, by perceptive consciousness. To experience means to relate what is sensuous to a universal, that is, to cognize in each singular its own inner connectedness, and its relatedness to other objects (the world). Sensuous apperception sees concrete objects as existing by themselves. The multiple properties of objects (or their internality, for example, the crystaline form of a grain of salt, its salty taste, etc.) are free from this (negative) bond of the singular object and also free from one another. Thereby, they are coming closer to that of universal matters.

The proximate truth of perception is that the general object is an appearence, while the internality is universal. The internality consists of multiple universals. This internality of the object is on the one hand, a sublated multiplicity of the sensuous manifold (the object), and on the other hand, it is itself a multiplicity. The difference between the above (i.e. a multiplicity that is sublated in the object, and a multiplicity that is contained in the object) underlies the realm of the laws of appearances. The passage from perception to understanding takes place when consciousness raises itself from "*the observation of immediate singularity* and from the *mixture* of the *singular* and the *universal* to comprehension of the *internality* of the general object, so that the general object is determined the same way as the ego". (Ibid, #422, italics given.)

The understanding consciousness possesses the truth of the objective world to the extent that it grasps their non-sensuous internality, which is the same as its own, namely, the self or the identity of subject and object. The truth of understanding is attained in the unity of subject and object. This unity is achieved in the understanding that the universality of reason that signifies the object is the same universality that signifies the subject. (My ego, *"which now includes the object within itself"*. Ibid, #438.) This comes very close to the notion of the (Spinoza's) immanence of substance in the object (mode). Hegel expresses a historical view of philosophical systems. He wants to make the history of philosophy integral to philosophy.

For Descartes, philosophy should be only systematic, what we need is a method. For Kant, philosophy is wholly a -priori. Both Descartes and Kant reject the idea that philosophy is historical. For Hegel, philosophy and the history of philosophy are integrated. The goal of human history is the realization of the idea of freedom, reason freed from dogma. He thinks that the central problem in philosophy is the problem of knowledge, and if the structured totality, the unity of subject-object has been demonstrated, then philosophy has come to an end. All previous theories are incomplete attempts to resolve the problem of philosophy, the subject-object unity.

Philosophy is the study of reason. Speculative philosophy is the activity of reason upon itself. Reason deals with itself, and is grounded in itself. Reason comes to grips with the whole of experience. Reason is the philosopher's tool. We need philosophy in order to bring unity to multiplicity. Philosophy aims at unity, a featureless unity, a unity that preserves the differences. One cannot isolate the result of the process from the process. He rejects the notion of understanding as productive of knowledge in the full sense. Reason needs to show that the opposites are relative. Understanding provides fixity of discreet entities. Reason relativizes these differences. The task of philosophy is to unite the differences, in a unity that underlies diversity. The Absolute is produced by reason, he is therefore present. Unlike understanding, reason is self-aware. The task of philosophy is to construct the Absolute for consciousness. Hegel denies the distinction between appearance and essence. Reason is connected to the Absolute. There is no opposition between subject and object, the finite and the infinite in the identity of the Absolute. The Absolute is produced as an objective totality, where each part is connected to the whole. Nothing starts outside reason. Knowledge can be infinite.

Exercises.

1. Truth is in the whole. Discuss.
2. The categories explain the primary structure of appearance. Explain.
3. What does Hegel mean by sensuous and intellectual intuition?
4. The sensory manifold is a manifold of particulars. They are united (bonded) in the object. Each particular taken by itself is also a universal. Discuss.
5. Is substance the binding force that holds the particulars together? Discuss.
6. To know an object requires both object and subject without either being the starting point. Discuss.
7. Philosophy is the study of reason. Comment.
8. What is, for Hegel, the difference between reason and understanding?

SECTION VIII.
MISCELLANEOUS TOPICS

Workshop 52. Some Ancient Views of the Organization of the Sciences.

Scientific thinking goes back to the Presocratic philosophers. Thales of Miletus was a naturalist. Water was the material cause of everything. Anaximander realized that not everything can be accounted for naturalistically. By bringing in the unbounded *(apeiron)*, he moved towards philosophy. Anaximenes provides an account for motion and change. Hot and cold, rare and dense are the moving principles. Air is the medium where motion takes place. Everything can be explained by air. Anaximenes may be thought of as a materialist monist. He is also the first experimental scientist in the sense that he relies on observation for his studies. Meteorological phenomena are explained in terms of rarity and density. He attempts to be systematic, and he takes Thales' naturalism as far as he can.

Xenophanes is dubious about the naturalistic account of the world. There are things that are not subject to our experience, and of these we can only conjecture. Xenophanes searches for wisdom. In this, he is a real predecessor of Plato.

For Heraclitus, *Logos* is the plan of the universe. It reconciles all oppositions. There is an underlying unity in the diversity. There is a unifying reality behind all change. This underlying coherence of things is expressed in the *Logos*. The *Logos* is the common and the rational. One may apprehend it or misapprehend it, but one must follow the common. The common *(Logos)* is the rational, and the universe functions according to natural law. Fire ("the world is an everliving fire") is the originative stuff of the universe. This would make Heraclitus a materialist monist. Fire may also be considered as another name for *Logos,* (fire as illumination), which would express a non-materialist view.

The Pythagoreans account for the plurality of things by mixing. Ratio or limit is the principle of mixing. The ultimate principle is the One (the limit). Out of the one, numbers are generated. The

Pythagoreans look for formal causes and essences of things. The latter are to be sought in numbers. The number series begins with two. One is not a number, it is the principle of number. Unlike the Ionians who were materialist monists, the Pythagoreans may be considered to be idealist- pluralists.

For Parmenides, genuine objects of knowledge are forever unchanging. The world of change and diversity is the way of seeming, not the way of truth. Truth sees being as one, unchanging and eternal. The way of truth is about truly intelligible objects. Some connect this to the Platonic forms.   Thought (the intellect) is directed towards being or truth. From a finite, (human) perspective, being that is immutable and one, appears as mutable and many. Truth is opposed to appearance, and a finite (human) perspective is opposed to an eternal one. The Eleatics are thought to be the founders of dialectics, through the use of refutation *(elencus).*

Empedocles developed a theory of cognition. Cognition is like by like. Things give off certain effluences that come out of the pores, and are received through sense receptacles. (In the Meno, Plato says that color is a film from the body, and depending how it fits, one sees it a certain way.) There are effluences from everything. The mind is likened to what it cognizes when it gets informed. (Like to like is later to become Aristoteles' theory of cognition.) Effluences are delicate mixings of the four roots. The mind is perfectly mixed, equally receptive to all.

The four roots (earth, fire, water, and air) are the ultimate beings. Everything is a mixture of the four roots. Love and strife are the causes of mixing and unmixing. Love and strife alternate in the cosmic cycle. Love is the principle of synthesis and coherence. It is the formula for mixing.   The sphere of Love is the ultimate deity, the ultimate intellect, and a harmony. It imbues the world with value. It is the formal cause of things. Strife is the principle of stress, separation, and decomposition. Decomposition or death leads to renewed composition. Empedocles had a rudimentary account of an evolutionary theory. In his zoogony, only those suited for existence would survive. Love *(aphrodite)* gave birth to the eyeball, and to seeing *(theoria).* Only air, fire, earth, and water have a nature of their own. All other things (trees, etc.) get their nature from humans who assign names to them.

Anaxagoras had a theory of matter (cosmogony) and a theory of mind *(nous).* The original single substance (matter) was a mixture of everything (everything in everything, except mind). The original matter includes innumerable seeds. These seeds are akin to prime matter. (For Aristotle, prime matter accounts for the transposition of one element into another.) Mind is infinite and self ruled. It is mixed with nothing and it consists only of itself, it is incorporeal and has no extension. *Nous* (mind) is an abstract principle that controls the cosmos. It is the cause of motion, and of all compositions as well as of all separations. It is incorporeal, and also the finest and the purest of everything that is.

Democritus, Loecippus and Epicurus held that corpuscular chunks or atoms are the building blocks of the universe. This is why they are referred to as atomists. Atoms exhibit infinite sizes, shapes and positions. All differences between physical objects are to be explained in terms of differences of shape, size and arrangement of atoms. Atoms are ungenerated, indestructible, and indivisible. There exist only atoms and the void between them. The latter makes movement possible. Atoms are always in continuuous motion, and they collide with each other. This leads to compounding, to change, and to separation. Quality is derived from quantity. Qualitative change is merely a kind of quantitative change, a displacement of atoms.

The atomistic theory is naturalistic. There is no human quality to the cosmos. This has lead Epicurus to state that death was nothing. One need not fear death. Once the uncertainty connected with death is overcome, there is no more reason to fear death. Sense perception is the ultimate criterion of science. Sense perception takes place through an atomic film that touches the senses. Epicurus modified the atomic theory of Democritus and Loecippus by introducing the doctrine of the slight swerve instead of straight path collisions of atoms. The slight swerve is meant to account for individuation and free will.

Plato and Aristotle.

In Plato's currriculum of the Guardian class, the first quadrivium (to age 17-18) consisted of arithmetic, geometry, astronomy, and harmony. Mathematics dealt with numbers or discrete quantities. Geometry deals with continuuos quantities. (Analytic geometry combines the two.) For the Greeks, mathematics was ontological. It dealt with things. Modern mathematics deals with symbolic numbers, irrational numbers and not with numbers of things. In Plato's curriculum, astronomy comes after the study of geometry. Plato gives a mathematical depiction of the heavens. The heavens are in the realm of approximation of the perceptibles. He uses mathematical descriptions as a way to make the phenomena of the heavens conform to our understanding of them. This is an instrumentalist (save the phenomena) approach to the philosophy of science.

The curriculum, between the ages of 18 and 20, consists of gymnastics. After that, (age 20 to 30) comes synoptics, that is, putting all the acquired knowledge together. At the age of 30 to 35, one learn dialectics. It means to give an account of things. The knowledge of the good is dialectic in a higher sense. The good is compared to being adopted. It causes pain. In the divided line

(Republic, Books VI and VII), Plato differentiates between the visible and the perceptible. The divided line is between the being of things and the faculties that comprehend them. In the lowest section of the line are the images of real things. The image is to the original as the perceptible is to the form. We apprehend the images through our faculty of imagination and conjecture. We apprehend sensible objects (trees, plants, etc.), through the faculty of trust. (We trust that the things are what we see.) This is the beginning of knowledge, but such knowledge is imperfect. It is more in the nature of opinion *(doxa)* rather than knowledge. In the upper half of the line, there are the perceptibles and the intelligibles (the Forms). Mathematics breaks out of the perceptibles. One uses perceptible objects (triangles, lines, etc.) as images of the original. Science begins with assumptions and one reasons from them. One assumes that there are lines. Philosophy asks: what are lines? The lowest cognitive state is conjecture. At the level of thought, we have the scientific or mathematical analogy to conjecture. In philosophy (dialectics) we try to justify the hypotheses or come up with higher hypotheses to justify the lower ones. In order to avoid infinite regress, we assume that there is an ultimate principle, the good. In the highest section of the line we don't use perceptible things at all. We use dialectics. We just talk. Philosophy comes after all the sciences. It is not foundational. To the extent that sciences deal with universals, they are on the third level, the level of perceptibles. The arts, (shipbuilding, shoemaking, etc.) do not fit in to this schema. Scientists keep us from knowing to the extent that they take their assumptions as ultimate. For Plato, the good is the ultimate original of which everything else is the image. All the forms are images of the good, and all the opinables are images of the forms. The knowledge of the good activates the soul. The good is analogous to the sun. As the sun is the source of all light and vision, the good is the principle of all, the *arche* and the ruler. As the sun is to the visible, so is the good to the intelligible. The sun - good analogy implies that one cannot stare at the sun or at the good for too long. The idea behind liberal education is to free man from the cave. The cave stands for the visible world of the senses, and the conventional world of the community. Each community has its own cave. After the escape from the cave, there are all the levels of the divided line. Can one drag anyone out of the cave? Plato answers: No. One cannot force education on anyone.

In the Timaeus, Plato presents a synoptic account of natural science. He defends the theory of Forms as the only entities accessible to knowledge. Of things that change, that is, of the sensible world, only opinion and conjecture is possible. In the Theaetetus, Plato says that we can make mistakes about timeless objects like numbers, and that we can know certain truths about the everyday world. In the Parmenides, he argues against the theory of Forms as the only genuine science. The sciences, for Plato, include dialectics, mathematics, astronomy, zoology, anatomy, and physiology.

Aristotle divides the sciences into: theoretical, practical, and productive. The theoretical sciences include first philosophy, mathematics, and physics. The practical sciences include ethics, and politics. The productive sciences include shipbuilding, architecture, rhetoric, poetics, etc. They are the applied sciences and the arts. The underlying principle of division is based on the purpose of knowledge. Theoretical sciences seek to know things as they are always or for the most part. Knowledge in the theoretical sciences is pursued for its own sake. In the practical sciences, knowledge is pursued for the sake of action, that is, to know the relative good in living well. In the productive sciences, knowledge is pursued for the sake of making, that is, to know how to make things.

First philosophy, (metaphysics or theology) deals with the changeless or the divine. Metaphysics is the science of being qua being. It examines the most basic *archai*, the first principles and causes of things *(ousiai)*. It asks, what is being, or *ousia?* It seeks to know the essence (the whatness) of things. How did this thing (the table, etc.) come into existence. The table is the outcome of a process. The necessary conditions of any process (or the reasons why) are as follows:

1. What is it? (The formal cause.)
2. Of what is it made? (The material cause.)
3. How and by what was it made? (The efficient cause.)
4. To what end was it made? (The final cause.) It deals with the why in the matter, the form, and the mover. It is that "for the sake of which", the thing was made. The first two causes (matter and form) are situated within the object, the other two (efficient and final), are situated outside the object. The causes can thus be divided into external and internal ones. Formal, final, and efficient causes often coincide (Physics, 198a 24.). Mathematics is the science of changeless things, (magnitudes, lines, points, surfaces, solids, and numbers). They are abstracted from things that change. Physics is defined as the science of things that change, (come into being and perish). It is the science of motion and process. Physics encompasses also biology, which deals with change that is peculiar to living things. This includes growth and decay. The practical sciences, politics and ethics, aim to discover man's function, and how to achieve it. The good for man is that what he seeks by nature (happiness). It is the fulfillment of his function. Politics is a branch of practical knowledge. It is part of ethics, which deals with men in groups. Man is a political animal and his nature is to live in communities (groups). The *Polis* (the city- state) is the best forum to serve man's ends, and the exercise of moral virtues.

The productive sciences are the sciences of how to make (produce) things, *poiesis*. The Topics deal with how to make an argument. Rhetoric deals with how to make a good speech. The fundamental concept in human production is art or *techne*. Nature makes things out of her own materials. Man makes things out of other things, (a house is made out of wood and bricks, etc.) Art completes what nature is unable to finish. Art completes nature. Art is *mimesis,* an imitation of nature. Nature is movement, action and process. Art imitates nature's way of acting. The four causes may be all reduced to the formal cause alone, since matter is the potentiality for the actualization of form, the efficient cause is the form in the mind of the maker (the artist), and the final cause is the end which is always for the sake of the form.

Exercises.

1. What is materialist monism? Materialist pluralism? Idealist pluralism?
2. What is a naturalistic account of the world?
3. Why did the Epicureans not fear death?
4. What is an instrumentalist approach to the philosophy of science?
5. How did Plato view dialectics?
6. Plato's divided line (Republic Book VII) is that between the being of things and the faculties that comprehend them. Discuss.
7. What is Plato's idea of a liberal education?
8. How does Aristotle divide the sciences?
9. Discuss Aristotle's causes of change.

Workshop   53.   Kant's   Aesthetics.

Kant (1724 - 1804) does not lay down a determinate concept as ground for art. The beautiful is not grounded in the good, the useful, or anything else. The origin of art is not determined by the principle of sufficient reason. The true   work of art is a product of pure imagination. The free play of imagination is harmonized with the reflective power of judgment. Imagination prompts reason to think. The purity of a work of art is not to be found in its structure but in its movement. The work of art opens the mind to a *telos* without teleology. Imagination mediates the world of nature and the world of freedom. The mirror through which we look at the work of art is in the imagination.   The work of art is purposive without purpose. The realm of order (nature), and the realm of imagination are conjoined. Imagination judges independently of ground. It is an indeterminate judgment. The universal is never at hand. There is the aesthetic search for a universal. (In a determinate judgment, the particular is subsumed under a universal which is given.) The pure work of art is not an object. It is a play of aesthetic and cognitive relations. Nature is viewed as freedom rather than as an object of cognition. Reason turns to imagination in order to expand the pure work of cognition. The aesthetic idea embraces reason and imagination. The movement of appearance as it appears in imagination supplements the epistemic world. The sensible is being judged for the use of the supersensible. Art bridges the gap between the phenomenon and the noumenon. A work of art is a distinct relation between mental powers, it points away from itself, and lets judgment be free.   The free lawfulness of imagination puts imagination in the service of understanding. It makes the free play of imagination possible. The latter is a source of great pleasure.

The beautiful is linked to the idea of taste. Kant elucidates four moments of the beautiful: disinterestedness,   universal communicability,   purposiveness,   and   social   necessity. Disinterestedness in the object is an essential apect of the beautiful. In Kant's words: "A judgment of taste,... is merely *contemplative*, i.e., it is a judgment that is indifferent to the existence of the object....Taste is the ability to judge an object...by means of a liking or disliking *devoid of all interest*. The object of such a liking is called *beautiful*. "[1] The exclusion of interest from the judgment of taste also justifies the claim for universal communicability. Judgments of taste are subjective, but can be communicated and shared by everyone, (second moment). The third moment is summed up by Kant in the following: "Beauty is an object's form of purposiveness insofar as it is perceived in the object without the presentation of a purpose."[2] And, the beautiful is an object of necessary liking   because the quickening of the imagination harmonized with the understanding (free harmony) is a source of pleasure available to everyone (the fourth moment).

The free play of imagination is related to an object that is beautiful. The beautiful is the relation of all four moments. The relation   highlights the beautiful as movement between imagination and contemplation. Purposiveness connects imagination with representation, ..."it involves... the relation of the presentational powers to each other...this relation, present when judgment determines an object as beautiful, is connected with a feeling of pleasure, a pleasure that the judgment of taste ...declares to be valid for everyone."[3]   The free space in pure taste is not dominated by any cognitive or moral rules. Pure taste is consonant with pure pleasure. Aesthetic purity is connected with aesthetic pleasure. The pleasure is purely intellectual. It is not the pleasure of the senses or of the good. The beautiful points to its disinterested nature.

The work of art is elevated to the pure realm of imagination. Disinterestedness is the very freedom of imagination. The pure work of art is the basis for universal communicability of the beautiful. The beautiful ought to be liked by everyone, not that it will be liked.   The pleasure of the pure work of art is derived from the freeing and the loosening of the cognitive dimension. The aesthetic rule is free of any individual cognition or moral will. It is a free pleasure. The purposive play of imagination is always a new play. The traditional relations between imagination and representation are loosened up. This loosening up of the bonds between imagination and representation is a renewed source of pleasure. There is the interplay of the aesthetic with the purposive. We have presentations between subject and object, but there is a disruption of the object. Subject and object dissolve. Kant radically deconstructs the objectivity of the object, although aesthetic reflection always takes place in relation to a particular object. Judging involves object and subject. It is a free judging however. The universal is no longer given.

An aesthetic presentation is in a state of flux with other presentations. Structuralist modes of representation are done away with, and deconstructed.   Art is invariably the production of freedom. The aesthetic relation must be a free relation. Art serves to free us from the contingencies of existence. The imagination is freed from the power of the will.   Imagination sees things different from reason or the understanding. In reflective judgment, pure ideas of reason are united with the power of imagination. The free play of ideas cannot however, offend our moral sensitivities. Kant's subject consists of   the transcendental and moral personhood.   In reflective judgment, the subject is critically reflecting on the object. Imagination is the play between subject and object. The free play of imagination reveals the transcendental aspect of Kant's aesthetic. The significance of subjectivity is being questioned.

The beautiful is neither a phenomenon nor a noumenon, it is a thing. It transcends both. The beautiful does not exists. It only provokes. It spiritualizes and it uplifts. We see the work of art through the imagination. The imagination mediates the world of the senses with freedom. There is an opennes in the realm of aesthetic in which the subject and the supersensible interact. The interaction takes place between nature (the world of the senses) and freedom. For Kant, imagination is a transcendental mode of thinking. The antinomies of reason compel us to look to the supersensible. It is the supersensible that gives us pleasure in the appreciation of the work of art. Imagination is in the service of the understanding. *Einbildungskraft*-imagination is the power to form images. To imagine the supersensible without imagining it. One cannot imagine the Jewish God, or the Infinite, the Absolute, etc. The supersensible is a dimension without objects.

To judge is to subsume particulars under a general rule (the universal, the principle, the law). In a determinate judgment, the universal is given. For example, when I say "this place is not a home", the universal (home) is given. Judgments of taste are reflective, not determinate. In reflective judgment, only the particular is given, the universal has to be found. In reflective judgment we don't know where we are going, the judgment is in search of a universal. In a judgment of taste (reflective judgment) the free flow of imagination is harmonized with the understanding. This harmony of the imagination and the understanding is not adduced to any definite concept. The work of art is neither an appearance, nor a thing in itself. The phenomenon-noumenon distinction is overcome in the work of art.

Objects are beautiful because they are purposive without purpose. (*Geistreich* or spiritual imagination, it is purposiveness without purpose). Nature is purposive without purpose. Purposive means that there is an intelligent design, the work is in accordance with a concept or plan. Nature discloses itself to us as art. Nature is purposive from the inside and has no purpose imposed on it from the outside. Purposiveness is freedom, the expression of the thing's inner nature. Purpose is the imposition of force from the outside, and is a limitation of the thing's freedom. The aesthetic conformity of nature to the pure play of imagination leads to the sublime and the beautiful. Reflective judgment contemplates Nature as being in freedom rather than as object of cognition. Reflective judgment is a source of a-priori pleasure.

A judgment of taste is both subjectively and universally valid. The mental state of free harmony is freely communicable to everyone. The cultivation of taste, and the appreciation of beauty is accessible to all. The free flow of the imagination harmonized with the understanding is a source of pleasure. Everyone can share in the mental state of free harmony that gives pleasure, but not everyone will see it in the same objects. Judgments of taste cannot be reduced to the agreeable or the good. Judgments of taste are devoid of any personal interest in the object of contemplation. It is disinterested judgment. The pleasure of beauty does not serve any given end.   A judgment of taste is purely contemplative.   It is not tied to the existence of the object.   If judgments of taste are independent of any subjective interest, they must equally hold for everybody, (although different people may have different disinterested preferences).

Judgments of taste are universally valid, because the pleasurable mental state can be shared by everyone. Without universal communicability, the work is *kitsch,* a private expression of taste. *(Kitsch* limits aesthetics to entertainment.) The pleasure is in the judging. The judging is a free play of imagination harmonized by the understanding.   Free beauty does not employ a concept in its composition. Dependent beauty does employ such a concept, as for example, the concept of a beautiful figure, or a beautiful face, etc. The mental state of free harmony gives rise to a feeling of pleasure. It is intellectual (not physical) pleasure.

Art gives insight into the supersensible, into what lies beyond experience.   Both natural beauty and fine arts satisfy intellectual interest.   An intellectual interest is independent of appetitve desire. The free play of imagination is not random. The imagination comes together and is organized around the expression of an aesthetic idea. The beautiful is the relation of the four moments of taste namely, disinterestedness, purposiveness without purpose, universal communicability, and social necessity. The free play of imagination is in harmony with the understanding. This harmony of the free play of imagination with the understanding is a source of pleasure. Art serves to free us from the contingencies of existence. The Greek idea of beauty is the ideal body, Kouros.   It expresses grandeur, simplicity, permanence. It exemplifies the powers of recreation. (The Greek beauty became a rule for judgment.) Sculptural beauty is detached entirely from human emotions. Greek beauty is disclosed in the free sculptural form of the body.

Exercises.

1. How does a judgment of taste differ from a cognitive judgment? from a moral judgment?
2. What is the function of the moments of taste in reflective judgment? What is the meaning of each: purposiveness without purpose, disinterestedness, universal communicability, and social necessity?

3. Can you describe the experience of pleasure in aesthetic judgment? What is the free flow of imagination harmonized with the understanding? Give examples from your experience.
4. How do you differentiate between beauty and Kitch (cheap entertainment)?
5. Is the delight and the pleasure of beauty in the contemplation of the beautiful? What is the source of the pleasure?
6. How does moral judgment differ from aesthetic judgment?
7. Is there a connection between good and beauty? Between truth and beauty?
8. What is the difference between the beautiful and the sublime? (Kant: The beautiful is connected to the understanding, the sublime is connected to reason.) Comment.

Notes

1. Immanuel Kant, *Critique of Judgment*. Transl. with an Introduction, by Werner S. Pluhar. Indianapolis: Hackett Publishing Company, 1987. pp. 51 and 53.
2. Ibid. p. 84.
3. Ibid. p. 66.

Workshop 54. Kierkegaard's Stages on Life's Way.

In *Stages on Life's Way,* Kierkegaard (1813-1855) discusses the three stages of human existence. The stages or spheres of existence come close to constituting a system, although Kierkegaard attacks systematic philosophy. The stages of human existence are not exclusive of each other. Neither do they follow chronologically from youth to old age. They overlap. One does not leave one stage behind upon entering another. The most telling characteristic of each stage is the direction, and the end of existence.

The first stage of human existence lies in the aesthetic sphere. There is both a desirable and an undesirable side to this stage. The desirable side lies in the artistic experience itself. Mozart and Aristotle's poetics are Kierkegaard's models. The undesirable side lies in the tendency toward seeing all life through the artisic prism. It is the tendency towards pleasure, and the hedonistic principle in life. In the fine arts we find the expression of the aesthetic stage of human existence. Human experience expresses itself in the fine arts. The fine arts point the way from the actual to the possible.

The second stage of human existence is the ethical stage. The ethical stage is qualitatively different from the aesthetic stage. The ethical man has a more profound understanding of life. He faces life with calm, and self-assurance. Socrates is the prototype of the ethical stage. The ethical stage represents the movement from the possible to the actual, (the real). This stage requires the stopping of reflection, and the making of choices. For the ethical man, it is the person's (ethical) character that is decisive in how one lives one's life, and character is what ultimately matters in life. Socrates acts on an ethical universal. He accepts the death sentence because its non-acceptance would lead to anarchy. Kierkegaard calls the ethical stage Religion A. Socrates believes in Religion A, the mediated presence of the Absolute. Religion A is natural religion. Religion A is ethics.

The third stage of human existence is the religious stage. The ethical stage is not ended but superseded by the religious stage. Faith rather than duty is the end of existence. Kierkegaard calls this stage religion B - revealed religion. Religion B is personal. It cannot be universalized, or stated in universal language. Suffering is a leap into the religious stage. The religious stage is the person's experience of God's transcendence immediated through ethical universals. Religion B involves objective uncertainty. It makes doubt an ally of faith. These two most important concepts (uncertainty and doubt) connected with religion B are generally overlooked. The religious stage exhibits an objective uncertainty coupled with a subjective commitment. This takes us to the subjective thinker.

Indirect communication is most appropriate to the subjective thinker. A subjective thinker is someone who takes a particular interest in the subject. It is not meant to be a denial of external reality. The subjective thinker has an existential interest in what he is thinking. Indirect communication expresses what cannot be said directly, because if it was said directly it would be falsified. In indirect communication, "the reader is asked a question, not furnished with an answer."[1] The subjective thinker cannot convey directly certain religious concepts or statements about existence, because others are liable to misunderstand, distort, or falsify them. One can always assume that initial statements (symbols) of any religion will be falsified. Therefore they cannot be communicated directly, but indirectly, as for example, in the biblical story of the burning bush. Indirect communication uses double reflection, a reflection of inwardness used by the subjective thinker. Double reflection requires double interpretation of what is said, and of what is meant. In irony there is double reflection. The irony of Socrates. Socrates: "I am only a midwife."

For Kierkegaard, the question of truth pertains not so much to objective truth, but of *"whether it is the truth to which the knower is related."* (The truth here stands for the truth of one's existence). It is more the question of the mode of the individual's relationship to the truth, it is the question of how intensely the individual seeks the truth. For, *"the individual is in the truth, even if he should happen to be thus related to what is not true. "* [2] Truth is in subjectivity. Existence is subjective. All essential decisiveness is rooted in subjectivity. Inwardness, passion, are subjective qualities. For these to be present, doubt is an absolute prerequisite. Unless there is doubt, there is no faith. It is doubt that helps produce the dialectic of inwardness. If passion is eliminated, faith would no longer exist. Faith does not result from a scientific inquiry. Faith is always a matter of subjective intensity. Objective thought looks for results. Objective communication expresses results, it uses reflection to reach results. Kierkegaard derides the professors and the *privat-docents* that pretend to portray objective truth impersonally. For them truth is just knowledge. It has nothing to do with life. Such professors neither know the truth, nor do they live in truth.

Subjective (indirect) communication puts the recipient in a process. It uses double reflection to produce inwardness. A double reflection leads the thinker to discover. The essential content of subjective thought is essentially secret, because it cannot be communicated. The truth as inwardness consists in personal appropriation. Appropriation is the process of becoming. The truth exist only in the process of becoming, the process of appropriation. Therefore it has no results.

Where appropriation constitutes the crux of the matter, the process of communication is doubly reflective, both for the communicator and for the listener. The purpose of subjective communication is to liberate the recipient. It is to make the recipient able to experience what leads to the discovery of truth. Receiving is active, it is the activity of retracing the steps. Subjective receiving is an active participation in what is being received.

The social principle, the principle of the many, is the illiberal principle. The public arena levels everything. Leveling is the lowering of some person or institution down to its lowest common denominator. The public is an abstraction created largely by the communicating media, but it has power by leveling. The communication media (the press and to-day's TV) appeal to the lowest instincts of the public. That is the meaning of the social principle being the iliberal principle. Kierkegaard strongly criticizes the phenomenon of leveling in modern society. Subjective truth requires doubt. Historical knowledge gives a kind of pseudo certainty. Historical events are contingent, not necessary. Accidental historical truths can never be truths of reason. It is doubt that helps produce dialectical inwardness.

The subjective thinker is always in the process of becoming. Becoming is the product of being and nothing. Similarly, spirit is the product of body and soul. For Kierkegaard the positive is illusory, the negative is more foundational. The power of the negative: it is constantly keeping non-being in mind. The negative causes the spirit to be striving, restless, unsettled, problematical. Human existence is the same sort of restlesss, troublesome, unfinished synthesis of all its components. The negative (nothing) is more respectful of the truth than the positive (being). The subjective thinker is aware of the precariousness of life. He endures isolation. (Kierkegaard defines the spiritual man by his strength of enduring isolation: "his rank as a spiritual man is proportionate to his strength for enduring isolation, whereas we men are constantly in need of 'the others' the herd;" "Spirit is precisely this: not to be like others."[3] The subjective thinker is as sensitive to the comic as to the pathetic. The things that are serious to us are for him comical.

What does it mean to be oneself? The subjective problem is about decisiveness. To become subjective is to be transformed through developed potentiality, infinite concentration, and intensified passion. Ethical passion produces freedom. From the ethical point of view, the individual subject is infinitely important. The ethical attitude teaches a person to venture everything for the sake of nothing. Our knowledge of the ethical is immediate. Our knowledge of the world-historical is only an approximation. The world historical process wastes individuals.

Exercises.

1. Explain Kierkegaard's "stages in life's way". How do you relate personally to these stages?
2. Explain Kierkegaard's statement: "truth is subjectivity." How does Kierkegaard characterize a "subjective thinker"?
3. What does the term "inwardness" mean, and what personal qualities does it represent?
4. Give examples of indirect communication and double reflection.
5. What is the difference between objective truth, and being in truth? Which is for Kierkegard more basic?
6. Can one come to know the truth of one's existence through an objective, systematic, impersonal, and detached analysis of one's situation? Is the latter possible?
7. Can the truth of one's life and of life in general be known totally, and with absolute certainty?
8. How does Kiekegaard define the spiritual man? Is this definition exhaustive? How do you relate to this definition? Can you endure isolation?
9. Explain Kierkegaard's concept of leveling. In what way do the media level people's values and tastes? Do you ever cringe in front of the TV, when they use erotic love to sell coffee?
10. Does Kierkegaard think that a science of history is possible? Why not?
11. Why is Kierkegard considered an existential thinker? What do you understand by the above term? Is existence contrasted with essence in the sense that essence is common to all and existence is individual? Or, is there a need to discern the essence of one's existence? Can you think of the essence of your existence?

Notes

1. A Kierkegaard Anthology, ed. by Robert Bretall, p. 19.
2. Ibid, p.211. Italics given.
3. Ibid. p.445 and p.467.

Workshop 55. Nietzsche: Philosophy Means Becoming a Person.

Freud on Nietzsche: "he had a more penetrating knowledge of himself than any other man who ever lived or was ever likely to live."[1]

It has been said that Nietzsche had a great fascination for life. He wanted us to savor life in all its fullness. He did not want to be inhibited by convention or false morality. He implored us to dare to be ourselves, to explore the hidden and the forbidden, not to be inhibited by convention, by guilt, by shame, and by the super-ego. He scorned false morality stemming from the fear of what others will think of one, and how they will judge one. He wanted us to be self-directed, to be capable of friendship, to do what the head and the heart dictate, and not to be held back by fixations and compulsions. For if you let go of your heart you soon lose your head too.

He had extreme confidence in our ability to experience rare and great events in life. His philosophy is concerned with maximizing our ability for cheerfulness. (He had a gracefulness for life itself.) We strive for the forbidden. The forbidden is what is simple, noble, and honest. We strive for the good, the beautiful, and the true. The beautiful, the good, and the true are to be found in the simple, the noble, and the honest. We must seek the truth in its nudity, strapped of all false appearances. The eyes see the mask only, they don't see the drama. What am I really doing, and why am I doing it? That is the question of truth. Life as such has no aim. I must give it an aim. I must give meaning to my existence. I must overcome myself. I must overcome vanity and weakness. I want to be alive, cheerful, patient, unpretentious, magnanimous in victory, and unbroken in defeat. I want to reach for the unfamilar, the new, and the dangerous. I want to conquer all the fears within me, and live dangerously. I want to have mastery over myself. I want to breath freely.

Nietzsche denounced all glorification and admiration of success. How much more beautiful was the possibility which was still there before I have arrived at the peak of success? I have to preserve a keen, balanced judgment, and reach out for the joys inherent in the unfamiliar, the new, and the dangerous. Conquer all your fears and live dangerously! To exist is to live dangerously. My inner worth lies in my breathing freely, and in my mastery over myself.

I have to be true to myself. I have to become what I am. I must give style to my character. I must seek the difficult, the good, and the holy. "With knowledge, the body purifies itself... it elevates itself...in the lover of knowledge all instincts become holy; in the elevated, the soul becomes gay."[2] You, lovers of knowledge, create your world!

To create your world is not to own it. It is not to be selfish. "Thinking of oneself gives one little happiness... The only happiness lies in reason; all the rest of the world is dismal."[3] The highest reason is embodied in the work of art. One should approach life as a work of art. To feel the flow of energy inside me, to be overtaken by the swiftness of feeling and thinking, that is what it means to be happy. It is to master life as the artist masters his work of art.

The free man craves for love. "A craving for love is within me. The command for today: Learn to love yourself." To love is to give. "I do not know the happiness of those who receive; and I have often dreamed that even stealing must be more blessed than receiving."[4] Noble souls always think what they might best want to give. "They do not want to have anything for nothing; least of all, life." [5] "To be valiant is not enough to wield a broadsword, one must also know against whom."[6] "In me there is something unbreakable and endurable like a rock: that is my will. I must face my hardest path! Alas, I have begun my loneliest walk."[7] "I am *that which must always overcome itself*.... Only where there is life is there also will... will to power"[8] Courage is the will to power over fear. "When power becomes gracious and descends into the visible - such descent I call beauty."[9] I have the power to be gracious and beautiful. Grace beautifies power. I don't want to be consumed by jealousy or revenge. The spirit of revenge only shows my impotence, "in the end, one experiences only oneself."[10] I am part of the universe. I am part of nature. Animals are part of nature. I can learn from animals, not only from humans. I can learn from nature. "To learn to love oneself... it is of all the arts, the subtlest, the most cunnning, the ultimate, and the most patient."[11] I must learn to resist the spirit of gravity. To be great is to be myself.

"The fervent will to create liberates the person. Willing is creating. Will is joy. "Will nothing beyond your capacity". Nietzsche opposes pity because pity does not involve the heart. "Suffering is a necessary part of creation. What does not destroy me, makes me stronger." "Man has felt to little joy. That alone is our original sin." "We should consider every day lost on which we have not danced at least once." "Brave is he who knows fear but conquers fear. "Oh happiness, how little is sufficient for happiness?"

"O Zarathustra, I am weary of it;... I am not *great* . I wanted to represent a great human being and I persuaded many; but this lie went beyond my strength. It is breaking me. O Zarathustra, everything about me is a lie; but that I am breaking - this my breaking, is genuine".... O Zarathustra, I seek one who is genuine, right, simple, unequivocal, a man of all honesty, a vessel of wisdom, a saint of knowledge, a great human being... I *seek Zarathustra* ."[12]

I want to think my own thoughts. I want to play with my thoughts. I want to create, and not be a mere creature. "The scholars, they are trained to pursue knowledge as if it were nutcracking....in everything they want to be mere spectators...they wait and gape at thoughts that others have thought... I am not like them. I love freedom and the air over the fresh earth"...[13] For Nietzsche, thinking is a reaching out to the limit, to penetrate the unthought and the unthinkable, a fusion of the horizon of the sensible with the supersensible. The flight into the horizon is also a descent into the abyss. Spirit is the very essence of nature, the absolute ground of the *Logos*. The Dionysian spirit, the affirmation of necessity, this is the spirit of life. We must take things more cheerfully than they deserve, *(amor fati)*.

In Greek tragedy, there is no gap that separates the world of man from the world of the Gods, (Aeschylus, Prometheus Bound). Prometheus suffers (vultures eat his liver) for giving mankind the privilege of fire (philosophy). He was punished by Zeus, but refused to submit to Zeus' will. Nietzsche's overman is directly related to Prometheus. Prometheus' stand against tyranny represents a heroic view of justice. Tyranny is a disease. One must fight it off. There is no easy way to escape from suffering and the contradictions of life. There is a strong redemptive value in suffering. Ancient drama was based primarily on suffering, on pathos, not on action.

In Nietzsche's *Birth of Tragedy*, we are exposed to the Dionysian world-view. (Tragedy derives from *traganon* = vinegar) The sour taste of life is transformed into wine. In song and dance, man expresses himself as a member of a higher community. Justice unites life's contradictions, it finds reason in madness. The Appolynian view represents the Greek genius for restraint, measure, and harmony. It found its highest expression in ancient Greek sculpture and architecture. Nietzsche's death of God,[14] may be viewed as negative ontology. The death of God signifies the end of Being. We must become what we are. We must become all we can be.

Zarathustra is thought to be a teacher of the Overman. A vision of time as the eternal return of the same. The eternal return of the same is a new seeing of time. The eternal return of the same signifies that everything comes back exactly as it once was. The death of God is the birth of Overman. The death of God frees man to become himself. The distant future of the *Kinderland,* the West's highest and supreme longing, is expressed as a fable.   Why characterize it as a fable? The fable represents the unity of man and animal (nature), the cosmic unity. The possibility that man can learn something from other (not human) beings. The possibility of man learning from nature.   Living is seeking out everything strange and questionable in existence, it means becoming a person. Philosophy means becoming a person. It means to have a fascination for life, to have the courage to think for oneself, to strive for the forbidden, for the simple, the noble and the honest, and not to run from greatness.

Exercises.

1. Select any of the above quotation and relate them to your life.
2. What does Nietzsche mean by "man needs to overcome himself"?
3. What is Nietzsche's view on suffering?
4. Nietzsche wants us to think for ourselves. Do we, as a rule, think our own thoughts, or do we think other people's thoughts believing that they are our own?
5. What does it mean "to breathe freely"?
6. What does it mean to have a fascination for life?
7. Nietsche said that he did his best thinking while walking. When do you do your best thinking?
8. What does Nietzsche mean by "living dangerously!"? Does it mean to follow your own instincts when they don't clash with reason?
8. Happiness, Nietzsche says, is the highest use of reason. Discuss.
9. Why is convention (the spirit of gravity) your worst enemy?
10. Nietzsche's will to power and Spinoza's conatus as the striving for self-preservation and self-elevation, are the same. Discuss.

Notes

1. The Encyclopedia of Philosophy, vol. 5 p. 505.
2. Walter Kaufmann, *The Portable Nietzsche,* New York: Penguin Books, p. 189.
3. Ibid. p. 50.
4. Ibid. p. 218.
5. Ibid. p. 311.
6. Ibid. p. 321.
7. Ibid. p. 264.
8. Ibid. p. 227.
9. Ibid. p. 230.
10. Ibid. p. 264.
11. Ibid. p.305.
12. Ibid. p.369.
13. Ibid. p.237.
14. Aphorism 25, The Gay Science.

Workshop 56.   What is Phenomenological Psychology?

Phenomenology is an introspective psychology. It reflects on mental states, and describes them. It derives universal laws that govern the mental life. We observe our perceptions and our thoughts about them.   Our mental life consists of a stream of consciousness, combining all perceptions and memories, with new perceptions continuously added on.   Our mental life (total experience) is like a river, a continuous flux. Things directly perceived are surrounded by things that are not directly perceived, and by the distant field of unknown things. This holds for every point in time.

Reflective, theoretical observation is the fundamental procedure of Husserl's (Edmund Husserl 1859 - 1938) phenomenology.   What is non-observable (God, the unconscious) is excluded. Wisdom consists in rational knowing, evaluating, and acting. The basic method of phenomenology is reflective.   Reflection means thinking about something. It also means looking inwards. Unreflective consciousness takes place when the object is the whole focus of our attention (trying to catch the bus, etc.) Reflective awareness deals with how the object presents itself to us. When we alter our attention to the object, the object changes in the way it appears to us. What the "I" engages in, is called intentive processes or intentive life.

Phenomenological reduction or *epoche* is a technique of suspending belief. There is a change in the attitude of the "I". *Ego cogito cogitatum:* I think thought. Phenomenology like geography explores unmapped teritory.   Life is nothing physical or biological. It is mind, psyche, experience, consciousness, intentive life. What is the "I"? It is what has habits, attitudes, inclinations, etc.   There are two views on the "I", pro-egological and anti-egological. The pro-egological view: The "I" accompanies our intentive life. I live through my intentional life, attending to what it presents, directing it, and being formed by it.   Sartre's (Jean Paul Sartre, 1905-1980) anti-egological view pertains only to transcendental consciousness. He holds, in fact, that cosciousness taken psychologicaly is egological.

Husserl uses the *cogito* as mental or intentive processes that we are actually engaged in, i.e. *Erlebnis.*   There is a self-awareness that accompanies all intentive processes. In an intentional lived experience like perceiving a chair, one is thematically conscious of the chair while being pre-thematically (pre-reflectively) conscious of being conscious of a chair, as perceived, etc.   Intentive processes can pertain to the past, future, present, expectations, motivations, frustrations, feelings, etc. There are innumerable distinctions of intentive processes. Phenomenology deals with reflective theoretical observation of intentive processes with the emphasis of how they are intentive, whether temporal, motivational, emotional, etc. Earlier intentive processes cause later intentive processes to be the way they are. (If I have never experienced love, it would be hard for me to know love.) An intentive process does not come back again in the same way. The "I" now and the "I" tomorrow are different intentive processes, but the same "I".

An intentive process flows in inner time. Inner time is different from outer time (a weed grows, etc.) We can reflectively observe intentive processes (anger) which are not located in space. We are intentive to things that are not in space and time, for example adding numbers, etc. We may intent to in a loving, hating, destroying, creating, believing, connecting way, etc. Intentiveness is like a road sign, if you look at it, you become aware of what it points to. The intentive process is always directed at something. Not all processes in the stream of consciousness are intentive, although they are part of intentive life. Anxiety does not have an object or the object is not very specific. The object is not a focal point. There is intentiveness without a focal point (mood focused on the present or the future, regret focused on the past, etc.)

The object *(cogitatum):* it is that which is intended to in an intentive process. In an unreflective attitude, these are just things. In the reflective attitude, it is an object as it presents itself to me. (We perceive the door abstracted from its function. To perceive the door while disregarding its function is to adopt a purely theoretical attitude toward it. To reflect upon my perception of the door however, involves paying attention to all the facets of it as perceived, including the perceived function.) The object as it presents itself to me is primarily a visual object, but it has textual qualities, sonorous qualities, etc. Of all the five senses, (sight, hearing, smelling, tasting and touching), touching is the richest. You are always touching something. All these spheres come together in perception. There are errors in perception but we are constantly making adjustments to our perception. Consciousness of internal time: protentive and retrotentive. Consciousness goes off into indefinite past or future. There is no discontinuity in the stream of consciousness. Intentive life keeps flowing.

In practical life we are more interested in explanation than description, thus we tend to overlook description. (Descriptive accounts of things don't address the why. They describe only the how). What we describe is affected by our rational explanation. We cannot explain without describing. If the descriptions are false, our explanation will be false. The descriptions that are most interesting in phenomenology are not factual. Husserl was mainly concerned with universals. Husserl's concern with facts was primarily in order to form ideations- ideas, essences. The cover is red. Red is a universal. Red is a color, this is an eidetic statement. We vary the description of the object in order to refine the account of it. The intentive process *(noesis)* and the object that presents itself *(noema)*. Things in time can be worldly or transcendental (not worldly). Concepts are things not in time.

Phenomenological psychology describes and reflects on mental states. A science of the mental, of the intentive life or consciousness. There can be laws (eidetic regularities) that hold for psychic life, the way natural science establishes laws that hold for nature. Constitutive phenomenology is based on reflective theoretical observation and the method of ideation. Ideation is imaginative variation. Ideations are procedures to gain eidetic knowledge.

The method of phenomenological-psychological reduction: The phenomenological -psychological reduction disregards all objective data concerning the world. The purpose is to discover the world as experienced and thought by a (or any) psychological subject, without engaging in a critical (transcendental) investigation of the evidence by which the world is known to exist. Such disregarding however, is not a suspension of belief in the existing world, of which the psychological subject is taken to be an actual or possible part.   Suppose we disregard the world as one existent reality. We also bracket the belief that our intentive life is part of the world. Our intentive life is in a transcendant state, i.e. as not being part of the world. Our intentive life exists absolutely, but the world does not exist absolutely. The world only exists relative to the intentive consciousness. It exists as phenomena. We suspend belief in order to get a clear way to analyze things. We have the (apodictic) certainty of the subject (intentive life), and the uncertainty (non-apodicticity) of the contingent world. Only the present intentive life is apodictic. (The now of another person is not apodictic). We exclude the past (memory) and the future. Because the present intentive life is not part of the world, it can be used to justify the world. The aim is a transcendent grounding of all knowledge.

The method of phenomenological reduction is purely reflective. It provides access to the purely psychic, the mental, and subjective state. It is a scientifically objective approach to the subjective. In the transcendental *epoche'*, subject and object are purified. The purpose of phenomenological psychology is to understand psychic life in its unity as lived experience. It does this through intuition and observation. Lived experience (intentive mental processes) consists of our internally interconnected states: perceptions, recollections, feelings, willing, etc. Phenomenological psychology is an intuitive, descriptive analytical psychology. An inner viewing that opens up the lived experience. To see what goes on in me when I perceive my cognitive life. Consciousness is always consciousness of something. It is the most universal characteristic of inner life.

Exercises.

See the exercises at the end of the next workshop.

Workshop 57. Husserl's Phenomenological Psychology: Basic Concepts.

Phenomenology may be defined as the science of consciousness. Events and objects in the ouside world appear to our consciousness as phenomena. We will consider some of the basic assumptions and propositions of phenomenological psychology.

1. Life Consists of Mental Processes.

Life is essentially mental (mind, psyche, consciousness, etc.). This is confirmed by the definition of death as the cessation of all mental functioning. The lived experience pertains to all mental states, (thinking, valuing, feeling, perceiving, recollecting, willing, etc.). All mental states are clearly subjective. Phenomenological psychology studies mental states objectively. It is a science of the purely subjective, and the purely mental.

Mental processes (inner experiences) take place within the person. Through introspection and reflection, we can become aware and describe such experiences. Through an awareness of what goes on within us, we can learn to understand our perceptive and cognitive processes. We accomplish this through reflection. Phenomenology can be thought of as an inner viewing of the consciousness.

To be conscious is to be conscious of something. Thus, consciousness is always intentional. All inner life (perceiving, valuing, reflecting, willing, etc.) and all mental processes are intentional. Intentionality is the most universal characteristic of our mental life or consciousness.

The subject matter of phenomenological psychology is to describe all aspects of the mental processes in their intentionality. Based on the description of intentional mental processes, phenomenological psychology derives universal laws that are applicable to (subjective) mental life. It is an a priori eidetic (i.e. universal) science of the psychic. Intentive or intentional processes point at objects, events, happenings, etc. The objects can be in the present, (I look at the tree in front of my window), in the past (I recollect an event from my childhood), or future (I expect to meet a friend tomorrow).

Perception can be reflective or unreflective. Unreflective perception is the direct experience of the object. I experience the object directly when I look at the door in order to get out of the house quickly. In reflective perception, I observe the object as well as my thoughts about the object, (including previous perceptions about the object, etc.). The object has a perceptual field, (surroundings, background, etc.), and a wider horizon. The object can be real or imaginary, and it can pertain to the past, present or future. Any given experience of an object is one-sided. When I change my perspective, (far, near, right, left, above, below, etc.), the object appears differently. Through reflection, I perceive the unity of the object in its multiple apperances (adumbrations). Every actual experience opens up a whole horizon of possible experiences in the past, present or future. For every given perception, there is an open horizon to be explored.

Phenomenological psychology seeks to arrive at a-priori or essential (eidetic) truths that underlie all intentive, mental processes. Pretheoretically, we experience the object with undoubting certainty. The object is always located in a time-space continuum, and stands in a causal relation to other objects. This we know with apodictic certainty. (Apodictic certainty means that we cannot conceive its non-being.) In our theoretical (as distinguished from practical) attitude, we seek to grasp the *"eidos"*, the idea or the essential "a-priori" of our experience of the object. We want to be apodictically certain of it. It does not matter whether the object is real or imaginary. (Truths are called a-priori if and when they precede factual existence.)

2.   The   Main   Categories   of   Phenomenological Psychology.

2.1. The "I" or the Ego.

The "I" consists of one's habits, attitudes, inclinations, character traits, tendencies, etc. The "I" (the ego) engages in encountering the object, and it is the "I" that accompanies the subject's intentive life. The ego synthesizes the manifold properties, and the appearance of the object. Husserl carefully distinguishes between passive synthesis, that does not involve any active participation by the ego (such as the synthesis by which a manifold of adumbrations presents one object), and an active synthesis in which the ego is actively involved with the objects already unitarily constituted for it by passive synthesis. Active synthesis for example, would pertain to the forming of subject-predicate relations amonng aspects of perceived or imagined objects. Intentive processes go on changing, the stream of consciousness flows on uninterruptedly, but the "I" remains the same. Some philosophers questioned whether a separate "I" can be distinguished from the mental operations that go on in the mind. William James (1842-1910), did not make any distinctions between them. Sartre (Sartre, Jean Paul, 1905-1980) denies the existence of a transcendental ego, because he insists that transcendental consciousness cannot involve one's habits, inclinations, character traits, etc. He accepts them however, as appropriate for psychological reflection. Husserl does not hold that the

"I" can exist apart from the stream of lived experiences. Such an "I" would have no way of engaging in encountering objects.

2.2. The *Cogito*.

The *cogito* pertains to the actual modes of perceiving an object. It relates to the mental processes that take place when the Ego encounters an object. (Husserl's term *Erlebnis* has been translated as lived experience or intentive mental processes.) The intentive processes *(noesis)*, as lived experience, include all mental states (perceiving, thinking, remembering, feeling, willing, valuing, judging, etc.). Phenomenology can be described as an inner viewing of our mental states. All mental processes are directed towards an object, (event, etc.). They are intentive processes. There are many kinds of various, distinct intentive processes, that can be identified.

2.3. The *Cogitatum*.

The *cogitatum* is the object as it presents itself to consciousness. It is that, which is intended to, in the intentive process. This is referred to as *noema*. In the unreflective attitude, it is just the thing that one sees. In the reflective attitude, it is the object as it presents itself to us. The object that exists, (the existent object), becomes *the meant, intended* or *experienced* object. Each object is both a harmonious unity, and a multiplicity of possible appearances (adumbrations). The identical thing appears in many different shades, shapes, and forms from different perspectives and positions. Any given perception is one sided. Every single perception has a limited perspective. In the reflective attitude, we can see (experience) the thing (event, etc.) from a multiplicity of perspectives.

2.4. The Noetic- Noematic Unity.

It is the reflective synthesis of the *cogito* with its *cogitatum*. Each intentive process, (i.e. *cogito* intending its *cogitatum*), has its own synthetic structure of multiple appearances, that can be described and analyzed. These structures are referred to as noetic- noematic compositions. They pertain not only to sensuous perception, but to all other modes of intuition. Thus, a potentially unlimited field for phenomenological research is opened up.

2.5. The Stream of Consciousness.

Our consciousness, and our mental processes are continuous. There is no break or discontinuity in our mental life. Consciousness is like a stream that flows continuously, and uninterruptedly. The intensity of the stream is not necessarily even. Sometimes we experience things with greater or lesser intensity. Intentive processes (as well as moods, anxieties, etc.) have their own time sequence, an inner time which is different from objective time. Inner time has a protentive and retrotentive structure. Through expectation or memory, consciousness goes of into the future or brings back the past. In the flow of the intentive life, a given perception becomes a past perception to be followed by a new perception, and the stream of consciousness keeps flowing uninterruptedly.

2.6.   Apodictic Certainty.

As has been referred to before, apodictic certainty means, that we cannot conceive of the object's non-being. For example, we cannot conceive of a real object not being located in time and space, and not being subject to causality. Similarly, we cannot conceive of the non-existence of a pure number.

2.7.   The Immanent.

It pertains to the purely subjective, internal elements that belong to a given perception. The purely immanent pertains to our perception of the object that is given to us externally. Through the method of phenomenological reduction (to be discussed later), we reduce an external perception to its immanent components. In the unreflective attitude, we are certain of the perceived object as existing. In the natural, reflective attitude, we look at the perception of the perceived object, (the object itself is irreal), but we are still certain of the object's existence as well as of all possible perceivings of it. When we reflect on the "modes of givennes" of the object, and our subjective ways of perceiving it, we direct our attention to the purely subjective, immanent components of the perception. We reflect on the phenomenon of the object as is meant and experienced by us, whether actually or potentially.

3.   Methods of Phenomenological Psychology.

3.1. Reflective, Theoretical Observation.

This is the primary means of phenomenology. Through observation, we are aware of the object (real or ideal) as given to consciousness. We can describe and explain it, (or possibly explain it). In the theoretical (as opposed to practical) attitude, we seek to know things. We know things through their *"eidos"*, i.e. through their essential idea or universal essence.   Phenomenological psychology is an "eidetic" (that is, thoretical) science. Through reflection, we observe and describe our inner mental processes. We look inwardly and engage in an inner seeing. Introspection is the core of phenomenology.

3.2.   The Method of Ideation Through Free Variation.

Every existent thing is defined by its *"eidos"* or essence. It cannot be defined without reference to its *eidos*. The *eidos* itself does not have any real existence. Eidetic statements are a-priori in the sense that they do not refer to, and are independent of, given facts (or factual existence). They do, however, inhere in the existing objects. The *eidos* is the invariant that is common to all possible variations of the object in our mind. Through the method of ideation, we come to comprehend the *eidos*. Starting from any (real or imagined) object, we freely and arbitrarily vary the object in our imagination. All variations must however pertain to the same class of objects. For example, I see a red car. I imagine all sorts of red cars, each one having a different shade of the color red. What is invariant in all the various shades of red is the eidos "red". I can define red in terms of range and frequency of electromagnetic waves. Such a definition however, would no longer be descriptive. It would involve an appeal to an objective-scientific explanation of the physical and psychological process involved in seeing, but not a description of what is seen, either in particular or eidetically. For a simple like red, no descriptive definition seems possible, except an ostensive one, namely, that red is what is found in common in the variations one has run through, and in all possible further variations.   Or, I see a rainbow. I can imagine many kinds of rainbows, with all kinds of real or imaginary colors, but the eidos "color" will be invariant to all of them. (The *eidos* "color" is a genus and the *eidos* "red" is one of its species.) I can apply this free varaiation to any object and derive its *eidos*. The *eidos* represents the essential and universal truth of any given object or experience. Any given experience opens up an infinite number of possible experiences in the past, present and future. By an inner viewing of our mental life, we can get at such universal ideas or truths.

3.3.   Phenomenological Reduction.

Through the method of phenomenological reduction, we can get to the purely immanent or the purely subjective components of a transcendentally objective, external perception. (The meaning of the purely immanent has been discussed previously). When we perceive an object in the natural attitude, we are interested in the object, we want to know its properties, and perhaps mentally or factually possess it. Our perception is thereby goal oriented.   When we exercise a phenomenological reduction, we consistently thwart our interest in the objective existence of the external thing (the world). We neither deny, nor doubt the existence of the outside world. We simply suspend judgment about it. We assume an attitude of neutrality with respect to our belief in the world. We parenthesize the existence of the outside world along with our experience of it. I am now free to reflect on my reflection of the perceived object. I experience the object as *meant and intended* by me. In the phenomenological reduction, the *"meant and intended"* become explicit in my act of experiencing the object. In this sense does the perceived object disclose itself to my consciousness as a phenomenon. I then describe the phenomenon strictly as it presents itself to me. The state of suspended judgment when performing a phenomenological reduction, is called *"epoche"*.

4. How Does Phenomenological Psychology Relate to Transcendental Phenomenology?

Transcendental phenomenology aims at a first philosophy that will provide a grounding for all specialized sciences. Phenomenology is the objective science of subjectivity. The aim is to arrive at a first philosophy grounded in absolute knowledge. All scientific judgment must be based on evidence (i.e. mental seeing). Apodictic evidence means absolute certainty. We arrive at apodictic certainty through the method of the phenomenological reduction and the transcendental, phenomenological epoche.

In the epoche, I suspend judgment about the existence of the world, including my own bodily and sensual experience. I put everything in brackets. The world becomes for me a phenomenon of being rather than a fact of being. I also suspend all beliefs, values, acts of judging, deciding, etc. that go on in my natural, non reflective attitude. I suspend (parenthesize) all my beliefs and positions I have had with respect to the world. This is the meaning of the exercise of a transcendental phenomenological reduction. By this exercise, I acquire a transcendental ego, where the world exists only in the form of my subjective thoughts of it, (as *cogitationes* of my *cogito)*. The world becomes for me a universe of phenomena. I am the pure stream of my *cogitationes*. Of this, I can be apodictically certain. The phenomena are phenomena of the natural world, but this natural world derives its whole sense and meaning from me, that is, from my own evidences, thoughts, experiences, as a transcendental ego.

The phenomenological *epoche'* opens up a new realm of transcendental experience. For every factual experience that there is, I can have a corresponding (correlate) imaginary experience. Thus, an a-priori science of pure possibilities comes into being. In this universe of transcendental self experience, the evidence consists in the harmonious structure, and the inherent unity of the experience. The real world with its constituent parts has its counterparts in consciousness. Any object appears as a multiplicity of possible perceptual appearances *(noemata)*, harmonized and synthetized into a unity (identification). There is a correspondence between the object and the multiplicity of its subjective appearances. Thus, we account for the object and the world, through our subjectivity.   Therein lies the relation between transcendental phenomenology and phenomenological psychology.

Exercises.

1. When you take a walk in the woods, do you see things reflectively, unreflectively, or both? Describe the circumstances of each.
2. We experience the world (objects, events, facts) as phenomena. The latter means how things, and objects present themselves (as presences) to our consciousness. Phenomenology deals with the mode of presence of things to our consciousness. Suppose I take an interest in you. Both you and my interest in you present themselves as phenonomena to my consciousness. Our primary contact with the world is through the phenomenon. Is it likely that the same facts will appear differently to me and you? Discuss.
3. How can there be a science of subjectivity, of subjective phenomena? Does the *"eidos"* unify the subjective phenomena? Explain and discuss.
4. Why is intentionality considered to be the essence of phenomenology? What does it mean to intend to an object as meant and experienced by me? Does it mean to give meaning to my experience of the world? Describe how you give meaning to your experience of the world.
5. What is the difference between objective and subjective determinations and analysis of events? Does it mean, that individual perceptions must be confirmed and validated by others? Is objectivity simply a matter of numbers of people arriving at the same conclusion, (for example, racism)? Or, is it a matter of a proper, unbiased attitude to the subject matter or event that is being investigated?
6. What is a phenomenological reduction? Is it an exercise or an attitude?
7. In the state of *epoche,* when the natural view of the world is bracketed, the world is experienced as a phenomenon of being. What is the difference between the natural scientific view and the phenomenological view of the world?
8. Why is the ego in the phenomenological reduction called the transcendental Ego?

9.   What is your inner clock? Observe your inner time. How is it different from objective time?

Workshop 58. Introduction to Hermeneutics.

Hermeneutics is a certain way of reading the text, or a particular kind of thinking in relation to the text. Critical reading is a precondition to the understanding of the text. Hermeneutics is grounded in understanding. Authority and tradition, they are two key prejudices. This does not make them unnecessary or entirely negative. Art challenges the hermeneutic circle. (The problem of the hermeneutic circle: the part and the whole. One does not exist without the other). The Greeks viewed art as the imitation of nature. (Art imitates nature, *mimesis*). Language is the essence of the hermeneutic experience. For Gadamer (Gadamer, Hans Georg), thinking is historical. It happens at a certain place and time. He views language as a mode (or the possibility of a mode) of communication. Language is unique. It allows for poetry and for science. A poetic description is wholly different from the scientific description: language experienced as light, as the poetry of speaking and writing.

An investigation into the nature of understanding exceeds philosophical and psychological considerations. The hermeneutic orientation is sceptical of the empirical orientation. The hermeneutical view tries to emphasize the total view. We can judge the empirical only if we can see beyond it. For Gadamer, hermeneutics is not a system of rules. He suggests that hermeneutics is rooted in the understanding of art. Philosophy is part of the experience and the understanding of art, but it exceeds art. Art by itself is not reflective. It needs reflection on its meaning, how the thing shows itself in itself. Gadamer does not understand hermeneutics as a subjective experience. Subjective does not mean arbitrary. Subjective refers to the consciousness of the subject, the ego, the consciousnesss of the self, the thinking I, the Kantian a-priori structure of the mind. For Kant, the a-priori structure of the mind (space, time, intuitiveness, the transcendental categories, substance, modality, causality, etc.) is a condition for the possibility of thinking, experiencing, and knowing. In Gadamer (and Heidegger) there is an attempt to go beyond consciousness. Most of the time we are not self conscious, we are not reflecting on our being, (Nietzsche).

For Nietzsche and Marx, the essence of man is not consciousness. The essence of man is historical. It is what we, as human beings, develop and cultivate. The essence of man is being, not consciousness. Hermeneutics struggles with the problem of the dialectics of being and consciousness. It is not the Cartesian consciousness but a historical consciousness of the subject. The emphasis is on being, existence, on the "I am", not on *"the cogito"*. Gadamer is concerned with dialectics, not with method, (as Descartes). He wants to move dialectics out of the history of method. Plato was very scientific, but he refused to confine philosophy to a system. He always remained open and playful. With Hegel, dialectic was no longer free. It was very powerful, dynamic, intense, but in the service of the rational, the Geist, Begriff, etc. Marx applied Hegel's dialectic to the understanding of society, and to the notion of social revolution. Dialectic was to be in the service of social spirit, the spirit of freedom. For Heidegger, being is time. The being, Dasein, the human being is ecstatic (rooted in experience), not transcendental (prior to or beyond experience). Time, for Heidegger, is the ontological foundation of man, time is free of consciousness. (Time as possibility, possibility is rooted in time.) In Kant, time is a principle of understanding, not limited to consciousness, (time and space - the transcendental super-categories). Transcendental refers to the a-prori structure of the human being. Transcendent refers to an Absolute, which for Kant, is no longer knowable. In Heidegger, we have a mystical notion of time. In the later Heidegger, it becomes a notion of space, *der Zeit Spielraum.*

Kant defines judgment as the power to subsume the particular under the universal. If the universal is not in sight, how do we make a judgment? We cannot discover the Absolute by reason. Prior to Kant, Reason was seen as leading to the knowledge of the Absolute. For Hegel, (and Marx), history is the science of God. (When justice exists, God will be.)

Gadamer builds a hermeneutics out of the question of truth. He looks at the question of truth as it emerges in the experience of art. He emphasizes the spirit in the *Geisteswissenschaften* (liberal arts). The human sciences cannot be determined by the inductive or the scientific method, a method based on observed regularities. (Method - the path, the way, that it is, and why it is.) Method does not lead to the truth. The truth leads to the method. The human being cannot be examined scientifically. Gadamer is not against scientific thinking. But science does not go deep enough in its thinking. Science does not ask the question of being, a more primordial question, (Heidegger). In science, we are more eager to know than to understand. Understanding transcends boundaries and norms, be they scientific or ethical. The human sciences are determined by a different kind of experience from the one that is determined by an investigation of the natural laws.

An important concept in hermeneutics, is *Bildung. Bildung* means self-formation, the cultivation of the self, the formation of personality. It relates to culture and education. For Marx, *Bildung* is reaching up to humanity, the formation of a revolutionary consciousness. For Nietzsche, *Bildung* means the formation of an ideal image of man, a life with great goals. It means more than the development of one's natural talents. For Gadamer, *Bildung* is more than culture. It is the cultivation of spirit, the formation of mind. The goal of *Bildung* is freedom. It is a becoming that leads to being. For Hegel, *Bildung* means being elevated to the Universal. It requires restraint of desire, the sacrifice of particularity. (Work is restrained desire).   Theoretical *Bildung* goes beyond the immediate experience, it necessitates the separation of ourselves from ourselves, and of finding ourselves again. *Bildung* means to recognize myself in the other, a self elevation to a theoretical attitude. As such, it is already alienation. It is an opening up towards a totality, an opening to the whole, the ground, the spirit. For Hegel, *Geist* is the home for all things, the very essence of all things, all humans. For Humboldt, (Humboldt, Wilhelm Von 1767-1835) *Bildung* is the development of tact, rather than the Hegelian spirit. Tact-*tactus* - *tangere* - to touch. The Universal does not touch. For Gadamer, tact is a particular sensitivity, a particular sense of knowing and of being. It includes the aesthetic and the historical dimension.

Sensus communis, the sense that creates the community. This sense of the communal is nourished by what is probable, rather than by what is ideal. It is more experiential than ideological. It reflects a moral attitude that is grounded in social freedom, and in human thinking. This goes back to the Stoa and to the Roman concept of human life. It entails a natural love for humanity. (Marcus Aurelius: we are made for cooperation.) The Romans are more concerned with *phronesis* (temperance) than with *sophia* (wisdom). Gadamer is very interested in this part of the Western tradition. He feels that it, the concern with possible and the practical, was neglected in German Idealism. Gadamer wants to go back to the Roman roots, rather than to the Greek roots, as with Heidegger. *Phronesis* means to look at oneself from a perspective of reason, a perspective that is no longer dominated by the subject. Reason judges intelligence. We have a lot of intelligence, a lot of technology, but what has happened to our reason? Technology has not made us better human beings.

The origin of Gadamer's hermeneutics is to be found in Plato's Symposium. The *"eros"*, man's desire for the beautiful, is to attain the truth which is directly related to the beautiful. In Plato, desire is linked to possession. Eros is goal oriented, satisfaction is rooted in possession, possession of the good or the beautiful. Kant introduces a theory of desire that is no longer linked to possession. He parts with Plato on this. Kant radically questions the link between desire and possession. The true form of the beautiful lies in the relation of judgment to feeling. This relation is like music without a text. (*Musike* = to make everything flow). True beauty, in contrast to dependent beauty, presuppposes no concept what the object should be. It is a free, or reflective judgment. Natural beauty, a flower, a landscape, etc. are examples of free beauty. Dependent beauty, like the beauty of a woman, a horse, a building, etc. serve a concept of purpose, the concept of perfection. It is a determinate judgment. In reflective judgment, there is an interplay between the particular and the general. Kant's reflective judgment is free from moral or political concerns. What does Kant mean by natural beauty, a free judgment of taste? The aesthetic experience is free, disinterested pleasure. For Plato, there is an ascent (a hierarchy), from the pleasant to the good to the beautiful. For Kant, there is a stepping back, you can represent the ugly beautifully. In the *Birth of Tragedy*, Nietzsche criticizes Kant's notion of disinterested beauty. Disinterested beauty is disinteresting. He brings back the Appolynian and the Dionysian, two key figures in Greek mythology.   The Apollynian beauty is a determinate beauty, and the Dionysian is a (free) orgy, a violent, supersensuous disruption. Nietzsche's *amor fati* is an acceptance of the Dionysian experience of suffering, joy, etc.   The Appolynian and the Dionysian together constitute the nature of the human experience. Nietzsche upholds the importance of the illusion.

The object of the sensuous drive is life. It expresses the natural world, the material being, the needs. The object of the form drive is *Gestalt*. It expresses the (formal) shape, *eidos*, idea, the physical appearance including a strong sensuous connotation. *Gestalt* expresses the rational drive in man. The play impulse, the third main drive, connects the two essential human drives. (Matter, form, and play are the three essential human drives for Schiller, [Schiller, Friedrich, 1759-1805]). Play expresses beauty in its widest meaning. For Hegel, the play impulse attempts to synthetize the sensuous and the non-sensuous, the finite and the infinite. Hegel's *Begriff* (the notion) is a synthesis of the finite with the infinite. When sensation and thought are joined, the expression is the beautiful. Play unites the world of the senses with the world of the *logos*. Play is neither subjective, nor objective. It is neither limited to the sensuous nor to the rational, neither internal, nor external. It is removed from the constraints of the world. All concrete things lose their seriousness. The human being should play with what is beautiful. The human being is complete when he or she plays. Play touches the very root of the human being. For Schiller, the inner essence of beauty is freedom. Freedom is the highest inner necessity. Reflection breaks down the power of nature over man. Man's play of imagination, a free movement not necessarily rooted in *Gestalt* or in thinking. The terrain of imagination, an appearing, a *schein*, an emerging, an *Aufschein*, an unlimited sequence of human ploys, an aesthetic illusion.

In Kant, the free play of imagination is related to goals. Schiller radicalizes the free play of imagination. For Spinoza, imagination is a fiction. For Descartes, imagination is secondary to the intellect or understanding.   A lot of Nietzsche's ideas are related to Schiller's emphasis on the importance of play in human existence. The

Appolynian illusion is an aesthetic illusion. The artistic illusion does not rest on need. Desire turns into love. Need turns into aesthetic taste. The aesthetic state unites thought and feeling. It completes the person. For Kant, the aesthetic experience is rooted in pleasure. For Gadamer, play is rooted in truth. It is the clue to the understanding of art. Play allows the exit from subjectivity. The idea of play is never exhausted by a particular play. Play lies in the attitude of the player. The movement of play has no goal that brings the play to an end. Play renews itself in constant repetition. In Nietzsche, the universe is a play of forces. In the Appolynian illusion, everybody is an artist. In the Dionysian experience, one image fades into another, *Erlebnis* fades into *Erfahrung, Erfahrung* becomes primary. It is an experience of being not dominated by the logocentric perspective, by a consciousness of the dialectic. The human being is a work of art, it is never complete, it is continuously forming itself, it is infinitely creating itself.

For Nietzsche and Schiller, play is related to illusion. For Gadamer, play is related to truth. It is a self- representation of the subject in play. There emerges a structure which loses the egocentricity of the subject. If we cultivate a sense of this play, we can employ it hermeneutically, as a way to truth. There is a recognition of truth in the experience of play, an illumination, and a freeing from all chance and variable circumstances. The aesthetic attitude is an essential part of play as play. For Hegel, art is the intuitive, sensuous manifestation of spirit (truth). Art and truth, subject and object are reunited by the historical consciousness (spirit). Truth manifests itself in a totality of understanding. Art must be understood as *Erfahrung,* not *Erlebnis. Die Erfahrung der Kunst* is related to truth. *Erlebnis* is related to subjective consciousness *(Bewusstsein). Erfahrung, dasein,* is related to the object of experience. Understanding is an *Erfahrung,* not an *Erlebnis* oriented category. For Heidegger, *Erfahrung* is letting the phenomena speak. It is not a consciousness or a subjective oriented understanding of phenomena. It is an attitude of *Gelassenheit:* let being be, a thinking free of willing.

Exercises.

1. How is the question of being and consciousness posed by Kant, Marx, and and Gadamer?
2. For Heidegger, being is time. Time is possibility. Discuss.
3. What is *Bildung?* Discuss the several dimensions of *Bildung.*
4. Temperance *(phronesis)* is to look at oneself from the perspective of reason. Reason judges intelligence. Discuss the distinction between reason and intelligence.
5. How do you understand the attitude of *Gelassenheit,* of let being be? Can you practice this for yourself?

6. "Play renews itself in constant repetition". Discuss.

Workshop 59. The History of Hermeneutics[1].

The word hermeneutics is derived from the Greek *hermeneuio* meaning, I explain, define, clarify, interpret, expose, bring to light, etc. The question of meaning in relation to the text: should interpretation be governed by author and tradition, or not? Martin Luther (1483-1546) began to question the traditional interpretation of the Bible. He postulated three possible meanings of a text: the literal meaning, (the flesh of the text), the deeper meaning (the soul of the text), and a still higher meaning in terms of the things to come, (the spirit of the text). In Latin: *corpus* = flesh, *anima* = soul, and *spiritus* = spirit. God made the *corpus* for those who lived before us, the *anima* for today, and the *spiritus* for the future.

In Jewish hermeneutics, there developed a fourfold theory of interpretation, named *PRDS (Pardes)* or enclosure. *Perash* to spread out is the literal meaning, *Remez* to hint is the allegorical meaning, *drash* to interpret is interpretation, and *Sod* secret is the mystical meaning. The word *PRDS* first appeared in Spain (13th cent.) In the Catholic religion, hermeuneutics is based chiefly on tradition, the unwritten light handed down from the past. For Martin Luther (the Protestant Church), it is the whole of Scriptures that guides the understanding of individual passages. Spinoza was the founder of Biblical criticism. He did not consider the Bible to be the work of God, but he refused to devalue its cultural and political dimension. It is due to his influence that hermeneutics was liberated from theological dogma.

Nietzsche in "The Use and Abuse of History," deals with the question of the hermeneutic circle: To find the spirit of the whole in the particular, and to grasp the particular in the whole. We examine the part and unite it with the whole. They are both one harmonic life. Knowledge of the particular presupposes knowledge of the whole, and knowledge of the whole requires the knowledge of the particular. The particular is a representation of one totality. The whole is prior to the parts. In Kant's transcendental apperception (the transcendental ego), every particular appearance reveals the whole of life. Life is present individually and universally.

Ast (early 19th cent. German philologist) defines hermeneutics as the explication of texts, as the unity of content and form, letter and spirit. To explicate a text, we must not only know the language of the time but also the spirit of the time. The spiritual understanding unites the historical and the grammatical understanding. To understand Plato's works, we must know the spirit of the epoch, the social and economic structure of the time.

Schleiermacher (Schleiermacher, Friedrich Daniel Ernst, 1768-1834) represented a turning point in the history of hermeneutics. With Schleiermacher, hermeneutics became an independent method, no longer limited to the Scriptures or to the literary text. It came to be related more closely to the interpretation of the text of life. It concerned the unfolding of the ethical problem of freedom, (Spinozas meaning of freedom). Schleiermacher relates the individual to society, and to history. It is necessary to understand history from the perspective of the freedom of the individual. The essence of interpretation lies in the reconstruction of the work as the living act of the author. The power of the universal over the particular is revealed in the language. The hermeneutic circle, (which is only apparent), can be surpassed. The goal of understanding is reached in the oppositon, as well as in the unity of the whole and the part, a superimposing of the whole on the part and the part on the whole. As we speak, we express a totality (language). Without it, we could not communicate. The particular presupposes a totality, a language. What is to be understood, is not only the words, but the individuality of the speaker, i.e. the author. There is another text that needs to be discovered in the text. Hermeneutics is ultimately a divinitory process, a placing of oneself in the mind of the author, a recreation of the creative act, a seminal decision, *a Keimentschluss*. It animates both content and form.

Schleiermacher's use of *Keimentschluss* is a modification of the Aristotelian idea of *entelechy*, to have one's goal in itself. *(Entelechea, the form realizes itself in the matter)*. The seminal decision relates to some general theme or feeling of the entire work, as it is suggested by the title. To understand the seminal decision of the work is basic to the understanding of the text. To observe the development of the seminal decision is in a sense to reconstruct the experience of the aesthetic art of genius. The seminal decision denotes the origin of the work of art. A work of art cannot be dissociated from life. Every interpretation has two dimensions: a linguistic dimension, the elementary unity of words, and the historical dimension, the unity of human life. Every allusion to the particular is only understood from the perspective of the whole.

Dilthey (Dilthey, Wilhelm 1833-1911), a student of Schleiermacher, projects a more historical approach to hermeneutics. He seeks to establish a critique of historical reason in order to lay down the foundation for the human sciences. Human sciences differ from natural sciences in their method and objective. How can human sciences be legitimized? They can reveal a historical knowledge, if they are founded on a theoretical ground, i.e. historical life. Life is historical. It is neither transcendental (Kant's-priori), nor empirical, but immanent. Life can grasp life. Life in the present rediscovers itself in the past. We insert our own understanding of life into every form and expression of life. We insert our own words (understanding) into the understanding of the life of others. Mankind is an object of the cultural sciences. Human sciences are grounded on life. The task of finding a basis for the human sciences is by finding the life soul. Hermeneutics, the theory of the art of understanding, goes beyond psychology. It is a historical hermeneutics based on *Lebensschule* (the school of life), defined as a process in which the sensuously given experiences of life are brought up to knowledge. It is an objectification of the subjective experience of life, (expression, experience, *Erlebnis*). A finite individual cannot completely understand the totality of history. This can be provided by the State, the Arts, the University, the Church, etc. It still poses the difficulty of how we can attain reliable knowledge of the inner experience of another person? Dilthey's life ground is determined by a desire for objective knowledge, an orientation towards a scientific ideal of the natural sciences. He seeks a rational foundation for the human sciences determined by life. There is a difference between explaining and understanding. The natural sciences explain, in the human sciences we try to understand.

In his lecture "On *Ontologie,* Hermeneutics of Facticity", (1923), Heidegger states that access to interpretation involves the being that is here. He is relating *Dasein* to the dimension of space in which the human being dwells. The being that stands in the clearing, in the light. *Dasein* emerges as self-understanding. *Dasein* is the possibility of being here, the possibility of being in the world. World is that which makes the place of the human being possible. World is the human being. We are always withdrawing from being, and through it we come closer to the sense of being. The human being emerges as play of absence and presence. The idea of withdrawing from the subject is important in Heidegger. Heidegger radically questions the position of self-consciousness, of subjectivity. To understand the human being from the perspective of being, and not from the perspective of being human. One of the most difficult problems, is who is *Dasein?* Is it the self, in so far as it is grounded in the possibility of self-consciousness? *Dasein* is a going deeper into the subject, a going into the origin of the subject. The withdrawal from the subject is also a penetration of the subject. The question of *Dasein* reveals itself in relation to the question of the meaning of being. A particular being that has forgotten the question of Being is called *Dasein*. Traditional metaphysics has revealed *Dasein* as being of substance. We need to rethink the distinction of Being and beings. In Spinoza, Being is the absolute, nature or substance. In Parmenides, it is the question of the One-*hen (henology)*. Plotinus: all things seen through the one *(hen)* that is above being. Heidegger understands Being from the question of time. Time is not understood from the perspective of the present. For Kant, time is a pure intuition. Time cannot be perceived in opposition to Being. Nietzsche frees Being from eternity, and relates Being to time. For Heidegger, Being is not an object of consciousness. Being is to let it be seen in so far as it shows itself. The phenomenological encounter of Being takes place in the facticity of *Dasein*. Thinking concerns the relation of subject and object. For *Dasein*, it is a disclosing, a revealing. Disclosure is the basic form of *Dasein*. A work of art is an experience of disclosure, a showing, *(schein)*. Nietzsche: the earth is the meaning of life. To get rid of alienation is to get rid of life. By cutting out evil, you cut out life. Accept your joys and sufferings (Dionysian).

Dasein emerges as disclosure of self, and as disclosure of being. This unique disclosure of Dasein is existence. Dasein has an ontological priority in relation to the understanding of itself that involves the understanding of the other. The self-disclosure of the human being in relation to its own being. Dasein emerges temporally in the world. It is the constitution of its own being. The being of the "I", the existentiality of the Self, the self-*verstehen*, as the self representing subject. *Verstehen* is not to be reduced to a cognitive activity. Understanding is a mode of being, a way of behaving towards being other. Reason is not the essence of *Dasein*, mood is the essence of *Dasein*. It is the way we find ourselves in the world. It is our *Befindlichkeit* - disposition. The self emerges as displaced, dislocated. The self as mirroring, mirroring the things that are, a mirroring in which the subject-object become one. Mirroring is a falling, an inauthentic dimension. The existent of *Dasein* is in its possibility to be transcendent. It is *Dasein's* almost possibility to be. Ontic beings lack the reference to self and time, they are not transcendent, they lack the possibilities that lie in that being.

The ecstatic character of temporality, it is that which enables us to transcend the everyday business of life. Heidegger does not understand temporality from a dialectical perspective. He does not understand history in a Marxist way. For Heidegger, history is art, art is history. The idea of history is based on the understanding of art. Nietzsche: we have exhausted the idea of God. We have to return to man what we have placed in God. The phantasy of God remains, higher than reality stands possibility. The possible is higher than the real, this is the actual hermeneutic relation. It is the possibility of the being of the self. *Dasein* is thrown into possibility. Heidegger's notion of the historical is not rooted in the real, but in what is not rooted yet, in terms of what will be (in terms of the future). Heidegger's view of history is determined by possibility (the future). He is not limiting history to what happened, but relates history to what has not yet happened. The traditional view of history suffers from the neglect of the problem of being.

Heidegger's idea of interpretation as *Auslegung*, a freeing in the opening of being. It is a primordial laying out of the self.

Hermeneutics is to be understood in relation to a philosophical vigilance. Hermeneutics is to disclose what is concealed in philosophy. It is to disclose the imagination, the unconscious, the Dionysian. There is a radical awareness in this disclosure.   To question consciousness is not to question awareness.   Awareness, a radical vigilance, (as in Buddhism) is a key concept in Heidegger's philosophy. It transcends particularity. It   discovers the unity of meaning by activating legitimate prejudices, authority and tradition.   Only what constitutes a unity of meaning is intelligible. The interplay of tradition with the movement of the present, the mediation between the horizon of the text and the horizon of the interpreter (the horizon of the present). The achievement of the right horizon of inquiry for the questions evoked by the encounter with tradition. The unity of horizons, horizon *Verschmeltzung,* this is a hermeneutic event. The task of hermeneutics is to ask, what kind of event, what kind of knowledge.

Exercises.

1. What are the multiple meanings of a text? Give examples.
2. Discuss the relation between the whole and the part.
3. With Schleiermacher, hermeneutics came to be connected to the interpretation of the text of life. What is the text of life? Discuss comprehensively.
4. How do you understand interpretation of a text, event, etc. from a historical perspective? Be specific and give examples.
5. What does Heidegger mean by the need to understand the human being from the perspective of being and not of being human? Comment.
6. Heidegger: "Awareness discloses unity by activating legitimate prejudices, authority and tradition." What prejudices are legitimate for Heidegger?

Note

1. This workshop is based on Professor Wurzer's lectures. (Wilhelm S. Wurzer, Duquesne University).

Workshop 60.   The Notion of Play in Gadamer's Hermeneutics.

Gadamer discusses the concept of play in the context of the aesthetic experience. For Gadamer, play is a way of overcoming the subjectivity of the aesthetic experience. As I contemplate or produce a work of art, I am at first dominated or absorbed entirely by the consciousness of what I am doing. However, the deeper I get into that state of mind, the less am I conscious of it. Eventually, there is an opening to the work of art, (or the beauty of nature, or the distant sound of music, etc.), a kind of rupture whereby the aesthetic feelings and impressions are free to come in. At that point, I am less and less aware of myself as the spectator or the producer of the work of art. My subjective consciousness recedes into the background, my thinking is no more dominated by it, and whatever I experience takes place outside of me. The work of art or the object of my contemplation opens up to me, and I experience it not from the confines of my ego, but free from them. Only then, do I fully experience the artistic beauty, the truth and the essence of the artistic creation.

This view of the aesthetic experience is different from that of Kant, for whom the experience is embodied in the subject, and is a source of pleasure. For Kant, pleasure is primary to the aesthetic experience. Not so for Gadamer. For Gadamer, the aesthetic experience is primarily related to truth, and pleasure is felt only as a derivative of truth. The opening up to the aesthetic experience takes place in the form of play. The free play of the imagination really takes over when the thinking frees itself from the consciousness of the subject, that is, when the subject is not bound anymore by the consciosness of his thinking. Thinking is no more dominated by the *logos* or by rationality. The free play of imagination is free from the domination of the subject, and thinking becomes free for the subject. This kind of thinking leads to truth because it frees the subject from his involvement with himself. Thinking therefore can get straight to the essence of the subject. The subject does not force or direct his thoughts in any given, predetermined way.   There is no given a-priori purpose to the person's thoughts. Thoughts are free to come and go. They are like a rhytmic flow, a movement to and from, changing directions, and lines. The attitude of the player is a serious one, but the play itself is a free play, not serious. The free play leads to the discovery or the recognition of truth. The truth does not lie, and is not fixed within me. It lies in the aesthetic experience that leads to it. Play becomes a way to the experience of truth. It leads to the essence, and to the beautiful. We find in true love perhaps the best example of play. In true love, no force is used, whatsoever.   The subject (the player) loses himself or herself in the artistic experience of play. He or she becomes intoxicated with the intensity of feeling. The intensity of feeling turns into a spiritual experience, where the ego has completely disappeared, and in its stead, the essential truth reveals itself in all of its majesty. All pettiness of the egocentric "I" dwindles to nothingness. The experience overwhelms and takes over the subject. The intense experience can be provoked by an ordinary happening, a walk in the woods, a distant soud of music, a dance, a work of art, natural beaty, etc. It does not depend on something extraordinary happening to us.

For Gadamer, the artistic experience of truth does not originate in the subject. It is not subjective. It does not take a special or extraordinary subject who can experience truth and beauty. Rather, beauty reveals itself in the experience of it. The subject changes through the aesthetic experience of art. This experience is related to truth. The aesthetic consciousness allows the truth to reveal itself, to come out. It is not committed to any one particular outcome, or any one particular kind of truth. This is the essence of play. Truth is more a recognition than a (rational) cognition. It is similar to Plato's notion of recollection. The person has known and experienced it before. The play presents itself to the player, and the player sees himself presented in the play. Self-representation is the mode of being of play.

When our thinking is dominated by the "I", the ego and the *logos,* when the thinking is egocentric and logocentric, it is not free to change direction or totally absorb itself in the experience. The more we get absorbed in the activity, (writing, reading, contemplating, etc.), the less conscious are we of it. The more we get away from ourselves, the closer we get to ourselves. Our involvement with the activity is greatest when we cease to be conscious of our separate existence. We lose self-consciousness precisely at the peak of our merging with the experience. Our impressions, thought processes, instincts, senses are sharpest when we are not conscious of them. Thus, we free thinking from the consciousness and the confinement of the ego. We lose ourselves in the artistic experience of truth in play. We become intoxicated.

We can cultivate an attitude of play and habituate ourselves to it. Play will be transformed into structure *(Gebilde),* a permanent image pattern which one can enter, leave or come back to. The structure loses the egocentricity of the subject. We come to recognize the truth in the experience of play. We learn to cultivate a sense of play, and use it hermeneutically in order to arrive at truth, not only of a work of art, but also of ourselves. Play frees me from the attachment to the object. It frees the aesthetic experience from the desire to possess the object. Play is disinterested of any selfishness. Pleasure ceases to be tied to having. I can enjoy things without the need to have them. (More often than not, possessing things may interfere with the enjoyment of them.)

Thus, I can overcome alienation and reification through play. It frees me to be myself. And, to the extent that I am free to be myself, I am also free to relate to the other in a natural, non-alienated way.

By cultivating an attitude of play, I become free of my egocenticity. I am more open to the mystery of nature, the world, and the other. I can free myself from my own alienation, and from the reification of the culture. I am no more bound by convention. I become free from the dependence on things. I do not allow them to blot my vision of who I am, and where I am going. I am free to find my essence in life. I am free to expand, and reach out. Where essence shines through, appearances matter less. I open myself up to the hermeneutics of life. What is the essence of life? To be able to answer this, I have to come back to the notion of play.

I have desires, plans, interests, etc. but all of these lose a certain fixity through play. I am not bound by them any more. Play loosens all my compulsions and fixations. I am free to find the truth through my projects (desires, plans, etc.) rather than them imposing their truth on me. Life does not depend, and is not exhausted by anyone of them. The totality (life) is greater than all of them. This understanding leads the way out of the hermeneutic circle, that we so often seem to get stuck in. For example, I cannot study because I cannot concentrate, and I cannot concentrate because I feel lonely, etc. Play allows us to break out of this circle. (The hermeneutic circle deals with the relation of the whole and the part. We can only understand the part as related to the whole, and we can understand the whole only as related and composed of its parts.)

Through play I become aware that life goes on, and that it cannot be reduced to any one of its parts. I am thereby at ease when I contemplate my desires, options, plans, activities, etc. I am at peace with myself and relaxed. There is no force involved in anything that I want or do. This relaxation does not change any of my projects. The only difference is, that I am now free to find that project, (work, idea, etc.) that is truly mine, the one that I truly want to carry out. The latter will be most compatible with the totality of my being. If I make a mistake in any of my plans, encounters, or if any of my hopes don't work out, both hope and life continue in a more rewarding and deeper sense, because I have come to know a greater truth of myself, and of my situation.

An attitude of play to life, makes my life more involving with my true self, and more compatible with my real interests and abilities. In this sense, play makes my life more serious, and even outwardly more successful. The attitude of play brings serenity and peace into my existence. I do the things that I really want to do, and the reasons for my doing them are not extraneous or alienated. What I do is what I truly want to do from within me. Socially, I am open to my fellow men. I relate to the other from the truth of my inner being. I don't have the need to hide myself behind a facade of appearances. Social intercourse becomes simple, natural, and meaningful. Since I am not preoccupied with my own self, I can freely direct my attention to the outside of me. I can have a real encounter with another person. (Recall Buber's I and Thou). This carries over into the political arena, too. I am now free to be a political human being. I can take a stand on issues, and can freely involve myself in the affairs of the community and the nation. Moreover, this involvement will be firm and unconditional, since it is based entirely on my own free choice.

Exercises.

1. Reflect on the following: Nature is a constantly self-renewing play, without exertion. To be natural is to be without strain.
2. Play allows you to observe the comedy or tragedy of life, as on stage. Since you are a spectator, the comic and the tragic aspects of play are interchangable.
3. Play gives you more room for yourself. You do not invest your thoughts, feelings, and outcomes with excessive emotionality. You don't put yourself into a straight jacket of forced outcomes. You can take yourself less seriously. It allows you to transcend your present self, and thus exercise judgment that is more in line with your real self. It enables you to become more rational, and view life from a longer perspective. Life is possibility, and there are always other possibilities in life.
4. Put yourself into a state of mind whereby you consider your most important project in life as play. Can you do that?
5. Stay with it for some time, and write down all the accompanying effects and reactions.
6. Does it make you more relaxed, more creative, more free, and more cheerful? How does it affect your friendships or your marriage? Are you more free to experience and enjoy beauty?

Workshop 61.   On Deconstruction.

1.   What is Deconstruction?

Deconstruction does not lend itself to a single or definitive interpretation. It is easier understood in terms of what it is not, than in terms of what it is. When Derrida was asked to explain it, he expressed it in terms of what it is not. Deconstruction is not negative. It questions everything that we have been used to accept without questioning. All oppositions, and all the logical categories that underlie Western metaphysics are subject to renewed scrutiny. Fundamental concepts, such as essence, appearance, presence, reality, being, thing, substance, inner-outer, etc. are deconstructed. There is no ultimate referent that is to serve as   foundational ground. Deconstruction does not accept a philosophical hierarchy of high-low, essence and appearance, *mythos* and *logos,* i.e. a hierarchy that prefers one of the oppositions as against the other. Such hierarchy is implicit in all binary oppositions of traditional metaphysics.

Deconstruction is etymologically linked to structure. Originally, structure referred to some spatial configuration of forms and sites, like in architecture. Later, the term was applied to verbal concepts, such as *eidos*, essence, form, totality, organism, state, composition, ensemble, etc. What is common to both spatial and verbal structures is the characteristic of closure, and of centering, (a point of fixed origin). A structure is an enclosed totality without an opening. A passage or an opening to another structure can come about only by a fissure or rupture, that is, by chance. Structures are to be reopened and decentered. "Structures were to be undone, decomposed, desedimented (all types of structures, linguistic, "logocentric", "phonocentric"... socio-institutional, political, cultural, and above all...philosophical)."[1] The undoing of structures is carried out for the purpose of their reconstruction and a better understanding of "how an ensemble was constituted."[2] The purpose is to discover new elements, and to gain new, previously unthought of, insights. A decentering of closed structures, (i.e. verbal terms and concepts that we have been using habitually and have accepted without questioning), will enrich our thinking processes, and open up new possibilities for deeper penetration into the complexities and realities of any situation or problem we might face. We will be better equipped to reassemble the old structures in a new way. This enabling operation of decentering the old and the familiar in order to arrive at the new and the unknown,   Gasche calls infrastructures. According to Gasche, that is what Derrida means by structures.[3]

Infrastructures open up the possibility of greater interaction, greater movement, greater exploration, and utilisation of the potential imbued in existing structures and forms. The term is borrowed from the physical use of infrastructure. Physical infrastructures, such as roads, telephone lines, sewers, bridges, airfields, etc. allow for an intensification of economic interchange, and a greater utilization of the possibilities imbued in a given economic system. Infrastructures mediate activities. By themselves (without mediation), they are of no use. Derrida's infrastructures perform a similar function. They are used as means for the exploration, revelation, and intensification of new possibilities inherent in traditionally closed concepts, such as truth, essence, being, etc. Infrastructures lead to the opening up of new insights, new angles of vision, and new meanings that have hitherto been undisclosed and trapped within the traditional binary oppositions of Western metaphysics. The infrastructures must be thought of as preceding or being outside the traditional oppositions of absence-presence, sensible and intelligible, being and nothingness, empirical and transcendental, Being and beings, etc. Derrida cites a number of ways (infrastructures) by which existing structures can be decentered, *differance* being the most known one. Other ways of designating infrastructures are: inscriptions *(ecriture)*, supplements, *gram*, trace, archtraces, hymen, *pharmakon* (which is neither remedy nor poison), spacing, etc.

We need to understand old concepts in a new way. The cause-effect connection must be looked at, and considered differently than we have been accustomed to. For example, cause-effect may be immanent in each other, they may be reversed from each other, there may be participating causes and effects not lined up sequentially, we may be mistaken about their connection and identity, etc. etc. The dialectics of the same and the other, of outside and inside, of the homogenous and the heterogenous, are to be scrutinized and reconstituted anew. The renewed scrutiny carries the double mark of overturning and transgressing. To overturn and transgress implies a refusal and an unwillingness to be bound by the traditional interpretation and understanding of old (metaphysical) concepts. It is both similar and different from the Hegelian dialectic of sublation or *Aufhebung*. To sublate *(aufheben)* means to destroy and preserve, to negate and affirm, to retain and supersede. Or as double negation, it is to supersede, to affirm, and to supersede again. For example, in Hegel's master - slave dialectic, self-consciousness (the individual) first thinks that it is what it thinks it is, (the way it appears to itself), then it thinks that it is what the other thinks it is, (the way it appears to the other, it thereby negates or supersedes itself), then it asserts itself by superseding its appearance to the other, etc. Hegel's Aufhebung however, still operates within the confines of binary opposition, because a new opposition supersedes the old one.

Differance operates at the limit of Hegel's sublation *(Aufhebung)*. *Differance* interferes and upsets Hegel's sublation because it does not allow any fixed new constellations to settle in. *Differance* cannot be fully determined or totally resolved. In writing, the syntax is of equal importance to the word. "Instead of investigating only the contents of thought, it is also necessary to analyze the way in which texts are made: *'In a certain way, thought means nothing'*. [4] Whatever goes for thought, can and should be contested. It should be deconstructed. Derrida questions the authority of "thought", the centrality of the logos. He wants to deconstruct logocentrism, the authority of meaning, the transcendental signified, idealism, and the *telos*. Deconstruction seeks to get out of tradtional metaphysical opposition altogether. Deconstruction does not accept any finite interpretation or definitive conceptual resolutions. In writing, there is production, and there is also non-production, an operation of discounting of what one writes, and a moving beyond of what one says.

Deconstruction is neither analysis, nor critique. The taking apart of a structure is not done with the aim of bringing it back to an *indissoluble origin*. [5] All the values that underlie this operation are themselves subject to deconstruction. Deconstruction is not a method. It is not a set of rules of how to read or interpret a text or an event. It is not even an act or operation exercised by a subject on an object. (Deconstruction questions both subject and object). It just something that can be done. "It can be deconstructed".[6] Deconstruction cannot be defined because it deconstructs all the predicates and all the concepts that we may use in an effort to define it. It can best be described as "a discourse or rather a writing that can make up for the incapacity of the word to be equal to a thought".[7] A word can never express all the possible shades of meaning that we can think of.

To deconstruct the binary opposition, for example, the opposition of theory and practice, we must first neutralize it. In order neutralize it, we must overturn its hierarchical structure. (The two terms of the opposition are not on equal footing, one governs the other, for example, light-dark, light rules the dark, sensible-intellligible, the intelligible rules the sensible, theory - practice, theory rules practice, *logos* and *mythos, logos* rules *mythos*, etc.) To take the example of theory and practice again, when we overturn its hierarchy, we get a new linking of theory and practice, such as theory guides and is guided by practice, practice guides and is guided by theory, theory is enclosed in practice, and practice is immanent in theory, etc.

2. What is *Differance?*

We single out *differance* as the infrastructure most often associated with deconstruction. *Differance* is a delay or postponement. Derrida enumerates several ways of what *differance* means:[8] 1. It is a movement that defers, (postpones or detours), presence. 2. It is what differentiates between (oppositions), i.e. nature-convention *(physis-nomos)*, appearance-reality, sensible-intelligible, etc. 3. It is also the movement that produces these differences. 4. We must move beyond it, beyond the difference, to *differance* which is both the unfolding, and also prior to the unfolding of difference contained in the binary opposition.   To briefly restate the above: *Differance* is that what defers presence, it is prior to differentiation and opposition, it is also a movement that differentiates and produces oppositions. *Differance* produces concepts and words, (such as gram, trace, spacing, supplement, etc.) but these are not new foundations or grounds. *Differance* is not a concept that lends itself to simple definition. To define *differance* or to ask what is its essence would mean to put a closure to it, precisely what   *differance* is trying to overcome. *Differance*   does not allow closure. It inherently questions the distinction between the thing and the signifier, between the word and its meaning, between the text and its content.

The science of signs and significations is called Semiotics or Semiology. Sausure (Ferdinand de Saussure, 1857-1913) was the originator of general linguistics and semiology. Every sign is a unity of two sides, the sensible (signifier) and the intelligible (the signified). The signified is inseparable from the signifier. Signifier and signified are based on and derived from differences of signs and significations. With a different system of significations, signifier and signified will mean different things. Deconstruction denies an independent content to the signified, i.e. a transcendental signified. For example, what we understand as a tree, would be something entirely different in an different system of signs and significations.

The concept of sign i.e. the separation and opposition of signifier /signified is necessary for translation and the passage of communication.   Deconstruction looks at signs and concepts as ..."formal play of differences. That is of traces."[9] *Gram* or trace introduces a new concept of writing. It is the movement of *differance* in writing. It is an interweaving of all elements in a chain or system, designated as writing. The play of differences prevents any simple element to be present by itself or to stand on its own.   Every element, is connected to every other, in an overall system of traces and differences that constitute the text. It is a spacing by which all elements are related to each other. Nothing stands on its own in the system. The *differance* is always active, it generates differences, it is dynamic as opposed to the static nature of *structure*. Differences are effects of transformations *(the differance)*, and they also leave room for the formation of structures. The silent *a* in *differance* represents spacing, by which a relationship to the present is always deferred. Every element in this system of traces conveys meaning only in relation to a past or future element.

3. Derrida and Hegel.

Derrida's relation to Hegel is very complex.. "We will never be finished with reading or rereading of Hegel, and, in a certain way, I do nothing other than attempt to explain myself on this point."[10] With regard to Marxism - Leninism, Derrida says that he has not as yet acquired a satisfactory protocol (of how to read them).[11] The works of Marx, Engels, Lenin are not homogenuos critiques. The Marxist concept of contradiction is still caught up in in speculative dialectics, it operates within the teleological confines of Western metaphysics.

Hegel relativized the two poles of opposition, i. e. apperance-essence, absence-presence, high-low, clean-dirty, etc. Heraclitus (fifth cent. BC.) and the Chinese philosopher Lao Tsu (sixth cent. BC.) did the same. Heraclitus: "The path up and down is one and the same"(Fr. 200.) Lao Tsu: "Opposites derive their meaning from each other. Reality is contradictory." (Tao Te Ching, Chpt. 2.) When the two poles of the opposition are relativized, they merge into unity (they become one). For example, in the opposition of absence and presence, we may have different kind of presences and absences, (I can be physically present in a meeting but mentally absent, i.e. I am present under the mode of absence, my friend can be mentally present with me but physically absent, ideas can be present in some minds and absent in others, I am present now, but a little later I am present differently, my mind begins to wander, and so on). When the opposition of appearance and essence is relativized (as Hegel did), essence is included in appearance, and appearance constitutes part of the essence. Appearance is part of truth. Spinoza deconstructed the traditional notions of good and bad, (good is what is useful to the human mode, bad is what is harmful). When old concepts are challenged, there is movement. When they become fixed and ossified, movement stops. The stopping of movement is not really a standing still. Reality never stands still. It is instead a going backwards, a retrogression. On the other hand, when everything that we hold on to is being relaxed, new challenges and possibilities open up, and we can move forward. Deconstruction is in a sense, a relaxing of all fixed determinations and positions.

Derrida deconstructs the metaphysical concept of history, as linear or circular progression of meaning seeking to fulfil itself. He would replace it with the concept of monumental history, a history full of contradiction, stratification, *repetition* and *trace*. [12] There is not one unique history, a Hegelian expressive totality.   There are many histories. Derrida wants to move out of the metaphysical concept of the essence of history, and deal instead with the question of the history of essence. We must deconstruct the traditional presuppositions and reappropriations, such as essence, truth, meaning, consciousness, etc. It is necessary first to overturn the traditional notion of history. Each of "history's" presuppositions must be investigated separately.

Exercises

1. What does deconstruction seek to achieve?
2. What are the potential rewards of deconstructive reasoning?
3. Is deconstructive thinking opposed to constructive thinking?
4. Can deconstruction be thought of as radical criticism?
5. Can deconstruction provide new insights into an area or problem previously considered as closed? Give examples.
6. Have you ever come to think 'unthought' thoughts? Describe the process.
7. There are no sacred cows in deconstruction. Comment.
8. Does deconstructon do away with ground and grounding? Or does it seek a a firmer and more certain foundation?
9. Can deconstruction be carried away as to lose the very ground it is standing on? Can it get you into an infinite regress?
10. Explain Derrida's *differance*.
11. Deconstruction is not logocentric. Explain how and why.
12. Deconstruction has been charged with circularity, i.e. it uses *logos* to criticize *logos*. Discuss.
13. Is there an alternative to *logos*, to reason? Elaborate.
14. What does Derrida mean by "making the word equal to the thought"?
15. Are signifiers (words) based merely on differences between them, or are they names for independent content to which they point? Discuss and reflect.

Notes

1. Jacques Derrida, Letter to a Japanese Friend. In *Derrida and Differance*. edited by David Wood and Robert Bernasconi. Evanston Il.: Northwestern University Press,1988. p. 3.

2. Ibid. p. 3.

3. Rodolpho Gasche, *The Tain of the Mirror*. Cambridge, Ma.: Harvard University Press, 1986. p.147.

4. Jacques Derrida, *Positions*. Translated and annotated by Alan Bass. Chicago: The University of Chicago Press, 1982. p.51

5. *Derrida and Differance.* p.3.

6. Ibid. p.4.

7. Ibid. p.4.

8. *Positions.* p. 24.

9. *Positions.* pp. 47 and 49.

10. *Positions.* p.77.

11. *Positions.* p.63.

12. *Positions.* p.57.

Index

Absolute, 292, 311, 346
Absolute Spirit, 181
accommodation, 55, 77
acting by non-acting, *wu-wei*, 143, 128
action (praxis), 269, 283

Adler, Alfred, 113
adventitious ideas, 295
Aenesidemus, 288
aesthetic illusion, 348
aesthetic sphere, 325
aesthetic stage, 325
alienated labor, 176
alienation, 13, 14, 25, 91, 103, 104, 105, 169, 170, 247, 253, 359
amor fati, 331, 348
analytic judgment, 304
Anaxagoras, 191, 197, 314
Anaximander, 187, 195, 261, 313
Anaximenes, 188, 313
anima, 60
animus, 60
Anselm, St., 215
antinomies, 303
anxiety, 7, 68
apeiron, 187, 195, 313
Appolynian, 331, 348, 349
Arendt, Hanna 270, 271
Aristotle, 1, 2, 3, 164, 191, 196, 199, 200, 204, 211, 221, 224, 225, 226, 230, 251, 265, 266, 270, 271, 273, 281, 314, 315, 317, 325
artistic beauty, 357
artistic experience of truth, 358
assimilation, 55, 77
ataraxia, 288
Atomists, 198
attribute of thought, 240
Aufhebung or sublation, 243

Augustine, St. 105, 207, 208, 213, 226, 229, 289, 290, 293
authentic existence, 252, 257
autonomy of the will, 276

Bacon, Francis 295, 297
behavior, 97; formational, deformational, 31
Being, 190, 196, 197, 251, 354
being (life), 108
Being and beings, 353
"Being for itself", 309
being in-the-world, 252
Big Bang, 239
blind spots, 90
Buber, Martin 23, 26, 360
Buddha, 100
Buddhism, 99, 100, 355
Buddhist state of Samadha, 128

call of conscience, 256
Capitalism, 170, 175, 176
Categorical Imperative, 275, 276
causa sui, 135, 137, 238
causal necessity, 136
cause-effect connection, 299, 302
causes of change, 199
character virtues, 266
Cicero, 3
city-state, 266, 282
civil laws, 159
clarity and distinctness, 296
class conflict, 172
clear and distinct ideas, 215
cleverness, 274
clues, 89, 94
cogitatum, 339
cogito, 296, 339
cognitive development, 53, 54
collective unconscious, 57, 129

learning, 29
learning environment, 78
Leibniz, Gottfried Wilhelm, 224, 225, 226, 295, 296, 297, 301
Lenin, Vladimir Ilyich, 171
Leucippus, 192, 198, 262, 263, 315
levels of abstraction, 293
levels of reality, 229
Lewin, Kurt, 67
liberation, 41
libido, 108, 109
light of reason, 283
Locke, John, 166, 185, 295, 297
logos, 188, 189, 195, 196, 223, 252, 313, 331
love, 7, 9, 49, 191
love of God, 159
lower Self, 107
Lucretius, 226, 263
Lukacs, Georg, 103, 180, 181,
Luther, Martin, 351
Luxenburg, Rosa, 171

Macciavelli, Niccolo, 185
manipulation, 16
Marcus Aurelius, 347
Marx, Karl, 103, 104, 169, 170, 175, 176, 178, 179, 180, 243, 282, 283, 284, 301, 345, 346
Marxism, 181, 282
Marxism - Leninism, 365
Marxist economics, 172
master - slave dialectic 39, 43, 44, 363
Materialism, 170
materialist monists, 314
Melissus, 190, 191
memory, 100, 208
methodical doubt, 214
mimesis, 318, 345
Mind, 192, 216

Mind and body, 216
mind-body unity, 83
monads, 224, 296
moods, 30
moral action, 290
moral character, 273
moral consciousness, 277, 278
moral excellence, 266
moral law, 276
moral purposiveness, 231
moral responsibility, 100
moral virtue, 271, 274
moral will, 276
motion and rest, 239
motion, (kinesis), 1
motivation, 91
Mozart, 325
mystic virtue, 131
Natura naturans, 137, 237, 239
Natura naturata, 137, 237, 239
natural light of reason, 212, 223, 296
natural rights, 158
nature and modes, 236
nature's freedom, 237
nature's perfection, 237
necessary succession, 100
negation, 39, 245
Nietzsche, Friedrich, 99, 152, 329, 331, 345, 346, 348, 349, 351, 353, 354
noema, 121
noesis, 121
non-being, *(thanatos,* despair or death), 108
non-evaluative feedback, 72
non-existent modes, 137
noumenon, 39, 243, 302, 303, 305, 319
noumenon-phenomenon, 241
nous, 199, 200, 294
Nous (mind), 314

objective truth, 283, 290
ontological proof, 229